Girls on Fire

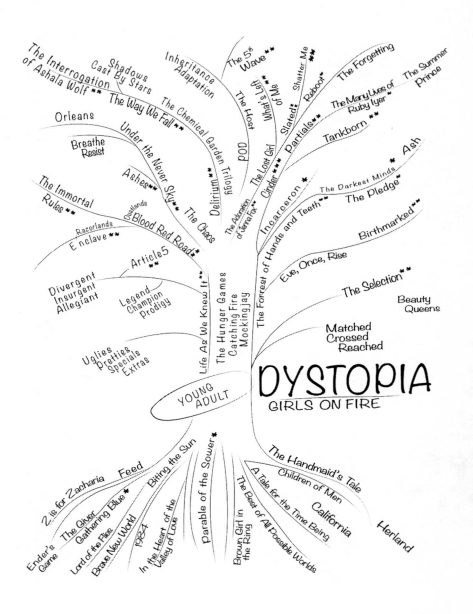

DYSTOPIA
GIRLS ON FIRE

YOUNG ADULT

The Interrogation of Ashala Wolf **
Shadows Cast By Stars
The Way We Fall **
Inheritance
Adaptation
The 5th Wave **
Shatter Me *
Reboot *
The Forgetting
The Summer Prince
The Chemical Garden Trilogy
The Many Lives of Ruby Iyer *
Orleans
The Host
POD
What's Left of Me *
Slated *
Tankborn
Breathe Resist
Under the Never Sky *
Delirium
The Lost Girl
Cinder *
Partials **
Ash *
Ashes **
The Chaos
The Adoration of Jenna Fox *
Incarceron
The Darkest Minds **
The Pledge **
The Immortal Rules **
Duelands
Blood Red Road *
The Forrest of Hands and Teeth **
Birthmarked **
Razorlands
Enclave **
Eve, Once, Rise
The Selection **
Article 5 *
Divergent Insurgent Allegiant
Legend Champion Prodigy
Life As We Knew It **
The Hunger Games Catching Fire Mockingjay
Beauty Queens
Matched Crossed Reached
Uglies Pretties Specials Extras
Parable of the Sower *
The Handmaid's Tale
Z is for Zacharia
Feed
Biting the Sun
Children of Men
Ender's Game
The Giver
Gathering Blue *
Brave New World
1984
In the Heart of the Valley of Love
Brown Girl in the Ring
A Tale for the Time Being
California
Herland
The Best of All Possible Worlds
Lord of the Flies

Girls on Fire

Transformative Heroines
in Young Adult Dystopian Literature

SARAH HENTGES

McFarland & Company, Inc., Publishers
Jefferson, North Carolina

ALSO OF INTEREST
AND BY SARAH HENTGES

Women and Fitness in American Culture (McFarland, 2014)

*Pictures of Girlhood: Modern Female
Adolescence on Film* (McFarland, 2006)

Frontispiece: As I imagine this body of Girls on Fire YA dystopia books, this image resonates. The roots include a variety of books that I explore in Part I—the mothers of YA dystopia's Girls on Fire and the foundational texts in American literature and YA dystopia. The trunk holds the most foundational works, and as the branches reach, the books get more critical. The growth is outward and upward and is complemented by the theme tree on page 112 (design by Sarah Hentges; digitized by Karyssa Upham).

LIBRARY OF CONGRESS CATALOGUING-IN-PUBLICATION DATA

Names: Hentges, Sarah, 1976– author.
Title: Girls on fire : transformative heroines in young adult dystopian literature / Sarah Hentges.
Description: Jefferson, North Carolina : McFarland & Company, Inc., Publishers, 2018. | Includes bibliographical references and index.
Identifiers: LCCN 2018003171 | ISBN 9780786499281 (softcover : acid free paper) ∞
Subjects: LCSH: Young adult fiction, American—21st century—History and criticism. | Dystopias in literature. | Heroines in literature. | Teenage girls in literature.
Classification: LCC PS374.Y57 H46 2018 | DDC 813/.609352352—dc23
LC record available at https://lccn.loc.gov/2018003171

BRITISH LIBRARY CATALOGUING DATA ARE AVAILABLE

ISBN (print) 978-0-7864-9928-1
ISBN (ebook) 978-1-4766-3144-8

Front cover image © 2018 Grandfailure/iStock

Printed in the United States of America

*McFarland & Company, Inc., Publishers
Box 611, Jefferson, North Carolina 28640
www.mcfarlandpub.com*

For all my Girls on Fire.
But mostly,
for Octavia E. Butler—
this is positive obsession.

Table of Contents

Acknowledgments

This book has also taken shape alongside my teaching of a 300-level elective, cross-listed between American studies, English, and Women's and Gender studies: "Girls on Fire: Gender, Culture, and Justice in YA Dystopia." My students in this class—spring 2015, fall 2015, and fall 2016—have embraced the subject matter and have taken it in a variety of directions that have inspired me as a teacher, a writer, and a person. If I could somehow encapsulate all of my students' perspectives and critiques in this book, we might begin to be able to appreciate the breadth and depth that YA dystopia can bring to the classroom—in this case the online classroom. But their work already extends the classroom and I include examples of their "action" projects as evidence of the reach of Girls on Fire.

I also have to thank my students for keeping me up-to-date on the many online conversations and articles related to our class and my research for this book. Through students' posts I found books like Ruby Iyer and sources that I may have overlooked (as well as many I had already collected). And, in the third iteration of this class a student shared a post that enraged her—it was exactly what I was looking for at the moment as I was trying to explain the ways in which these books speak to a middle-aged female audience as well as young adults. The articles and links students found also helped to give me an idea of what was most striking and poignant about these novels and what online conversations spoke to them.

So many of my students are passionate and committed. So many are brilliant. Jessa Edney's work brought feminist frameworks and contemporary examples to every discussion board and she helped me to expand and extend my ideas about the queer aspects of the Hunger Games. She also helped inspire me to think more about cyborgs and androids and to pay more attention to social media. Michaela Bragg also dominated the discussion boards, taking on our subject matter with a critical eye and a teacher's heart. Both became TAs for the course the second time I taught it. Jessa continued to develop her research projects and Michaela took her experience into her own classroom. In fact, many students who took this class were already teachers and they brought these books and ideas into their classrooms in powerful ways; and then they brought these experiences back to our classroom discussions.

I cannot begin to thank my research assistants Lauren Verow, Kendralee Tessier, and Elizabeth Barnhardt-Roderick for their work, especially on those details of citation and development of lists. The number of sources and resources were overwhelming at times. Lauren shares my love of YA dystopia and gave me many early suggestions. Plus she is just a super-cool nerd. Kendra's attention to detail and competence are second to none. And Elizabeth Barnhart-Roderick was there with her eye for detail when I most needed such help. (She is also a super-cool nerd.) Karyssa Upham helped to save me from the daunting task of tracking down book cover images and other important tech-related details, including photographing the covers. Most importantly, she brought my dystopia tree designs from pen and paper to digital image—an important visual that represents my vision. Thanks is certainly deserved for Tessa Pyles who forwarded me a link to Victoria Law's blog on bitchmagazine.com about girls of color in YA dystopia before I was ready to look for it. That was the moment that I decided I had to write this book.

And when I decided I had to write this book, I cannot thank enough our Director of Library Services, Ben Treat, for listening to me babble, offering insights, and helping me get the books I needed. Carla Billiteri and Mazie Hough also helped get me resources that I could not access. Cindy Dean, Lorien Lake-Corral, Lisa Botshon, Elizabeth Powers, Jen Mascaro and Kati Corlew helped inspire my work in a variety of different ways—through critique and through fandom. Amie Doughty and Sean P. Connors also deserve thanks for supporting my work in its early stages and publishing my related articles. Sean has also contributed thoughtful reflections on YA dystopia, as an editor and a critic. I admire his passion for teaching YA dystopia.

But most of all, I have to thank Octavia E. Butler. Through her work I rediscovered my love of reading, and when I ran out of her books (and re-read them multiple times), I went searching for something like Butler, which eventually led me to discover YA dystopia. All I knew about *The Hunger Games* when I picked it up was that it had a strong female protagonist and that it was going to be made into a film. A few pages in and I was hooked. More than 140 YA dystopia books, and many more dystopian, science fiction, speculative fiction and fantasy books and films, and I am still re-reading Butler's novels and short stories. And I am still in love.

Preface

I have always been a fan of science fiction and speculative fiction—books, TV, films, and stories more generally—because they imagine differently. They comment on today's problems through a lens focused on the future. This has been my entertainment for decades, my not-quite escape from reality. Thus, I had read a lot of young adult dystopian literature before I decided to transfer my love of reading to my love of scholarly inquiry. I knew that what I was reading would resonate with my students. And I found that YA dystopia extended some of my previous work and inspired some new directions. "Pictures of Girlhood" has become "Girls on Fire" and the intersections and dimensions in my academic explorations of texts and contexts illuminate girlhood—in all of its complexity—providing cultural negotiations through literature, film, culture/media, and feminism.

But the concept of "Girls on Fire" is richer and more complex than "Pictures of Girlhood" could hope to be. And while these girls still manifest in films, their primary realm is good old-fashioned books (and e-books). In my nascent explorations in *Pictures of Girlhood: Modern Female Adolescence on Film*, I was a green scholar, and the films I explored were a brand of feminism that was young. Girls were just getting a spot on the pop culture map; third wave feminists were putting them there. Girls on Fire are the progeny of the girls I explore in *Pictures of Girlhood*. They are still fighting for justice. But the battlefield is more complex and more is at stake. This book is about real and fictional girls, in real and fictional worlds, facing real and fictional problems, and finding real and fictional solutions. Through an interdisciplinary framework, this book takes a big picture look at girls and girlhood as they illuminate our world through fictional futures. The lines blur.

This book is complicated and simple, layered and interconnected. It is for those who read every piece of YA dystopia they can get their hands on as well as those who are familiar with the Hunger Games but might not be familiar with the wide breadth of works that comprise this genre and pop culture phenomenon. I hope readers will find new books to read (and pass

1

on to other readers), new ideas to think about, and new perspectives on YA dystopia as well as our collective future. Mostly, YA dystopia is an entertaining and compelling read for those who want to simultaneously escape the world we live in and ruminate on the ways in which our world can be a better, more just place. Imagination rooted in reality and a critical mind are the two necessary tools.

Ultimately this book is about where we are—girls, women, hu(man)kind—and where we're going (and a bit about where we've been). All readers will find value in this book's discussion of gender, race, sexuality, community, culture, power, love and its interdisciplinary approach. For students, this book makes connections between and among books and between books and life. There are many starting points for further exploration. For teachers, this book provides a variety of resources for understanding and teaching these dystopic books in their interdisciplinary complexity. For readers who are lovers of YA dystopia, this book aims to give us another layer to the books we love to devour. What is it about this genre that entertains readers while also providing a context to unpack the past and the present as well as the future? I hope all readers will appreciate the valuable depth and breadth of the cultural work that YA dystopia lends itself to. The body of work I study—mostly books and some films, mostly young adult dystopia and some (adult) dystopia, mostly girls but some boys and men and women—inspires imagination and action and provides tools for transformation.

* * *

This book has come together over several years of reading for pleasure, a couple of years of research and more reading (still pleasure), a lot of note-taking, Google searches and scholar alerts, a failed attempt at a research grant, a scrap of course release time, and more reading and research. The bigger the reach, the deeper I got. It has been developed through a conference presentation at the national PCA-ACA conference in New Orleans in 2015 organized by Amie Doughty, among many other YA and YA dystopia panels. This presentation became a book chapter in *Children's and Young Adult Literature and Culture: A Mosaic of Criticism*, "Othered Girls on Fire: Navigating the Complex Terrain of YA Dystopia's Female Protagonist," the blueprint for this book. This conference presentation also connected me with Sean P. Connors and I wrote an article for *SIGNAL*, "This Class Is on Fire! (and Online): Teaching YA Dystopia and the Girl on Fire Through Themes, Contexts, and Actions" about some of the more practical aspects of teaching YA dystopia as well as the idea of "Girls on Fire." I've also published some popular articles through my website and blog and "Girls on Fire: Political Empowerment in Young Adult Dystopia" for *The Conversation*. Pieces of these works are echoed (and quoted) here, providing a foundation for the expanded argument that I make in this book.

* * *

I have worked diligently to accurately represent the details of these works, while focusing on bigger picture ideas. I read many/most of these books before I ever read a word of scholarly—or even popular—criticism and I have re-read many books/series during this process. The pop culture resources related to this research roughly span 2012 through early 2017 but reach forward and back beyond this time frame. An interdisciplinary/intersectional framework is the glue. I hope to honor the rich variety of scholarly analysis that exists and inspire some future directions, or at least provide a flexible resource. But the many threads I bring together are rich and deep and I can only sample the pool. I will inevitably drop important pieces like television, comic book, and video game representations that might be considered to be about "Girls on Fire" or a variety of scholarly or popular analyses whose depths I can only gloss over (or have to set aside). There's a reason why so many scholars and students want to write about Katniss and Tris and female protagonists who I call Girls on Fire—these are compelling and hopeful subjects. This book seeks to pull together many texts, through a variety of lenses and a particular framing, in order to continue to move this conversation forward.

Because of the range of material, there are several appendices and embedded illustrations that may be helpful while reading. Readers should also note that when, for instance, *The Hunger Games* is italicized, I am referring specifically to the book and/or the film. When it is not italicized I am referring to the series (or to the actual games in the book). Also, I rarely spell out young adult and opt for the YA abbreviation. Some of my sources abbreviate science fiction as SF or sf. Appendix 1 includes the books that comprise the body of work that I refer to here as Girls on Fire and YA Dystopia. Listed by title of first book, each entry includes the name of the author and the series (if relevant), the Girl on Fire (the female protagonist), and other related electronic books and films through 2016. This list provides a reference point to help the reader navigate my text as well as the Girls on Fire texts themselves. In addition to a list that catalogs these works by title, all of the Girls on Fire books are also listed as works cited (by author). I also include "Something Like a Rating System," which offers some brief details and connections about individual works and groups of works. The charts included throughout the book also provide a quick overview of the specifics and general patterns. Throughout the book, book cover images represent some of the visuals that shape so many people's outsider—and insider—perspectives on YA dystopia.

This is an ambitious project that attempts to do justice to the diversity of YA dystopia, to imagine a better world for girls and a better future for us all. It asks for ambitious readers. It speaks to all kinds Girls on Fire, especially those who want to transform ourselves and our world and actually believe we can.

Introduction: Girls on Fire

The Popular and Critical Terrain

In the past decade, female protagonists have begun to explode on the popular culture radar. The popularity of *Twilight* (beginning in 2006) and *Harry Potter* (beginning in 1997) revealed that readers were hungry for young adult stories that blended reality and fantasy, adventure and romance. And with Bella and Hermoine building upon the past popularity of other female protagonists, readers—and popular culture fans—were ready for female protagonists of a new grade. And then *The Hunger Games* changed the game, and YA dystopia exploded on and off the page. As Sean P. Connors points out, in 2010 millions of copies were in print in the U.S. and the popularity of the Hunger Games also led to an increase in popularity for young adult literature more generally. Further, more than half of the young adult books sold today are purchased by people over 18 and most are purchased by people in their mid–30s to mid–40s (Conners 2014). The Hunger Games trilogy sets the standard for young adult literature generally, and for the Girl on Fire as a cultural force to be reckoned with—symbolic and real. The female protagonist as a Girl on Fire is complex, intelligent, brave, and a triumphant survivor of impossible situations. As individual characters, these girls have their own challenges and most tell their own story. As a genre of Girls on Fire, these girls speak to an important cultural moment and an optimism that shapes the future.

It is not difficult to imagine why dystopia is a popular subject for contemporary writers and a popular reading choice for contemporary U.S. readers. As many have casually or seriously pointed out, the U.S. shares many dystopic qualities with the fictional settings imagined by writers and devoured by readers. When Stephen Colbert interviewed author Edan Lepucki about her 2014 book *California*, a dystopic novel that examines interpersonal relationships and pregnancy as well as community and power, he took advantage of the opportunity to connect the "unrealistic" aspects of dystopia. The novel is described by critics as "dark" and "chilling." With the dead-pan delivery he is known for, Colbert notes, "So, California." We laugh, but this joke is not far from the truth.

It's also not difficult to imagine why YA dystopia in particular would catch fire (pun intended) with a young adult audience (Blake, clo0701, Scholes, Zemier, Polatis). As Christine Seifert argues in her study of virginity in YA literature, "YA literature—and other pop culture aimed at young adults—is a profitable industry, and there's no likely end in sight to the mass production of YA entertainment" (152). Most of these novels echo the romance of *Twilight* and/or the friendships of *Harry Potter*. And with the exception of some supernatural elements, a few vampires, a handful of zombies, and some technological advances, YA dystopia is sometimes frighteningly realistic. Dystopia adds a variety of new worlds for readers to explore, with characters who are (most often) compelling and complicated. These worlds and characters give us endless opportunities for entertainment, critique, imagination, and revision.

When I was a girl, the choices of Girl on Fire female protagonists were limited to Princess Lea and Wonder Woman. I had to extrapolate from male characters to imagine the hero was me. These heroes have been re-imagined with new strong female leads for the Millennial generation—but still suffer from under-representation and exploitation in the male dominated spaces of future-oriented stories like Star Wars, Star Trek, Superhero films with Superman and Batman, The X-Men, and other books, films, comics, video games, cartoons, and entertainment media. But in today's YA dystopia, girls do not have to look far to find a female character—a strong, brave, struggling female protagonist who finds herself with no choice but to work for the greater good. And there are also plenty of female protagonists who aren't exactly "Girls on Fire," but make their own stories regardless. The Girl on Fire is rarely a perfect, infallible hero; she is most often a real girl struggling to find herself and keep her friends or family safe against impossible odds. She wants to discover the truth that has been kept from her, and from the populace more generally. She wants to cut the ties that bind and bring freedom to oppressed peoples. She is an outcast, a rebel.

Girls on Fire and Identity: Norms and Exceptions

Identity	Explanation	An Example	An Exception
Age is sometimes not overtly stated.	Most are 15 or 16. Some are 17 or 18. Stories usually span a year or less.	All protagonists are teenagers, adolescents, young women, girls.	Ruby in The Darkest Minds is 10 when she is institutionalized. Most of her story she is a teenager.

Identity	Explanation	An Example	An Exception
Race is mostly physical description.	Most are defacto white. Book covers often feature white girls.	Lena, in Delirium, is short and plain with brown hair.	Despite the ambiguous cover image for *Partials*, Kira is not white.
Class is reflective of hegemonic society	Most are lower class, poor, survivors living on little.	Saba in Dustlands scrapes together a meager living for her family.	June in *The Summer Prince* is a "tier-eight brat."
Gender is sometimes negotiated but always "girl."	Almost exclusively biological girls. Many balance feminine and masculine traits.	Katniss plays up her feminine qualities for the cameras, but some argue that she is more masculine than Peeta.	Petra, in *Beauty Queens*, is transgender (and a former boy band member).
Sexuality is often minimized, often implied, and acted out mostly through kissing.	Most assumed heterosexual. Some have sexual intercourse.	Juliet in *Shatter Me* knows Adam will always be patient.	Fen, in *Orleans*, never expresses a preference or engages in any romantic or sexual activity.
Ability does not hinder impact but influences sense of self.	Most are ordinary girls. Some are outcasts and some have special powers.	Tris is plain and unassuming as Abnegation. As Dauntless she falls short but perseveres.	Alex, in Ashes, has a brain tumor that becomes a "monster" and has its own power.

All of the Girls on Fire are an amalgamation of their identity traits, shaped by their life experiences and the dystopic conditions they live through.

She is sometimes successful, and sometimes not. Sometimes brave, sometimes vulnerable. She struggles and encounters hardships, sometimes losing nearly everyone and everything she has, sometimes losing many times over. Most often she endures and lives on her own terms, sometimes she just survives. Most often her story ends happily—which most often means with the boy/the love she cannot live without. But sometimes this scenario is more complicated, nuanced, or ambiguous. And sometimes this scenario is unique and empowering. Regardless, most of these books are full of mystery and adventure and weave places that imagine new worlds. And readers imagine further new worlds. Imagination is a powerful tool.

It is also no wonder that YA dystopia is read not just by girls and boys in the intended YA audience, but also by adult men and especially by adult women. Many of us describe the reading experience as a kind of addiction, bringing books with us everywhere we go, sneaking a few pages under the dinner table, staying up late into the night, devouring book after book. The readable nature makes these books enjoyable, but it is the ideas that they examine—the possibilities for the future and the present—that keep our attention. This book is ultimately about these dystopic ideas. What we do with these ideas—the future(s) they create and inspire—is only limited by our inability to see beyond our own narrow world.

Framing Wide from Narrow

YA dystopia may sound like a rather narrow subject, especially when we further limit the category to consider books that focus on a female protagonist.[1] Further, some of the politics of YA dystopia are, indeed, narrow and repetitive—romance as compulsory and heterosexual, the role of choice as of primary importance, the assumptions of whiteness. The narrow conventions of romance are the most tiresome aspect of these novels; however, this convention also tells us a lot about hope, love, and commitment to something bigger than ourselves. Love—romantic or not—is also in comparison with a variety of other relationships from friendship to family. The assumptions of whiteness are the most troublesome aspect of this collection of work because the possibilities of new worlds are limited by unexamined expectations of the old world; however, what this collection tells us about race and diversity is richer than the surface appears.

Not only is this collective of fiction not narrow, it is complicated and messy, layered and interconnected, creative and contested. Many scholarly and popular works take up the subjects of dystopia, YA dystopia, and YA dystopia with female protagonists and provide a variety of compelling and illuminating arguments about characters and plots, environment and romance, and many other topics that *Girls on Fire* considers as well. The wealth of scholarly and popular press and media attention to YA dystopia is deep and wide as much as it is shallow and narrow. Part I highlights, complicates, and extends these studies. But this book offers something that is simultaneously wider and narrower than previous studies—it considers the "narrow" category of young adult dystopia with female protagonists in its comparative wider depth and breadth, in and out of academia, on and off the page, and in the world and into the future.

In other words, this book establishes YA dystopia as framed by previous scholarship and then it goes wider and deeper and innovates interdisciplinary and intersectional ways of considering this genre/mode/cultural object. (I use the term genre throughout this book though it is not always the best descriptor.) Rather than consider a few key works in the larger genre, as most scholarly studies tend to do out of necessity and academic convention, this study considers more than 140 books and a wide variety of themes and subgenres. My work here contextualizes this body of YA dystopia within a variety of contexts and conversations including the necessity of interdisciplinary inquiry; contemporary culture as dystopia; the structures, themes and patterns of the genre; and applications and understandings of the ideas these works inspire. My net is cast wide and some of the details slip through the net, some of the critiques and approaches get overlooked, but overall, the contents are representative of what's in the wide, unknowable sea of the future.

The way this book approaches the topic of YA dystopia is shaped by the object of study. After establishing the base of understanding, my argument branches off in multiple directions, establishing lines of inquiry and theories that define and illuminate the vast and variegated terrain of YA dystopia and Girls on Fire. I work from the assumption of the power of literature and culture to shape rather than simply reflect. I work to complicate the center and illuminate the margins. The most popular books tell us a lot, but the less-well-known books are an integral part of the conversation.

Framing Narrow from Wide

The study of YA dystopia—specific and comparative, collective and individual—has been framed in a variety of ways by scholars and critics for decades. Each of these frames has to be adjusted for considerations of YA dystopia as separate and distinct from something else—like the long tradition of utopian literature and philosophy or the larger body of young adult literature—yet intricately related to each of the particular frames. Since the tendency in contemporary cultural criticism is toward specialization, individual works are more likely to be narrowly critiqued within these frames while the frames themselves are left as solid structures. This book more closely examines not only YA dystopia texts themselves, but also the way we understand and contextualize these works as scholars and critics and readers and students (and fans and haters). I reconsider the scholarly frames that shape critical analyses and offer new frames toward depth, connection, expansion, and empowerment.[2] These bigger pictures establish frames, structures, and possibilities.

Frames, Structures and Possibilities

Such a large and diverse body of works lends itself to a large and diverse number of frames, structures, and possibilities. I divide Part I and Part II as theory and practice. Part I, "Excavating Theories and Legacies," lays a foundation for understanding YA dystopia through interdisciplinarity and critical cultural studies. It is, essentially, an extended introduction to the threads woven throughout this book. I make some preliminary connections here to

YA dystopia, but Part II digs more deeply into the body of texts, providing comparative analyses and revealing diverse ties that bind this literature with life, culture with identity, and stories with activism.

The first chapter establishes the critical space of YA dystopia through an interdisciplinary/intersectional frame that can unpack, encompass, and extend the frames explored in chapter two and three. In other words, I look at some of the ways in which interdisciplinarity—working between and among disciplines—gives us a richer base for exploration of YA dystopia. An American studies lens also provides a critical frame, especially for understanding the political and cultural contexts that shape YA dystopia. Women's studies sheds further light on gender and sexuality. Some of the frames of dystopia and girls' studies speak to interdisciplinarity explicitly or implicitly, but in this first chapter I build upon what are mostly multidisciplinary models to demonstrate how interdisciplinarity and intersectionality (developed further in chapter 6) shape a mode of inquiry that can elucidate the complexity and possibility of YA dystopia.

The second chapter considers dystopian (and utopian) literary traditions more generally, especially as vehicles for social critique. Considering YA dystopia with female protagonists next to YA dystopia more generally, I illustrate the way boys and men have dominated many of our visions of the future. I then call on the mothers of dystopia and build a "transcendent community" of women writers and female protagonists that speak to the complexity and importance of the body of Girls on Fire YA dystopia. This chapter concludes with a brief review of some of the poplar and academic criticism of *The Hunger Games* and the female protagonist.

Chapter three considers girlhood and popular culture through the lens of women's studies, psychology, and girls' studies. These frames are important for understanding the role of the female protagonist and the cultural weight that she carries. YA dystopia gives girls opportunities that are still limited in the real world of contemporary American culture and politics. Gender and sexuality are navigated and negotiated by Girls on Fire and these personal struggles are connected to the expectations of the patriarchy. These books speak back to the institutions and structures that continue to limit girls' roles and opportunities. More importantly, they speak to the possibilities of transformation on the individual and structural levels.

All of these frames—interdisciplinary inquiry, dystopic legacies, and women's studies—reveal important aspects of YA dystopia, but they are all incomplete because they have to be. They are all pieces of the critical puzzle. *Girls on Fire* critiques and reconfigures the critical puzzle that we have been using to understand YA dystopia and seeks to add to these frames and open more space. The feminist critiques that chapter three discusses are important; however, they suffer from some of the limitations of both traditional and feminist critical and activist approaches—the unintentional reinforcement of white supremacy.

The frames that we typically use to understand this genre—literature, YA dystopia, and the female protagonist—are incomplete not only out of critical necessity, but also because they are each shaped by dominant approaches and "Anglo" tastes. They are, like virtually everything, white washed, not because of evil intent, but because of legacies of cultural and scholarly processes. The difference for YA dystopia as the object of critique—as opposed to other forms of popular culture—is that these books are exploring a future that is related to our contemporary world—our dystopic reality. To continue a pattern of white supremacy and its intersections with capitalism, patriarchy, heteronormativity, and exceptionalism is in direct contradiction with the ideas and ideals embodied in YA dystopia. And yet, like so many other cultural forms and scholarly inquiries, issues of race are pushed to the periphery and multivalent texts and analyses are left out or reduced. This dynamic is not necessarily intentional, but it is inevitable without active resistance and re-orientation. I try to harness critical legacies toward more radical ends.

Between the theory of Part I and the practice (or praxis) of Part II, "Interlude: Fangirling: A Passion for YA Dystopia" acts as a reminder that the visceral pleasure of reading is ultimately where the power lies.

In Part II, "Excavating Fiction, Imagination and Application," I put interdisciplinary and intersectional critical frames to work, illustrating and illuminating the characteristics that make this genre diverse despite is reoccurring themes. Chapter four explores our contemporary dystopia and the conditions of the present that authors and readers have to play with as we create and consume, process and use YA dystopia. This chapter defines the issues that illuminate the specific contexts—and many variations—of YA dystopia. Time, place, technology, disaster, decimation, invasion, slavery, nature, cyborgs, and zombies build the context and foundation of these stories—future worlds full of limitations and possibilities.

These interdisciplinary and intersectional dystopic themes pave the way to consider other defining structures and themes, characters and patterns. Chapter five extends my previous analysis of specific texts and considers the whole body of works as they overlap, intersect, and extend. The "YA Dystopia Tree" visualizes the body of these works and their relationship and a variety of charts help to compare and contrast the individual works that make up this rich and varied genre. Here I consider the importance of voice and narration, art and culture, violence, social control, walls as metaphor and reality, and choice as hope. I also consider the role of boys and men as the role of friendship. These many strands reveal the power and potential of the genre as a whole. The structures, themes, and patterns I consider in this chapter show us not only what these books reflect, but also what they build.

The sixth chapter begins by framing an intersectional approach and focuses on "Othered Girls on Fire" with particular attention to race and sexuality. Love and romance and sex outside the boundaries help us reconsider narrow readings and narrow representations. This chapter also considers whether while supremacy is an "unshakable structure" and how we might represent race responsibly in future scenarios. Two sections dig more deeply into several texts that highlight intersectional and indigenous stories. Drawing on intersectional feminism, I consider YA dystopia's Girls on Fire as implementing tools outside the master's control as well as the ways in which Girls on Fire go from being survivors to community-organizers to world-makers.

Chapter seven extends beyond the page, beyond the screen, into—and beyond—the classroom, considering pedagogy and process, interpretation and action, power and empowerment, as inspired by and through these texts. The mainstream books and engagement through a variety of pop culture forms and forums, often yield what appear to be more superficial results, but the power of a text cannot be contained. Moreover, just as we cannot limit the ways in which these texts will be interpreted by readers, we also cannot assume that reading and interaction that appears to be more shallow is not also transformative and, at least, influential in positive ways. With the right (dystopic) circumstances, and when presented for discussion and critical understanding, YA dystopia can inspire consciousness and action. My students prove this over and over; their sparks might just catch fire. And spaces at the edges, or outside, of the mainstream—like self-publishing and social media—hold potential toward transformations that go beyond the individual, beyond the page. At the very least, we cannot take the present for granted when we see what possible nightmares the future may hold. But we also should not burn ourselves out and can take self-care inspiration from Girls on Fire as well.

The trajectory of these chapters matches a process for understanding the power and potential of these texts when considered as a whole—as a specific context with multiple frames and a bigger picture. YA dystopia, even when we narrow the defining characteristics of the category, is a rich and vibrant object/subject. YA dystopia's Girls on Fire provide a platform for considering "Utopian Visions for Dystopian Realities" and my conclusion shows how utopia and dystopia are complementary—characteristic of our conflicted legacies and lives.

The power of YA dystopia and American futures resides with the Girl on Fire. Ordinary girl or extraordinary girl, she embodies hope. She is not the acted-upon ancestors or the "acting out" of her age group. She is the actor, the center. How we understand her reflects how we understand ourselves, how we understand YA dystopia and contemporary American dystopia, and how we understand the world(s) we simply inhabit or painstakingly alter.

ONE

Interdisciplinarity and Intersectionality
Modeling the Complex World[1]

"We are no longer naïve concerning the arena in which social problems exist—they exist entangled with every aspect of society.... Interdisciplinary studies may provide the means to finding creative and alternative solutions to contemporary world problems, especially where social-political issues are entangled in the material remedies. This can only be achieved if a dialog of social justice engages both the physical sciences and the liberal arts.... These overlapping worlds have been treated as distinct for far too long" [xxi].
—R.P. Clair, *Zombie Seed and the Butterfly Blues: A Case for Social Justice*

We live in an interdisciplinary world. YA dystopia—in its texts, critiques, and applications—is interdisciplinary. Interdisciplinarity is not stagnant. It is changing. It may very well be that in another 30 years new disciplinary structures have arisen; or perhaps there will be none at all. Academic knowledge can only try to understand, make sense and order of, the world around us—part natural, part constructed, and much contested. This is what Cassia does in *Matched*. She is a sorter. She explains, "The government has computers that can do sorts much faster than we can, of course, but we're still important. You never know when technology might fail" (32). Sorters are part of a larger system of order and specialization. "Such specialization keeps people from becoming overwhelmed. We don't need to understand *everything*. And, as the Society reminds us, there's a difference between knowledge and technology. Knowledge doesn't fail us" (32). But knowledge, without a full context, has already failed.

Interdisciplinarity is a kind of sorting, but rather than narrow and specialized, interdisciplinarity brings order to the chaos of "*everything.*" We don't need to understand everything, and we need a certain amount of specialization, but we also need to understand ideas and realities between and among, across and within. In short, interdisciplinarity crosses traditional disciplinary lines (like English, Biology, Music, Sociology…), working between and among them to apply multiple perspectives and develop new syntheses for a deeper understanding of a topic, issue, or problem. The topics, issues, and problems are, themselves, interdisciplinary. One lens is not enough to understand the world or the self.

The legacies in chapters two and three provide an important basis for understanding YA dystopia in interdisciplinary ways. These foundations are particularly demonstrative of segregated critical approaches simply by virtue of being a part of a segregated society/culture. This segregation speaks to the importance of interdisciplinary and intersectional approaches as a tool for a deeper and wider understanding of texts and their real-world contexts. Interdisciplinary approaches recognize the rich variety of material that these books tackle, including the important elements of science and technology as well as the sociological elements of world-building and the psychological elements of character development. Interdisciplinarity plus intersectionality teases out the social justice elements of YA dystopia. As R.P. Clair argues, "Bringing seemingly disparate fields together through novel approaches may give new insights into the entangled worlds in which we live, giving social justice a chance to surface and spread" (xxi). The "novel" approaches of YA dystopia are both literal and figurative, and an understanding of interdisciplinary theories and structures brings forth the intersectional and social justice aspects of this pop culture phenomenon explored in part two.

Connecting with the Segregated Sciences

Science fiction has the ability to bring together the segregated spaces of the Humanities and the Sciences, often seen as distinct, and opposite, approaches in academia. Not only do students and professors in the Humanities tend to fear and avoid math and science, the approaches and worldviews in the Sciences are often posed as opposite from those in the Humanities. But R.P. Clair argues, "Science is meant to touch and improve our lives, not alienate us from ourselves. Social problems cannot be so easily segregated these days" (xx). What science can bring to the Humanities is important for a more integrated world-view as well as for a richer understanding of YA dystopia and possible futures.

Scientists also collaborate with social scientists, bringing a more human connection to the insights of science. Social science can provide insights into scientific studies that are social and cultural. Social science can also bridge the gap between science and people. As John W. Rowe argues in the introduction to *Interdisciplinary Research*, interdisciplinarity is "vital for the well-being of science *and* society ... whether in the form of scientific research and scholarly inquiry or interventions and policy aimed at improving individual health and social well-being" (446). Individual health as well as the well-being of society are more complex than science can measure and evaluate. But scientific topics are taken up in YA dystopia as Girls on Fire navigate health concerns like *amor deliria nervosa* (Delirium), Delta Fever (*Orleans*), the plague (Legend, *Shadows Cast by Stars*), environmental disturbances (*The Forgetting*, Breathe), the flu (Last Survivors series), reproductive control (Eve, Chemical Garden series), manipulated brainwaves (Ashes), reconstructed bodies (Cinder, Tankborn), and epidemics of all kinds (Enclave).

Scientific language, relationships, and advances can be difficult for non-scientists to fully understand or accept; this makes collaboration between science and the humanities a challenge. As Craig Calhoun and Cora Marrett explain in their foreword, there's a "difference between simply transporting a technique from one field to another, or citing research across disciplinary boundaries" (xxii). Such integrative work is difficult in fields where techniques, language, and process can be very different. As Aletha C. Huston notes in "A Path to Interdisciplinary Scholarship": "truly interdisciplinary scholarship requires participants to learn how to think in the lexicon of other disciplines, at least to some degree" (266). As a result, in many interdisciplinary endeavors, sciences are often segregated from the Humanities. But in YA dystopia, the lexicon is both from our real world as well as the world built for the book (a word that inevitably also reflects our own). Science is integrated into the plot; it is not segregated, it is re-imagined. It saves and enhances the life of the Girl on Fire in *Cinder* and *The Adoration of Jenna Fox*. Both girls struggle with the artificial aspects of their minds and bodies. It controls societies—monitoring and restricting basic needs—in *Matched*, where food delivered for each meal and all refuse is monitored and processed, and *Breathe,* where oxygen is distributed based on class. It modifies brains and personalities in Uglies and *The Summer Prince*. Science holds many possibilities in the future and reflects our struggles with fast-moving, all-consuming technologies in the present.

Sherri L. Smith, author of *Orleans*, considers how speculative fiction "gives us a place to ponder the direction long before the science puts us on the path" (40). She explains, "I'll lump SF and dystopia together under speculative fiction and say that the value of speculative fiction is the value of humanity. We dream. We question. And we try to find answers ... [it] has served as a collective conscience for society, warning us away from god complexes and totalitarianism" (40). Speculative fiction is where we find the stories that connect us through our shared future and dystopia reminds us what's at stake.

Stories Are the Stuff the Connects Us

One connection between the sciences and the Humanities is stories. The stories told by and about Girls on Fire integrate science and technology with the impacts of these on the lives of humans and on the balance of societies or civilizations. Stories, as R.P. Clair argues and illustrates, also link to social justice. Adhesion, integration, application, transformation—stories are bigger than just words on a page (or a screen). As Anderson and Blayer argue, "Stories are sticky. They adhere to many surfaces, such as when you cannot get one out of your head but more fundamentally they bond all manner of things" (1). Stories connect and extend. Many critics, across a variety of fields, have written about the importance of stories in a plethora of historical and cultural contexts. Literature—of the capital L variety—as well as the popular and the pulp have been understood through their power to tell stories and explored from a variety of angles. In *Minds Made for Stories*, Thomas Newkirk argues, "We rely on stories not merely for entertainment, but for explanation, meaning, self-understanding. We instinctively make connections of cause and effect, and always have. To deny the centrality of narrative is to deny our own nature" (16). Stories are, he argues, "hardwired" into our brains (28). He means this literally. We create stories where there are no stories; we become engaged with ideas and subjects we might not otherwise pursue if there's a good story to relay the information or persuade us to think a certain way about something. We tell stories about ourselves.

The power of stories has been recognized through the Social Fictions Series, a project of Sense Publishers, edited by Patricia Leavy. As R.P Clair explains In *Zombie Seed and the Butterfly Blues: A Case of Social Justice*, one of the foundational ideas to the social contexts series is that "there is much to learn through fiction" (n.p.).[2] The books in this series are considered part of the "arts-based research movement" and "each book includes an academic introduction that explains the research and teaching that informs the book as well as how the book can be used in college courses." They provide a tool and a theoretical/pedagogical context for the stories and part of the potential power is in the way that "the books are underscored with social science or other scholarly perspectives and intended to be relevant to the lives of college students—to tap into important issues in the unique ways that artistic or literary forms can" (n.p.). Artistic and literary forms are spaces where interpretation can roam more freely; they are a part of a culture of possibilities.

As Anderson and Blayer, argue, "Narratives breathe life into culture even as they draw sustenance from it, a flexible, frequently contested relationship" (3). The reciprocal relationship between narratives and culture can move us forward or hold us back. Science fiction generally, and YA dystopia specifically, can play an important role in the futures we imagine. Raymond Williams argues, in "Science Fiction" (in 1956), "Fiction is a kind of fact, although it takes some people centuries to get used to it. To point out that its substance is imaginary, or fantastic, is no criticism of it, for that is the kind of fact it is: a thing man has thought or imagined, rather than observed or made" (Milner 13). The power of fiction is central to a variety of interdisciplinary studies, particularly in critical humanities areas like cultural studies.

The centrality of stories to our understanding of ourselves has been foundational long before we had print and they will continue to be foundational as the modes for storytelling continue to change. As Cass notes in *Shadows Cast by Stars*, "words hold power…. They make the impossible real" (97–8). While YA dystopia adheres to many of the qualities of dystopia (as capital L literature), its intended audience of young adults/teens—and its unintended audiences that span a variety of groups, particularly middle-age women—means that this particular literary form has a power to reach further than Literature. And it does, through movies, e-books, and mass-marketed paperbacks as well as films, music, magazines, blogs, memes. Thus, these literary frames extend into popular spaces. These popular spaces can be better understood through interdisciplinary approaches like cultural studies, American studies, and women's studies.

Cultural Studies: Interdisciplinarity Beyond Humanities

The Humanities is often seen as the realm where stories circulate. Humanities speaks to the classical traditions—the arts and letters, the capital L literature, the Greeks, the past. Humanities celebrates texts for their creativity and ability to speak to and about the human experience. Humanities is many different things at once and brings together similar fields like Literature (English), History, Philosophy, Art, and Music. "The Humanities" have a specific history, rooted in the works of ancient cultures, and an evolving canon of texts that recognizes the historical and contemporary, traditional and innovative. But the Humanities are under attack. The situation is so dire that Zhange Ni argues, in "A New Defense of Poetry: Viral Power, Bio-Capitalism, and Ally Condie's *Matched* Series," "regarding the marginalization of the humanities, it is no exaggeration to say we are living in a dystopian world" (177). Ni offers a brilliant analysis of the Humanities via the Matched series. She argues that "this renewed vision has implications for our understanding of the radical possibilities of not just the poetic genre but poetry standing for creative arts and the humanities in general" (165). She explores the characters—Cassia (the poet); Ky (the pilot); and Xander (the physic) and "the collaboration of poetry, science, and politics" (171). Ultimately, Ni Argues, "the virus of poetry has taken advantage of the popular dystopian trend in young adult literature, an unexpected site where humanities can be investigated and reconceptualized, not just defended in their current shape" (180). YA dystopia can save the Humanities and maybe even the world.

While Humanities is often a buzzword and concept used to preserve traditional ideas, Cultural Studies questions tradition and argues for the importance of all voices, all texts, especially those of the oppressed and marginalized. The qualities that unite Humanities—in method and subject— make interdisciplinary movement among them more fluid; they are textual and open for interpretation. For instance, history informs literature. Cultural Studies integrates social sciences (like economics, sociology, political science, and psychology) and, thus, crosses disciplinary lines more than the interdisciplinarity among the Humanities. Cultural studies ferrets out the stories that are not on the surface; it finds stories in all kinds of places and in patterns and practices as much as texts.

Cultural Studies is both wider and narrower than Humanities. Cultural studies is a shared commitment to critical analysis and political engagement. It is practiced within disciplinary boundaries and between and among them. As Klein describes, "Cultural studies is a general form of the bottom-up model" (59). Cultural studies takes the Humanities outside of their narrow box—it expands and explodes the object to "culture" and "texts" of all kinds. It pushes Humanities to engage us personally and politically. Cultural studies is "critical humanities." And critical dystopias are a key example of how texts can be shaped by political ideas and ideals. As Miller notes, the focus is gender, race, class, and sexuality in everyday life, under the sign of a commitment to progressive social change (108). This is also one focus in my study of Girls on Fire.

What also distinguishes Cultural Studies from other fields is self-consciousness, positioning, and transparency. When considering YA dystopia through this lens, we can see the more powerful and empowering aspects of this pop culture phenomenon. But Cultural Studies lends itself to all kinds of interdisciplinary connections and is a larger umbrella for American studies, which elucidates the elements of place, space, and nation, and Women's studies, which focuses on gender, sexuality, patriarchy, and intersections and often centers social justice.

American Studies and Women's Studies

In order to get to the critical root of YA dystopia we have to unpack legacies in criticism and fiction, legacies of our culture. In my teaching and research American studies, women's studies, and cultural studies are virtually the same thing with complementary structures but a different focus. And all of these fields are contested: what is the "American" in American studies?; "women's studies" does not speak to the field's elements of gender, sexuality, race, class, and other intersections; and "culture" can be defined in about a million different ways. But these challenges create important points of conversation and help us to see what is American about texts that focus on gender, for instance, and how literature can become a powerful cultural symbol.

Critical interdisciplinarity must take on multiple lenses. American studies brings a critical lens that elucidates the ideologies of nationalism and the ways in which old ideas of American exceptionalism, American identity, and American politics play out in our stories. American studies provides radical perspectives considering root issues and the centrality of social change and transformation. Women's studies makes the female protagonist a worthy focus of study with her own multidimensionality, her own place in the cultural imagination, her own power as symbol and social actor. Both fields aim to work toward social justice, to hold the U.S. accountable to its ideals and ideologies, to make gender equality a reality instead of a fantasy. The relevance of the interdisciplinary field of women's studies to YA dystopia's female protagonists is obvious, and I explore these theories and legacies further in chapter three.

What is also American about these texts is a mix of location, politics, tradition, culture, and—most often—the ramifications of living the way we live in the present. The Rusties of Uglies and the Wreckers of Dustlands have damaged the earth that the future generations inherit, for instance. Our Western lifestyle and American values are often the cause of the problems in future worlds. *Orleans* takes place in a future where The Outer States have separated from their Southern troubles. In *Legend*, The Republic and The Colonies divide the east and west of what was the U.S. Co-protagonist, Day, wears a quarter dollar (from our present) that represents freedom and possibility— the United States was real despite what people have been led to believe. Some American elements of these texts are contested.

Kat Zhang, author of The Hybrid Chronicles, creates a world where hybrids—two people sharing one body—are oppressed. In "the Americas" hybrids are illegal and are blamed for all of society's ills. The Americas are isolated and underdeveloped compared to the rest of the world. The government lies to the populace and works to eliminate recessive souls between birth and ten years of age. The similarities to our world are blunt objects: a country created after the Great Wars, ruled by the same President and his family for a century. Zhang expands the U.S. to "the Americas" but the book clearly takes place in what could be the United States. In *Never Fade* (second book in Darkest Minds series), the connections to the U.S. are clear: "All along, President Gray had been insistent in his weekly addresses that Americans were pulling themselves up by the bootstraps and taking care of themselves and their countrymen" (364). The United Nations has put economic sanctions on the U.S. The markets have crashed; and President Gray insists that "Americans would help Americans" (364). Americans suffer from this philosophy in both of these series because the state has made enemies of potential allies.

What is also American about these texts is the ways in which we relate to the rest of the world—ignoring it, controlling it, wondering about it, fantasizing about it. In *Article 5* the Federal Bureau of Reformation has been established, "the branch of the military the president had created at the end of the war three years ago … to halt the chaos that had reigned during the five years that America had been mercilessly attacked" (12), though we never learn who has attacked America, only that cities have been destroyed and evacuated. A few texts are set outside of the United States, or what was formerly the U.S. *Cinder* takes place in a future China (The Eastern Commonwealth), but this text is totally American. *The Summer Prince* is set in Brazil, but has been influenced by immigration and is part of "The Americas" of the future. In *Shatter Me*, the United States reaches across the world through The Reestablishment which is "struggling to root itself as a new form of government across all international societies" (32). The Reestablishment is an "initiative that was supposed to help our dying society" (1). It "had its hands in every country, ready to bring its leaders into a position of control … the inhabitable land left in the world has been divided into 3,333 sectors and each space is now controlled by a different Person of Power" (31). The Reestablishment justifies its power and control as well as "killing all the voices of opposition" as "the only way to find peace" (31).

Some texts are American in the continental sense like Canada (North America) and Brazil (South America), and some are not "American" at all in setting or author origin (Australia and The U.K.); but these books are a part of the cultural imagination, accessible to a U.S. reading audience through Amazon.com, for instance. These multifaceted contexts are important not only for comparative American studies, but also because our future is a shared collective endeavor. American studies asks us to consider "America" as it exists in the cultural imagination, in the world outside U.S. borders, and in the shared concerns of the global environment. Borders, social control, choice, political process, and geography, along with social and cultural traditions, language, and identities are some of the elements elucidated by YA dystopia's Girls on Fire.

While there are many elements of these texts that are "American," and while these elements lend themselves to "American studies" in its simplest understanding and application, ultimately, what is "American studies" about my analysis is the critical approach. This critical approach is also foundational to cultural studies, as I discuss above, and utopian/dystopian studies, as I will further explore in chapter two. This critical approach is also foundational to feminist women's studies. But, it is important to note here that in deploying interdisciplinary theories and critiques, we must remain critically vigilant in recognizing our power and privilege.[3] The self-reflexivity that is central in these fields cannot only reflect upon those elements that are most present in the text, but also those elements that are rendered invisible. Interdisciplinarity that is also intersectional must interrogate white supremacy and heteronormativity, among other vectors of inequality and oppression that operate on individual and structural levels. Cultural criticism continues to evolve toward intersectionality, and YA dystopia's Girls on Fire can bolster these critical frames.

* * *

Interdisciplinarity in American studies and women's studies also speaks to the diversity of topics and ideas that give us time and space to think about the future, and how to get there. Without intersectionality, interdisciplinarity suffers from a lack of perspective, particularly global perspectives and perspectives that center the experiences of women. For instance, as we consider disaster stories, we should also consider that many places in the U.S. and around the word are already suffering from this form of dystopia. Climate change, exacerbated by waste in the developed nations, directly impacts the lives of these nations that are in danger of losing their homes in the next few decades. We might also consider that women around the world are responsible for the majority of food, water, and fuel needs for their families. Half of the world's women are cooking on open fires. People are living with the techniques that our protagonists use in the dire circumstances of dystopia. Women are disproportionately impacted. Girls carry the weight of the future today. Girls are already heroes—in fiction and in life.

Before we can explore the stories of YA's Girls on Fire, and the girl heroes who spark our imaginations, we need to better understand the foundations of these texts and our popular and scholarly understanding of YA dystopia and its many contexts—literary and cultural, popular and academic, mainstream and revolutionary.

Two

Shaping Dystopic Literature as Young Adult, Feminist and Critical

As the larger umbrella for (YA) dystopia, the wide category of science fiction holds the power to explore worlds that are not our own but bear important resemblances. The power of social critique in science fiction has become more developed in the last several decades, but it is particularly relevant in our contemporary world. In *Scraps of the Untainted Sky* Tom Moylan argues, "at its most significant, [science fiction] can be a part of the process of mobilizing the cultural imagination. It can be part of making the world 'legible' in a way that not only delivers pleasure and knowledge but also the joys of joining in the collective, historical work of bringing a more just and free society into being" (28). My work here seeks to harness this very power, illuminating the pleasure and knowledge of YA dystopia with female protagonists and highlighting the voices of girls—a group whose voice is often excluded from "the collective, historical work of bringing a more just and free society into being."

Science fiction has played this role for centuries even as it elicits criticism for its imaginary mode of social critique. As Moylan explains, "The infamous 'escapism' attributed to sf does not necessarily mean a debilitating escape *from* reality because it can also lead to an empowering escape *to* a very different way of thinking about, and possibly of being in, the world" (xvii). Many different types of literature provide escapism and YA dystopia certainly includes this element, particularly through its romantic aspects. However, as Moylan argues, "such works can bring willing readers back to their own worlds with new or clearer perceptions, possibly helping them to raise their own consciousness about what is right and wrong in that world, and even to think about what is to be done, especially in concert with others, to change it for the better" (xvii). Consciousness and action are important here, and as

Moylan continues, "Throw in the particular modality of utopian and dystopian narratives and the possibilities get all the more interesting—and all the more useful and dangerous" (xvii). In fact, dangerous is exactly what Girls on Fire are.

Of course, also like any other literature or cultural product, the category does not guarantee transformational power. Moylan argues, "To be sure, many sf stories fail to deliver on this larger critical potential, for they deliver no more than a one-dimensional extrapolation or a simple adventure" (xvii). Many of YA dystopia's Girls on Fire offer simple adventures and some female protagonists fall short of being a fully self-actualized Girl on Fire. The overt or covert or unintentional reinforcement of mainstream ideas are one way that Girls on Fire can fall short. But even in the most "one-dimensional" works there is value to the collective swath of this genre and the meanings we make from it. Through discussion, critique, and context, every YA dystopian text has critical or oppositional potential in varying degrees; together they are on fire.

Legacies of Utopia/Dystopia

It is not uncommon to hear critics and fans refer to dystopia as the "opposite of utopia." This is not incorrect, but it is an oversimplified understanding of a long legacy. A sweeping view considers "Utopia" as encompassing dystopia. As Raymond Williams illustrates in his 1978 piece "Utopia and Science Fiction," utopia and dystopia are "comparative rather than absolute categories" (Milner 94) and he details four types of "alternative realities" that can be explored through utopia or dystopia. As Milner explains, what distinguishes these from science fiction is, in part, the necessity of having an "'implied connection' with the real: the whole point of utopia or dystopia is to acquire some positive or negative leverage on the present" (93). Dystopia certainly leverages the present, and YA dystopia's Girls on Fire is wired into the pulse of contemporary girlhood, a different cultural foundation from classical utopian writings and critical traditions.

And, of course, these designations of "utopia" and "dystopia" continue to be contested and articulated by scholars, critics, writers, and fans. For instance, Sharon Wilson notes in her introduction to *Women's Utopian and Dystopian Fiction*, titled "Utopian, Dystopian, Ustopian, Science Fiction, and Speculative Fiction," that "little agreement exists about distinctions among science fiction, fantasy, speculative fiction, utopia, and dystopia" (1). Unfortunately, her introduction does a poor job of elucidating these categories. Regardless, utopia imagines what the future can be; dystopia imagines what the future will inevitably be … without intervention in the present. Plenty of conversation on the subject exists in and out of academia. I am less concerned with the dividing lines, and when we center YA dystopia in this matrix, the classic, contemporary, and nascent understandings are developed through new dimensions. Further, when dystopia is so intricately linked with the conditions of our present, we can see how not only the negotiation of these dystopian conditions, but also the creation of settings where the rules of the modern dystopia do not apply (not technically utopia), are an important part of this genre.

One of the best examples of utopia/dystopia in the Girls on Fire stories is the world created by *The Forgetting*. Greed and corruption are responsible for the turn as much as the unforeseen effects of flora and fauna and a comet that sets The Forgetting into motion—an event that wipes people's memories clear every 12 years. The people of Canaan, we find, are actually from earth, sent to this planet with two directives. One hundred and fifty people were screened and selected for this mission. The first directive, which everyone knows about, is "to build and populate the first civilization created to exist in harmony with itself and its environment … to live without bloodshed, without money, without industry, without waste … with respect for the land … with minimal technology" (217). The second directive, that is only known to some, is to explore the planet and find the natural resources that can be plundered. When they have found these resources, they are supposed to signal earth so that mining can begin. It is this fact that brings the utopic settlement to civil war just before the first Forgetting happens. And, despite the fact that Janis has been manipulating people's lives and the entire society for generations (in an attempt to activate that signal), it turns out the signal had already been activated and has been sending the signal for over 100 years. No one has arrived. After a vote, they turn off the signal and focus on re-building a society that has survived the worst of dystopic circumstances. Going forward, utopia might just be possible.

In the Shadow of the Canon: Where the Boys Have Been

When we think of dystopia—in academia and in popular culture—the "classic" literary texts, largely written by men, are the texts that come to mind and to popular culture references. Lois Lowry explains how she was required to read classic dystopian texts like *Fahrenheit 451*, *Nineteen-Eighty-Four*, *Brave New World*, and even *Animal Farm*, which Lowry notes is a kind of dystopia in its own right. Among these classics, the classic feminist texts have established a strong voice in science fiction, but still remain segregated as "feminist." With occasional nods to Ursula LeGuin, Margaret Atwood (who won a 2017 lifetime achievement award from the National Book Critics Circle), or Octavia Butler, science fiction texts by men—especially in popular culture—remain the standard by which legitimate science fiction and dystopia are measured.[1] Browse any list of the "best" science fiction—films or literature—and the women are largely absent, like any other list of cultural "bests." Lists of feminist science fiction are often a different category with separate lists.

Classic dystopian texts join the classic science fiction texts, which are also heavily dominated by male protagonists and masculine pursuits. Lowry also notes that later, "as a housewife who read a lot" she "loved Margaret Atwood's *The Handmaid's Tale*," which she partially attributes to the shared Cambridge, Massachusetts setting. This text reminds women how quickly our bodies can be used for someone else's reasons, a lesson that resonated with many housewives who read a lot—a lesson that was transmitted via Lois Lowry's imagined society where people have no idea what they are missing in their controlled, safe world. But Lowry's classic YA dystopia text follows the masculine tradition. Jonas is designated keeper of people's memories. Thus, writers also invest in masculine legacies. It is more common to see women writing about male protagonists than it is to see men writing about female protagonists. Lois Lowry also notes that it is easier to write female protagonists (Conners). In fact, only three of the YA dystopia books/series I consider here, as YA dystopia with female protagonist, were written by men (and Dan Wells also bravely tackles race in the Partials trilogy). As Rojas Weiss notes, online conversations where male authors who "shy away from writing female characters" defend their reliance on male characters can cause "major drama in the young-adult novel blogosphere." These patterns reflect our social and cultural norms and they deserve more critical attention.

Masculine, patriarchal legacies—in and out of science fiction—shape YA dystopia. Categorization of children's and YA books often determine a book is for girls if they include a female protagonist, but are considered to be for a general audience if the protagonist is a boy. This is an obvious result of sexism and the way it has shaped our expectations of what is and is not interesting or important. We are sending a message to boys that they should not be interested in girls' lives and experiences, that girls are somehow not worthy of the same opportunities let alone the role of protagonist. Further, in all of pop culture generally, girls are often tokenized—the solo female character among a cast of boys—what Katha Pollitt referred to as the "Smurfette Principle" in a 1991 *New York Times Magazine* article. "The message is clear," she writes, "boys are the norm, girls are the variation; boys are central, girls are peripheral; boys are individuals, girls are types…. Girls exist only in relation to boys." This principle is alive and well today and can be seen, for instance, in Star Wars films, The Lord of the Rings books and films, the Harry Potter franchise, *The Maze Runner* dystopian novel and film, and in

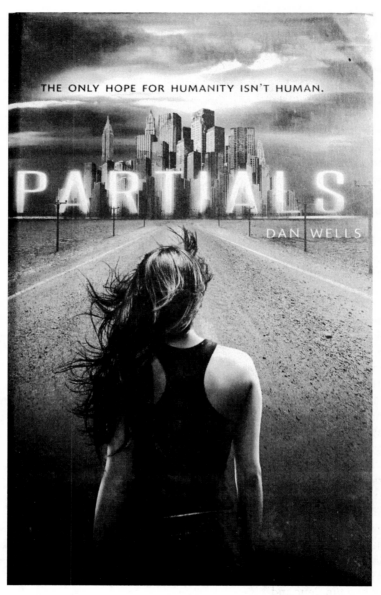

Kira's retreating figure exemplifies a frequently used pose on the cover of these books. Showing her from the back is an easy way to obscure her race and a good example of whitewashing. Kira is explicitly identified as a girl of color and the author, Dan Wells, writes overtly about racism, but this cover doesn't represent this content (Blazer + Bray [HarperCollins]. Jacket art ©2012 by Craig Shields. Photo of girl ©2012 by Howard Huang. Jacket design by Alison Klapthor).

just about every action film (if women are present at all). We invest in these legacies.

Some of the most popular and seminal works like *Ender's Game, The Giver, Maze Runner,* and *Feed* all feature boys in ways that reinforce male dominance, even as these texts also sometimes try to challenge assumptions about gender. For instance, *Ender's Game* (and the extended series) includes a few strong female characters like Ender's friend Petra, and while she is equally brilliant, her ability to come through under pressure is questioned. And, in *Feed*, ideas of masculinity are challenged as Titus takes pleasure in being a man through rather shallow and stereotypical gestures like protecting Violet and hugging her "like a man" (75). These empty symbols of manhood are all he knows—masculinity has been filtered through decades of advertising propaganda and mind control. And the love interest, Violet, plays a pivotal role in opening Titus's eyes and heart (like the boys of YA dystopia's Girls on Fire books) and expanding the landscape of his world amidst a cacophony of cultural noise. She challenges the feed and pays the price. It takes Titus longer to figure things out; and when he does, it might be too late, not just for him but for the planet and all of human existence.

While *The Hunger Games* proved that a female protagonist can be just as engaging for boys as for girls, many critics make assumptions that certain books are more or less appealing to boys. Books about girls that are touted as more "gender neutral" or "for boys as well as girls," tend to be more action-oriented and largely ignore gender rather than engage with its possible consequences in the future. *Uglies* is the best example of a book about a girl that might as well be about a boy, and the series as a whole fails to engage gender, even as it challenges ideas about beauty. The majority of the books are spent travelling around, and narrowly escaping, on hoverboards. It is certainly an interesting and entertaining read but having female characters without depth should not be mistaken for being "gender neutral." In the world of Uglies, gender does not really exist and the markers of female are forced in *Pretties*, like through dreams of princesses.

Some writers balance the female protagonist with other main characters who sometimes share narration (which will be considered more fully in chapter five). These voices are varied—female foils, friends, the love interest. Other writers attempt to balance the female protagonist with a male protagonist like Susan Beth Pfeffer in *Life as We Knew It* and its companion novels, *The Dead and the Gone* and *This World We Live In*. In *The Dead and Gone* we are introduced to the same set of events as they unfold in the life of Alex Morales, a Puerto Rican American in New York City. While *Life as We Knew It* is told through Miranda's diary entries, Alex's story is told in third person as he looks after his two younger sisters after the disappearance of both his parents. In the third book, we shift back to Miranda's diary as her life intersects with

Alex's. Likewise, in the Lunar Chronicles, Meyer creates two strong female protagonists in Cinder and Scarlett (and two struggling to be "strong" and succeeding in the end, Cress and Winter), but balances them out with the "bad boys" of Wolf, an ex-gang member and street fighter, and the escaped convict, Carswell Thorne. Both are heroes despite their faults, and are more complicated than surface appearances. Both are also good looking, of course. And both become coupled with our female protagonists: Wolf and Scarlett as the alpha male and female and Thorne becomes the good-hearted hero Cress always wanted him to be.

All of these examples of YA dystopia and male protagonists also center around white characters (except, for instance, Alex, who is Puerto Rican, an identity that shapes his narrative in rather stereotypical ways). When diversity is a concern, there may still be an emphasis on male protagonists. For instance, the edited collection, *Diverse Energies*, includes a rich variety of dystopia that still remains focused on male protagonists. The book's cover description explains:

> In this stunning collection of original and rediscovered stories of tragedy and hope, the stars are a diverse group of students, street kids, good girls, kidnappers, and child laborers pitted against their environments, their governments, differing cultures, and sometimes one another as they seek answers in their dystopian worlds. Take a journey through time from a nuclear nightmare of the past to society's future beyond Earth with these eleven stories by masters of speculative fiction.

Of the 11 stories in this collection, only three have female protagonists (though there are five female contributors) and one of these is Ursula K. LeGuin's Nebula winning short story, "Solitude." Malinda Lo's story "Good Girl" and "Uncertainty Principle" by K. Tempest Bradford round out the female protagonists.

Both editors of this collection, Tobias S. Buckell and Joe Monti, speak from their individual mixed identities and extrapolate the diversity of the future and the real and fictional needs. Buckell's short preface relates his experience growing up "split between two worlds" where books "never looked like the world in which [he] lived" (9). Monti similarly describes the "wonderful, blended, messed-up world" that he grew up in on the East coast (308). The books Buckell loved were "tales of fantasy, strange lands, strange worlds, strange futures, and adventure" (10). But these books offer "only one kind of hero, one kind of face on the cover./ When I moved to America, I realized why" (10). He explains why he is committed to writing books with diverse characters: "It's the future face of the world. It's us. All of us. And we all deserve to be seen in the future, having adventures, setting foot on those strange new worlds" (10). Indeed.

The book jacket for *Diverse Energies* promises such stories: "The future is here. Are you ready?" and "In a world gone wrong, heroes and villains are not always easy to distinguish and every individual has the ability to contribute something powerful" draw the reader into a vision of the future that is more diverse than the typical YA dystopian offerings. Monti explains that *Diverse Energies* is "an anthology about a wonderful, blended, messed-up future not as a role model, but a touchstone" (309). The editors and authors provide a collection to draw inspiration from. Monti continues, "Having people of color/Caucasian/LGBT protagonists in stories by these writers is not a brick thrown at a window; it is the continued paving of a path" (309). Monti ends his afterword with a quote by LeGuin: "the children of the revolution are always ungrateful, and the revolution must be grateful that it is so" (309). The path that YA dystopia continues to pave remains focused on the actions and stories of boys, but the Girl on Fire challenges the Smurfette Principle and patriarchal institutions and legacies.

* * *

Despite the continued importance of boys' texts and experiences, the Girl on Fire is prolific. In the YA dystopia category, she outnumbers the male protagonist, even as he is almost always by her side, on the side, in the background, or in some other pivotal role. In fact while female protagonists dominate the genre, the supporting cast of characters is not often made up of girls. Boys clearly have an important role as comrades in the struggles to save the world (or to save themselves at least). Fathers are important parts of stories whether they are evil, gone, or sometimes even doting parental figures. Brothers are protective of their sisters, even when they are Girls on Fire, and men and boys play the role of helper sometimes as well. So, even as girls take center stage, they do not do it all on their own and they are often up against masculine power. But they are the center—the one on fire. The fact that they have a plethora of supporting characters who are men and boys only makes sense. Boys stoke the fire in formulaic and novel ways and, perhaps, challenge traditional patriarchy. Girls who are only allowed power in the roles and spaces where girls are allowed to have power, are only figments of the patriarchy's imagination. Dan Wells, one of the few male authors in this body of books, knows this. In the Acknowledgments section to one of the Partials books, he writes:

> Last of all, this book owes perhaps its biggest debt to the ultimate models for Kira and Heron and every other awesome girl in the Partial series: my two daughters. May you always have heroines to inspire you, role models to look up to, and the freedom and courage to make your own choices, no matter how simple or scary or hard or eternal they may be [452–3].

Girls on Fire have been simmering and smoldering, creating a foundation for the recent explosion that this book considers. But their mothers establish roots and foundations.

The Mothers of YA Dystopia: A Transcendent Community

Science fiction by men is allowed to tackle the issues of the times in a way that favors masculine themes and supposedly neutral issues. It confirms the world as patriarchal because it does not (or cannot) imagine it as anything else. Narrow conceptualizations of gender, and limited access and encouragement, tend to keep power structures in place in fiction and criticism. Feminist science fiction writers and critics have been making this argument, and creating their own spaces, for decades. Feminist science fiction often occupies its own category—a segregation that speaks to dominant power structures as much as to the power of a tradition in science fiction that illustrates the unique quality of feminist texts. The tradition is separate, in part, because feminist science fiction critiques the very structures of patriarchy that ensures that it will be marginalized because of its content. There are not always direct lines to draw from Mothers to the Girls on Fire of YA dystopia, but the tradition of women writers and feminist writers and critics has made space for women and girls to write, read, critique, and expand dystopian visions.

Very few people have probably ever read or even heard of Margaret Cavendish's 1666 *The Blazing World* or Charlotte Perkins Gilman's feminist and socialist serialized novel, *Herland* (and perhaps even less so, *With Her in Ourland: Sequel to Herland*). Both of these texts turn the world of men upside down. Few probably consider how Mary Shelley essentially invented science fiction in 1818 when she wrote *Frankenstein* as a teenager (Pharr and Clark). Some of us discover Margaret Atwood's *The Handmaid's Tale* in a college (like Lois Lowry), or maybe high school classroom. (And more will discover this book through the 2017 Hulu original series.) Science fiction by women—to be true to the nature of the genre—must confront the way in which the world is organized along gender lines in ways that texts by men do not have to. The absurdity of the inequalities of gender lend themselves to the kind of social and cultural critique that science fiction provides. Women and girls—and their allies—understand this.

The connections between fiction by women for girls and fiction by women about girls create a web of influence that transcends many boundaries, including time. Joy James's idea of transcendent community is fitting for a consideration of YA dystopia and feminist science fiction. As she explains in *Shadowboxing: Representations of Black Feminist Politics*:

> Transcendent community reflects a theory of knowledge based on experience, reflection, judgment, and action. In this epistemology, the experiences of living thinkers produce reflections that incite judgments to inspire ethical action that renews the cycle—with new experiences, self-reflections, judging, and organizing [37].

Feminist authors of dystopia, as well as their protagonists, are certainly "living thinkers" as they inspire us to think differently about ourselves and about the future. Living thinkers, in the form of readers, critics and fans, also "inspire ethical action." "Living thinkers," James argues, "mirror worldviews that present service and community as indispensable; knowledge and responsibility as intergenerational; and community as a changing and thorny tie" (39). These worldviews are also mirrored in YA dystopia's Girls on Fire texts. A transcendent community crosses time and space, gathering together ideas and voices that exist before and after, here and there. A transcendent community meshes with the transcendent quality of YA dystopia. The plots, spaces, and places require a stretch of the imagination that extends from our world, but transcends the possibilities and probabilities of reality. This is why both classic and contemporary dystopian texts are important for an understanding of YA dystopia. While there are many texts we might consider in this transcendent community, I focus on a few texts whose connections provide a rich ground for explorations throughout this book.

* * *

I first encountered Cavendish's *The Blazing World* (originally *The Description of a New World, Called the Blazing-World*) in graduate school in a required British literature course. Since I was already a fan of science fiction, this book was a lifeline in my least favorite realms of literature (pre–1800 and British). Cavendish was well aware that her world was limited and writes in response: "since Fortune and the Fates would give me none, I have made One of my own." The world she made was "an Appendix to [her] *Observations Upon Experimental Philosophy*" which she notes is not something that most women are interested in. Instead, she gives them the "fantastical." Clearly, the "blazing world" is a direct connection to the fire theme that weaves throughout YA dystopia and Cavendish was certainly a trailblazer. But Cavendish, and other early women writers, had class advantages that has helped ensure their work was known in their time and helps it persist throughout time. Cavendish is, ultimately, writing to the "Noble and Worthy Ladies" that she addresses and her husband provides a preface to her work ("But your Creating Fancy, thought it fit/ To make your World of Nothing, but pure Wit"); she even notes that her world is certainly not a "Poor World, if Poverty be only want of Gold, and Jewels." She has plenty of gold, but her soul is lacking such riches. These early platforms remind us that the roots of YA dystopia's Girls on Fire run deep. They run so deep that second wave feminists had to excavate the ground to reveal these roots. Girls on Fire often lack these roots to the past because they have been forgotten, buried, erased, and skewed by time and by power that is threatened.

During the late 19th and early 20th century, utopian writings were popular in an America that was uncertain and optimistic about the future and our ability to shape our country for the better. As my colleague, Lisa Botshon, noted at a discussion group on the book, 160 utopian works were published between 1880 and 1900. (As a comparison, my study includes over 140 young adult dystopia books published between 2008 and 2016.) One of the first mothers of YA dystopia, Charlotte Perkins Gilman, was rediscovered by Ann J. Lane, one of the first Gilman scholars. As Lane notes, "Gilman had an enormous reputation in her lifetime, but she is almost unknown in ours" (ix). I had been introduced to Gilman as most English students are—through her canonical short story, "The Yellow Wallpaper," and I taught it in English classes for years before I had time to read *Herland*. "The Yellow Wallpaper" captures the cage-like existence of women who have few options and little control over their lives or their bodies. Her 1915 utopian text, *Herland*, reflects Gilman's time as well as her feminist and socialist philosophies. Lane notes that Gilman was writing in a time period when the socialist and feminist movements were both growing; "Gilman sought to unite them by demonstrating their essential and necessary interdependence" (vi). Today's Girls on Fire have far more movements to demonstrate such necessary interdependence.

Gilman's classic text not only examines common assumptions about masculinity and femininity, but also establishes the importance of interdisciplinary approaches and comprehensive, integrated education. In fact, Gilman was a sociologist as well as a literary figure. Mary Jo Deegan explains, "she held fiction, rather than nonfiction, in the highest regard. As a sociologist, she wanted to transform the 'facts' of sociology into the 'art' of fiction. In this way she intended to shape culture itself" (47). Gilman saw the power of fiction. Deegan also notes that "because of men's interests, their control over publishing and distribution, and their control over readers' consciousness" (47) fiction was "severely circumscribed" (47). The powers that be also saw this power and options for women were limited on all fronts.

So Gilman did what any Girl on Fire would do, she serialized *Herland* in a monthly magazine, *The Forerunner*, an enterprise that she published (and was the sole contributor to) for seven years from 1909 through 1916 (Deegan 8). This publication included Gilman's poetry and fiction, like *Herland*, as well as critical essays, book reviews, and more; its seven years of content was equivalent to 28 full-length books (Lane vi). *The Forerunner* also published *With Her in Ourland: Sequel to Herland* in installments in 1916; the false split of these two novels with the recovery of the "lost" novel of *Herland*, Mary Jo Deegan argues, obscures Gilman's feminist politics and sociological approach. It is clear, Deegan notes, that Gilman conceived of these two texts as "interconnected parts" (8). Herland is not about escapism or "feminist separatism," Deegan argues, "but calls for reason, social action, and cooperation between the sexes" (2). So, while *Herland* is mostly understood as a utopian text; it is most certainly connected to the dystopic world that Gilman inhabited. As the "most significant Western feminist theorist of the period 1890–1920" (Allen 1) Gilman was on the frontlines of the first wave of feminism, a movement that is still fighting the same battles today.

In an Introduction to a 1979 publication to *Herland*, Ann J. Lane notes a rebirth of "the utopian novel as a literary form"; this rebirth, a "uniquely feminist expression," includes Marge Piercy, *Woman on the Edge of Time* (1976); Joanna Russ, *The Female Man* (1975); Ursula LeGuin, *The Dispossessed* (1974) and others. Lane notes that "many of the ideas in these books are reminiscent of notions expressed in *Herland*" (xx). Because of the feminist nature of these utopian books, Lane notes, they are "not comparable to the classic utopian form" (xx). While utopian texts were popular in the mid–1970s, in the mid–1980s the turn to dystopia marks "anxiety about the body" with *The Handmaid's Tale*, *Children of Men*, and *V for Vendetta* (Brown, Patrick). This wave inspires the "explosion" of young adult dystopia, and a turn to romance, that this book considers.

Another clear mother of YA dystopia, Atwood's text is frequently cited in relationship to the "classic" science fiction writers often recognized as *the* American science fiction tradition (as previously noted). Margaret Atwood's text, *The Handmaid's Tale* (1985), is a clear template for many YA dystopian novels that take up the subject of compulsory reproduction and the enslavement of women for the purposes of reproduction. For instance, *Eve's* feminist premise is apparent immediately. It begins with a quote from Margaret Atwood's foundational feminist dystopian/speculative fiction text, *The Handmaid's Tale*: "*Maybe I really don't want to know what's going on./ Maybe I'd rather not know. Maybe I couldn't bear to know. The Fall was a fall from innocence to knowledge.*" This quote could preface so many YA dystopia books and *The Handmaid's Tale* also gets a nod in *The Summer Prince* where it is a text being studied in June's class.

The election of President Trump and the fear of the loss of reproductive freedom has re-established this classic texts alongside *1984*. In February of 2017 on *AM Joy* on MSNBC, Joy-Ann Reid discussed how *The Handmaid's Tale* is not far off of the bills that conservative men (and some women) are attempting to pass through state legislatures. After explaining House Bill 1441, which would require women to have the permission of a male partner in order to get an abortion, she says, "This is not a dystopia…. It's Trump's America." The conversation on Twitter continued the comparisons and reflected the impact this novel has had on women. One comment even suggested: "I'm guessing dystopian tales will be very popular. We need a field guide for the 'New America.'" Girls on Fire are providing such a field guide.

The Primary Mother and the Original Girl on Fire

While these are certainly not the only "mothers," the primary mother—and the source of the original Girl on Fire—deserves her own subtitle and section. As Ytasha L. Womack writes in *Afrofuturism: The World of Black Sci-Fi and Fantasy Culture*,

> In a hypermale sci-fi space where science and technology dominate, Butler provided a blueprint for how women, particularly women of color, could operate in these skewed realities and distant worlds. Butler set the stage for multidimensional black women in complex worlds both past and present, women who are vulnerable in their victories and valiant in their risky charge to enlighten humanity [110].

Womack traces Butler's influence across a variety of cultural spaces including writers, filmmakers, musicians, visual and performance artists, teachers, and community organizers and traces the rise of an Afrofuturism movement that goes back to recontextualize the works of the past; Octavia Butler is one of Womack's pillars of this movement. Womack continues, "She gave many women a voice and validated their mashed-up mix of women's issues, race, sci-fi, mysticism, and the future" (110). And while I will explore these Afrofuturistic elements of YA dystopia later, it is also important to note that while Butler holds a special place in the past, present, and future of black people in America and the Afrofuturism movement, she is also a foundational *American* science fiction, speculative fiction, and fantasy writer. Her work spans many different contexts from a time traveler in slavery times, to an alien invasion, to space travel, to telepathic abilities, to vampire communities—a body of work impossible to capture in all its complexity and glory here. Her lifetime achievement represented by her MacArthur Genius grant, speaks to some of her importance as a cultural figure.

As Moylan argues, "Butler's [Parables] story is of great consequence to readers because she explores the psychological and spiritual repercussions of racism on a disintegrating country that illustrate the importance of examining attitudes, assumptions, and feelings by which society has conditioned everyone" (21). A central aspect of YA dystopia is exactly such an examination. Butler's text is a model for many YA dystopia texts and female protagonists, and I connect YA dystopia's Girls of Fire and their stories to Butler's Lauren Olamina and her coming of age and coming to power story.

Octavia Butler's *Parable of the Sower* as "Young Adult"

Qualities That Inspire YA	Why Parables Is Not YA
Today's world is reflected in the story. Many of these books echo the problems that shape Butler's dystopia.	The dystopian context is too close to reality.

Qualities That Inspire YA	*Why Parables Is Not YA*
Butler explains, "I considered drugs and the effects of drugs on the children of drug addicts. I looked at the growing rich/poor gap, at throwaway labor, at our willingness to build and fill prisons, our reluctance to build and repair schools and libraries, and at our assault on the environment" (337).	Some of the parents and older people can remember when things were not so bad and they think that, once again, the good times will come back and things will get better. Lauren—being young and seeing the deteriorating world from behind a wall—knows that it is just inevitable the wall will come down.
"The idea in *Parable of the Sower* and *Parable of the Talents* is to consider a possible future unaffected by parapsychological abilities such as telepathy or telekinesis, unaffected by alien intervention, unaffected by magic. It is to look at where we are now, what we are doing now, and to consider where some of our current behaviors and unattended problems might take us" (*Parable of the Sower*, "A Conversation with Octavia E. Butler," 337).	YA gives us scenarios that are far enough away that they *could* happen. Parables is a future too close to home.
Survivor(s). Olamina is a Survivor. She is a victim of sexual violence while she also has a healthy understanding of her own sexual desires.	There is too much sex, generally, and too much honesty about sex and rape. Many students identified the treatment of sexuality or graphic violence (particularly rape) as the reasons why this novel is not in the "YA" category.
Disability. Olamina is a "sharer." While she experiences pleasure and pain that she sees, there is far more pain to experience in her world. Guns. The violence in Parables is, in part, shaped by the presence of guns. Lauren's father makes sure his kids are familiar with guns and at age 15 the kids go out to practice shooting.	Realistic violence and detailed descriptions of violence.
Olamina has romantic relationships with a boy, a man, and almost with a woman.	Her main love interest is a 57-year-old man.
Voice. Girls in YA dystopia certainly hold their own when it comes to voice through first-person narration.	Lauren Olamina tells her own story through journal entries. A few other texts follow this format, like *Life as We Knew It*, but most books are written from a first-

Qualities That Inspire YA	Why Parables Is Not YA
Lauren shapes a belief system that creates a community. She has agency. Lauren Olamina is a shaper of ideas and of community—of people.	person point of view—the Girl on Fire talks directly to her reader. There are exceptions (multiple narrators, third-person), but the most powerful voices and the most powerful texts are first-person.
Fire shapes her life. For Lauren, living in drought conditions in dry Southern California, fire is a constant threat. As she and her gathered community travel North by foot, fire threatens to consume. Fire is also renewal as one of the Earth-seed verses offers.	There is no "reluctance" in Lauren as pro-tagonist. Lauren is aware of the problems. She is learning and preparing for the worst. The worst is far worse than she really imag-ined.
The only constant of the universe is change.	Olamina's Earthseed vision not only out-lives the political threats and violence of her times; it is used to start to build a new society.

The ways in which Octavia Butler's text speaks to, and through YA Dystopia's Girls on Fire not only speak to Butler's genius, but also the possibilities of change in the future.

When Butler's work is recognized, it is often for the ways in which she tackles race. In "Imagining Black Bodies in the Future," Gregory Hampton explains, "Her vision is unique because she has located black and brown bodies at the centre [sic] of her speculative dystopian visions of the future" (181). Because of the lack of other science fiction writing by black women and people of color more generally, and because of the lack of science fiction that imagines race as a central theme, Butler's work is essential for laying intersectional and interdisciplinary foundations. Octavia Butler's *Parable of the Sower*, and her female protagonist, Lauren Olamina—who is mostly Lauren in *Sower* and almost exclusively Olamina in *Talents*—is the original prototype for the Girl on Fire and the YA dystopia novel/trilogy. She sets the bar for considerations of race, class, gender, and sexuality and critiques of American culture, politics, history, community, and more. The influence of Octavia Butler and the centrality of her work to the burgeoning YA dystopia movement

Opposite: **Over its many years of publication, several different covers have been designed for Octavia E. Butler's** *Parable of the Talents.* **This particular version makes it clear that this is not a YA dystopia book. A confident and strong young black woman stares directly at the reader. She looms large, emanating rays of light, above images of imprisonment and one member (her brother) looking back as he is walking away (Aspect [Warner Books]. Cover design by Don Puckey. Cover illustration by John Blackford).**

cannot be underestimated. But it is. Butler's work establishes a multidimensional dystopic setting and the fundamental defining aspects of the Girl on Fire in ways that no single protagonist can, not even Katniss Everdeen.

The biggest difference between Butler's Girl on Fire and the majority of Girls on Fire of contemporary YA dystopia, is that Lauren Olamina is black and her race shapes her identity, family, and community as well as the way she is seen by people outside of her community. It is common for my students to not realize that Lauren Olamina is black, at least until she explicitly identifies her race. Even then, some students miss it; and despite the overt discussion of race and the issues related to it, some students feel that race is not really an important element of the book. Other students have a more sophisticated view. One student even wondered about whether Butler waited to introduce the character's race until we had gotten a chance to identify with her. This is an important frame for the Girl on Fire; she can't be white because she is the future. But in the future definitions are different. Whiteness is the fading norm of our times.

It is no surprise that sex, sexuality, and gender are also navigated in important ways in the texts that sit at the margins of literary analysis. While YA literature fetishizes the virgin, as Christine Seifert argues, dystopia for adults includes frank and graphic sex and more complicated love stories. This is a quality shared by several YA novels by women of color, about girls of color. Octavia Butler's *Parables* make sex and sexuality a fact of Lauren's existence, not something that drives her actions or ambitions, but something that shapes who she is. For instance, when she has sex with her boyfriend Curtis, they are certain to use condoms for protection. Lauren does not want to get pregnant and have another reason to be stuck behind her neighborhood wall for life. When she and Bankole get together the first time they simultaneously pull out condoms. Lauren Olamina is a practical girl who protects herself and her future.

Other norms—of economics, exploitation, environmental degradation—are common, in varying degrees, in both the present and the future. In addition to paying attention to the politics of her times, Lauren also manages life and school and friends and struggles with her father and brothers and stepmother, until the walls of her community and all illusions of safety are shattered. But Lauren saw it coming and prepared. She was able to see through the illusions of safety. She leads herself out of immediate danger and then she leads other people toward something better. The literal and metaphorical walls—and the leadership to overcome these—are important qualities of the Girl on Fire. And then, of course, there is the element of fire—another powerful metaphor and reality. And the guns—a stark reality of survival. Lauren's father made sure that he and his family, and his neighborhood community, were armed and knowledgeable about firearms. This training and knowledge is a major asset for Olamina—in her survival and in her leadership and community-building.

Some female protagonists in YA dystopia take up this same fire that follows them from their ancestors through to their dystopian context—Fen de la Guerre in *Orleans*, Cassandra in *Shadows Cast by Stars*, and June in *The Summer Prince*, are some of the most articulated racial and ethnic connections. But, regardless of overt and articulated visions of protagonists of color, almost every YA dystopia book with a female protagonist connects to Lauren Olamina's story and Butler's vision. Throughout Part II, I explore the connections between Butler's work and the YA dystopia texts with Girl on Fire, elucidating not only Butler's influence, but the larger cultural importance of these texts. Looking backward, and forward, as well as at our present moment, Butler's *Parables* are transcendent and instructional.

Widening the Transcendent Community

Just as the genre of YA dystopia covers a wide variety of ground, the texts that speak to this genre can be found wide and far. These mothers provide important insights through their work. When we consider YA dystopia as a transcendent community, we also widen the scope of possibility, especially in terms of a wider representation of non-white racial and ethnic identities and politics and more overt discussions around sex and sexuality. These "adult" novels provide female protagonists of color in contexts that are often urban. They also offer complex characters, discussions of overt sex and sexuality, and a variety of elements, endings, and continuing visions.

Cynthia Kadohata wrote a literary work that can be seen as a young adult dystopian novel. The misleading description on the back of the book explains the setting: "In the year 2052, America is deteriorating: water and gas are rationed, disease flourishes, and everyone is regarded as a stranger. The one-time promised land, Los Angeles, is now a petrified landscape where people disappear and corruption is rampant." Even at its 1992 publication date, the world that *In the Heart of the Valley of Love* creates is hardly unfamiliar; it is not a far stretch from our contemporary world, as is the case for many dystopias. It is definitely not the "unfamiliar and frightening world" that the book-cover description claims. But perhaps the setting is described in this way because the novel is not considered dystopic. It is a future world that is a pretty natural extension of Los Angeles circa 1992. As protagonist Francie notes, "the fear became just another part of your life…. You still have to eat, work, walk, talk, sleep, love" (64).

Much of the book is going through the motions of life while also trying to have hope and love. Francie is doing what she needs to do to survive. The book description further explains the plot: "This is where nineteen-year-old Japanese-American Francie has lived with her beloved Auntie Annie and her aunt's boyfriend since her parents died. But when tragedy strikes, she must venture out on her own into a world gone mad, a place where survival takes precedence over everything else." This definitely rings true of YA dystopia, but this is not accurate to the novel. The disappearance of her aunt's boyfriend alters their lives, but such disappearances are common place. Francie hardly has to "venture out on her own"; she has many connections to community. She decides to go to community college and works on the school paper. She meets her boyfriend Mark and several friends and they do what they can to survive as well as to help each other deal with the ramifications of this "world gone mad."

One important element to *In the Heart of the Valley of Love*, however, is its creation of a future where people of color dominate and where the policies of the rich and powerful have led to corruption and environmental degradation. The segregation of the past haunts the future as "every city had a richtown" (5), a segregation of socioeconomic class present in most dystopic novels (as well as increasingly in our real-life world). Race is also overtly discussed. In the second chapter her race is identified as she notes her "yellow-brown legs—the yellow from my Japanese mother, the brown from my Chinese-black father" (22). It's a future where being mixed is the norm and being white equates with advantage: "before nonwhites became the majority" (76). What is most important to this book's contributions to this transcendent community, is the optimism, strength, and endurance that Francie demonstrates. Like other YA dystopia female protagonists, she loses her parents. Her parents want to leave her knowledge as they die, but she knows that the world is changing and the kind of knowledge they are offering is of little immediate value. She says, "I believed it was not my knowledge but my skill and my strength that would help me conquer the future, the present, and even the past. They didn't know I felt this" (22). Like YA dystopia's Girls on Fire, Francie develops her own agency early in life and it gives her strength and perspective.

Eden Lepucki's 2014 dystopian novel has a similar geographical setting to Butler's *Parable of the Sower* and Cynthia Kadohata's *In the Heart of the Valley of Love* (1992). Lepucki is a contemporary older sister to Girls on Fire in YA dystopia; her novel, *California*, exemplifies the main difference between dystopia and "YA" also through overt sex and sexuality, but also through hopelessness. The protagonist never had an opportunity to be a Girl on Fire. Instead, she enjoyed baking and smoking pot. She fell in love and now she finds herself isolated and without any options and few, if any, distractions. She is bored. And while she has some feminist sensibilities, "Frida thought that the worse things got, the more women lost what they'd worked so hard to gain. No one cared about voting rights and equal pay because everyone was too busy lighting fires to stay warm and looking for food to stay alive" (66).

Privilege plays into the shape of the dystopia but is not framed or examined as such: "In L.A., when Cal could no longer improve the world by growing food, he had resolved to escape the wretchedness, take Frida to the edge of the world, and start over…. How impossible, though, to turn one's back on all the horrors in the world; there had to be another way to live" (299). Cal's attempt to escape the chaos of L.A. does not pay off. When Frida sees the opportunity to join a gated, surveilled Community, she justifies her choice: "She and Cal, they were lucky. Frida knew she was thinking only of her own family, that she had begun to see them as special: separate from the rest of the world with all its attendant suffering and corruption. Maybe it was wrong, but it is the choice she had made" (388). In the end, it is clear that the Communities are not what they had hoped. Instead of water and electricity and schools and the comforts of money, they find no produce (only protein powder), limited electricity and hot water, no more meat, and antiquated gender politics. The future remains bleak and uncertain.

Biting the Sun by British author Tanith Lee also existed before the YA category, and has a variety of interesting dimensions in common with *Uglies, Feed,* and *The Summer Prince. Biting the Sun* is about the Jang—the youth of the Utopian society run by Q-Rs, androids with no "life spark" (soul or consciousness). Q-Rs have humans' best interests in mind, and they uphold strict laws on the free-loving youth who are expected to engage in experimentation, vandalism, excess, indulgence in food, drugs, sex, and upper-ear music to control moods. The protagonist tries out all sorts of different bodies and does all the things that the youth are supposed to do, but she feels empty and wants to move on to the next stage in her life.

The novel (or set of two novels, published in 1976 and 1977) challenges gender and sexuality, making space for Girls on Fire to play and grow outside the confines of today's formulaic approach to sex as, essentially, kissing (maybe some "heavy petting"). The Jang can inhabit any body they choose; in fact, when they are done with one body they just "commit suicide" and get a new body. People are predominantly male or female, but they try out different bodies and identities. There is much experimentation with gender and sexuality as well as skin color, hair styles, appendages (number and type). One of the characters, Hatta, wants to be ugly because it is the person inside that matters, a sentiment that Shay echoes in her pleas to Tally in *Uglies.* Jang language and customs create a unique world that leaves the protagonist searching for meaning outside of society's youth constructs.

The similarities between the youth society of *Biting the Sun* and that of the youth in *Pretties* are instructive in the more radical nature of *Biting the Sun.* Not only are the parties and the surgeries nearly identical in *Uglies,* but

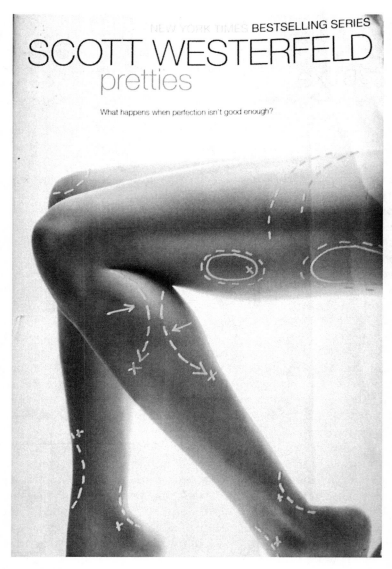

There are two different sets of covers that represent the Uglies series in different ways. One set relies on the close-up of a striking face, similar to the covers for the Delirium and Tankborn books. These covers reflect how the popular novels align with the standard imagery of the genre. The second set of covers, represented by this *Pretties* cover, focuses on body parts and allude more directly to plastic surgery and the other modifications that are central to the plot of these books (Simon Pulse. Cover designed by Russell Gordon. Cover photography © 2011 by Monica Stevenson).

so is the theme of seeing beyond the surface of things. However, the means, techniques, and results of seeing beyond the surface differ greatly. Lee's book is rife with a variety of experiments with gender and sexuality. For instance, while pretties can get surge to modify their appearance, the Jang of *Biting the Sun* can become male or female and can look any way they can imagine (much like the youth in Diego who are not required to follow the rules about appearance set in Tally's home city). So, throughout this experimental youthful phase, people are male and female and have sex with whomever they like whenever they like. Or, rather, they can have "marriage" for any length of time before "having love" (sex). The youth party and do crazy tricks, and are protected from hurting themselves in both of these books. But because there are no brain lesions in *Biting the Sun*, there is nothing to placate the youth and dull their brains and actions. In *Uglies*, Tally also counts down the days until her "pretty surgery," lamenting that her friends are in line before her. But in *Biting the Sun*, advanced technology is paid for through energy, and eventually the protagonist tires of this life. She begins to question the inanity of youthful space and can't imagine playing in this space for the many years required before she can be taken seriously by adult society.

Another contemporary mother is found in the character of Violet, making the male author a mother as well. M.T. Anderson's *Feed* is a sanitized version of the kind of freedom that Tanith Lee imagines. Sex is a reality for the teens in the book; it is casual and mostly inconsequential. Girls get jealous of other girls, but no one is really able to be emotionally invested enough for relationships to last long past the "fun" stage. Titus is looking for fun, and he—like his fellow adolescents and citizens more generally—is not emotionally mature enough to know what love is. When he connects with Violet, he has a glimpse: "We stood, looking out at the shrubs, and the motorboat up on a trailer, and I felt like I was in love, and our arms were around each other" (75). When he tries to express this to Violet, he can only get out a few awkward words: "I really like you" before she "hit [him] on the back of the head. That'll do, she said" (144). Violet doesn't need inadequate words. And in *Feed*, few words are adequate by today's standards of communication.

Titus tells the reader, "Being with Violet was great…. It was like she took my hand, or I took her hand, and we ducked through doorways, and together we went to an old place, and it was a new place./ We went there holding hands" (88–9). Although Titus has been sexually active in the past, he does not initiate "fun" sex with Violet. Eventually, she initiates a weekend getaway, which turns into a break up when Titus doesn't want to have sex with Violet because he keeps "picturing [her] dead already" and he feels like he is "being felt up by a Zombie" (211). Titus cannot deal with Violet's slow decay because she is the only person he really feels anything about; he just cannot process his feelings through his feed.

Violet is different from everyone Titus knows, and her relationship with Titus is awkward, sad, and as broken as she is. In fact, through a disability lens, the story of Violet is evidence that the cyborg girl suffers a harsh fate that can be rectified in the YA dystopia genre by characters like Cinder. Violet's feed malfunctions, in part, because she is at the lowest strata of society. Her father saves up for a year for her to visit the moon, something that Titus and his friends can do for "fun" any time they want to. Because her feed was installed later than most, and it is a sub-standard model, and because she cannot fit a customer profile, Violet's feed malfunctions and she cannot get the help she needs to have it repaired or removed. As Violet dies, the civilization is also crumbling, though no one takes much notice. She asks Titus,

> Do you know why our skin is falling off? Have you heard that some suburbs have been lost, just, no one knows where they are anymore? No one can find them?.... Almost nothing lives here anymore, except where we plant it?.... We don't know any of that. We have tea parties with our teddies. We go sledding. We enjoy being young. We take what's coming to us. That's our way [214].

He doesn't want to hear these truths. She dies and he refuses to be "called her hero" (207). She doesn't have the technology she needs to live, so she pays with her energy.

Eventually, when it is far too late, he goes to visit her near-corpse (she's at 4.6 percent functionality) and tells her: "There's one story I'll keep telling you. I'll keep telling it. You're the story. I don't want you to forget. When you wake up, I want you to remember yourself. I'm going to remember. You're still there, as long as I can remember you. As long as someone knows you" (234). He cries and tells her "the story of us," which is like a trailer for a film, or the description of a formulaic YA dystopia story:

> It's about this meg normal guy, who doesn't think about anything until one wacky day, when he meets a dissident with a heart of gold.... Set against the backdrop of America in its final days, it's the high-spirited story of their love together.... Together, the two crazy kids grow, have madcap escapades, and learn an important lesson about love. They learn to resist the feed. Rated PG-13. For language ... and mild sexual situations [234].

His only response is his own face "crying, in her blank eye" (234). But Titus has done something powerful. It is Violet's story that survives; and he gives it a positive spin. She gets the love that was denied to her. She gets the resistance and triumph against the feed that she wanted. She gets everything that the Girls on Fire get (most of the time) in their stories. Except a full life.

Violet provides an important prototype for some of the Girls on Fire in this study. As the female love interest, Violet plays a role similar to the role that the male love interest plays in YA dystopia novels with female protagonists. The fate for Violet is far more harsh than it is for any of the male love interest characters in any of the Girls on Fire books. In fact, the Girls on Fire rescue their boys from abusive situations and questionable futures. Violet tries. Titus's emotional stunting caused by the culture he lives in—the constant noise of the feed that, Violet argues, eats his brain—causes him to neglect Violet as she lies dying. The Girls on Fire, at least, have the agency that she never had. As Richard Gooding argues in "Our Posthuman Adolescence," *Feed* "presents a model of activism through Violet that can succeed in the world that Anderson's novel has reference to, ours" (126). Violet is, thus, a "mother" in this transcendent community.

* * *

Nalo Hopkinson's work has been compared to Octavia Butler, and her creation of black female protagonists brings a cross-cultural and mystical mix. Her YA novel *The Chaos* also provides an interesting example that falls within the YA dystopia umbrella. A one-day event, a temporary alteration of reality causes death, destruction, and transformations of all kinds (people into objects, objects into animals, hybrids of all kinds, a witch with a live flying house that eats people, headless horse men, etc.). One interesting element of this novel is its frank treatment of sex and sexuality. The protagonist is slut-shamed and bullied and sexuality is overt and challenges mainstream conventions including polyamory, gay, and lesbian sexualities (11, 18, 42). Further, race is overtly discussed and negotiated. She is black but not dark enough to be black like her mother, brother, boyfriend, and best friends. She refers to people's race when characterizing. When the chaos passes, her skin has been transformed and she is darker than her mother. She is pleased to be darker (239). In the end, things return to "normal" but Sojourner (Scotch) is inspired to find "something different."

Perhaps more interesting as a foremother is Hopkinson's first novel, *Brown Girl in the Ring*. Nalo Hopkinson's *Brown Girl in the Ring* is a multicultural milieu combining a dystopic future Toronto, Afro-Caribbean magical realism, and a female protagonist that establishes an important basis for the Girl on Fire. When I finished reading *Brown Girl in the Ring*, l was surprised to see that it had originally been published in 1998. This is a first novel by Nalo Hopkinson, re-issued in 2012. I did not read it until 2016. This is part of the power of the Girls on Fire transcendent community.

In fact, it is this novel's resemblance to Detroit that has increased its visibility. Dan Hartland writes in a 2016 book review, "From its depiction of a near-future Toronto hollowed out at a broken centre—which reflects with eerie extremity the current experience of Detroit—to its profoundly intersectional themes of power, identity, and solidarity, the novel speaks to our moment somehow with a greater urgency than it may even have done at the time of its writing." Recognizing the relevance of fiction to our modern problems allows this novel to have another life like *The Handmaid's Tale*. As Lee Skallerup Bessette writes in *The Atlantic* in 2013, "with recent news that a political candidate in a wealthy Detroit suburb is actually proposing that a wall be built along the border of the now-bankrupt city, Hopkinson's dystopic vision has become a disturbing reality—and is well-worth revisiting."

Hopkinson certainly makes space for a merger of cultures, a sense of place, and magic. The language that mixes English with Caribbean, the stories and myths that enable magical realism, and the traditions and rituals that mix with a dystopic future—all of these speak to the diverse and intersectional themes of YA dystopia's Girls on Fire. At the end, Ti-Jeanne is surrounded by community, a gathering to honor her grandmother and to "calm the dead spirit and point out its way to Guinea Land, sent off with the love of the living it must leave behind" (242). Ti-Jeanne is poised to make her own decisions about how she wants to live her life, how she wants to raise her child, and how she wants to live in her community and world. She is a mother and a community leader.

While Hopkinson's fiction establishes her as a mother of YA dystopia, so does her work as a critic and an editor. Co-edited with Uppinder Mehan, *So Long Been Dreaming: Postcolonial Science Fiction & Fantasy* is a collection of "stories that take the meme of colonizing the natives and, from the experience of the colonizee, critique it, pervert it, fuck with it, with irony, with anger, with humour, and also, with love and respect for the genre of science fiction that makes it possible to think about new ways of doing things" (9). Thinking about new ways of doing things is one of the foundational aspects of dystopia, and one of the key aspects of my work in this book. As Mehan notes in his "Final Thoughts" on postcolonial writers, "So many of us have written insightfully about our pasts and presents; perhaps the time is ripe for us to begin creatively addressing our futures" (270).

Critical Dystopia as the Standard

While all science fiction has a critical edge to it, scholars like Thomas Moylan and Raffaella Baccolini, in the introduction to *Utopia Method Vision: The Use Value of Social Dreaming*, have distinguished the "critical dystopia" as a category of dystopia that exhibits the "stubborn presence of utopian hope" as well as hegemonic challenges, self-reflexivity, and "genre blurring" (14). This seminal volume in Ralahine Utopian Studies, the publishing project of the Ralahine Centre for Utopian Studies, establishes an important turn in utopian studies, which is interdisciplinary and international as well as collaborative.[2] The edited collections, monographs (classics), and republished and recontextualized work (readers) provide a rich body of scholarship on the topic in its broadest definition.

Moylan further develops the idea of critical dystopia In *Scraps of the Untainted Sky*. Drawing on the work of Lyman Tower Sargent, Moylan describes "critical dystopia" as "a textual mutation that self-reflexively takes on the present system and offers not only astute critiques of the order of things but also explorations of the oppositional spaces and possibilities from which the next round of political activism can derive imaginative sustenance and inspiration" (xv). What better than the world of the "young adult" to find "spaces and possibilities" and to inspire "political activism and imaginative sustenance"? Moylan draws from the work of Baccolini in "Gender and Genre" and argues that feminist "new dystopias" provide "preferred sites of resistance" (190). Moylan argues that these texts are intersectional; they are "not only feminist but also anti-capitalist, democratically socialist, and radically ecological" (190). These dystopian texts still play with identity politics, but also take "the political imagination into the larger realm … of transformative politics that are capable of both rupturing that [political-economic] system and forging a radical alternative in its place" (190). I'd like to extend this argument to the "new dystopias" of YA dystopia's Girl on Fire, which are also dominated by women writers, characters, and readers. The potential of critical dystopia speaks to the potential of YA dystopia's Girls on Fire.

These texts, Moylan argues, "have rekindled the cold flame of critique and have thereby become a cultural manifestation of a broad-scale yet radically diverse alliance politics that is emerging as the twenty-first century commences" (xv). He sites Kim Stanley Robinson, Octavia Butler, and Marge Piercy as the "most eloquent" examples and these texts are absolutely setting the bar for dystopia as critical and potentially transformative. YA dystopia, particularly *The Hunger Games*, may not be the "most eloquent" examples, but they may have the power of a wider cultural appeal and a bigger sphere of influence. Girls on Fire reach a youth audience as well as adult, national and international, print and screen. They challenge convention and rewrite rules. They hold down dystopia while diversifying the genre.

Another power of critical dystopias, Moylan argues, citing Baccolini, is that "critical dystopias more often 'blur' the received boundaries of the dystopian form and thereby expand rather than diminish its creative potential for creative expression" (189). As I will discuss in more depth throughout this book, the genre that I am considering is messy and crosses other genres and encompasses a wide range of themes, symbols, and, etc., even as it has a particular structure of its own shape and design. Baccolini shows, Moylan argues, "that dystopian narrative is further rendered as an 'impure' text that can renovate the 'resisting nature' of dystopian sf by making it more properly 'multi-oppositional'" and able to consider "multiplicity and complexity" as well as "partial and situated knowledges" and "hybridity and fluidity" (Moylan 189). This is exactly what YA dystopia offers through individual texts and the larger cultural trend and exactly what inspires this book.

Othered Legacies of Utopia and Dystopia

When it comes to issues related to race, optimism about the power of science fiction to tackle the problems surrounding difference is fraught. As Lavender argues in *Race in American Science Fiction*, "Even though sf seems to be uniquely suited to the critical study of race … sf critics pay scant attention … [these texts] make clear matters of racial and ethnic contact, where prejudices, discrimination, hatred, and stereotype, as well as empathy, tolerance, patience, and acceptance, take place because of difference" (10). Lavender's critical attention here is focused on many of the classic science fiction texts and his argument makes an important point for our consideration of YA dystopia's female protagonists. They are largely whitewashed, especially in their most popular iterations. Further, since "critics pay scant attention," texts that deal critically with race are less likely to expand beyond critical spaces. Thus, part of my argument in this book hinges on the lack of critical engagement with race in critical dystopian YA texts and scholarship—symptoms of the larger structure.

Lavender compares science fiction with the actual landscape of his life and concludes, "The remains of segregation resonate powerfully across time and place. My surreal experience is the stuff of science fiction (sf). This rumination caused me to think 'what if…'" (2). Fortunately, for the Girls on Fire of YA dystopia, there are women of color whose "what ifs" give a texture to the genre that lacks in many of the less gritty mainstream texts. But the problems and possibilities with the "what ifs" is that the cultural (racial, ethnic) roots can become any variety of branches, leaves, or fruit. Just like a text more generally, once it is out there it cannot be controlled or owned.

In *Scraps of the Untainted Sky*, Moylan specifically notes the intersectional nature of critical dystopias; as I note earlier, these texts are "multi-oppositional" and able to consider "multiplicity and complexity" as well as "partial and situated knowledges" and "hybridity and fluidity" (Moylan 189). However, we need to remain critically vigilant in order to ensure that interdisciplinarity is also intersectional. Dawn H. Currie critiques the problem of what Valerie Hey describes as "sectional rather than intersectional" (Currie 30, citing Hey 18), but she also works toward a solution for a problem that is not "empirical…" (30). More of the same reproduces critical structures and fails to illuminate the intersectional. More of the same often means that race is not engaged.

Lavender illustrates how race is often overlooked in science fiction criticism except when in relation to Octavia Butler or Samuel Delany, suggesting these are the only texts where race is a relevant topic (10). This omission of race is dangerous; it suggests that the future will be a fantasy projection not of the reality of global demographics, but of a projected white supremacist vision, however mild, benign, or intentionally racist those visions may be. As Lavender further explains, "science fiction often talks about race by not talking about race, makes real aliens, has hidden race dialogues. Even though it is a literature that talks a lot about underclasses or oppressed classes, it does so from a privileged if somewhat generic white space" (7). YA dystopia is, largely, this kind of generic white space, at least on the surface, and many texts include hidden race dialogs as well as stories that highlight the underclass or oppressed class. As we unpack race and racism in YA dystopia we can see that the problems and potential are messy.

The most famous female protagonist of YA dystopia not only supports this legacy, but also interrupts it.

Foundational Girl on Fire: Some Critical Explorations of The Hunger Games

While there were female protagonists before Katniss Everdeen, and I point to Butler's Lauren Olamina as the original, the world of female protagonists and the field of YA dystopia are totally transformed with her appearance. Pop culture and academic analyses abound. From articles in *The New York Times* and other print and online newspapers and magazines, to companion books, essay collections, blogs and websites, Tumblr posts, Facebook groups, and a number of scholarly books—monographs and edited collections. The sheer amount of books, articles, conference presentations, popular articles, and student analyses in my classes make it nearly impossible to capture all of the shades of Katniss and the important impact of the Hunger Games, let alone to chime in on all of the critical and scholarly analyses. Many of these focus primarily or exclusively on the Hunger Games and/or Katniss, while some also include other well-known or similar works and other female protagonists including Tris of the Divergent series, Lena of Delirium, and Tally of the Uglies. To consider the bulk of such scholarship and popular criticism here would be impossible. Instead, I offer a few important works and the way they shape our understanding of Girls on Fire. The works that I focus on not only overlap with my analyses and provide a wealth of critical consideration of characters, plots, power, gender, and much more, they also model some of the varied scholarly approaches in this book.

The Girl Who Was on Fire, edited by Leah Wilson, provides analyses by young adult authors that highlight some of the important themes in the Hunger Games like romance, PTSD, and community. The first edition was published before the films, and an expanded version includes a few essays about the films. These essays are accessible and a helpful way to introduce students to related concepts without too much theoretical language. For instance, Jennifer Lynn Barnes argues in "Team Katniss" that this series is not about who she ends up with, but "about who she *is*—because sometimes, in books and in life, it's not about the romance./ Sometimes, it's about the girl" (18). Barnes illustrates the many roles that Katniss plays and the many dimensions of who she is as well as the many hardships of what she survives.

The 2014 publication *The Politics of Panem: Blurring Genres*, edited by Sean P. Conners, considers the Hunger Games trilogy from a variety of theoretical frames showing "what reading the Hunger Games trilogy from the standpoint of theory potentially reveals about its complexity and sophistication" (8). Connors argues for "young adult literature as a complex body of literature capable of challenging readers of all ages" (2). While this claim might seem obvious to those of us who read YA, many authors seek to prove that studying young adult fiction is a worthy scholarly pursuit. At the very least, scholars can attest to the ways in which our students are moved by and engaged with this literature. As Conners notes, *The Hunger Games* "participates in social criticism [and] invites readers to imagine other ways of interacting with the world and other possible social relationships" (155). *The Politics of Panem* makes a variety of important contributions to the study of young adult literature and YA dystopia, and I consider several of its chapters in other sections of this book.

Jamey Heit's book provides a more narrow view of "politics" than, for instance, the *Politics of Panem* book edited by Sean P. Connors. In Heit's book the "political" context for the Hunger Games is placed within a man's world— his world. Heit cites films like *Gladiator, Braveheart,* and *The Bourne Ultimatum* as well as political texts by a range of historical figures from Machiavelli to Hitler and Thomas Jefferson to Martin Luther King, Jr. These are important contexts to read in relation to the Hunger Games since the very project speaks to the weight of the Hunger Games as a cultural text of importance. These contexts also illuminate the political aspects of the novel as they align with classic cultural texts. He notes that there is "a creative element" to his interpretations and that he does "not want to claim that these patterns were [Collins's] conscious intent" (8). He continues, "My reading is just that: my own. It is one of many readings of how politics unfolds in the series" (8). While all cultural texts are fair game to all sorts of interpretations, and no reading "excludes possible other readings" (8), it is important to note that how we (critics) read texts also shapes the critical field itself. Heit's book neglects the organic context for the Hunger Games by placing it within traditional political contexts.

Not all single-author books take such a narrow view as that provided by Heit. Tom Henthorne's *Approaching the Hunger Games Trilogy: A Literary and Cultural Analysis* provides a text that offers a variety of angles and interdisciplinary approaches through which to understand this trilogy and Collins's work more generally. Henthorne frames the cultural phenomenon and then he explains that "most chapters begin by introducing a theoretical approach and then applying it to the trilogy" (3). He also illustrates messiness and complexity with character, genre, and theme, arguing that his "volume plays in the Collins mess rather than try to clean it up.... Indeed, one of this book's underlying assumptions is that messiness is a good thing, at least when it comes to fiction, since it reflects the way life really is" (6). With its glossary of characters and terms, biography of Suzanne Collins, and its questions for further study, this book also provides a resource for use when teaching this trilogy. The lack of endnotes and academic jargon makes this book an enjoyable lens through which "general readers" can expand their knowledge of some of their favorite reads from a variety of angles including: literature and cultural production, gender and sexuality, representations of war, philosophy, media studies, dystopian novels, psychology, and digital culture, many of the overlapping frames that I also consider here, which illustrate the depth and range of these books.

Of Bread, Blood and The Hunger Games: Critical Essays on the Suzanne Collins Trilogy is an edited collection that was published the same year as *Approaching*, by the same publisher and attempts to "fill that gap" (Clark 2) in scholarship about the Hunger Games. This collection provides a variety of ways of considering some of the same themes that Henthorne considers— and as I consider here—and "assesses the Panem novels as a paradigm of Millennial anxieties and human complexity set within a cross-genre, cross generational narrative that is itself proof of the validity of human creativity in a seemingly inhumane world" (Pharr and Clark 17). The single-authored chapters allow for a bit more depth and breadth and provide more of a variety of voices and "a range of evaluative tools, probing the trilogy's meaning by using theories as varied as historicism, postmodernism, feminism, humanism, cultural studies, political studies, queer theory, and media studies" (Clark 2). The book gives an extensive overview of young adult dystopian literature and reminds us that "the literary fire set by Suzanne Collins blazes on!" (Clark 3).

This blaze is especially fierce in *Space and Place in The Hunger Games: New Readings of the Novels*. This edited collection has scholarly rigor and theoretical framing that provides a "radical" departure from its predecessors. As the title states, this collection is connected through the themes of space and place: "how places define us and divide us"; "how space can be used politically and socially to wield power and create social hierarchies"; "how space and place can be conceptualized, carved out, imagined, and used" (Garriott, Jones, and Tyler 1). So, not only does it not reiterate the same ways of considering the trilogy, it also pushes the boundaries of critical analysis. Notions of space and place are challenged and the well-worn themes are "disrupted," the authors argue. Taking the idea of a safe space as well as the ideas that literature plus analysis can set the world on fire, the title disguises the rather radical approach of this text. The "new readings" are not simply new—they are challenging the ways in which we do such analysis in the first place as the introduction's subtitle illustrates, "Taking Up and Entering Critical Space." This approach coalesces with its reading of the Hunger Games, and with my reading of YA dystopia "inspired by the spirit of the Girl on Fire, we engage in fanning the flames of critical discussion, disrupting the world just a little, so that rebuilding can begin" (Garriott, Jones, and Tyler 13).

Each text or collection is careful to note that it offers only one approach among many and that it hopes to inspire further directions from the rather banal desire to "encourage a new way of reading and watching" (Heit 8) to the more incendiary "ember to fan the flame of activism and scholarship" (Garriott, Jones, and Tyler). What all of these works have in common is a focus on the Hunger Games in all of its richness and as a serious subject for scholarly analysis. This means that the female protagonist is considered— how could she not be? But the idea of the female protagonist beyond the revolutionary role of Katniss—within and beyond the texts—does not occupy the central position that she does in other works like Leah Wilson's *The Girl Who Was on Fire* and the collection of scholarly analysis in *Female Rebellion in Young Adult Dystopia*. There are so many moving and weaving strands in this messy, complex, and enduring series. But there are other (and Other) Girls on Fire who deserve our attention.

* * *

The literary and critical legacies considered in this chapter are part of the bigger picture of YA dystopia's female protagonists. Since Katniss and the Hunger Games have produced so much academic ink, it should be rather obvious that she has exploded on the popular culture scene and a number of online discussions, popular books, memes, gifs, and other forms are proof that Katniss has captured the attention of American popular culture. She moves conversations forward on topics related to gender, class, poverty, sexuality, violence, and more. She was in the right place at the right time. In chapter three, I look more closely at girls and girlhood and legacies of girls' studies. As Roxane Gay notes, "Girls have been written and represented in popular culture in many different ways. Most of these representations have been largely unsatisfying because they never get girlhood quite right ... girlhood is too vast and too individual an experience. We can only try to represent girlhood in ways that are varied and recognizable" (53). The cultural legacies of girlhood and theories of feminism provide an important complement to literary frames, but also perpetuate the divide between white and black, mainstream and oppositional.

THREE

Girls' Studies
and Popular Culture
Segregated Feminisms

YA dystopia is a literary phenomenon, but it is also cultural. These books reference contemporary popular culture as well as classic literary texts. Food, fashion, music, businesses, sports, and any assortment of icons and activities are connected within and beyond the text. The films bring the books to the screen and beyond, inspiring trends in birthday parties, toys, hairstyles, baked goods, and fashion (Siesser, Martinson, Close). The films and characters dominate popular culture, but this trend is also mocked and revered in pop culture. Many representations shrink it down to a love triangle, a maneuver that promises to exasperate many YA dystopia fans. An episode of *The Simpsons* TV show mocks the phenomenon of the Hunger Games when Lisa takes up with a group of older girls and ditches her father to see the film *The Survival Games*. She croons and giggles like the other girls, and in the back of the theater Marge shushes Homer's interruptions as she watches: "Shh, she's trying on dresses." This satiric portrayal mocks YA dystopia in predictable ways, making the savvy Lisa into a giggling school girl. And because Marge is drawn into the spectacle as well—perhaps even more superficially than the girls—women are also implicated.

While this TV show episode is an anecdotal example of a pop culture reference, this example speaks to what the mainstream—in this case the adult (masculine) world—does to disempower empowering texts. As Bradford and Reimer argue in their introduction to *Girls, Texts, Cultures*, since "texts and textuality are crucially implicated in the socialization of girls and their identity formation" (9), and since texts can "unsettle dominant discourses" and "afford the potential for subversion" (11), the texts that girls consume, as well as the texts that we consume about girls, are important for an understanding of the roles that girls play in life and in our imaginations. U.S. culture mocks and reduces potentially empowering texts with the intention of minimizing their impact, or assumes that anything that involves girls must be frivolous. Girls are buying the pop culture texts, but they are not buying a dismissal of their economic or cultural power.

The girls of YA dystopia are far from frivolous. They are surviving, fighting, learning, leading, loving, and caring for others. As Bradford and Reimer argue, "In contemporary Western societies, girls and girlhood function to some degree as markers of cultural reproduction and change" (12). YA dystopia is all about interrupting such reproduction and advocating for change. Katniss Everdeen is the pop culture icon that embodies the trend of the female protagonist. And as much as Katniss might be mocked or criticized, she is also revered. For instance, on the third season of a TV game show called *King of the Nerds*, when her mistake causes one of the contestants to face elimination in the Nerd Off challenge, the guest celebrity declares, "I volunteer as tribute!" The nerd contestants and the TV audience know immediately what this reference means. It's a joke, but it is loaded with the love Katniss has for her sister, and her bravery and loyalty. And not only nerds use this cultural reference; it has seeped further into popular culture and is a common reference. Katniss is a cultural icon that reaches beyond the "narrow" category that created her. Old ways of categorizing girls is exactly what YA dystopia counters. Here girls are the center, the heroes (even when "reluctant").

They don't do it all alone, even when they want to protect other people and take on burdens and responsibilities that others cannot or will not. Katniss, as well as Tris from Divergent, are the most visible pop culture heroes for girls, but many of the Girls on Fire from YA dystopia are also *American* heroes. They are not always right, or brave, or intelligent, but they exist among a field of heroes dominated by men. For instance, in *Monsters* (third book in the Ashes trilogy), Alex reflects on her situation as the series comes to a close: "She didn't want all this on her. Yet … every step she had taken since the Zap had been because of someone else. She might still be lost if not for Ellie and Tom and Chris. Even Wolf. All those connections led her out of those woods, from a very black place, and pulled her from the brink of a leap where there was nothing and no one waiting but death" (565). She shoulders her responsibility, but she doesn't forget who she is a hero for or why she survived at all. While Katniss and Tris are the two most popular Girls on Fire—in part, because of the films that bring these books to life—they are a small sampling. And Girls on Fire are even more fitting as American heroes because they are complex, conflicted, sometimes reluctant, sometimes blindly focused, sometimes selfish and sometimes selfless.

There are many similarities in the female protagonists of YA dystopia, but they also have their unique qualities and struggles, influences and environments. The variety, even across sameness, is perhaps one of the most feminist aspects of YA dystopia as a whole category. These female protagonists have different settings and backgrounds, different shades of hair and eyes (and sometimes skin), different interests and abilities, different families and friends, different challenges and ambitions and different stories and futures. Their differences give the collective of YA dystopia layers and degrees. But the sameness across the category speaks to segregated feminisms—traditions of girls as white, privileged, upper class, and heterosexual are challenged in degrees rather than in character. In fact, most of the female protagonists are fighting for survival and/or are from poor or working-class origins. They are "Othered" girls. But whiteness and heteronormativity dominate these texts. Pop culture texts and criticism of these texts also suffer from segregation. Because of this segregation, critics and fans are able to set aside questions of race and ethnicity, and even questions of sexuality, in order to celebrate the female protagonist. And we do need to celebrate the female protagonist, because even in at her peak of popularity she is subject to a variety of criticism, skepticism, and marginalization.

From Pictures of Girlhood Past

In my 2006 book, *Pictures of Girlhood: Modern Female Adolescence on Film*, one of my main arguments was that the mainstream coming of age films that feature female protagonists (*Clueless, Bring It On, 10 Things I Hate About You, Mean Girls, She's All That*) are limited and limiting. What we know of girls and girlhood is whitewashed and shined up. I argue that if we had more mainstream access to films that feature "othered" girls (*Just Another Girl on the I.R.T., Whalerider, Manny and Lo, But I'm a Cheerleader, Whatever, Girls Town*)—and themes that speak to the realities of girls lives like violence, homelessness, pregnancy, lesbianism, and structural racism—then we would have a very different idea about girls in mainstream America and, thus, more potential for empowerment, equality, and social justice. These "girls' films"— the body of coming of age films in collective conversation—are potentially transformative, but the stories of "American girls" are segregated spaces where difference is erased, absorbed, ignored, and reduced in the mainstream.

New Pictures of Girlhood:
Shared Themes in Girls' Film and YA Dystopia

Theme	Girls' Film	YA Dystopia
Mainstream Girls/ popularity	Clueless Mean Girls Bring It On	Uglies Beauty Queens The Selection

Theme	Girls' Film	YA Dystopia
Vampires, Zombies, Horror	Buffy the Vampire Slayer Ginger Snaps Scream	The Immortal Rules Forrest of Hands and Teeth Enclave Ashes
Fairy Tales	Ever After A Cinderella Story Ella Enchanted	Incarceron The Selection Eve Cinder Ash
LGBTQIA	All Over Me The Incredibly True Adventures of 2 Girls in Love Show Me Love But I'm a Cheerleader	Adaptation Beauty Queens The Summer Prince The Hunger Games (?)
Experiences of Girls of Color	Just Another Girl on the IRT Bend It Like Beckham Rabbit Proof Fence Whale Rider Girls' Town	The Hunger Games Orleans Tankborn Shadows Cast by Stars The Interrogation of Ashala Wolf The Summer Prince
Outsiders/Outcasts	Welcome to the Dollhouse Whatever Slums of Beverly Hills	Birthmarked Under the Never Sky Shatter Me The Darkest Minds
Feminism	10 Things I Hate About You Foxfire	Eve Ash Prized The Pledge and The Essence Beauty Queens The Summer Prince

My argument here is not all that different. YA dystopia's female protagonists extend and expand the "pictures of girlhood" and the feminist characters, ideas, and plots offered in these films of the late 1990s and early 2000s. These girls' films exploded in this time frame, just as YA dystopia (and YA literature more generally) has exploded in the years since *The Hunger Games* was published (or *Twilight* or *Harry Potter* depending upon where we begin measuring). In her study of virginity in YA literature since *Twilight*, Christine Sefiert argues that *The Hunger Games* "ushered in an unprecedented demand for young adult dystopian books set in future worlds where governments control people and require extraordinary and often barbaric feats of its people" (55). The Hunger Games puts a lens on our contemporary world that makes it impossible to ignore the way we are headed—and girls are at the center. They are conduit and tool.

Girls on Fire are contemporary, interdisciplinary, contradictory "pictures"—the amalgamation of written texts, films, and other pop culture texts—that offer a variety of pop cultural functions, simplify and complicate girls lives and identities, and provide an overt political message. These novels are coming of age stories, but the stakes are higher than in the girls' films of my 2006 study of girls' culture. These YA dystopia books have a stake in life and death situations, revolutions and transformations. But they also have many elements in common with teen films—and girls' films: a strand of fairy tale interpretations, fashion themes, school struggles, conflict with parents and authority figures, and a divide between mainstream and marginalized or "othered" girls.

The female protagonists of YA dystopia, the editors of *Female Rebellion in YA Dystopia* argue, "seek to understand their places in the world, to claim their identities, and to live their lives on their own terms" (3). These qualities are key to coming of age narratives and describe the plot and progression of almost every girls' film I consider in *Pictures of Girlhood*. But, "Further, and perhaps more significantly, these young women also attempt to recreate the worlds in which they live, making their societies more egalitarian, more progressive, and, ultimately, more free" (3). Some girls' films of the 1990s and 2000s reach from the individual toward the structural, but none work to transform their world like YA dystopia's Girls on Fire do out of duty as much as necessity. (Consider, for instance, Cher's charity drive in *Clueless*.) This rich body of literature and culture makes "Girls on Fire" a significant cultural phenomenon that is more than an extension of "girl power." In *Pictures*, I highlight the "oppositional" qualities of these films and the cultural work they do. Here, I do the same, but more is at stake. A foundation has been set for Girls on Fire by the third wave feminists of the 1990s and 2000s, and there is more potential for individual and collective transformation in the wave that follows.

From "Othered" Girls on Fire

My arguments in *Pictures of Girlhood* have shaped not only my love of reading and writing about YA dystopia, but also the ways in which I posit Girls on Fire and center the Otherness of these characters. In a world full of vanilla portrayals of girls, the ways in which the female protagonists of YA dystopia are positioned as not pretty, as outcasts, as unpopular girls, is an important element of these works. More importantly, the little bit of space that this genre makes for girls of color has the potential to crack pop culture wide open. In my chapter from *Children's and Young Adult Literature and Culture: A Mosaic of Criticism*, "Othered Girls on Fire: Navigating the Complex Terrain of YA Dystopia's Female Protagonist," I argue that "when we layer non-white racial and ethnic identities with those that dominate popular consciousness, we democratize/complicate/deepen/transform YA dystopia in ways that might mirror the larger cultures—real and fictional—that YA dystopia is a part of" (238).

In "Othered Girls on Fire" I lay a foundation for the female protagonist as Girl on Fire, which is exploded here. I illustrate the ways in which segregation in literature and criticism shapes our ideas and ideals, and I discuss some of the racial futures of YA dystopia. In the section "All Female Protagonists are 'Othered'" I argue that "many are loners and/or are struggling to survive. They are poor. They are outcasts. They are victims of violence. They have lost parents, siblings, and friends, and have to be strong and brave. They are different" (237). But this "Othered" status is not simply about being an "outsider in the text; her story is outside the realm of mainstream YA dystopian texts" (238). I further argue that "if we consider YA dystopia without considering the stories of the Othered Girls on Fire, then we continue to perpetuate the kind of world we live in—a dystopia where not only our reality, but also our fiction, is unequal, unjust, and uninspired" (244). These are foundations for my arguments here, but in this book there is more space for breadth and depth. The power of the diversity of Girls on Fire, the intersections and critical consciousness that they exhibit and inspire—can be illuminated. But first, the foundations of the Girl in culture and criticism. In the remainder of this chapter, I extend these arguments about girlhood and girls' studies to conclude Part I—excavating and rethinking theories and legacies that further set the stage for excavating fiction, imagination, and application in Part II.

Excavating Girlhood and Girls' Studies

One of the most important frames that *Female Rebellion in Young Adult Dystopian Fiction* brings to our consideration of YA dystopia is of Girls' Studies, a sub-field of Women's Studies. Since one of the defining arguments of Girls' Studies questions the ways in which adult women study girls, the relationship between women's studies and girls' studies has been contested and interrogated. Despite the contentious relationship, the symbiosis of girls' and women's studies provides critical perspective on girls' cultures from women who also have perspective on their own experiences. YA dystopia makes a similar connection between the women who dominate the genre, the girls they write about, and the girls and women who read themselves into or from these books. And, yet, women—as writers as well as readers and critics—can be inadvertently dismissive of girls' agency.

The collection, *Girls, Texts, and Cultures*, edited by Clare Bradford and Mavis Reimer, provides important frames for YA dystopia and Girls on Fire through its approach to girlhood and girls' studies. It considers both the scholarly divide between traditional approaches to girls' studies and girls' literature as well as the reasons why intersectional analysis is generally lacking in scholarly considerations of girls and girlhood. "Academic research," Currie argues, "plays a role in re/constituting what it claims to have discovered: girlhood" (31). And this collection of essays considers girlhood as a diversity of experiences, texts, and contexts. The real-life experiences of girls, girls' cultural production, and texts for and about girls are brought into conversation among multi-disciplinary scholars.

One of the editors' arguments speaks to the patterns of segregation that I argue undergird both scholarship and cultural production. The editors critique the segregation between Girls' studies as it developed in the 1990s, "after male domination in academic institutions had eroded and when feminist scholars turned to research on girls' experiences and practices" (1) and the study of children's literature, which emerged during the 1970s and "is frequently downgraded in the academy" (2). The editors detail the development of both of these fields and the ways in which they have understood girls and girlhood, which helps to explain the remaining "divide between studies focusing on girls and their cultures, and studies of texts for and about girls" (2). This divide was also the focus of the conference that inspired the *Girls, Texts, Cultures* collection; it is but one divide.

Another important frame for considering YA dystopia's Girls on Fire is the play between past and present—and the future that dystopia interjects. The editors find that "feminist scholars of children's literature have been more interested in past locations, practices, and texts of girlhood than have scholars from the disciplines of sociology, education or media studies, who typically focus on contemporary practices" (7). This divide is particularly interesting to consider in relation to YA dystopia—a set of past texts, set in the future, that speak to contemporary practices. Currie cites Valerie Hey; she notes, "As Hey reminds us, 'In building new feminist futures we might need to be alert as to how our investment in things past regulates a misconception of the present'" (31). The "new feminist futures" of YA dystopia's Girls on Fire invest in things past as they replicate, for instance, heterosexual romances; and they might be accused of providing a "misconception of the present" since some books offer alternative presents instead of far-flung futures.

To extend the editors' argument, "understanding how formations of girlhood have functioned in other times … how they have secured, negotiated, or contested dominant values, and which of these structures of feeling have entered the present, can allow researchers to ask better questions about girls' cultures in contemporary contexts" (7) *as well as future contexts*. In considering the future of girls and girlhood, we are not only imagining the women these girls become and better understanding ourselves as women, we are also imagining the potential of the idea of girlhood and the space it occupies in the real world and the cultural imagination. The texts and contexts of Girls on Fire "unsettle dominant discourses" and "afford the potential for subversion on the part of their audiences" (11), as the editors note of several articles in the collection.

Currie argues that "reflexivity is necessary if girls' studies—itself a textual practice—is to remain committed to the feminist goal of enlarging *all* girls' potentials" (18). "Such an approach ["girlhood as a textually mediated social relation"]," she argues, "directs researchers to different kinds of texts" (31). This approach might also begin to direct readers—and mainstream popular representations and engagement—to different kinds of texts. The reader who chooses YA dystopia finds that the struggles and triumphs of the Girls on Fire resonate beyond the text. The power of the female protagonist in YA dystopia transcends what "girls" are allowed to do in fiction as well as real life. The Girl on Fire suffers from these same contradictions—of structure and generation and identity—in addition to the limits of adolescence.

Adolescence Beyond Liminal Spaces (Excavating Psychology)

Theories of adolescence play a central role in criticism of YA literature generally, and YA dystopia specifically. In "The Treatment for Stirrings" Joseph Campbell makes some interesting metaphorical connections between adolescence and the genre of YA dystopia as he discusses the state of American adolescence and how the genre shows how "society constructs the adolescent subject" (178). Inevitably, society's construction is an attempt to define and confine. It is no surprise that YA dystopia is a popular choice for teens since it models—in a metaphorical kind of way—the struggles and processes of adolescence, including a coming of age that calls into question the status quo of the world we live in.

In "Our Posthuman Adolescence," Richard Gooding argues that in *Feed*, "adolescence becomes the dominant subject position for all ages" (113), a subject position that is, perhaps, assumed because of the language used in the text. For instance, the way the narrator speaks and tells his story is not different from the ways that the adults also speak, and this is assumed to be result of the dumbing down of the people as a whole. Does this stilted language equate with adolescence as a subject position? Gooding notes that this adolescent subject position is "a result of the conflation of consumer culture and information technologies" (117), which is a state now—and in the imagined future—that more than just adolescents occupy. The fact that most everyone is part of the feed, embedded in this conflation, speaks to the state of this part of dystopia. In fact, the world of *Feed* resonates with the world of the film *Idiocracy*, where lower class breeding, not technology and corporations, is blamed for the people's inability to string together more than a few coherent words. Adolescence might be a transitional state, but it is not necessarily an ignorant one. In fact, Girls on Fire, even when ignorant of certain skills or knowledge, have a subject position of strength that straddles the personal and the political.

Negotiations between the individual psychology of adolescence and the structural shaping of our cultural landscapes happen in YA dystopia as well as in real life. When we consider how psychological concepts can inform our understanding of both the audience of YA as well as the structures of the stories themselves, we can see the power of interdisciplinary approaches. The edited collection *Female Rebellion in Young Adult Dystopia* establishes a kind of metaphorical understanding through the psychological concept of "liminality" to describe the "in-between" space of adolescence, "of individuality and conformity, of empowerment and passivity" (4) even as they extend this space, conditionally. "Liminality" frames how these characters "occupy the role of active agent rather than passive bystander" and "illustrate the ongoing challenges of redefining what it means to be a young woman" (4). This is powerful, but contained. The focus on rebellion and liminal spaces in *Female Rebellion* suggests inevitable acts of adolescence before settling down into adulthood and responsibility. The idea of the liminal is a major focal point, but this version of rebellion is deceptively simple.

Within the diverse frames through which we can view the female protagonist, a heavy focus on a particular psychological concept/theory of adolescence limits our understanding of these texts as well as our understanding of adolescence. We might also consider some other psychological concepts that illuminate and extend YA dystopia. In her book, *Finally, A Song from Silence (Poetry from When I Was Young)*, Laura Kati Corlew, a scholar of community psychology, sheds light on adolescence through psychological concepts and her own excavated writings from her "at-risk" adolescence and early adulthood. Some of these concepts also illuminate YA dystopia—its form and function in theory and practice. For instance, she describes the psychological concept of the "personal fable," as "the belief that adolescents' ordinary lives are particularly extraordinary, and that no one has experienced the same level of good or bad that they experience. It is the belief that every experience they are having for the first time in their lives is being experienced for the first time ever in the world" (5). YA dystopia takes the "personal fable" to an archetypal level.

Perhaps ironically, popular culture often creates the "epic" quality of "crushes" in YA dystopia that seep over into the ways in which we perceive aspects like love triangles. In fact, there are few "crushes" in dystopia—almost all opposite sex relationships are the stuff of everlasting love stories. What could be more epic? Love, as much as the stakes of the future of the world, is epic. And such epic stories are always bigger than themselves. Corlew pairs the "personal fable" with the "imaginary audience" which "is the sense that everyone is watching, constantly—watching with jealousy, with judgment, with awe" (5). And, of course, in YA dystopia, the story told by the protagonist—The Girl on Fire—is one that everyone is watching/reading/experiencing. When the text is brought to film, the impact reaches further. Corlew continues, "They may know that they are not the center of the universe, but it certainly feels to them like they are" (5). In the epic and desperate stories of YA dystopia, the Girls on Fire are the center of their own universe. They are often the center of at least one other character's universe. They are at the center of the reader's universe. They are the center of this book.

The drama associated with adolescence in our privileged world is something different in dystopia, but the similarities are also empowering. Intense emotions, empathy, and optimism need not be seen as negative states nor confined to adolescence. As Corlew argues, "It is common for teens to recognize that there is something wrong with the world, with society, with politics, with whichever cultural narratives bind or restrict them inexplicably and often invisibly" (152). She further explains that "adolescents are able to critically process complex social narratives and explore hypothetical realities and futures with roughly the same cognitive capacity as adults" (152). This would explain why YA dystopia books are popular with teens; these books are an opportunity to "critically process" a "social narrative" that has provided the often-confining structures of our society and culture. These texts give readers a stake in a collective future. Further, these texts find adolescent readers just as engaged with their adult-like cognitive capacities.

And in fiction, the Girls on Fire process the wrongness and, perhaps "because they [like adolescents more generally] don't have the same level of life experience that fills out social and political reasoning of adults, they are more prone to a political and activist belief that we can and should mold life into our ideals" (Corlew 152). We can imagine an ideal life. We have a stake—a *should*—and there is a strong tendency in YA dystopia for Girls on Fire to be overwhelmingly idealist. While in life it may take "decades" before teens can "fully parse out the elements of this wrongness" (152), the Girls on Fire don't have nearly this amount of time for their own processing. They are required to take action long before their psychically unformed adolescent brains can catch up. Corlew continues to explain the impact that can result from teens' critical processing:

> Activism and rebellion are two sides of the same coin—teens perceive (rightly, I might add) that many of the "truths" they are told to accept are half-truths, lies, or just plain wrong, and they lash out against the world to effect change or at least in a statement of non-compliance. They often feel betrayed by adults and world leaders who push an agenda based on ideals, but who simultaneously enforce unjust social structures [152].

In almost every YA dystopia text, there is an uncovering of lies. Sometimes these lies are huge and shape the structure of the Girl on Fire's world, and sometimes they are personal and impact the character development and action. In *What's Left of Me*, Eva notes that the government lied and the president lied. And, like in *Eve* and *Matched*, the teachers lied, "or didn't even know the truth of what they doled out in class" (338). When Girls on Fire "lash out," it is sometimes a result of adolescent angst and "non-compliance," but it is also sometimes a successful attempt—individually and/or collectively—to "effect change." Further, the betrayal of adults coalesces with the betrayals of "world leaders" and the very "ideals" and "unjust social structures" are the impetus of Girls on Fires' action—whether this action simply sustains their survival or significantly shifts their society's structures.

The structures/rules that contain girls socially and culturally—and the rules that hold down an entire population—are parts of the same system. As Girl on Fire Ashala argues, "the government loved its rules" (69). The boys in YA dystopia feel the oppression of the rules as well. In *Delirium*, Alex notes the similarities between rules and walls and cages and his experience of living in Portland: "rules everywhere you turned, rules and walls, rules and walls.... I felt like I was in a cage. We *are* in a cage: a bordered cage" (228). Lena is shocked because she never "thought of it that way" (228). Railing against these rules cannot be dismissed as adolescent rebellion alone. These rules also apply to adults. These stories speak to the need for large and lasting change, an end to rules that define and confine us in individually and structurally damaging ways (Corlew). As Dan Wells writes in his dedication to *Partials*: "This book is dedicated to the rule breakers, the trouble-makers, and the revolutionaries. Sometimes the hand that feeds you needs a good bite."

The idea of liminal space deepens our reading of the female protagonist, but what is missing from *Female Rebellion* illustrates one of my core contentions here about segregated criticism—all of the examples discussed in the editors' introduction skirt the issue of whiteness and race and structural racism and privilege. The liminal as a space of privilege is not important. YA dystopia's female protagonists are considered through lenses that are already whitewashed and narrow. What is different for the "Girl on Fire" compared to *Female Rebellion*'s "contemporary girl protagonists" (3)? While there is certainly overlap and common ground, there are also some important differences. Corlew recognizes that "activism and rebellion are two sides of the same coin" and Gooding recognizes Violet's activism as a model for our contemporary world. Rebellion is not just teenage angst; it is a potential for revolution—inside and outside the text.

The Female Protagonist as Girl on Fire

Girls, and America more generally, are ready to make Girls on Fire stories a permanent fixture of our soon-to-be, if-not-already dystopic culture—the explosion of YA dystopian fiction speaks to this lack and desire. As cultural texts re-create the superhero Ms. Marvel as a Muslim teenage girl, and the re-made *Ghostbusters* movie imagines a team of women fighting to save the city, and *Logan* brings a girl who may be better than Wolverine into the X-Men story, we can imagine the shifting cultural currents and/or the simultaneous fact that the female protagonist is a hot cultural commodity and marketing tool. Thomas Newkirk argues in *Minds Made for Stories* that "we seek the companionship of a narrator who maintains our attention, and perhaps affection" (146). Girls on Fire tell compelling stories, and they are almost always loved if not by the reader, then at least by the male love interest and often by a population of people indebted to her. This genre provides diverse characters and repetitive tropes that speak to girls' lack of power and potential for power and empowerment—ultimately the core subject matter of this book.

But just because we have discovered where the girls are does not mean that we don't have to keep the fire burning. Even the women responsible for bringing us strong female protagonists undercut their cultural capital. In an interview, Veronica Roth and Marie Lu (both young and cute) give one-word answers to a series of things, indicating like, dislike, or neutral (Lanfreschi). The first item on the list was "female protagonists," and despite their famous creations of strong female protagonists both authors showed an immediate dislike for this term (even as they celebrate the female protagonist elsewhere). They are both of a generation that can take for granted the right for the female protagonist to exist, let alone to dominate the imagination of popular culture. And they are also a generation that resists being pigeonholed as "feminist" as much as being "female." But these young women also carry a lot of responsibility as popular authors and, thus, pop culture icons. Their response undercuts their power.

* * *

When considering the female protagonist as Girl on Fire, we are also easily deceived by appearances—ironically, a lesson that texts like *Birthmarked* and *Uglies* try to instill in readers. Many texts appear to be empowering, many female protagonists appear to be Girls on Fire, but critical attention may be so focused on superficial markers that we miss the bigger picture. One chapter in *Female Rebellion* considers another popular series that is recognized for a strong female protagonist. In "The Three Faces of Tally Youngblood" Mary Jeanette Moran assumes the novel portrays "some advances" toward gender equity "from a feminist perspective" (127). In a footnote she cites a lack of patriarchal structure and a lack of men in positions of power as well as the fact that the most powerful woman is female and men and women of both genders "demonstrate qualities" across traditional gendered expectations as "advances" (127). If these are our measure of gender equity, we are setting our standards far too low.

The conventional way of reading Tally reveals that she is a Girl on Fire. She is the center of the story, and she wins in the end, even though she also loses a lot in the process (not unlike Katniss, but far less bleak). The lack of direct mention of any gender norms in the first book makes Tally feel like a universal character. The second book can remind us of Tally's femaleness because she has already been established as not being that kind of girl. She eschews fashion. She literally dreams of being a princess. She is disgusted by the oppression of women exhibited by the primitive peoples she encounters. Tally can take on these feminist and feminine qualities. And she can leave them behind just as easily when she becomes a Special in book three. But if we read the first book (and to some extent the rest of the series) with different lenses on gender and sexuality, some important trends and problems in YA dystopia are revealed. If we read the first book with Tally as gender neutral or as a male character, not a whole lot changes. Even the romantic aspects are fairly neutral though certainly not absent.

Romance and Limitations of Virginity as Lens

Romance allows us to step out of the realm of the ordinary struggles of relationships, love, partnership, expectations, and responsibilities. It gives us an escape, but also a microscope to better understand ourselves and our needs and desires. The context of material desperation that comes with many dystopic settings means that sex and sexuality can easily be pushed to the side. And yet, there it is—sex and affection and power fighting their way into the narrative through the trope of romance and the theme of love. Romance—and, more, a romantic ideal of love—undergirds almost every one of these books. And romance is not just the sappy stuff of love triangles, fate, and unquestioned support and devotion. Romance is often a stand-in for sex and sexuality that can both obscure and reveal. But if romance is only read through a lens of sexuality—as a mirror to our cultural obsession with virginity, for instance—then we are misreading the romance.

Like I conclude in *Pictures* about girls' films of the 90s and 2000s, Seifert concludes that the narratives in Matched, Delirium, and The Selection end in marriage or the assumption of marriage (59). Two of the three novels she considers are categorized as "implied long-term relationship"; however, ending in marriage and ending in "long-term" isn't exactly the same thing. One is entering into a legal institution; the other is sometimes implied by an optimistic or ambiguous ending. Further, at the end of *Pandemonium*, Lena and Alex reconnect, but as the story ends there is no promise that they will work out a relationship. It is implied, but perhaps only because we—the reader and the fan of the genre—expect and hope that this is the suggested outcome. What they have worked out is their enduring love, "a kiss that promises renewal" (388). Without building a new world, there will be no place for this love. The focus on the closing pages is the tearing down of the wall, not the romantic relationship. Further, this is one incident among Lena's survey of the people and responsibilities in her life. She holds Grace's hand as she notes Bran and Hunter, Pippa, Coral, her mother, Julian. For a moment she feels "a sense of overwhelming grief: for how things change, for the fact that we can never go back.… But it's not about knowing. It is simply about going forward" (390). It's about "watching the border dissolve, watching a new world emerge beyond it" (391).

Seifert also minimizes these characters, taking away potential power (or empowerment) when she notes that "they are still heroic, but their virginity—the constellation of characteristics that define them—matters more than what they actually do" (59). This is a stretch in all three of these novels, and in the genre more widely. Seifert, for instance, reads The Selection as hinging on America's "purity," but this is hardly her most visible quality. In fact, she is poorly behaved in this setting (and annoyingly whiny and indecisive most of the time), but also conflicted and frustrated with a process where she has no power. She stands out because of her lower class characteristics more than her perceived "purity." She stands up for what she thinks is right.

Ultimately, Seifert concludes that "popular YA dystopian novels suggest that girls can be heroines and change the world but only if they are pure enough and only if they are fighting to maintain the right to engage in long-term committed heterosexual relationships" (82). While a bit skewed and overstated, it is clear that "popular" texts reinforce limited and limiting ideas about sex. As Roxane Gay notes, "It's disturbing that within the world of the Hunger Games, it is perfectly acceptable for teenagers to kill one another and die or otherwise suffer in really violent ways, but it is not at all acceptable for them to explore their sexuality" (140). Is it not acceptable in the context of the future world, the context of the YA genre, or the context of *our* world?

While romance is overplayed in the genre/mode as a whole, romance acts as more than just a conventional convention. In many books, Girls on Fire come to know themselves, to believe in themselves, at least in part through the love of a boy/young man. The cultural weight of this arrangement is saturated by the age-old hetero-romance narrative. But if we look more deeply at the ways in which romance and love are negotiated in this group of books, we can see that sexuality is more complex and fluid than first glance. Seifert's study is a necessary maneuver because "analyzing how we fetishize virginity is one way of understanding—and pushing back against—images of young girls as objects—the blank slates that we use to live our misguided fantasies" (19). But what if the "blank slate" girl is powerful—not the object of our shared sexism and misogyny, but the subject of our hope and possibility?

Excavating Heteronormativity and Sex

Just as these novels are overwhelmingly white, they are also overwhelmingly heteronormative—or straight. They are also very often romances and almost all of the books have a male/female romantic relationship dynamic. Such romantic elements are not reserved only for YA dystopia or YA literature, and the oppositional elements of romance have been argued by countless critics, following Janice Radaway's 1984 *Reading the Romance: Women, Patriarchy, and Popular Literature.* But since almost every text I consider here includes a romantic element, we also need to consider how this trope defines and defies. These novels model relationships and attitudes that are sanctioned by mainstream American cultural expectations; sometimes they challenge convention.

Some of these romantic dynamics are problematic, if not downright disturbing. For instance, the over-marketing of the love triangle diminishes the other elements but also misrepresents the range of relationships in these books. From the creepy control of Saba's brother, Lugh, in Dustlands to the boys competing for the privilege of spending time alone with a girl in *Prized,* the love triangle is rarely what the hype reflects. For instance, Saba is used to doing what her brother tells her to do: "Lugh goes first, always first, an I follow on behind./An that's fine./That's right./That's how it's meant to be" (1). Her words on the first page of *Blood Red Road* echo her last words. When Lugh sees she has feelings for Jack, Lugh acts like a jealous boyfriend. But it's not just her brother and her love interest that make this triangle. The heart stone (that guides her to her heart's desire) leads her to DeMalo (the bad guy) as well as Jack; when she has sex with DeMalo and things get really complicated. Further, Tommo, DeMalo's estranged son, has a crush on Saba. When her brother dies, she is distraught, crying that her *"golden heart is gone"* (*Raging Star* 383), but at other times she recognizes that "Lugh don't own me" (*Rebel Heart* 193). In other cases, the love triangle is a powerful symbol of something bigger than two people. As Zhange Ni illustrates, in the Matched series, "the trite convention of heterosexual romantic love in young adult literature, is replaced by the triangular interaction (not to be misread as a love triangle) of Cassia the poet, Xander the physic, and Ky the pilot" (171). This trio speaks to the important shifts of society and culture and the need for interdisciplinary approaches to the problems that we face.

A few novels interrupt the heterosexual narrative in passing (pun intended). In *Delirium*, where love is a disease, and all love is outlawed, "every so often people make mistakes" (52). They let their passions run wild, beyond the bounds of what's acceptable and lawful. Lena explains that the disease of love is "biological, a result of the same kinds of chemical and hormonal imbalances that occasionally lead to Unnaturalism, to boys being attracted to boys and girls to girls. These impulses, too, will be resolved by the cure" (52). With just a few sentences, homosexuality is recognized, equalized, and dismissed. These impulses of attraction are not "same love" beyond another brief mention in *Pandemonium*—a lost opportunity to challenge heteronormativity. Except, Lena considers one "Unnatural" to be a close friend, so we should assume that being homosexual is okay outside of the rules of society. The Unnaturals, we might assume, leave society so that they can love whoever they love, and in this novel this situation is just like it is for any other citizen. All love is outlawed. But this connection to an othered sexuality is not developed in this series. This one example suffices.

Plenty of books take even less of an opportunity to challenge heterosexuality. In a genre that avoids sexuality more generally, this is not surprising, but it is also not excusable. There are plenty of opportunities to challenge heteronormativity, but authors may not take these opportunities for any variety of reasons from the restrictions of the genre, to their own beliefs and feelings, to the perceived backlash from parents and teachers. In her study of virginity in YA literature, Christine Seifert compares the explicit sexual nature of Judy Blume's controversial and resonant young adult novel, *Forever*, which "has always been challenged somewhere since the time of its publication" but seems "less controversial in the 1970s than it is now" (2).[1] Today, while gender, sex and sexuality are becoming more fluid and open, particularly among young people, YA novels reflect mainstream mores about what kind of sexual material should be available to teens. In fact, because any sex is controversial, Seifert actually has to make the explicit point that the presence of sex in a novel (like rape in the novel *Speak*) is not a simple promotion of sex, but an

opportunity to understand it as an aspect of the teenage (and human) experience. The power of perceived "parental uproar" is a powerful shaper not
only of what young readers consume, but also what writers and publishers
produce.

In Seifert's evaluation of popular literature and sex-positive literature,
nothing contemporary can rival *Forever*; instead, YA literature has been
shaped by more conservative attitudes about sex and sexuality. Seifert identifies four virginity tropes established in the Twilight series that are played
out in YA literature over the last decade: "Innocence and Naiveté Are Inexplicably Attractive"; "Virgins Need Virginity Guardians"; "Virgins Have Des-
tined Soul Mates"; and "Danger Is Sexy and Tempting." While Seifert makes
a strong case for these tropes in paranormal and contemporary YA literature,
her arguments are less convincing in the diverse genre of YA dystopia (which
I examine more closely in Part II). Regardless, we cannot deny the fact that
when it comes to YA literature, romance sells. *Twilight's* sales have squashed
Forever, Seifert argues, and "publishers pump out series after series that rely
on *Twilight's* tropes" and "barrage us with simplified, stereotypical, and often
contradictory messages about sex" (16). These contradictory messages are
cultural power plays that result in robbing girls of agency in terms of sexuality,
which connects to all kinds of agency in her life.

But there are some spaces and fissures in a variety of YA dystopia texts
that may not appear to be "sex positive." At the very least, Seifert notes that
"dystopian romance series present tropes similar to those of paranormal
romance novels, but the dystopian romance novels are significantly more
complex" (59). Sex is part of a rich landscape, even if it is restricted to kissing
and romantic, forever kinds of love (which are also more complicated). Sexual
pluralism is important to bring forth in YA dystopia as youth are exposed to
far more open and diverse sexualities, in life and in other mediated contexts.
The power of the reader's interpretation—and pop culture as a space to play—
means that even less open texts can be explored through a critical eye and
voice to bring forth the subtle navigations of sexuality as well as race, class,
gender, culture, power, and the possibilities of transformation.

Beyond Race and Gender: Segregated Dystopias and Finding Common Ground

With all of the influence of feminism and all of the possibilities of a
future that has not yet been written, why do we get so many versions of the
future that are whitewashed or conceive of their female protagonist in flat or
narrow ways? The answer lies, of course, in a culture that continues to suffer
from segregation, sexism, racism and a population that cannot help but

subscribe to the imposed limitations of this system because they lack the tools for developing critical and oppositional forms of consciousness. Segregation impacts writers and critics, publishing trends and reader's tastes. Thus, who chooses to write, what/who they choose to write about, what gets written, what gets published, what gets read, what gets critiqued and promoted and shared and awarded, is shaped by a system invested in what feminist critic bell hooks calls the white supremacist, imperialist, capitalist, patriarchy. Better understanding how these interlocking systems limit our present possibilities and our future potential—as well as our individual and collective imagination—can help us better understand what's on the table and what's at stake, what's up for negotiation and what will break before it bends, and what tools we have and what tools we need.

While the female protagonist has been considered in a variety of anthologies about YA dystopia, and the prototype of the female protagonist—the Hunger Games' Katniss Everdeen—has been written about in volumes, a closer look at these feminist frames reveals that just because a book has a strong female protagonist, does not mean that it is a feminist text or an example of critical dystopia. And, just because a text engages with dystopian ideas does not mean that it is original or progressive, insightful or inspiring. In fact, YA dystopia illustrates well the tensions and contradictions that exist within feminist traditions that frame not only feminist literary traditions, but also American culture more generally. For instance, Tally and Ember are rather superficial measures of a "female protagonist" pushed to the edges of criticism, not to mention a low standard for the threshold of "advances." The female protagonist as Girl on Fire can do better. When we place this symbol in the context of interdisciplinarity and intersectionality, we establish a female protagonist who has more at stake. When we mediate space for the female protagonist to be bigger than the confines of girlhood, we open the possibilities for all of us. And when we place the female protagonist in the contexts of woman of color feminist ideas of third spaces, world-traveling, decolonization, oppositional consciousness, and transcendent community, we see very different aspects than the feminist critical tradition that shapes most of our mainstream understandings of girls and girlhood.

In criticism, questions of race can be compartmentalized in anthologies like *Female Rebellion* where only two chapters engage with texts or themes that include racial or ethnic dimensions. As I note in "Othered Girls," when critics take on race, they most often are tackling a book or a singular representations. For instance, Couzelis's important arguments about how "the future is pale" is based upon a small sampling of books, which may or may not represent the whole of YA dystopia or young adult literature more generally (6). However, when we gloss over race, it is often convenient because our focus is elsewhere. For instance, *Female Rebellion's* critical focus on

"rebellion, romance, and hope," narrows the critical field and its connections
to "contemporary adolescent womanhood" (11) can be read as code for white
girl experiences. The focus on "signs and symbols of their rebellion" (12) and
"place, space, and population" (12) highlight dimensions of these texts seemingly empty of racial signification. They offer "insights into the intersections
of adolescence, dystopia, and rebellion" (12). This collection aims for an
understanding of how "the larger picture created by considering the myriad
representations of rebellious adolescent womanhood also calls attention to
the broader impact of such stories" (12). If this "broader impact" is whitewashed then it is not an accurate representation of redefinitions of "the young
women themselves but also their place in their own society and the impact
they may have on future generations" (12). If we only listen to the stories of
the mainstream (white, heterosexual) girls, and if we let these stories define
the whole category of "young women" then we are not doing justice to the
very spirit of the Girl on Fire. I make this argument in *Pictures of Girlhood*,
and it is just as relevant in this context a decade later.

* * *

While *Female Rebellion* establishes a number of important frames for
considering the female protagonist, it also inadvertently illustrates an important quality of segregation in American literature and culture as well as scholarly inquiry. As a result of the frames offered by this critical text, the
consideration of race fades into the background as if its invisibility makes it
unimportant. In fact, the opposite is true. The assumptions of progressive
(or even contested) politics in texts that fail to engage with questions and
issues of race, for whatever reason, only makes this aspect more important.
It is easy for white authors and critics to assume the playing field is equal—
the future is a blank slate. But the future that is available, and often mass-
marketed, is one that is based upon the blinders, blanks, fissures, and assumptions that shape the contemporary political atmosphere regarding race and
bleed into the future through fiction.

Many of these science fiction, young adult, and feminist traditions are
predominately white, and considerations of the treatment (or lack of treatment) of race in science fiction can be heated. Many of the feminist traditions
that shape women's studies and feminist scholarly inquiry are also segregated;
thus, centering in on the ways in which race and ethnicity are—and are not—
represented is important for considering the full diversity of the genre as well
as our criticism.

If we fail to expect a diverse set of representations, we get female protagonists who set their world on fire—a controlled blaze. We deserve more.
American girls deserve more. YA dystopia deserves more.

And it can do more.

Building upon the genius of Octavia Butler (and other "mothers" discussed in chapter two) science fiction has become more diverse, and young adult dystopian literature takes on race, ethnicity, and nationality in interesting ways. But not only does scholarly criticism largely ignore these texts—and obsess about others—such criticism also lacks the tools and interdisciplinary perspectives needed to unpack texts as rich as those of YA dystopia's Girls on Fire. The threads woven throughout Part I where I have excavated the theories found in studies of utopia/dystopia (and speculative fiction more generally) as well as cultural studies, American studies, and women's studies are the tools that help us to challenge legacies of racism and white supremacy, sexism and misogyny, heteronormativity, and oppression in the stories we tell, share, consume, and unpack and apply. The future is diverse; it can also be intersectional.

The next four chapters use these tools of interdisciplinarity and intersectionality to illuminate cultural contexts and the connections to our real world, which is the inspiration. These tools also examine the significant themes and patterns that establish the interlocking web of the collective of YA dystopia and the possibilities and potential for a better future. But first, an interlude that reminds us why these books are important texts—we love the experience of reading them.

INTERLUDE
Fangirling: A Passion for YA Dystopia

I love a good story. I get absorbed in a book and entangled. If I read the first in a series, I become invested in finishing the story (at least the vast majority of the time). I become a part of that world and sometimes have trouble adapting to reality after a heavy reading session or a haunting book. YA dystopia is particularly suited to such entrapment. I call them my crack books because I cannot stop reading one more page, one more chapter, one more book. I can't and won't put them down. When I finish a series, I am instantly disappointed that I will never be able to read it again for the first time. My favorite books are re-read and the experience is new again because it is more than it was the first time. Good books only get better.

When I finished the Hunger Games series I was afraid that I would never find a book like it again. It didn't take long to realize that there were many more books—they were being churned out. I read a lot of books about boys and then I found the books about girls. Jackpot. But it wasn't until I discovered Victoria Law's *Bitch Magazine* column "Girls of Color in YA Dystopia" that I became bound and chained to YA dystopia. It became more than just a good laugh from the library staff on my campus as I stalked the desk waiting for my next book to arrive. I suspect the friend/colleague who sent me the link suspected just what I would do with what I found. My obsession became a mission.

This is when I started to think about YA dystopia in scholarly ways.

This is when the web of connections began to weave itself into my brain. I love patterns and big pictures. I am an undisciplined structuralist/deconstructionist. I love stories that mean something, that argue for a transformation of ideas, peoples, structures, myths—that challenge what we think we know and what we think we want. The argument that Girls on Fire books make as a collective, is powerful. I am a fangirl of revolutionary change and of thinking about how to create change.

74

Yet I still enjoy every book, every word I read. Even if I am rolling my eyes, sighing heavily, or crying, I am still enjoying the visceral and intellectual reading experience.

Fangirling shapes my relationship to this literature as a teacher, a scholar, and a critic. I have never shied away from teaching and writing about popular culture; I have always encouraged my students to critique the things they most love. I share the wisdom of W.E.B. DuBois:

> But the hushing of criticism of honest opponents is a dangerous thing. It leads some of the best of the critics to unfortunate silence and paralysis of effort, and others to burst into speech so passionately and intemperately as to lose listeners. Honest and earnest criticism from those whose interests are most nearly touched—criticism of writers by readers, of government by those governed, of leaders by those led—this is the soul of democracy and the safeguard of modern society [462].

Fangirls can be too close to our subject, but we can also provide insights that a reader without a passion for the text might not. These books we love shape the way we see the world. YA dystopia books are criticism—the "soul of democracy and the safeguard of modern society."

* * *

Late in the process of writing this book, I came across a blog based on a book of essays called *Bad Feminist*. I was attracted to the title of this work, which is layered and ironic, and I love layers and ironies as much as patterns. Quotes from Roxane Gay pop up all over my book because what she writes about makes interesting connections to, and insights about, what I write about. Roxane Gay is also a fangirl and an academic. In her book, she writes about a variety of cultural texts, especially focused around issues of race and gender and sexuality. She writes about being a writer. She also writes about herself. She weaves the personal and political in deft ways. After navigating several essays that deal with sexual abuse and rape, Roxane Gay shares her own story. Gay weaves her essays together masterfully, slowly unfolding her own personal trauma, contextualizing it within a larger culture where she is hardly alone. She opens her chapter "What We Hunger For" by noting how often "representations of a woman's strength overlook the cost of that strength, where it rises from, and how it is called upon when needed most" (137). In the middle of her gushings about the Hunger Games, she shares her own story of sexual assault—a gang rape that happened when she was in middle school. While I anticipated that this story would be told at some point (I saw the pattern being woven), I did not expect to find it sandwiched in the midst of her visceral descriptions of her love of the Hunger Games—the books and the films. It is this juxtaposition, or this complementary narrative, that makes me appreciate the wisdom and insight of Gay's work.

While I do not feel close enough to anything to not also be a critic of it, I can understand where Gay is coming from when she writes: "As a critic, I recognize the significant flaws, I do, but *The Hunger Games* is not a movie I am able to watch as a critic. The story means too much to me" (140). Just before she tells her story she tells us: "I am fascinated by strength in women./ People tend to think I'm strong. I'm not. And yet. I identify with Katniss because through the trilogy, the people around Katniss expect her to be strong and she does her best to meet those expectations, even when it costs her a great deal" (141). What we find in the characters of books not only helps us to see ourselves more clearly, these stories also help us escape into another world where we can see other women fight similar battles. What Gay and I do have in common is that "reading remains one of the purest things I do" (175). To think about how little most Americans read is simply tragic— another example of contemporary dystopia.

So, now I am not only fangirling YA dystopia, I am also fangirling Roxane Gay. I am also fangirling Sherri L. Smith, Ambelin Kwaymullina, and Alaya Dawn Johnson. Their books are perfection and these authors are modeling what intersectional feminism plus YA dystopia can be and what it can do. Johnson joined my Race, Class, Gender, and Sexuality class for a presentation and informal conversation via Google Hangouts in the spring of 2016. Having the opportunity to hear her speak about her work in the context of this class was invigorating for me as well as for my students. I was already fangirling her book; the person behind it was added to my list.

* * *

Fangirling can also shed light on the relationship of the author with her dystopic work. Toward these ends it is interesting to note the difference between Lois Lowry and Sherri L. Smith. Lowry, author of the foundational YA dystopia book and series that begins with *The Giver*, notes that she did not set out to write dystopia though she "had to read the classic dystopian literature" when she was majoring in English at Brown. As previously noted, Lowry states that "as a housewife who read a lot" she "loved Margaret Atwood's *The Handmaid's Tale*," which she partially attributes to the shared Cambridge, Massachusetts setting. While it is not what she is drawn to, her work has made space for other dystopic fiction. As Connors notes, "*The Giver* may not have been the first young adult dystopia, but it is among the genre's most recognizable titles, a result of its having been taught and embraced by a generation of teachers and students in American schools and elsewhere" (24). Lowry's text has been institutionalized in American education and continues to influence (young and not young) readers.

Smith, on the other hand, explains, "I am a speculative fiction fangirl at heart. I grew up reading fantasy and science fiction, and always assumed that would be what I wrote. I was actually a bit horrified to realize that wasn't what came out of my pen on my first novel" (37). When Smith "came home" to speculative fiction, she produced a masterpiece as well. But her masterpiece will be, as Connors describes it, "lauded by critics for its thoughtful portrayal of a strong female protagonist who is also a person of color" (37). It is also a piece that is specific to the regional ramifications of Hurricane Katrina and her real and imagined aftermath. It is less likely to be "taught and embraced by a generation of teachers," and yet, it is a seminal work in American literature, generally, and YA dystopian literature specifically. It *should* be taught in American schools. It could be taught alongside materials about girls' experiences with Katrina, with cultural texts like the film *Beasts of the Southern Wild*. It can be used to talk about climate change and poverty. It can be used to put the past, the present, and the future in context. It is just as relevant and "universal" as, for instance, *The Giver* or *1984* or *A Handmaid's Tale*.

But the thing about Fangirls is that we not only love very popular texts, we also love obscure texts. In fact, we like to like things a lot before they become popular and somehow sell out to the manipulations of the mainstream. But, as Roxane Gay exhibits, we still love and enjoy these mainstream renditions. And we can't help but love the fact that more people get to enjoy the texts we love. My fangirling is for the visceral and highly personal act of reading, but it is also for the orgy of ideas—the opportunity to live in a future that is but one of infinite possible futures. I hope that my work to elucidate and illuminate the stories of Girls on Fire inspires fangirls (and fanboys and fanwomen and fanmen and fandogs and fancats and fan beings of all kinds) to take the ideas of the Girls on Fire and run with them like wolves.[2]

FOUR

Contemporary Dystopia
Living the Future

The world we live in has many qualities in common with fictional dystopias—not simply because our contemporary culture informs these works of fiction, but also because we *are* a dystopia (Dean; McCrayer). In the past, what we imagined about the future—flying cars and robot servants, for instance—is far from the present dystopia realities of food shortages, climate change, and cyber warfare, for instance (Ali; Dvorsky; Geek's Guide to the Galaxy). Naomi Klein argues that all of the films and books, the "cli-fi" or the science fiction or dystopian stories "tell us is that we're taking a future of environmental catastrophe for granted." Further, our lack of being able to find solutions to these future problems speaks to a culture that has had a hand in them: "It seems easier, more realistic, to dim the sun than to put up solar panels on every home in the United States," states Klein. "And that says a lot about us, and what we think is possible, and what we think is realistic" (Geek's Guide). But Klein underestimates the power of stories.

References to American dystopia are not uncommon when people write and talk about the election and inauguration of Donald Trump. *The Daily Show* aired a dystopian episode that imagined what Trump's election would do to the U.S. It was comedy; it wasn't supposed to come true. When it did come true, Joy-Ann Reid cited the increased sales of *The Handmaid's Tale* in relation to dystopic conditions. Lists like College Humor's "5 Reasons We Are Already Living in a Terrible Dystopian Future" are plentiful on social media (Bridgman). Samantha Bee, on her feminist comedy news show, *Full Frontal*, referred to "Trump's dystopian agenda." But America has had dystopic qualities that began before the 2016 election. Even with obvious signs of dystopia, many of us fail to see dystopia as a valuable lens on our present that also sheds light on the future. We think dystopia stories are unrealistic because they are fictional or because they are specific or because they are fantastic. Or because girls are heroes.

Dystopia is not "unrealistic." In fact, some contemporary realities are another version of dystopia as Darling-Brekhaus argues of the gender dynamics in North Dakota, for instance. War, disease, famine, natural disasters, and hunger, violence, and abuse are daily realities for many people and communities in the U.S. and around the world. The U.S. has created dystopic conditions in Iraq, for instance, bombing water treatment plants and imposing a decade of sanctions. In Aleppo, a war-ravished city looks like an image from a science fiction film set. In the developed world, one event of the right magnitude, the right domino and the "Doomsday Preppers" will be fortunate that their obsessive compulsive behavior prepared them for the aftermath of a variety of catastrophes. If, in fact, they survive the initial blow. And, if, in fact, they plan well enough and get lucky. A 2016 episode of *Odd Mom Out*, a show on Bravo that spoofs the society women of New York (a scripted drama un/like Bravo's "real housewives"), recognizes this dystopic quality of our contemporary world as several of the women detail the contents of their basements and other doomsday amenities. "You have to have a plan," one woman remarks just before the news that kale has been declassified as a superfood sends them all into a screaming panic. Even better, in the season two finale shit really hits the fan when a Madoff-like financial manager is arrested for his Ponzi scheme and chaos ensues as the rich people realize their money is gone. How will they survive?

Dystopia creates more extremes. It intensifies through use of time or disaster or invasion or decimation. Things are similar to modern times but then, for instance, the aliens' presence is proven (*Inheritance, Article 5,* and *The Host*) or the grave human errors of the past are exposed (*Uglies*) or the government's secrets are exposed (*Matched*). And then the short history is exposed. And then the long history is exposed. Ambelin Kwaymullina, author of *The Interrogation of Ashala Wolf* explains in her author's note, "The world that Ashala occupies is not Australia, of course. There is no Australia in Ashala's time, and no anywhere-else-that-exists-now, either."[1] The earth itself has been transformed and the people have evolved. But even as the earth is healing, the people in power cannot live and let live, they cannot accept that things change or accept "the world as a web of living, interconnected beings," as Kwaymullina describes. It is easy to ignore a future that we won't be around long enough to see, but that future is not as far away as it might seem.

Climate change scientists have been warning us of dire consequences for decades, but we have made little collective progress toward their suggestions (Stollarz). We are taught that we can solve these environmental problems through individual acts like recycling—or if we're really being controversial, through our vegetarian diets. While such actions are important, they cannot change a system that has produced environmental crisis on a global scale. In fact, Clare Echterling argues in her award-winning article "How to Save the

World and Other Lessons from Children's Environmental Literature," individual actions "do little to encourage civic engagement that would call into attention the intertwined ideological, economic, and political factors preventing profound environmental change." But these personal solutions are the actions, Echterling argues, that are taught to children through "most contemporary children's environmental picture books and easy readers" and "do little to prepare young people for the socio-environmental challenges we face now and in the future."

If children are getting these individualistic messages, it is no surprise that Preppers, and the rich more generally, seem to be missing this bigger picture; those who have the means to save themselves and their loved ones might not care to invest in the preventative measures that would make the need for doomsday prepping far less necessary. Some see the problems as too big to fix, individually or collectively. They collect cans and boxes and weapons and water that they may, or may not, have the chance to use. And sometimes their supplies might still be there for the lucky survivors who do make it through disaster. (YA dystopia's characters sometimes benefit from these stashes like when Alex and Miranda find a house full of food guarded by a dead man and his dead dog in *The World We Live In*.) Dystopia takes these huge problems and gives us a story, a protagonist to anchor us, and hope. As Moylan argues, "Dystopian critique can enable its writers and readers to find their way within—and sometimes against and beyond—the conditions that mask the very causes of the harsh realities in which they live" (*Scraps* xii). These books also give readers a sense of the very real implications of our lifestyles today and foster an appreciation for the natural world. The "harsh realities" differ and the setting, as well as the social and cultural structures created through the author's world-making, shape the fictional settings.

What all YA dystopia texts have in common is that the world—the environment, in particular—is in a state of temporary or prolonged suffering, maybe even chaos. If the chaos has been quelled, it is kept at bay with strict rules and leaders who rule with an iron fist. The ending of most of these stories is continued dystopia, continued struggle. And yet dystopia gives us hope. It gives us characters who reluctantly, or with clear focus and purpose, or more likely conflicted feelings, work to change the problematic circumstances of the present or the projected (dystopian) future. Sometimes there are fantastic elements introduced like vampires, aliens, or zombies. Sometimes the stories are realistic, inevitable trajectories—natural disasters, economic collapse, evolution of human abilities. Kwaymullina explains: "A dystopia imagines the end of the world. But in an animate reality, where everything has spirit and consciousness and agency, life cannot be easily extinguished. So to conceive of the end of the world is also to conceive of its beginning./ Everything lives, and nothing dies." The end of the world that each of these Girls on Fire faces generally falls into one of a number of categories—time, technology, disaster, invasion, decimation, or an amalgamation (layered against the political, social, personal)—and tell us much about the dystopia we live in as well as the many possible dystopian worlds that we are creating. And in all these dystopic mixes, the power and politics as well as the personalities and problems of people are compounded and compounding. Very few of these books provide a vision where the rich and powerful use their resources for the collective good. Instead, the rich often have access to protected communities and limited supplies; they are immune to the kale shortages and even economic collapse. When old worlds are rebuilt, class inequality (or age or gender or race) persists. And this is the very power that Girls on Fire contest and transform from within desperate times and desolate places.

The End of the World ... Types of Dystopian Settings

Dystopian Element	*Types*	*Examples*
Time	Alternative present, Near future, Distant future.	The Last Survivor series—alternative present. Cinder—distant future. *Orleans*—near future.
Technology	A lack of technology because of a lack of power or the development of new technologies that range body modifications, weapons, environment, or reliance on old technologies.	Partials—who is human? Cinder—cyborg as Cinderella. Uglies—pretty surgery. *The Summer Prince*—mods and tech, pyramid city. Under the Never Sky—smart eye.
Disaster ... often leads to decimation	"Natural" disasters. Relations to fire and climate change.	*Life As We Knew It*—meteor hits the moon. Ashes—electromagnetic wave. *Beauty Queens*—plane crash.
Invasion ... often leads to decimation	Aliens, zombies, vampires ... or just the enemy. Or, the poor and desperate. May include a theme of slavery.	The 5th Wave—aliens. The Immortal Rules—vampires and zombies. Ashes—brains are transformed; Zombies result.
Disease ... often leads to decimation	A known illness like the flu; a new threat; a plague.	Delirium—*amor deliriosa ner vosa.* Chemical Garden Trilogy—girls die by age 20, boys by 25. Legend—plague (manufactured). *Orleans*—Delta Fever.

Dystopian Element	Types	Examples
Decimation … not just apocalyptic	Whether by nature or man (or both) … in some cases directly blamed on man. Population is reduced, sometimes confined.	Birthmarked/Prized—lack of genetic diversity. Blood Red Road—Wreckers. *The Summer Prince*—war by men; decimation of Y chromosome. *Breathe*—we have destroyed environment. Pandemonium—the Blitz (41). Enclave—the second apocalypse.
War—civil or global, past or present	War may be the result of invasion or a political conflict (past or present) or the plotting of a totalitarian leader.	Hunger Games—Suzanne Collins has stated that this series is about war. Partials—a war that threatens the survival of humans and partials. Legend—June's world is shaped by an ongoing war and military culture.
Amalgamation of a variety of forces	Not all dystopic contexts are so easy to categorize because they reflect the complex conditions of the contemporary world.	For instance, in *Parable*, Lauren Olamina refers to "The Pox" as the culmination of social, cultural, political, and environmental.

Time

Many dystopias are set far in the future where speculation and world-building are less tightly tied to contemporary and historic conditions. Other dystopias are set in a near future where our present problems are illuminated in sometimes frightening ways. The stories that offer an "alternative present" aren't too far from a near-future. In YA dystopia, *Life as We Knew It* could happen tomorrow. The 1998 film *Deep Impact* explores a similar event from a different perspective—following adult journalists and scientists, for instance. *Life as We Knew It* tells the story from a fairly stereotypical rural American teen. Beth and her family were not well prepared, but realized that shit was hitting the fan and were able to prepare better than others. Beth's story becomes one of survival and isolation. Her diary entries are intimate and she sees very few people besides her immediate family. Most everyone they know dies. A close future reminds us that it doesn't take much for things to change dramatically. We can only control and predict so much.

A far future makes room for magic, but we don't know what kind of changes that shifts in environment or biology might create. In the Darkest Minds series, children develop abilities as a result of IAAN, a disease that kills 98 percent of America's children. Or, In Ilsa Bick's Ashes, an electromagnetic pulse alters children's brains in ways that connect to puberty and hormones. These uncontrollable, but sometimes engineered, events keep the present close even as the circumstances of life can become nearly unrecognizable. But even the far-flung future often keeps the present close. In the far future of the Lunar Chronicles, there are recognizable cultural arrangements coupled with fantasy, fairy tale, space travel and a race of Lunars who've colonized the moon/Luna. A world like this takes far more time for all of these factors to evolve and change dramatically. Cinder is a cyborg and this series takes on almost every element of science fiction and dystopia: androids, cyborgs, space ships, disease, genetic modification, and the moon is occupied by Lunars with special powers, ruled by a queen. It also reimagines the Cinderella, Rapunzel, Snow White, and Little Red Riding Hood fairy tales. It imagines dystopia on a global scale, something few YA dystopia books do. Uglies branches out to other settlements and, in the last book, to another continent, but The Lunar Chronicles imagines a global governance system not unlike the Ender series where governments on earth interact with space-based governments.

Some far futures still make overt reference to our contemporary world and its responsibility for the shape of the present. For instance, the Uglies series makes sustained references to the Rusties and the civilization that failed and damaged the earth. (In Dustlands, the same ancestors are called Wreckers.) The rebuilding produced several cities where circumstances vary, but all rely on advanced technology and social controls. They all have a pact to preserve the natural world that the Rusties nearly destroyed. They do not cut down trees, but they also do not clean up and clear out the human waste—the namesakes to the Rusties nickname. The world of the Uglies series is far enough in the future that extreme surgeries, advanced technologies, and restructured societies are all believable. But they, like all YA dystopia settings, have explicit connections to our present world. Even the highly crafted future world of the Lunar Chronicles makes reference to "second era" music, for instance, which Cress enjoys in her isolated satellite prison and childhood home.

Some novels play with time like *Pandemonium*, the second book in the Delirium trilogy. In this book, Lena's story unfolds between alternating chapters of "then" and "now." The "then" chapters tell her story following the first book, her survival in The Wilds after she escapes from Portland. The "now" chapters tell her story as a part of the Resistance, living under an assumed identity in New York. Not only does time shift, but the setting does as well—from the beautiful and cruel natural world to the structured (and cruel) world of the territories inside the fences. *The Interrogation of Ashala Wolf* also plays with time, moving back and forth as we discover how and why Ashala has been detained and that there is a bigger plan. Likewise, *Orleans* gives perspective to the present time of the story through Fen's past. As Marotta notes, "By intermixing Fen's memories and her present day accounts, Smith highlights the influence of her various communities on the formation of her identity" (61). We get a better picture of Fen by understanding her parents as social scientists, and especially through the story of how she became a blood slave and escaped by badly burning herself. This window on her past helps explain how her present world evolved.

Time is often running out. In the Chemical Garden series girls die at age 20 and boys at 25. The society is missing a key generational demographic and it changes people. And it changes society. In the Hunger Games Katniss plans to die in the arena, twice. But she is a survivor, and she is a symbol. Her time does not run out. It stretches in front of her, shadowed by her past. In *The Forgetting*, Nadia (and Gray) have to find a solution to The Forgetting before no one remembers who they are and what has happened over the course of the last 12 years. They make it, for the most part (and with much trauma and violence), just in time.

Place

Time also shapes place. The specifics of place can shape the plot, characters, and other elements of a story; these places are also powerful connections to today's dystopias. Urban, suburban, and rural settings are all explored. And specifics of place can shape stories in powerful ways. As previously noted, the New England setting of *The Handmaid's Tale* resonates with readers and Hopkinson's *Brown Girl in the Ring* provides an urban setting that speaks to today's crises. In "Brown Girl in the Ring as Urban Policy," Sharon DeGraw notes the ways in which "Hopkinson builds on contemporary urban trends in cities like Detroit, Michigan: urban flight, unemployment, corrupt government, gang and drug problems, and a breakdown of municipal service" (193). Dystopia takes these real elements and gives them a different time, a different space that lets us reimagine place. DeGraw continues, "At the same time, Hopkinson offers positive, mitigating reactions to these devastating trends through a reimagined Toronto" (193). The power of re-imagination of place has contemporary and future implications; it offers a new historical trajectory.

* * *

In *Dispatches from Dystopia: Histories of Places Not Yet Forgotten,* Kate Brown connects the "modernist wastelands" from Eastern Europe and Central

Asia with those of the American West and the Midwestern United States. She explains, "I do not mean to equate the economic devastation of my hometown with the near total decimation of the communities of Right Bank Ukraine. These experiences are of two vastly different orders" (145). These are places where "the forces of destruction were so outsized they were impossible to miss—Ukraine, Kazakhstan, gulag territories, and nuclear wastelands" (150). And these are forces of destruction that are dystopic in the present as well as the future.

She describes the relationship between where she grew up in Elgin, Illinois—an American wasteland in the Midwestern rust belt—with similar sites abroad: "not to be mistaken for belly-up Appalachian mining towns, blighted inner cities, or failing Western railroad and farm towns" (143). It is not coincidence that the first similar wasteland is the setting for *The Hunger Games'* District 12; the second, the site for *Divergent, The Immortal Rules,* and *Delirium,* among others; and the third is central to novels like *Life as We Knew It* and the classic, *Z Is for Zachariah.* In both novels the female protagonist is isolated; in the latter she is almost the only person who survives. Such rural settings are also the backdrop to many other YA dystopia novels where devastation leaves isolated pockets of people.

As Brown explains, "For a wealthy country blessed with wealth and political stability, the United States has a surprising number of places that possess a half-abandoned quality, communities that have been bulldozed, shattered, and scarred with bullet holes, yet have suffered no war" (143). Nicole Bruce features striking images of such places in her *Thrillist* piece "The Most Insane Abandoned Places in the Midwest"—factories, ski resorts, schools, churches, malls, power plants, ships, correctional centers, transportation hubs. These places in the present resemble the dystopic scenes of the future in YA dystopia. Brown's descriptions of the "muted" sights and smells that these places hold in common echo the scenes set by dystopian authors—desolation, decay, "depression and despair" (144). The "Rusties" of the Uglies series are direct descendants of this world. Brown explains of today's world: "The rust belt, in short, serves as a metaphor to express anxieties about the economy, society, race, and the nature of human life" (148). This metaphor is extended into the fictional future through the Uglies series where the failures of the Rusties are nearly always present.

Brown predicts that "because capitalism is a cyclone pushing across the globe, the number of chroniclers of modernist wastelands will continue to grow" (149). In fact, we might see the trend of YA dystopia as a set of such chronicles. The connection between the real/the modern and the possible future of YA dystopia is an unbreakable, but infinitely moldable, connection. Like the Levi's ad she analyzes, there will be "those who profit from destruction through corporate raiding, foreclosures, and legal fees, and in the cleanup

and gentrification that ensues; and those who pay the cost of continual abandonment with their livelihoods, investments, health, and futures" (147). This
basis of the haves and the have nots is also central and critical to YA dystopia.
Most of the Girls on Fire are a part of the legacy of those who have been
abandoned, and they are almost always fighting the oppression and injustice
of "those who profit" and pass on their legacies. Coupled with environmental
devastation, social and cultural control create the dystopic conditions that
shape the "dispatches" from YA dystopia's Girls on Fire.

Food, Water and the Have Nots

While there are many variations on the theme, most every book in this
study has a version of the age-old societal division: the haves and the have
nots. Some dystopian societies like in *Ashala Wolf*, try to address the "pollution, the overcrowding, and the terrible disparity between rich and poor"
(23). Almost all of the Girls on Fire fall into the have not category. As Bea
asks in *Resist*, "Can Premiums be so self-involved they completely fail to
notice how ninety-five percent of us live?" (139). The Premiums control the
food and air, and the health and well-being of Auxiliaries suffer. In *Parable
of the Sower*, water has to be bought from peddlers and may or may not be
safe. In *Requiem*, the river is cut off from its source and causes temporary
panic before the government moves in to obliterate the displaced population
in the Wilds. In the Darkest Minds water pollution is the source of the children's development of abilities. Clean water is scarce in *Orleans,* and Fen is
looking to acquire bottled water to feed Baby Girl in order to avoid Delta
Fever. But for June in Legend, food, water, and shelter are not a concern. She
lives in a rich sector and these needs are easily met and when she finds herself
disgusted by the filth of the poor sectors, she reminds herself that her brother
"had told me to never judge the poor like that" (97). Later she tells Day that
"sometimes it feels like we're the same person born in two different worlds"
(304). Both are prodigies; both had perfect scores on their Trial, but Day and
his family were sacrificed with many other have nots who scrape together
survival and hope to avoid the Plague.

Given the centrality of food and water (and air) to the basic survival of
individuals and the collective survival of humanity, it makes sense that these
play an important role in many novels. The Hunger Games makes food a
central facet, obvious through the title of the first book and the name of the
game central to the plot of the first two books. Katniss's knowledge of edible
plants—she's named after one, after all—is key to her survival. It is also key
to her ability to subvert the power of the Game Makers and President Snow
in the first Hunger Games, at the end of the first book. The poison berries

are a symbol and a means of resistance. In Dustlands, Saba's discovery of a seed bank recovers knowledge and a means to remake society. The few with literacy skills are needed to sow the future as they "discover the secrets of the seedstore" (*Raging Star* 420). Saba notes it is a "gift from the past to the future and she is "hopeful fer New Eden. Fer the earth an the sky. The water an the trees. The beasts an the people" (420). The Hegemon who wanted to control New Eden is defeated and everyone can have the New Eden that Saba and the Free Hawks fought for—"good land an clean water…" (*Raging Star* 3).

Violet's role in *Feed* illustrates the disposability of the poor as well as the apathy of the sidetracked through young people. As her health fails as a result of her dysfunctional feed, and she is faced with the inanity of the population she's a part of, Violet screams at the other youth playing spin the bottle:

> Can I tell you what I see? Can I tell you? We are hovering in the air while people are starving. This is obvious! Obvious! We're playing games, and our skin is falling off. We're losing it, and we're making out…. *Look at us! You don't have the feed! You are feed! You're feed! You're being eaten! You're raised for food! Look at what you've made yourselves!* [160].

Violet's call for consciousness falls on deaf ears. The place she lives is one that really has no place anymore. People live virtually in the feed—distracted by consumerism and entertainment—and the real world is dying. The world and its people are being consumed as feed for a failing system.

While food, water, air and other resources necessary for survival create challenging circumstances for populations and for the societies of the future, in many books there is a portion of the population that essentially plays the role similar to slaves or immigrants in contemporary and historical America. They are like Violet's description of feed. In *Breathe* and *Resist*, these are the stewards, people who essentially become human test subjects. The Avox in the Hunger Games have their tongues cut out and are forced to serve the elite in silence. The Factionless in Divergent refuse to be categorized and find the means for survival outside the Faction system. The Libbies in Sylum are forced to live at the margins of society and are not allowed to be mothers to their children. In *The Forgetting*, the evil Hegemon and Council head, Janis, selects the people who should be made "Lost" based upon her tests and observations and crooked belief that she needs to select the 150 best people in the community to go back to earth and rule like kings. Her warped vision isn't too far off of the God complex that contributes to the division of the rich and poor, the haves and the have nots, the oppressed and the oppressor. Those who oppose the powerful are punished in a variety of ways including social status and quality of life, if not also pain and humiliation. These groups are on the outermost margins of a society that has a large population of disenfranchised or controlled individuals—the zombies or sheep, metaphorically.

In *Shatter Me*, Juliet explains how this division developed: "A new generation comprised of only healthy individuals would sustain us. The sick must be locked away. The old must be discarded. The troubled must be given up to the asylums. Only the strong should survive" (60). "They," she notes, are creating this divide so that "the new citizens of our world will be reduced to nothing but numbers, easily interchangeable, easily removable, easily destroyed for disobedience" (38). In the Darkest Minds, protesters send the message: "WE ARE YOUR TIRED, YOUR POOR, YOUR HUDDLED MASSES" (*Never Fade* 112). But these protestors, identified as probably being college students, are dealing with the conditions of the deterioration, not with the same circumstances of being assumed to be dangerous criminals. In *After Light*, Charles argues to the powers that be: "all you're accomplishing is reinforcing in America—throughout the world—that the word *different* means *bad, ugly, dangerous*." Thus, Girls on Fire are fighting for the rights of the disenfranchised as much as they are fighting for their survival and for the people that they love. There is always more at stake and the powers that be often have more tools in their arsenal.

Technology

Technology is often a dividing line between "those who profit" and "those who pay." Technology builds cities (*The Summer Prince*), creates luxuries (the Hunger Games), provides safety (*Under the Never Sky*). Technology can alter people's appearances or extend people's lives. This is certainly the case for *Feed*'s Violet, but she does not have the resources to access life-saving technology. In the Lunar Chronicles series it saves Cinder's life, provides a damper for her Lunar abilities, shapes the personality of her best friend's artificial intelligence, and shuttles people to the moon and back. Technology can feed people and structure society efficiently like in the Matched trilogy. Meals are nutritionally sound, delivered consistently, and recycled efficiently. Technology can provide means of communications, the necessities and luxuries of life, and tools for brainwashing (Uglies).

A marker of our contemporary dystopia includes the ways in which communication shrinks our world, making all kinds of communication easier, faster, and more reliable. Communications technologies have transformed the way we live our lives and have given us the ability to cross vast distances. But, these communication abilities are still a luxury of the privileged and the promises of such communication have not been a panacea for cross-cultural communication. Even so, if these lines of communication were destroyed, we would be more isolated than ever. We would have to figure out older technologies like radio; we would lack the ability to call for help, let alone to connect outside our local spaces. The world would instantly shrink. In *Eve*, Caleb tells her about a radio code. She uses a radio to contact him through this code, not realizing that she is using an old code and giving away her location. People die; she goes on the run. In *Ashes*, all electronics are destroyed, but radio waves are used as a kind of communication—to control the unusual brainwaves of the youth, the Chuckies.

The technology in a book often depends upon other elements of the story. *Biting the Sun* offers a world that is shaped by the technology that keeps the population in check, much like Matched, Uglies, or *Feed*. The way technology has evolved, the way it has been used to make people's lives easier, can also trap them in an unsatisfying reality (to say the least). In *Biting the Sun*, characters "commit suicide" when they become bored and want to change their gender or their skin color or add a tail and some horns, for instance. Some characters in the world of the Uglies series choose not to have the pretty surgery and live in alternative (hidden) communities like The Smoke. Because the pretty surgery also alters the brain, it is not just a superficial change; it makes people obedient. In *Matched*, the society's controls have made a complacent population that is easily controlled through their food, their work, and their leisure time.

Some novels are shaped around a very particular kind of technology that only exists in the future—the pretty surgery of the Uglies series (which is not just physical, but mental as well) or the device that dampens Cinder's Lunar abilities, for instance. But many novels rely upon the more general technology, and long American tradition, of guns to move the plot along, empower characters, and connect with contemporary interest in guns in disaster-prepping scenarios. In most books, those with power have guns. But in some books, everyone has guns. In *Ashes*, guns play a big role from the beginning. Alex has her father's gun; Ellie (whose father died in Iraq) knows her way around a gun. Later in the series, the zombies are trained to use guns, making them more lethal than the average zombie. In *Orleans*, guns are a huge threat to a society that has little medical care and a great need for blood. In the humidity, they don't last long, but guns need only a little time to do a lot of damage.

Contemporary American gun violence is not restricted to war or mass shootings or gang warfare; guns play a large role in the American imagination of power and masculinity. Further, it makes sense for guns to exist in dystopic contexts since the Preppers who are preparing for the future are stockpiling weapons and ammo in addition to their food and water. But, guns are only as good as the available ammo and the maintenance of its mechanics. Olamina is careful to maintain her group's guns and to clean them and take care of them. In some futures, the technology simply no longer exists. For instance, in the utopia that turns quickly to dystopia in *The Forgetting*, they have knives for utilitarian purposes, but there is not a single mention of guns, even when they review footage of information about Earth.

In some future scenarios, particularly wastelands like in *Dustlands*, technology is archaic compared to our contemporary standards. Oftentimes people have to learn old skills in order to survive. In *Enclave*, they have developed a form of mushroom that can be grown underground with no light and can provide nutrition and protein. This keeps them from having to go to the surface where Freaks (zombies) dominate. In *Orleans* and Partials people survive on what was left behind. In disaster situations, technologies that we take for granted like washing machines, stoves, and cars are often not available. Miranda and her mother jump into action, running the dishwasher and clothes washer and vacuuming when the power comes on.

In *The Summer Prince*, technology is advanced, but the Aunties limit tech, especially biomodification and weapons. When Auntie Maria conspires with a programmer from the Verde and tech gets out of control, two young people are killed, which is unheard of in this society. This incident starts a divide between the technophiles and the isolationists. June is torn between these two sides, not only because she can see the problems and promises of both sides, but also because Enki and Gil are divided by these sides. Enki is the embodied symbol of the technophile—interacting with the city through the mods he has illicitly obtained. And because Gil can see the havoc those mods wreak on Enki's body and mind, he can't help but be an isolationist. When the media try to pin June down, she says, "'You can't dance in a data stream' … and remember[s] that Enki loves to dance too" (165). This balanced view may reek of maturity, but also makes room for complexity. Further, the lethal tech was introduced by an Auntie to bolster the isolationists' agenda, not the waka she framed.

Human and Not Human

Technology might enhance or inhibit our human qualities. Being human is an important part of many YA dystopia plots, whether humanity is about making connections with others or whether being human means not being a zombie, a cyborg, or a monster. The zombie is both literal and figurative, often mindless, infected, unconscious. But the monster is often created from an experiment or a miscalculation or an oversight. The cyborg is part human and part machine and the dividing line is blurry. Technology creates the ability to be more human—or less. In *The Lost Girl*, Sangu Mandanna imagines a world where a replacement daughter can be created by Weavers for wealthy families as an option, just in case she's lost. Eva explains, "the Weavers create us, but they don't love us. They stitch us together. They make sure we grow up knowing, always, that we belong to them" (4). Eva becomes Amarra after Amarra dies in a car accident. Eva is illegal and has to fight for the right to exist outside this pre-determined life.

The cyborg—the human with enhanced capabilities of body and/or mind through technology—is a reality and metaphor used by Donna Haraway in "A Cyborg Manifesto," published in her 1991 book and reproduced in the 2000 publication of *The Cybercultures Reader*. A cyborg is, according to Haraway, "a cybernetic organism, a hybrid of machine and organism, a creature of social reality as well as a creature of fiction" (291). The hybrid of the machine need not be the literal melding of flesh and bone; we are all cyborgs, addicted to our phones and dependent upon Google for knowledge. Some of us are more literally cyborg through medical technologies—replacing limbs, enhancing hearing and sight, and improving functionality. The female representation of android or cyborg is not uncommon in science fiction texts from *The Stepford Wives* to *Ex Machina*.[2] Sometimes she is object; sometimes she is victor.

Haraway uses the cyborg to think about gender, noting the "utopian tradition of imagining a world without gender, which is perhaps a world without genesis, but maybe also a world without end" (292). The cyborg is, of course, complex and much-debated and extended over the past 30 years and we can further extend Haraway's arguments about the cyborg to speak to the feminist roots of YA dystopia and allow for an exploration of intersectionality. As Haraway notes, "a cyborg world might be about lived social and bodily realities in which people are not afraid of their joint kinship with animals and machines, not afraid of permanently partial identities and contradictory standpoints" (295). Girls on Fire books feature all kinds of cyborgs who give us imaginative space to think about the qualities of being human and the relationships we have with our "tech." After all, as Haraway states, communications technologies and biotechnologies are the crucial tools recrafting our bodies" (302). Recrafting our bodies might undermine gender constructs, limitations to sexuality, permanence of racial features, or debilitating disabilities.

In YA dystopia, sometimes the human/not human dynamic is a direct commentary on sexism or racism; other times it skirts the edge or speaks more generally to discrimination or to disability. As Moya Bailey argues in "Vampires and Cyborgs: Transhuman Ability and Ableism in the work of Octavia Butler and Janelle Monáe," Both Octavia Butler and Janelle Monáe present problematic examples of disability: "For Butler and Monáe, transhuman disabled bodies offer possibility and freedom that simple humanity forecloses.… Butler and Monáe open up conversations about disability that are messy and fraught, but they do so in arenas that traditional disabilities studies scholarship neglects."

Violet, in *Feed*, is a prototype and sacrificial lamb for female protagonists in YA dystopia, but she is also a prototype for YA dystopia's cyborg protagonists. The rest of society is barely functional as they are attached to the Feed.

She functions within the Feed while still remaining autonomous—she can write, for instance. And, more, she challenges the Feed. But, because her Feed is dysfunctional, she cannot survive. Similarly, Adrienne Kertzer considers The Jenna Fox Chronicles through the lens of trauma and identifies both her near-fatal car crash, as well as her "realization that she is now a cyborg" (7) as trauma. When Jenna destroys her computer backup and, perhaps more importantly, the backup her father made of her friends whose bodies could not be saved in any capacity, Kertzer argues that this act makes Jenna human: "first by making her mortal" and "second by making her morally superior … a cyborg who empathizes is more 'human' than a human who does not" (8). The cyborg who empathizes with humans teaches us to be more human.

Dan Wells and Karen Sandler both use the cyborg to complicate the racialized futures they imagine. While it is clear from the beginning of Tankborn that Kayla is a cyborg, we do not know until later in the Partials series that Kira, who has been fighting the Partials, is, in fact, a Partial herself. Likewise, Kayla is obviously a cyborg, but we find out later that she was actually made into a cyborg, and the antidote exists to transform her back into fully human. Regardless, both of these girls break out of the norm of the typical white female protagonist. Racism is a key consideration in Tankborn not only as cyborgs are considered to be slaves, but also as a caste system based on class and skin color is in place. Racism in Partials, on the other hand, is explored more metaphorically through the differences and hypocrisies visited upon the Partials by the humans. Partials just want to be people too. In fact, it turns out they were engineered to co-exist with humans, that humans and Partials were engineered to need each other in one of the most basic human functions—breathing.

The fairy tale genre is combined with the struggles of the cyborg in one of the foundational YA dystopia texts, Marissa Meyer's Cinder and The Lunar Chronicles series. (It also combines space travel and cultural difference.) In Cinder, the cyborg is created because she is burned to near death and is put back together as part girl, part machine. She is considered the property of her step-mother, and she is basically a servant and a second-class citizen. (And then we find out that she is also Lunar. And she is also the heir to the throne, assumed dead at the hand of the evil Queen Levana.) As a cyborg, she is marginalized, but she is also enhanced in a way that gives her a kind of special power. This is the exact reason why laws against cyborgs exist; people fear that cyborgs might overpower them if given the opportunity. Her disabilities actually give her enhanced abilities. But these super-power abilities grow when she finds out that she is also Lunar and that she is able to manipulate people's bioelectricity, and, thus, control them. This is the only power that is going to be able to defeat the evil queen and deliver freedom to Luna's manipulated and enslaved citizens.

But Cinder continues to struggle with her cyborg status until she finally accepts it (and works to change things for other cyborgs): "After five years of wishing she was like everyone else, now she missed all those conveniences that had come with being cyborg" (667). She stops hiding her cyborg parts, but more importantly, she comes to terms with her own vision of herself and the way in which she has been labeled as something "grotesque, unnatural, disgusting" (753). She feels bad for seeing Levana's disfigurement as grotesque because "she had once been a victim, as Cinder had once been" (753). But Cinder reasons that Levana's monstrosity is not what can been seen on the outside, when her glamor fails, "her monstrosities were buried much deeper than that" (753). And Levana proves just this as she fakes a surrender and stabs Cinder in the heart.

Cinder also has an android best friend, Iko, who is like a pre-teen girl. Iko is a chip that can be transferred from body to body, and as a clunky robot servant she dreams of being able to wear fancy clothes and live the life of parties and popularity. Cinder's evil stepmother dismantles Iko and sells her off for spare parts. Cinder keeps Iko's personality chip because it is "defective" and no one would want it. Iko is unhappy when she finds herself installed as the auto-control system of a large starship, but in this body she is able to play a pivotal role in the action, as well as continue to deliver comic relief through her classic android sarcasm. But Iko wants to be feminine, beautiful. She's happy to find—and hold onto—her escort droid body.

In addition to a difference between artificial intelligence and enhanced humanity, the difference between the android in YA dystopia compared to the android more generally, is a wide sexual divide. In YA dystopia, the potential sexual functions of the android are virtually ignored. However, despite their cyborg bodies, these girls still feel, still fall in love, and sometimes even develop an attitude. Cinder's android sidekick, Iko, is a perfect example. When she finally gets the body that she wants, it is an "escort" model. She is gorgeous, of course, and everything Iko hoped to be. And because she has a personality chip that has evolved, she is able to function beyond the scope of the escort android. Her escort body is worn down through her battles, and Iko hates looking like "a broken machine" (717). "She'd gotten used to people looking at her like she was human. Not only human, but *beautiful*. But now she was stuck with a flopping arm and shredded skin tissue" (717). But Iko chooses not to trade her escort body in for a new model, even though Cinder reminds her that "it would be more cost-effective" (809). Iko "had grown attached to this one" and since "none of her friends' bodies were disposable, … why should hers be?" (810). Haraway suggests that "the machine is us, our processes, an aspect of our embodiment. We can be responsible for boundaries; we are they" (315). If we can embody and be responsible for such boundaries, we can be empowered, but if we are not responsible, we will pay the price.

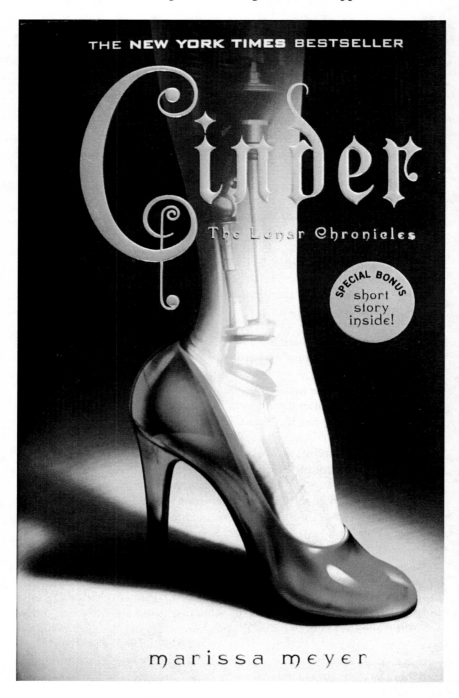

Cyborgs and androids may struggle to be accepted as fully human, but many Girls on Fire also feel that their difference makes them monsters. In fact, the struggle to accept one's monstrosity appears in a variety of forms in YA dystopia. As Haraway notes, "monsters have always defined the limits of community in Western imaginations" (315). In fact, Cinder finds a common link between her and the mutant soldiers the queen produces: "they were both unnatural. Only, instead of being pieced together with wires and steel, these creatures were a jigsaw of muscle tissue and cartilage" (*Winter* 434). But Wolf proves that no amount of genetic manipulation can make someone into a monster. He may think that "after years of fighting to avoid becoming one of the queen's monsters, it had happened" (*Winter* 546), but when it comes to Scarlett, he is able to remember who he is and what his priorities are.

In Ashes, Alex struggles with the boundaries of her monster—the tumor in her head that first threatens her life and then becomes a means to save not only herself, but also her friends and her enemies. She feels threatened time and again by the monster: "Maybe the monster was tired of the game and had decided to flex its muscles, take that great, big, drippy—final—bite. She thought that might be all right. But the world didn't fade" (450). She persists, in part, because the monster needs her, and she needs the monster. But, Haraway reminds us that "cyborg imagery can suggest a way out of the maze of dualisms in which we have explained our bodies and our tools to ourselves" (316). In the final book, *Monsters*, Alex notes that "no one can help but stare at the monster, because horror is a cousin to awe" (579). And, yet, that awe is a reaction to the ability to control minds and actions and outcomes. Alex is much more human and she and her monster, like Cinder—and like Girls on Fire more generally—topple the power structure. "Cyborg imagery," Haraway argues, "can suggest a way out of the maze of dualisms in which we have explained our bodies and our tools to ourselves" (316). Girls on Fire are beyond dualism.

Disaster and Decimation

One of the first young adult books, *Z Is for Zachariah*, is essentially a disaster novel—and a really poorly adapted 2015 film that completely changes

Opposite: The cover of *Cinder* features a high-heeled bright red transparent glass slipper, an obvious and modernized shout-out to the classic fairy tale it borrows from, but here the bewitched shoe encases a transparent lower leg and foot, revealing its wearer as a cyborg (Square Fish [Macmillan]. Cover illustration by Michael O. © 2012. Based on original art work by Klaudia Jakubowska. Cover design by Rich Deas).

the book, especially the ending (and even adds a third character who creates more conflict, mostly as a romantic interest). But the original novel was a result of imagined nuclear fallout, tapping into the anxieties of post World War II America and the nuclear arms race. In contemporary YA literature, a whole sub-genre of disaster fiction shares many qualities with dystopia and many texts overlap both of these categories, but few deal with nuclear fallout. Instead, disaster may be natural or man-made and decimation often has a variety of causes: disease, invasion, fire, flood, atmospheric disruption. In most books the population has been greatly reduced, and in some the world is virtually empty compared to our population in the 2010s. Some of these novels carry with them the kinds of messages about environmentalism that Echterling calls for; others, like the bestselling Last Survivor series beginning with *Life as We Knew It*, rely upon an unlikely (but entirely possible) event— like a meteor hitting the moon—to create environmental crises which results in the catastrophes that its characters navigate.

In "The End of Life as We Knew It: Material Nature and the American Family in Susan Beth Pfeffer's Last Survivor Series," Alexa Weik von Mossner notes the popularity of the disaster branch of YA dystopia with a "flood of publications that turn toward environmental or ecological concerns and their consequences for human existence" (149). These books enjoy "phenomenal success in the marketplace" (149), she argues, in part because they are compelling and believable. An unexpected, catastrophic event completely transforms the world, and this sudden change requires people to adapt—and get lucky—in order to survive. Specifically, "Susan Beth Pfeffer's Last Survivors series has been especially successful with North American teenagers" (149). The accessible voice and style of diary entries, may be another reason for this book's success. Pfeffer "imagines the possible social, political, and personal costs of sudden radical environmental change in the very near future" (149). Miranda's life changes fundamentally, but it does not change enough to give her control over, or responsibility for, her own life or the lives of others, at least not in more than small doses—sharing food with neighbors, nursing her family back to health when they get the flu. Miranda's mother stays in charge and still exerts what parental authority she has. Miranda's world is entirely local.

Citing Claire Curtis, von Mossner notes that The Last Survivor series books "do not offer young adult readers the space to resist the reality of their imaginative future world and, by extension, the inequalities and unsustainable practices of their own twenty-first century world" (161) but do "inspire their teenage audience to reflect critically on their lives and their current assets" (160). In other words, we might assume that the world was just fine before the meteor hit the moon and "shit hit the fan," as the Doomsday Preppers like to say. We don't know what is happening on the larger scale; however, because the population has been virtually wiped out, first by volcanoes and tsunamis and then by flu and starvation, we may believe that "the people in charge" are either sequestered or decimated as well. In later books we know that there is some structure as well as safe havens for those who are rich enough to buy their way in. For those less fortunate, like Miranda (rural) and Alex (urban), what remains important is scraping together resources, maintaining family, and surviving to see another day. Caragh O'Brien supports such survival in real life, donating some proceeds from her Birthmarked series to The Global Greengrants Fund, "a non-profit, international grassroots organization that provides small, pivotal grants to people dealing with environmental destruction." The people of Wharfton do not have such aid.

In her author's note to *Enclave*, Ann Aguire speaks to the apocalyptic future she imagines: "It's hard to envision the end of the world or predict what it might be like." She then relates her resources for the post-apocalyptic world, the "nebulous future," that she has created. She imagines society would break down within 100 years, spurred by biological weapons and manufactured plagues: "I pulled my projections of what the cities might be like from what occurred in New Orleans, after Hurricane Katrina. Thus, the poor remain in these wrecked, abandoned cities, still devoid of hope or resources, taking their rage out on one another. Therefore, the gangers are violent, vicious, and patriarchal." She also bases her story on a controversial book, *The Mole People: Life in the Tunnels Beneath New York City* by Jennifer Toth, a "non-fiction" book that lends itself well to fiction since the book's truth is widely and narrowly debated. When disaster and decimation force people underground, new worlds are created.

* * *

Beauty Queens also creates a new world. The book begins with a disaster—a plane crash—and uses parody as well as humor among some elements of dystopia. Being on the island helps the girls to see the dystopic qualities of the world they live in. As Shanti remarks, "It's kind of a mixed-up, messed-up world we're inheriting.... When we get back, we should do something to change that" (253). Overall, *Beauty Queens* is more of a survival and rescue story than a dystopia, but it has elements of government control, explorations of gender and sexuality, a variety of voices and most importantly the beauty queens have to build their own world. They rise to the occasion as "the whole thing had come to resemble a giant science fair" (119). It's a *Lord of the Flies* for girls of our modern world, which these savvy beauty queens recognize (176–7). In this book, disaster gives the beauty queens an opportunity to act, think, and be outside of their narrow image. When Taylor wants them to focus on their pageant skills, Adina says "look at us—look what we've built here" (154) and Miss New Mexico says that the pageant "doesn't seem like

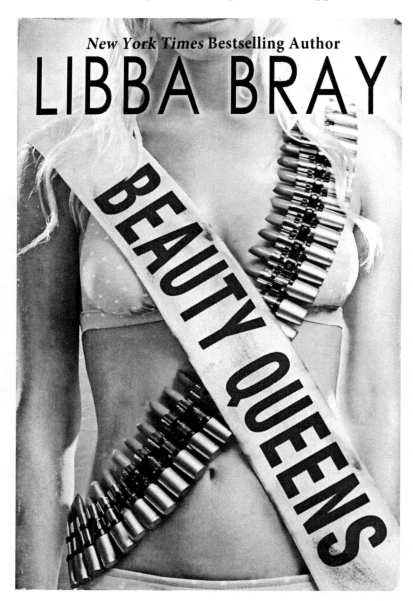

Perhaps the cover of *Beauty Queens*, with the pageant winner sash, counter-sashed with an automatic round of lipstick "bullets," and draped over the bikini-clad torso of a woman shown only from her lips down, exploits the female body, but it also highlights the book as a parody of beauty pageants and hints at the kick-ass Girls on Fire characters within (Scholastic. Cover image ©2011 by Michael Frost. Cover design by Elizabeth B. Parisi).

enough anymore" (154). Some of them die. Some find love. Some find themselves. In fact, Mary Lou notes that "maybe girls *need* an island to find themselves. Maybe they need a place where no one's watching them so they can be who they really are" (177). On the island, "they were no longer performing. Waiting. Hoping./ They were becoming./ They were" (177). YA dystopia is this kind of island—a place where girls can be, even if we are watching them by reading them.

While the disaster in *Beauty Queens* creates a world for women, in several novels decimation means a shift in sex and gender. In Eve, a plague has wiped out the vast majority of the population (98 percent) and there are more females than males (63). Because of this, and her education, Eve assumes that she is "every man's type" (*Eve* 63). In *The Summer Prince*, 200 years in the future, gender has reached an even distribution of male and female, but women continue to dominate politics and control the shape and direction of the society. June thinks: "We're walking through the mess men made of the world" (246); this is the ideology that drives her society. Enki tries to explain to June that this arrangement is not equality and June "want[s] to say that maybe boys don't have as much representation, but they have plenty of freedom" (246), but when she thinks this justification, she also thinks that she sounds like an Auntie and she doesn't want to think the same way that they do. In *Dustlands: Raging Star* this shift in thinking promises "something good an right an hopeful" (419). While DeMalo had a vision, the future "won't be the story he intended" (419). Instead, "at the centre of New Eden will be a council of nine wise women" (419). The work of healing the earth and rebuilding society will take many lifetimes.

* * *

Orleans has, perhaps, one of the most realistic disaster plots. Climate change experts have noted that tropical storms will become more extreme and weather patterns will be unpredictable and devastating. We can already see these disastrous impacts across the U.S. and all over the world. Smith builds a world that traces the development of the line of demarcation—a series of hurricanes—that establishes Orleans by separating it from the United States both physically and politically. The aftermath of this disaster provides an opportunity for the environment to flourish even as the people tear each other apart.

Hurricane Katrina, and similar weather-related incidents, speak to a future where weather extremes are directly connected to social, cultural, political, and economic emergencies around the world. In the science-fictional future of the 2006 film (and novel) *Children of Men* global climate change, rising water levels, and rising temperatures are directly connected to health (infertility) and to population shifts (immigration). The DVD documentary, "The Possibility of Hope," further contextualizes the film's fictional vision of the future with the current realities of a changing world. This film provides a foil and complement to conscious constructions of the future like Octavia's Butler's *Parables* books and Sherri L. Smith's *Orleans*, particularly since the perspective provided by the documentary is steeped in privilege, making claims like "natural selection," and not the current arrangements of wealth and poverty (rooted in past and present colonialism and imperialism), will be responsible for who does, and doesn't, survive global catastrophes.

What many of these future environments think less about is what the people might look like and live like as a result of power and privilege acting as "natural selection" for those who survive disaster, decimation, economic collapse, or violence. The whiteness of the future characters we find does not reflect the demographics of a mostly non-white world, but their characters do reflect the demographics of the people most likely to survive—the rich and privileged, the overwhelmingly white (or lighter, or simply richer) around the world. They do not reflect the demographics of those most impacted by environmental disasters and emergencies—the poor and disproportionately people of color. In too many future visions, those with power (white Northerners with money) retain power and prosper while the poor, of color, from the South are assumed to perish due to their lack of desire (not *means*) to move. Most dystopian novels inadvertently reproduce these prejudices by not engaging with elements of race and class and geographic inequalities. Very few of these novels, for instance, consider the necessity or impacts of immigration or migration, at least not on global levels. For instance, many books do include an impetus that causes people to have to relocate, but these instances are usually rather local—across, around, and throughout the United States, for instance. *The Summer Prince*, on the other hand, directly considers the migration that will happen as a result of, for instance, a catastrophic climate event or a world war. The city of Palmares Três has a strict immigration policy and June's family is descended from a great grandfather who is white/European. He and his daughter, April, walked to Palmares Três. April was killed (and also, most likely, raped) when she was working with refugees. These elements not only add to the storyline, but they also help explain some of the racial politics in Palmares Três.

In his Master's thesis, "Decolonizing the YA North: Environmental Injustice in Sherri L. Smith's *Orleans*," Micah-Jade M. Coleman notes that "this novel offers YA readers a holistic understanding of climate change as an integral, local, and ultimately global issue, one whose consequences differ by race, class, gender and region" (2). Hurricane Katrina certainly dramatized and visualized these racially-divided consequences, particularly through news coverage and reactions and critiques from artists and celebrities. The impact of the storm can be explored not just through the ways in which the physical world has transformed or the ways in which cultural critics have responded. Coleman notes that "*Orleans* invites readers to reflect on the trauma associated with the storm and the ecological disorder the storm portends" (1). The near and far effects can be compared in ways that help us to see how to change the present to positively impact the future.

Invasion

Some disaster and decimation elements are shaped by the invasion of alien life forms or zombies. Two seemingly opposite forms of invasion can happen: the threat that comes from within and the threat that comes from without. In some cases, they are the same thing like in *The Host* or *The 5th Wave* where the aliens take up residence inside of humans. An alien invasion might lead to decimation, or it might lead to an altered human population. In *The Host* humans resist their alien invaders and negotiate a more humane means of coexistence. In the 5th Wave, they fight themselves and the enemy. Alien invasion often comes with fear and a lack of control, let alone a lack of knowledge of what's happening and why.

POD, a little-known book, alternates between the story of a girl stranded in a parking garage and separated from her mother and the story of a boy trapped in his home with his father. Both suffer from hunger and dehydration. She faces the dangers of gang takeover though she avoids sexual violence. She has to be resourceful; and she has to hide and evade. He has to deal with the monotony of spending so much time with his father, of being unable to leave the house. He also has to face his father's sacrifice. They are running out of food. In Malinda Lo's duo, *Inheritance* and *Adaptation*, alien invasion also comes out of nowhere but much of the rest of the population is mostly free to live their lives as if invasion never happened. Reese and David cannot ignore it. When they go back to life, Amber Gray is assigned to keep her eye on Reese. Amber and Reese end up having an affair and this relationship shapes the books and provides a means and opportunity to peacefully coexist with the aliens. The opposite is true in The 5th Wave where alien invasion means genocide or enslavement.

Slavery

Generally, America's cultural roots are intertwined with slavery, but we have not been able to rectify and move on from this past. Post Civil War, Jim Crow laws did the work of incarceration. In contemporary America, we prosecute the poor and maintain racialized trends of punishment. Today, our most oppressed are also our most imprisoned. Growing poverty, multiplying mandates for drug possession and nonviolent crime, and the increasing parameters of enslavement shape the lives and communities of people of color and poor people today and mass incarceration of young black and brown people predicts the eventual enslavement of those displaced by globalization and climate change, those replaced by machines and cheaper labor. While social services and spending on education decrease, spending on prisons exponentially increases. The impact on black Americans is undeniable. In the future, such parameters are drawn through similar and different lines. But when the laws shift to accommodate the unemployed, when private prisons are some of the fastest growing businesses in the U.S., and when more people in the U.S. are incarcerated than at any other time or place *in the history of the world*, then we have lost perspective and the conditions of *Talents'* "Camp Christian" seem all the more realistic. Contemporary American prisons are dystopic places.

Slavery is not always spelled out as such in YA dystopia, but reference to slave-like conditions in the Darkest Minds series also draw upon these legacies and contemporary realities of slavery. Children with special powers are dangerous and are held in concentration camps; when the conditions of these camps and the corruption of the government is exposed, largely through the efforts of the children enslaved, the new power structure wants to put them into special communities. Of course, these communities are only glorified camps. Charles argues against these communities, but the book's resolution fails to fully engage in the problematics of segregation and slavery.

In *Eve*, Eve learns that the boys don't go to school; instead they are sent to labor camps. When Caleb tells her that boys have suffered, she doesn't quite believe it. "I couldn't stop from scoffing. It was always women who'd suffered at the hands of men. Men were the ones who'd started wars. Men had polluted the air and sea with smoke and oil, ruined the economy and filled the old prison systems up to their limits" (71). Eve has been conditioned to think of men as those responsible for the downfall of the country. But she also becomes well aware of the reproductive slavery that is slated for her future. For many Girls on Fire, sex slavery, reproductive slavery, imprisonment, and other methods of bodily control shape the only reality these girls know. For instance, in *Eve*, Eve discovers that she, and the other girls in her graduating class, do not have a future of possibility ahead of them. Instead, they will be chained to a bed and forced to breed until they are no longer useful. This kind of reproductive slavery for girls is complemented by forced-work camps for the boys. Such stories are common in this future and survivors often bond out of shared misery. They do their best to endure—whatever it takes. People are equally frightened by, and desensitized to, the violence all around them.

* * *

Like in *Parables*, some aspects of YA slavery are directly tied to the legacies of the U.S. In her article in the *Journal of Science Fiction*, "Sherri L. Smith's *Orleans* and Karen Sandler's *Tankborn*: The Female Leader, the Neo-Slave Narrative, and Twenty-first Century Young Adult Afrofuturism," Marotta writes about *Tankborn* and *Orleans* as Neo-Slave narratives. Through the title we can see the framing of this article, and it takes up several dimensions of YA dystopia that are often overlooked. Dystopia, for instance, is replaced with Afrofutrism and contextualized within the current and forward-looking twenty-first century. Thus, Marotta considers the female protagonist, the Girl on Fire, as "The Female Leader" and connects this leadership role directly to black women during the era of slavery. (We could also make this comparison to Olamina, a female leader of epic proportions.)

Marotta argues that both authors could have done more to emphasize "ethnicity" but at least they bring "much-needed attention to African American females in twenty-first century YA SF" (69). But this attention is through a narrative that relies upon past narratives and legacies. These may be twenty-first century African American females, but in Marotta's argument they are being framed by the past instead of being understood in the future they occupy as characters. Even so, this past legacy does speak to important aspects of this future. As Marotta notes, "Smith's Fen and Sandler's Kayla place themselves figuratively in the role of mother, specifically the twenty-first century version of the slave mother—the community leader" (57). The community leader aspect of both of these characters is tied to a kind of motherhood that speaks to the motherhood endured by the "slave mother"—she has to take responsibility for all of the children and rarely has the opportunity to care for her own children. Fen takes on an abandoned newborn and Kayla fights for the children who, like her, have been taken from their families.

Marotta traces these characters' development through a strict lens and notes that "though Fen and Kayla both free themselves from their objectified states in the end, the process of doing so for Kayla requires more developmental stages than it did for Fen" (66). Fen's development is accelerated by her circumstances and her need to grow up quickly; the world she lives in is far more dangerous than Kayla's relatively comfortable world. Kayla is more literally enslaved, working for rich people, and genetically modified to do so. Fen is not technically a slave, though she escapes the fate of a slave and is literally (and figuratively) scarred for life as a result. She burns her arms after she is raped and drained of her blood, and she can no longer be used as a

The covers for the Tankborn series all feature a girl's face, but from different angles and distances. The covers make it blatantly clear that the Girl on Fire is a girl of color. Further, the model's face is obscured with the tech that makes the Girl on Fire, a GEN (genetically engineered non-human). On the cover of the first book, the meaning of tankborn is revealed through the bubbles that contain fetuses (Tu Books [Lee & Low Books, Inc.]. Cover photograph of girl © 2008 Roxana Gonzalez; cover photograph of fetus © 2010 Chris Downie; cover photograph of bubbles © 2010 Tryfonov Ievgenii. Jacket design by Einav Aviram).

slave. Kayla also has three books (Fen, one) to complete this development and she also has a story that ends with her triumph, not her death.

Marotta writes about both *Tankborn* and *Orleans* as examples of neo-slave narratives, an important part of the racialized roots of these characters. *The Summer Prince*, on the other hand, provides a powerful connection to slavery that includes critiques of slavery and the past. These roots explode through Enki's antics as summer prince—through his simple dress and bare feet to his choreographed slave dance that brings the audience into its folds and creates a massive celebration/protestation. *The Summer Prince* illustrates a redemptive and transformative story of slavery that cannot be buried beneath the stink of the catinga. But this story is about a lot more than slavery. This past is a motivation, an inspiration, a tool of rebellion and it blooms through art and love.

Olamina, and her people, act as reminders that there is some hope in all this misery. When Olamina finds her brother for sale she does not hesitate to rescue him, a pattern she establishes early in *Sower* when she cannot resist helping people, especially people with children. Both Fen and Kayla are rescuing children as much as they are escaping from slavery. They are acting in the interest of others and putting those others ahead of themselves.

Zombies

There's another kind of slavery imagined through the zombie story. While the literal zombies trap people behind fences and walls, and while zombies are imprisoned in their in-between state of existence, the zombie is also a powerful symbol. The Forrest of Hands and Teeth, Enclave, The Immortal Rules, and the Ashes trilogies all include a kind of zombie—a symbol of what the world has become, how much humans have lost. These zombies might be created through any variety of processes—known or unknown—and the people who encounter them often fear infection—enslavement as a zombie—more than death.

The way R.P. Clair contextualizes the zombie aspects of her story in *Zombie Seed and the Butterfly Blues: A Case of Social Justice* illuminates a fascinating history of Zombie representation that Girls on Fire extends. She summarizes the history of the zombie theme and its racial implications and provides contemporary examples of the influence/interest in the zombie. She notes, "Zombies are far more than a cultural cliché; they are a symbolic icon of crucial importance in the history and practice of oppression and resistance" (xvii). YA dystopia taps into this cultural icon as well. The books don't call zombies by this name, but the monsters born of anything—from experiments gone wrong to environmental disasters—occupy an important role in many of these novels as zombies. Ashes has "Chuckies" and "The Changed"; Enclave has "Freaks" and "Muties"; The Forrest of Hands and Teeth has the "Unconsecrated"; Blood of Eden has "Rabids" (Vampire zombies). In Ashes the zombies have a complex society and evolve as the story progresses. They also have wild sex orgies, learn to ski and shoot guns, and one group even adopts the habits of wolves. Their fate is intimately linked with the people who have not been transformed and Alex cannot help but identify with the zombies; she too is a monster, or has a monster inside her head. "What she had with the Changed was like a bizarre kind of empathy, like a sixth sense that was growing stronger./ Because *she* was changing?" (241). The line between Changed and unchanged is not a clear one.

The role that zombies play in YA dystopia goes beyond the literal monsters. R.P. Clair explains what the zombie means in this more abstract form: "the current image of the zombie who walks through life without critically thinking, without addressing political issues, without participating in civil discourse or democratic entitlements" (xvii). In *Delirium*, for instance, the people who have been cured are seen as zombies by the "Invalids" living in The Wilds. The people of Portland see the Invalids as being on the same level as werewolves and vampires, while the people of The Wilds see the cured as zombies in a more figurative sense. Zombie is another name for those who've had the procedure because "the cure turns people stupid" (*Pandemonium*

35), as Sarah explains to Lena what Raven has told her. When Lena goes back into "Zombieland" she notes that "someone is always watching. There is nothing else for people to do. They do not think. They feel no passion, no hatred, no sadness; they feel nothing but fear, and a desire for control. So they watch, and poke, and pry" (*Pandemonium* 81). Many Girls on Fire escape from populations that follow corrupt governments like zombies. For these sociocultural zombies, the options are worse and the consequences can be deadly, but these people also want to *live*.

Girls on Fire could never be zombies. They are too invested in their worlds, too busy trying to survive (and sometimes surviving by fighting the real or figurative zombies of their world). Instead, the zombies are a constant threat and danger as well as a reminder. Thus, while "fantastic" and "unrealistic," the zombie is symbolic of the importance of consciousness. All of these circumstances produce survivors—girls who make it through circumstances that are beyond trying.

On Fire and Through Nature as Means to Enlightenment

A reality and powerful symbol throughout these books is fire. In the crowded, parched, impoverished conditions of Butler's science-fictional future there are many dangers. Fire is an extreme threat and destroys homes and lives regularly. Fire is used as a distraction by thieves. It is used as a form of recreation for drug-users (the "Pyros") and as a political statement about poverty and wealth. And, later, in the dry California climate, in the midst of dry grasses and highway, fire is a threat as the nascent Earthseed community looks for a home. Fire is a constant threat and a symbol of the chaos of the times. It destroys and yet it is also a necessity for the homeless as well as a phoenix and a cleanser when Acorn, the first Earthseed community, is destroyed. Olamina describes the event in her journal: "Most of us had seen our homes burn before, but we had not been the ones to set the fires./ This time, though, it's too late for fire to be the destroyer that we remembered. The things we had created and loved had already been destroyed. This time the fires only cleansed" (261). This cleansing—this fire—is needed to overcome slavery, torture, rape, and a variety of other hardships that the people of Acorn, Earthseed, the surrounding area, and unfortunate indigents all experienced at the hands of religious fanatics. Here, the fire brings the possibility of growth but only after the past has been destroyed. Fire in *Dustlands: Blood Red Road* is used by the Free Hawks after rescuing Saba and Epona and Saba rescues Jack from burning alive. In *The Forrest of Hands and Teeth* fire threatens the safety of the community since they are protected from the

Unconsecrated by their wooden fences. Fire can be used as a force of destruction, but it can also be used as an act and symbol of renewal.

Symbolically, Katniss is the ultimate Girl on Fire. The fire theme is woven into each book and evolves throughout the story. While Katniss is a spark, while she is passionate, and while she is a role model, she is also burned again and again, literally and figuratively. As the Mockingjay, she is a strong symbol, but she is a broken girl. In *Shadows Cast by Stars* Cass is also set on fire. In her battle with evil, all of her hair is singed off by the lightening she calls. While she wonders what she looks like, Bran says she looks beautiful so "for now, a goddess is what I choose to be, and I don't really feel like breaking that spell" (430). She has a new image of herself.

Lena, also, is reborn in *Pandemonium*, emerging as a new version of herself after losing everything she has ever known and the boy who convinced her to leave it all behind. As *Pandemonium* opens she reflects on her past and notes that "the old Lena is dead too./ I buried her./ I left her beyond a fence, behind a wall of smoke and flame" (3). While this image of fire is figurative, as we turn the page we find that it is also literal. Lena's story goes back to "then" and the literal meets the figurative: "In the beginning, there is fire./ Fire in my legs and lungs; fire tearing through every cell in my body. That's how I am born again, in pain: I emerge from the suffocating heat and darkness…. I am not born all at once, the new Lena./ Step by step—and then, inch by inch…. Fingernail by fingernail, like a worm./ That is how she comes into the world, the new Lena" (4–6). While fire is a powerful symbol and reality, nature more generally than the element of fire, can be a means toward enlightenment.

And for all of our Girls on Fire, fire also symbolizes something powerful and unordinary. As Auriel explains in *Dustlands: Rebel Heart*, "There are some people, she says, not many, who have within them the power to change things. The courage to act in the service of somethin greater than themselves" (110). She also warns Saba that DeMalo can see this power and that his interest in tapping into this power is dangerous. And DeMalo does understand Saba and her fire: "You have a rare fire within you. The power to change things. The courage to act in the service of something greater than yourself. And you lower yourself to this shabby misadventure" (*Raging Star* 31). However, like all our Girls on Fire, responsibility ultimately lies with Saba and she sacrifices part of herself for the greater good. While New Eden is changing to "something good an right an hopeful," she hopes "that beyond the horizon, somewhere, someday, I can live with myself an what I've done…. I'm done here. I hafta move on. An keep movin" (420). The fire keeps blazing.

* * *

Amidst the rot, decay, and destruction some relics of the old world remain, shaping the new world without context to its origins. Sometimes these relics are backdrops; sometimes they are mystery but they are often embedded in the natural world that has begun to reclaim itself. Nature often takes precedence over the man-made world. Many Girls on Fire are connected to nature, to the environment, and to a different way of thinking about her world through the lens of the natural world. In fact, being shut off from this world can negatively impact a Girl on Fire. As Juliet explains, "There aren't as many trees as there were before, is what the scientists say. They say our world used to be green. Our clouds used to be white. Our sun was always the right kind of light. But I have faint memories of that world. I don't remember much from before. The only existence I know now is the one I was given. An echo of what used to be" (2). The world outside of her prison cell has been compromised, but she has also been compromised. In *Breathe* and *Resist*, the characters live in enclosed environments that supply oxygen and food that supposedly cannot be produced outside of these controlled environments. But, when Bea leaves this regulated (and stratified) society and environment, she finds that people are living outside. Because they are a threat, they must be destroyed. In Under the Never Sky a similar environment exists, but people who survive live in communities shaped by the landscape and environmental conditions. In both examples, life for Girls on Fire is different on the outside than it was on the inside. While outside there is risk, there is also room to grow.

The Girl on Fire is always compromised by her environment, but she is

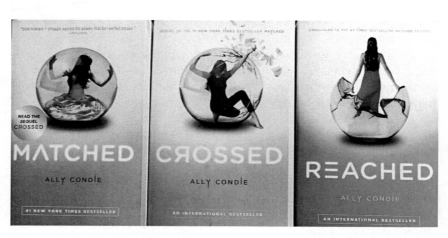

These covers show the progression of Cassia's storyline in the Matched trilogy. On the cover of *Matched* she is encased by a bubble, pressing her hands against the transparent enclosure. On the cover to *Crossed* one of her arms and one of her legs have shattered through the surface. The design of *Reached* shows her emancipated from the bubble, strong and standing and turning her back on the Society she is leaving behind (Speak [Penguin Group, Inc.]. Cover design by Theresa M. Evangelista. Cover photos by Samantha Aide).

also inspired by the environment she finds outside the structures of society. As McDonough and Wagner argue in "Rebellious Natures," the Girl on Fire "In *Uglies, Matched,* and *Delirium,* Tally, Cassia, and Lena discover within nature opportunities to pause away from their daily lives long enough to reevaluate everything" (168). This isn't just time out to think, but time to live differently, experience differently. Not only do the girls experience nature, they also experience different people and different societies. Place shapes the way people live and think. The authors argue that "the place of nature has permanently marked Tally, Cassia, and Lena, leaving them with a sense of hope. Hope occurs not only because the female protagonists have been awakened, but also because each of them has found a place endowed with enough value to allow them to claim their agency" (169). This hope comes from the possibility of a new way of living and being, not just for the girl herself, but also for her society. The authors note that "this sense of hope … is integral to young adult literature" (169). Hope is part of the power of these books and "all three novels end with the possibility of change and the promise that anyone can find her place" (169). This place is found through juxtaposition between the natural and the constructed worlds and it is a place that can be free.

Once again, *Parable of the Sower* offers an interesting connection to YA dystopia. Olamina describes the "Stars casting their cool, pale, glinting light" (5). She can see the stars because there is a lack of city lights to obscure the vision. She prefers the stars, but the adults miss the comfort of the lights— the world that had such luxury. Olamina thinks, "The stars are free.... We can afford the stars" (6). The stars also play a role in Dustlands, *Shadows Cast by Stars,* and *The Interrogation of Ashala Wolf.* In these novels, nature— the environment—is alive and integral to the protagonists' lives, cultures, traditions, and power. Ashala and Conner are described as binary stars. After her grandfather spirit helps to save Conner, Ashala remarks, "It hadn't occurred to me before to wonder what happened to a binary system if one star fell from the sky, how hard it might be for the other one to create a stable orbit on its own" (364). Her grandfather's voice on the wind remarks: "*He lives. You live. We survive*" (365). Ashala's fate is Conner and the fate of her world. Saba remarks that "if you know how to read the stars, you can read the story of people's lives. The story of yer own life. What's gone, what's now an what's still to come" (2). Stars continue to play an important role. After Saba confesses that she "don't know who I am no more" (422), Jack explains: "We don't choose the times we're born in, he says. That's the business of the stars. The only choice we got is what we do while we're here. To make it mean somethin" (422). Stars are symbols of other worlds, future possibilities. And Cass reminds us that "the brightest stars cast the deepest shadows" (428). Nature is powerful, deep, and full of possibility.

* * *

The themes that grow from setting—from time and place and disaster and invasion—are foundational to dystopia. Whether a small-scale place or a global vision, a variation on our present or an imaginative distant future, dystopia provides imaginative space for all kinds of issues, ideas, and possibilities. It also makes a clear, visceral connection with dystopic elements of the present. These connections are exploded when we dig below and beyond the surfaces of our dystopian contexts.

FIVE

Themes, Patterns, Trends and Transgressions

Layered with dystopic settings, the themes we can consider in relation to these books (like love triangles and choice) are rich and varied. While the characters and plots, approaches and trends can be tiresome, the worlds they create give us diversity. Many lines of inquiry, lenses for interpretation, focal points, and other ways into these texts shape our understanding of these texts and their contexts in scholarly and popular realms. Across this diversity, individual interpretation makes room for readers to develop their own understandings and meanings. What these texts mean to young readers may not match what they mean to adults. What these texts mean to women might be different from what they mean to men; queer people will read them differently than straight people. This is the beauty of literary and cultural texts. Among and beyond these multiple framings and readings, there are structures, themes, patterns, and prisms that speak to the bigger picture of what YA dystopia means for American culture and for the Girls on Fire who occupy their pages, as well as those who have their imagination sparked by these pages. And there are interruptions to norms and limitations.

To even begin to comprehend this genre, we have to acknowledge the many variations and look for themes and patterns, trends and transgressions. My definitions here are loose rather than strict, in part because this is the nature of the subject matter itself. The many strands that I have brought together in this book are not easy to manage. They do not make easy lists; they don't make simple Venn diagrams where overlap can be illustrated. As I read book after book, I began to chart the elements into linear, logical categories and subcategories, but the more I attempted to capture these details, the more difficult it became to distill the essence of YA dystopia.

And then dystopia provided the perfect image—the gnarled branches of a desiccated tree. The "Dystopia Trees" signify the dystopian landscape through relationships of books as well as themes. The first tree (see frontis-

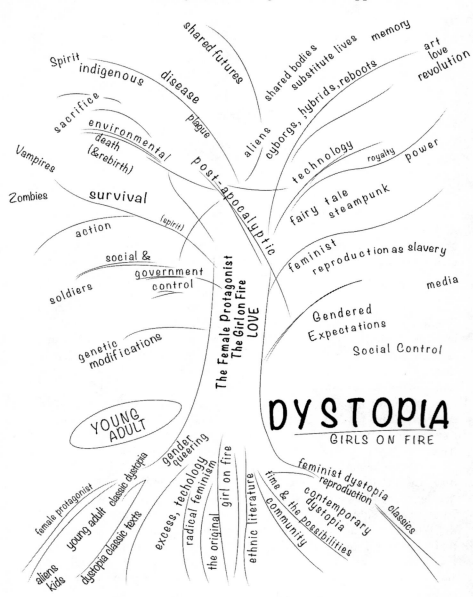

This dystopia tree complements the dystopia tree of the frontispiece and shows the overlapping themes as clusters of branches. The trunk is the heart of YA Dystopia and Girls on Fire and these themes are living and growing (design by Sarah Hentges; digitized by Karyssa Upham).

piece) maps the titles of YA dystopia as if they were the tree itself, growing out of the roots considered in Part I. This second tree adds the layer of dominant themes. While there are a number of relationships between and among these books and themes that cannot be captured through these illustrations, the visual evokes the growth of the genre as well as the growth of the characters—their coming of age—and the readers' coming to consciousness.

Voice

The role of voice for the Girl on Fire cannot be underestimated. In *Pictures of Girlhood* I argue that attitude, voice, and awareness are three important elements of empowering girls' films. When girls tell their stories in voiceover, or when they talk directly to the camera, they break the "male gaze" (Laura Mulvey) of the camera and their voice cannot be ignored. The voice of Katniss was the biggest element missing from the films. We have to rely upon Jennifer Lawrence to emote what Katniss is thinking and feeling—a feat impossible for any actor, no matter how talented. An important part of Katniss is lost when the films take away her inner monologue that the reader knows intimately. Divergent's films do better and allow Tris some opportunity to narrate. Films are visual and auditory. In the silence of books, voice is our direct connection, our lifeline. Saba's voice, for instance, is offered throughout Dustlands without interruption for direct quotes. Italics provide flashbacks as well as emphasis when she is talking to herself or when she is hearing Lugh's voice in her head. We hear other characters through her voice and her voice is grammatically unique. Only the first chapter of the second book, "Jack," is told from third person. Many novels tear the female protagonist back and forth between conflicting emotions: joy and fear and love and jealousy and anger and disappointment. Adolescence stirs up emotions, but dystopic conditions exacerbate these emotions. A lack of sleep, proper food and shelter, and adequate water will make anyone more emotional, less able to focus, and more likely to stumble, physically and mentally. When we hear this voice, we are closer to the character's reality.

In *Shatter Me*, Juliet literally writes her story (we assume) because there are parts crossed out, and yet still visible. For instance, she crosses out observations about her parents or about her interest in Adam. She describes him and crosses out gorgeous and replaces that word with "dangerous" (3). "~~Maybe I will die today~~" becomes "Maybe a bird will fly today" (28). She repeatedly crosses out a page full of "I am not insane" (20), with the last iteration left un-crossed. She crosses out the things that she writes that are the things that she wants to say, but knows she should not. Writing is the only means she has to try to understand herself. This writing is so important that she uses books as a metaphor when she describes herself:

> I've spent my life folded between the pages of books. In the absence of human rela-
> tionships I formed bonds with paper characters. I lived love and loss through stories
> threaded in history; I experienced adolescence by association. My world is one inter-
> woven web of words, stringing limb to limb, bone to sinew, thoughts and images all
> together. I am a being comprised of letters, a character created by sentences, a fig-
> ment of imagination formed through fiction. They want to delete every point of
> punctuation in my life from this earth and I don't think I can let that happen [70].

Her metaphor helps to keep her together. Her narration empowers her and she remembers that she has a voice. At the end of the book, she has a super-hero identity to build from.

As passed on by Lauren Olamina, the strongest Girls on Fire narrate their own stories. Very few books are not written in first-person. Birthmarked is one important exception. Even though the books follow Gaia, and Gaia is the clear leader and protagonist, her story is told in third person. Under the Never Sky is also told in third person with chapters alternating between Aria and Perry. Partials, Uglies, and The Lunar Chronicles are action-oriented; they need the constant shift of perspective and location, all the different aspects of the larger plot, a way to pull together all of the threads of the com-plex plot, especially in The Lunar Chronicles. While Cinder is the center and each book extends her story as the overarching narrative, each character has her story to play out. And because all of these stories are so interwoven, the omniscient voice resolves their stories together in the end (and happily ever after, of course). In *Beauty Queens*, each of the Miss teen Dreamers has voice through the omniscient narrator as well as through her own "Miss Teen Dream Fun Facts Page!" The omniscient narrator gives the story reach and perspective as well as background about what The Corporation is plotting and the interspersed commercial breaks that give the novel its dystopian fla-vor. But in Uglies, lack of voice is, perhaps, what makes Tally so one-dimensional.

Some books share narration. In *Delirium* and *Pandemonium*, we hear only Lena's voice, but in *Requiem*, she alternates chapters with Hana. In *Leg-end*, June and Day alternate chapters and the print is different colors and fonts. In the Legend series, it is Day's voice we hear first and we might wonder whose story *Legend* is to tell. In *Matched* Cassia narrates, but in *Crossed*, she shares with Ky and in *Reached* Xander and Ky narrate chapters alternating with Cassia. Zhange Ni notes the dimensions that each narrator brings to the Matched series:

> In the first novel, the utopian surface of Society is present from the point of view of
> Cassia, with that of Ky added in the second novel, which reveals the dystopian reality
> of Society. The third novel is narrated from three interchanging perspectives, Xander

becoming the third voice. The three young people become disillusioned with the rebellion … [and] embark on a cause of their own … through artistic creation and the collaboration of poetry, science, and politics [170–1].

In *Breathe*, two Girls on Fire narrate as Bea and Alina share narration with Quinn, a Premium and Bea's love interest. In the companion book, *Resist*, more voices join in. In *The Summer Prince*, Enki's voice is woven throughout in italic chunks that Johnson refers to as "his interstitial bits" (class visit). He is speaking to June in these bits and when the novel concludes, only this voice remains of Enki. June keeps his flame burning.

Voice plays an important role in *Orleans*; Fen's voice and dialect is unique among Girls on Fire. Her voice, like Saba's in Dustlands, *sounds* different. Marotta argues that "Fen's story is juxtaposed with Daniel's, but it is Fen's voice that is first heard from Orleans" (58). The fact that we hear Fen's voice first makes it clear that we are reading her story and that she is the central character. But Marotta interprets this differently. She explains, "This type of narration serves to temporarily place Fen in a subordinate position. Daniel's point of view—the voice from the Outer States—appears more valuable than Fen's" (58). This assumption is one made by this reader/critic, not one established by the way the story is written or the way the characters' voices are posed. Daniel's voice is not one of authority at all, though by today's standards it should be. He is educated, a published scientist, and in the military, and he is a man, but we know that he is risking all of this because he feels the need to cure a disease that took his younger brother from him. He is arrogant enough to think he can do it alone and immediately Daniel's authority is questioned; he is rebelling from his own privileged context and he is not prepared for Orleans. He is misinformed and naïve. Marotta notes that "eventually in the novel, Fen's voice will dominate Daniel's" (58), but Fen, when recognized as a Girl on Fire, is dominant from the beginning. The reader can spot Daniel as an idealistic fool. Fen is clearly the hero even if she cannot change her world or her fate.

Some girls grow into their voice through their struggles. But many voices are strong despite the dystopic, totalitarian, and/or sexist conditions, or they become strong, or they become stronger. But voice is only one tool girls can use; they can also use art.

Art and Culture: Propaganda and Empowerment

The power of art and culture to transform our world is no secret. The body of YA dystopia may just be one of these powerful and empowering forms of pop culture propaganda, and many of these novels/series highlight the power and potential power of literature, art, and culture to shape our world as well as our individual lives. The texts of a past that is off limits are foundational to many of these texts. In many futures, certain works are banned. In some futures, the meanings of these texts are manipulated toward social control. In The Selection, not only are stories from the past banned, but so are the diaries of the founding leader, which covers up his less-than-noble intentions. When Maxon gives America a copy, he sets himself up for a brutal beating. Literature is propaganda as much as it is a tool.

In *Delirium*, *Romeo and Juliet* is a "cautionary tale" as far as Lena knows, until Alex introduces her to love poetry. Similarly, in *Eve* classic literary texts teach girls the dangers of men. Every book the girls read is twisted around to teach a certain lesson about the dangers of men and the attributes of women. She has exams on the "Dangers of Boys and Men," a class where they were also taught about rape (25) and "all the ways women were vulnerable to the other sex" (40). They study *Romeo and Juliet* for their "Manipulation and Heartache unit" (40) and also have units on "Domestic Enslavement" and "Gang Mentality" (41). But one thing she hasn't learned is survival skills. As Arden reminds her, Eve is book smart (50). She knows nothing of the real world or how to survive outside the walls of her school. And she has been taught very particular interpretations of the art and literature they study in school.

Caleb knows how to read and he owns books. He teaches Eve other ways of reading and practicing critical thinking when her reading of *To the Lighthouse* proves just how skewed her education has been (140–1). And he also teaches her the necessary skill of how to swim. For a moment she forgets that Caleb is a different sex (148). She begins to see beyond the definitions she's been programmed with. She realizes that "somewhere inside me, there was deeper knowledge. It held a place that even fear and a carefully crafted education could not touch" (156). She knows that Caleb is "a good man" (157). She realizes that her education has been manipulative and skewed. She has been fed propaganda as truth.

In *Matched*, the 100 approved pieces of literature, art, music, etc., keep culture controlled and predictable; there is no longer space for creativity, imagination, innovation. Cassia notes, "My hands that, like almost everyone else in our Society, cannot write, that merely know how to use the words of others" (81). Not only are they stripped of written literacy, they are also robbed of the power of words and literature that can come through literacy. After reading the Dylan Thomas poem her grandfather secretly leaves her, "Nothing I have written or done has made any difference in this world, and suddenly I know what it means to rage, and to crave" (97). She continues, "There's a reason they didn't keep this poem./This poem tells you to fight" (98). In *Matched*, Cassia harnesses the power of past texts; more importantly, in *Reached* she works to inspire people to create their own art. Her step toward freedom of expression is also a step toward connections and community-building in *Reached*. Cassia is sorting and trading and then begins a gathering to share things that people make—writing, singing, carving, sculpting, designing, dancing—creating and experiencing art. She notes, "I am not the only one writing./ I am not the only one creating./ The Society took so much from us, but we still hear rumors of music, hints of poetry; we still see intimations of art in the world around us.... We took it in, sometimes without knowing, and many still ache for a way to let it out" (157). Society takes only so much when it utilizes cultural power—past, present, and future.

The Summer Prince is the best text for understanding the true potential of art as radical and transgressive since "good art has a habit of breaking boundaries" (125). June pushes right up against the boundaries her society has set: "They'd call it a prank at best, petty vandalism at worst. I'd tell them that transgression is part of what makes art *work*, but I admit I am a little afraid that the Aunties might agree with them" (90). She wants to shock; she wants to "force people to remember" but she doesn't "want to go too far" (90). At one point, Enki accuses June of "playing at being radical" (136) and asks her how much of herself she is willing to give to win (92). She is, after all, an upper-class "brat" who has been allowed to pursue her loves and talents in ways that are unavailable to the lower-tier wakas. When she sacrifices her anonymity to save people's lives, it is "no price at all for all the beauty of the art [she] created" (136). Enki forces June—and the reader—to consider how June's art might be implicated by her privilege and whether or not she can really transform society for the oppressed. He decides—perhaps in part because of her privilege—that she can do better than the complacent Aunties. While June does not choose to be queen, many Girls on Fire fight for freedom and for choice; they have to be strong to survive a violent world and corrupt power structures. Sometimes they have to fight fire with fire.

The Wall Is Coming Down

While the walls are often a result of the dystopic circumstances discussed in chapter four, and the need for the powers that be to keep control and impose order, or provide safety. A wall or a fence or a dome or an enclave or whatever it is that is keeping the people inside safe and the people outside segregated, will cease to exist. This is a trend in today's world that plays out in the future, as Emily Badger notes in her *Washington Post* article, "The Wealthy Are Walling Themselves Off in Cities Increasingly Segregated by Class." In *Parable of the Sower* people's status and safety is determined by the amount of wall they have between them and the "others" outside. Some other privileged neighborhoods are reinforced through the technologies and power of the rich. But most neighborhoods lack walls and are the constant victims of violence and theft. Lauren's family is part of a walled neighborhood of seven households of varying size, 20 miles out of Los Angeles. These physical environments directly dictate the quality of life of its residents—their limited choices and promises. After a lifetime of relative security inside these walls, Lauren's predictions come to fruition—the wall is violently breeched and all but a few residents are killed (and raped) as a statement by a group (The "Pyros") that burns, rapes, and pillages the rich (or "rich") in the name of the poor. Ultimately the wall is only an illusion of safety, a safety from the dangers of urban spaces. In the science-fictional future this safety no longer exists. In fact, such "luxury" becomes a target for violence.

In *The Hunger Games*, Katniss slips under the fence to hunt for her family. When she leaves her district and sees the reinforced walls of District 11, she notes how much more oppressed this district is compared to hers. When she returns home in *Catching Fire*, she slips out to enjoy the freedom she used to have. When she tries to return home, she finds that the fence is suddenly electrified and the Capitol is cracking down. As *The Forgetting* opens, Nadia lays on the narrow top of the wall that encloses her town, Canaan, fearing the flogging that she will earn if she is noticed. In her town, "*We stay inside the walls because that is what we know, and where we are safe*" (50). But the wall is not what people think it is; in fact, they don't really know what is outside the wall since they have all forgotten how it was built and how long it has existed. Later they realize that there used to be gates. As Nadia notes, it's what is inside the walls that should be feared.

Almost every book/series has some version of a wall. The intent is safety, the effect is illusion and often oppression. The wall works in conjunction with the corrupt power structure, but it is also a symbol on its own. One thing about walls that YA dystopia makes clear: they get broken down. Their failure is inevitable and often violent. With or without closed national borders, some YA dystopia places are walled in, or even underground. In *Enclave*, Deuce has never been above ground. When she gets above ground, she finds the world infested with zombies. She cannot just be free; she is still enclosed. *The Forest of Hands and Teeth* begins in a world that has never known anything but zombie infestation. The past has been lost. A fence encloses isolated communities that often don't even know that other communities exist. And within walls that keep zombies out, strict rules are enforced in the name of safety and continued survival, much like District 13's strictly controlled society in *Mockingjay*. When some rebellious teens break these rules and bring potential infestation to the whole town, Mary escapes into a maze of fences that will shape her new world.

In *Delirium*, the wall is around the United States. "The border is guarded constantly by military personnel. No one can get in. No one goes out.... This is for our own protection. Safety, Sanctity, Community: That is our country's motto" (42). Further, these walls aren't just the physical barrier; social and cultural structures impose just as many walls through their rules (*Delirium* 228). But outside of these walls are "the Wilds" where the "Invalids" live, and people in the city pretend that they don't exist. Like in *The Hunger Games*, the fence is a threat, sometimes electrified, sometimes passable. And the fences are replaced by a wall when the Resistance starts to make the Invalids impossible to ignore. In *Orleans*, the wall is erected to separate the United States—The Outer States—from the hurricane and disease-ravaged Delta. Armed soldiers ensure that no one crosses, and Fen is shot so that Daniel can cross back over with baby Enola.

In some books and series the wall is an enclosed structure, a set of walls. For instance, in The Selection series, even when America leaves the palace grounds to go home after her father dies, the bulk of these books take place within the palace walls, for the protection of Prince Maxon and the woman-girls competing for an opportunity to be princess. There are small setting changes—the smaller house and poorer circumstance of her family, the gardens and roof and safe rooms, the territory of the Northern resistance—but all of these are temporary escapes from the tightly regulated and highly monitored setting. Outside the palace walls, the people are suffering, especially the lower classes. Likewise, in The Chemical Garden series, Rhine is isolated under the protective (and sinister) watch of Linden's mansion. The Hegemon, Linden's grandfather, makes these walls possible with his money and power. When she escapes, she finds herself a caged prisoner in a disturbing carnival settlement, a different place but part of the same world. Inside the mansion she is protected from the sinister world outside. The price she pays for this protection is too much, but she accepts it because she has no choice and because she cares for her co-wives who are still captives, however willing. They have no option.

In *Birthmarked*, Gaia lives in Warfton outside of the wall that encompasses the Enclave. She hands over babies to the Enclave to keep the balance. Their wall has created a limited gene pool. In the second book, *Prized*, she finds herself in Sylum, a matriarchal society that has been isolated by an environmental phenomenon that drugs its population into addiction; people cannot leave because the withdrawal symptoms kill them. This phenomenon also creates imbalances in the population's reproductive systems and the society's imbalance of sex (and gender). While both of these populations are impacted by problems that root from genetic isolation, the results on these societies are vastly different while also being similar in their corrupt and tyrannical political structure and fear of change. When Gaia brings the two together, the results are more struggle.

In *Breathe* and *Under the Never Sky*, the wall is a dome. It is an enclosure that keeps a controlled atmosphere and ample oxygen supply for its citizens. In *Breathe* these citizens are offered different benefits according to their social standing, and the elite corruption produces second-class citizens who barely dare to breathe let alone use more oxygen than they can pay for. Exercise, sex, anything that requires more oxygen is strictly limited. In *Under the Never Sky*, those who live in domes are the fortunate survivors; when the dome is compromised, Aria has no choice but to escape and seek something else, somewhere else.

In *Eve*, the walls are both physical and mental. Like other Girls on Fire, Eve lives behind walls—in this case, the walls of her school. "We'd spent most of our lives inside the compound walls, never knowing the forest beyond it…" (1). Beyond there are dangerous men, violence, packs of dogs. Later she realizes that she has been protected by the walls and all the brainwashing they came with, but only mortally. Outside "here it was, waiting for me all along: death, inescapable death, everywhere. Always" (124). She also comes to realize that these walls were not only protecting her, they had also been molding her into a passive second-class citizen. Graduation day is the day they have been waiting for, the party they have never had, the promises that New America has made them. "I had been told there was a plan for me—a plan for all of us" (14). This plan is not the City in the Sand that she fantasizes about—full of art and music and freedom. This plan is reproductive slavery, at least for all of the girls whose father does not happen to be the king (which she does not discover until the second book, when she is expected to become a princess). Still, Eve must weigh the reality of her imprisonment when she is captured. "None of it mattered. It was over. No way to escape the bars, the burning sun, this man with the cracked yellow teeth. I was trapped again, new walls holding me in, bringing me to the King. The City gates would open and close behind me, another cage" (212). What awaits Eve is not exactly the scenario she imagines, nor is it the worst case scenario (reproductive/sexual slavery, for instance). She's given an opportunity to effect change, but she has to work for it.

Walls that are physical and mental—walls used for social control—often create conditions that are more amenable to violence. In *Never Fade*, when the temporary government announces that the kids who refuse to undergo the procedure that may cure them (and could kill them) will be housed in special communities, Chubs argues, "A community with barbed wire fences? Armed guards? … There's no rehabilitation in that" (526). The walls will remain in a new form. When walls cannot be maintained, as well as when they cannot contain, violence is often the result.

Violence

There is no doubt that dystopian futures are dangerous places. People are going to die. (At least most of the time.) People are going to get hurt.

Girls on Fire are going to have to fight. Sometimes they have weapons; sometimes they have no training or experience. Violence is the norm of navigating some of these future scenarios, especially if surrounded by zombies or in the Hunger Games arena. In fact, the violence of the Hunger Games made parents question whether these books were appropriate for their children, and the films definitely downplayed the violent aspects. They were not erased, but they also weren't exaggerated Hollywood-style. Violence is a reality of the world that Katniss survives and it is important to recognize the reality of this violence in order to understand other aspects of her story like her PTSD and her choice to marry Peeta and eventually (and arguably, reluctantly) have children. Katniss is forced to use violence, but she does not finds the means worth the ends despite her relative success.

Olamina represents the larger struggles, past, present and future, against prisons and state violence more generally. Throughout *Sower* Lauren reminds the reader that the cops cannot be trusted. Revealing these authority figures as corrupt and dangerous establishes a subversion of authority figures that rearticulates and rebukes the violence of the past. It also arms Girls on Fire. Community members are better equipped to take care of one another—people within the community can be trusted while authority figures cannot. This belief is further supported throughout *Parables*—and in almost all YA dystopia Girls on Fire texts—as police and other authority figures are corrupt and often ruthless. Olamina's view of cops extends the feelings of many racial and ethnic minorities, past and present, who have dealt with police misconduct from Watts, to East L.A., to Chicago, to Baltimore, to Standing Rock and on and on—even in Seattle in 1999 when police beat and gassed peaceful WTO protestors of all colors. Violence plays out in similar ways in the Darkest Minds series. Ruby, and thousands of other children, are imprisoned because they develop abilities that threaten the adults. Their existence is policed by corrupt PSFs as well as camp controllers, all the way up the line to the President. The kids are not treated with caution; they are treated like the dangerous criminals they are perceived to be.

Some girls are trained to administer violence and defend themselves from violence. In the Legend series, June is a prodigy who works for the government. She is efficient in hand-to-hand combat among a plethora of other skills. Tris is trained by her faction—the Dauntless—as well as by her love interest, Four (Tobias). This is what ultimately allows her to embrace her Dauntless designation. Ruby is conditioned as a soldier for the Children's League; she is a valuable asset with her orange abilities. Deuce is trained to fight and defend her enclave from the Freaks that roam the passages beyond their underground settlement. Others like Saba in *Blood Red Road* have to learn quickly because they are literally fighting for their lives, sparring in a cage fight against other prisoners.

Girls Who Fight for Their Lives

While almost all of our Girls on Fire fight for their lives and for the lives of others, many are specially trained or particularly adept.

Book/Series	Type of Fight	Special Skills/Tools
The Hunger Games	Fights for her life in the HG arena and then in the war against the Capitol.	Hunter turned soldier and symbol. Adept with a bow and arrow. Builds community.
Divergent	Fights to prove herself as Dauntless. Insurgence, War.	Tris trained to be "Dauntless" and becomes skilled in hand to hand combat as well as with guns.
Dustlands: Blood Red Road	Saba takes on cage fighting after she is imprisoned. Called The Angel of Death.	Intelligence, drive to survive. Perhaps fated to make a difference in her world.
Enclave	Deuce trained as a Huntress; has to fight the Freaks/Muties.	Her identity is wrapped up in her ability to defend her people.
Ashes	Alex fights with her mind, but is also strong in body.	Father trained her with firearms before kids started changing into "Chuckies."
Legend	First a part of the power structure; later a part of the resistance.	June is a prodigy and a child soldier at 15.
The 5th Wave	Survival against soldiers.	Guns are the primary method.
Orleans	Fen fights for her survival; then fights to get Baby Girl over the wall.	Intelligence and experience; culturally adept.
The Darkest Minds	Ruby trained in combat techniques by the Children's League.	Ability manipulates people through control of their minds.
The Immortal Rules	Survival against zombie-vampires	Learns the art of the sword.
Cinder	War, insurgence.	Her special powers as a cyborg and then her Lunar abilities of mind control.

Book/Series	Type of Fight	Special Skills/Tools
Breathe/Resist	Resistance against the Hegemon	Meditation and breath control.
The Interrogation of Ashala Wolf	Resistance and revolution against the government.	Able to walk in her dreams; thinks violence is a means to freedom.
Matched	A battle of ideas through art, but also a war—Ky fights, Xander heals, and Cassia gathers the hearts and minds.	Poetry (and guns).
Shadows Cast by Stars	War defending the Island against the Government; supernatural battle.	Boys go off to fight; Cass is a healer but also fights in the spirit world.
Under the Never Sky	Fight for survival in shifting environment.	Aria has acute hearing and other auditory abilities.

Some girls who lack fighting skills are threatened sexually, though this kind of violence is rare and often downplayed but not invisible in YA dystopia. In *Life as We Knew It*, Miranda stumbles upon some men with guns and hides. In the companion book, Alex is offered a trade for his younger sister and he refuses. He also rescues her from a big man trying to drag her off the street, hitting him with a can of pineapple and then lamenting the loss of the can of fruit. He already had to protect his sisters out of familial duty, but now he realizes the threat to their safety is more sinister than they know. In *Resist*, Bea is nearly gang raped before Ronan appears and rescues her. But not all girls have older brothers or friends to watch out for their safety. In The Chemical Garden series these violent sexual realities are closer to the surface. Rhine is abducted among other girls, some of which are disposed of (shot in the head, for instance) when they are not chosen. Girls who are not chosen also face violent realities that include being raped or used for their reproductive potential. Rhine is one of three wives chosen for Linden; the other two wives are obviously having sex with him even as Rhine chooses not to and he respects that choice. This narrator protects her "purity," but is really conflicted by her feelings for another boy. But for girls like Fen in *Orleans*, there is no element of control or choice—she is raped by a man when she is a child. This experience makes her wise and cautious and hard. Instead of being protected by a man, she saves herself by escaping her captivity as a blood slave and joins Lydia's gang of O positives. She learns how to survive. As Coleman notes, "Smith positions her future setting in terms of Katrina's real causes and effects" (9), and one of these is violence.

While much of the violence in these novels is a matter of survival, violence also shows the inequalities and powerlessness. In almost all cases, the balance of power is enforced through a show of force and those in power have weapons that are often not available to the oppressed populations. As Day states, "only one side has the advantage of guns. Guess who's winning" (*Legend* 252). Guns are one means of keeping social order and control. They are as much a symbol of power as they are a means of force. In some cases, the Girls on Fire gain access to guns. In some cases they gain special training. In some cases guns are only available for those with power. In most cases, guns are described in great detail. Some are realistic like in *The 5th Wave* and *The Darkest Minds* and some are guns imagined in dystopian futures like in *Divergent* and *Legend*. In *Never Fade*, Ruby describes her relationship with her gun: "My fingers curved around its familiar shape. It was the typical service weapon—a black SIG Sauer P229 DAK—that still, after months of learning to shoot them, and clean them, and assemble them, felt too big in my hands" (14). She has a familiarity, but the "too big" feel illustrates that this weapon does not feel natural to her. Whether this discomfort is with the inferred violence or her female gender, is unclear.

* * *

Sexual violence is often given a light touch, but the possibilities are not completely erased. In *Breathe*, Bea reflects on what Alina told her: "especially the girls, have had to offer up their own bodies to the stewards in exchange for safe passage through Border Control" (221). In *After Light*, Ruby remembers one of the PSFs "who liked to press himself up against the girls, hassle them to get them flustered, and then punish them for reacting in any small way. It hadn't made sense then, … now I had a pretty good sense of what he'd really been doing, and it lit my fury" (475). While this incident is not spelled out, the sexual aspect of this situation is clear. However, in *Never Fade*, the connection to sexual abuse is even more clear. Knox, an imposter for the hero "Slip Kid," is cruel. He has control over a group of Blues by sheer intimidation, humiliation, and bullying. Knox strips girls of their power. Ruby describes, Olivia, who has been badly burned and disabled: "The Olivia I had known had been so full of fire, she could have brought the whole warehouse down to a pile of simpering ash" (228). Knox keeps scantily-clad, emaciated girls nearby to grope, abuse, and demean. When Ruby and her friends are captured, Knox sends the others out into the cold without their jackets, but says, "The hot piece [Vida] will stay and keep us entertained" (229). The focus then shifts to what's happening outside the warehouse, rather than inside. Outside kids are freezing, starving, and dying; most are incredibly ill and near-death. Olivia takes care of the outcasts. It is clear what happens to the girls inside the warehouse; but we know that Vida can hold her own in the situation, even if we don't see her shut Knox down. Instead, Ruby takes him down when she realizes she can get into his mind without touching him (a new development in the evolution of her power).

In *Eve*, a group of boys take her in after Caleb rescues her from a bear attack: "These boys who looked at me as though I were something to be devoured" (103). She remembers what she learned about "Gang Mentality" by reading *The Lord of the Flies* (106). But, this is not when Eve learns just how dangerous boys can be. When the boys go on a raid for supplies (which include candy and beer) Eve finds herself navigating a world she doesn't understand. Eve has very little knowledge of how the world outside her school works; she has even less knowledge on the real "dangers of boys and men," despite this being part of her school curriculum. After she gets in an argument with Caleb, Leif moves in. Later she realizes she overreacted in her conversation with Caleb. She stays awake replaying the events in her mind, and then Leif finds her and starts kissing and touching her, trying to force her participation (Cass has a similar experience in *Shadows Cast by Stars*). She is confused even as she recognizes what is happening. "What Leif had done was wrong. And yet…. Had I given him some unspoken invitation? Had my kisses seemed like something more?" (198). In the moment she is confused, but later she knows that he misinterpreted "kindness as invitation" (201). This scene speaks to contemporary issues of date rape and blaming the victim. Even in this future scenario, Eve can clearly see that she is not at fault and she has to confront the realities of the world she now lives in. She has to see how Caleb and Leif are different; she has to face the realities that other girls and women are not so lucky to avoid. After Leif sells her to bounty hunters, she notes, "Some men saw women purely as a commodity. Like fuel, rice, or canned meat" (221). Girls on Fire challenge their commodified status.

In *Enclave*, where Deuce is raised, anyone who attempted to "breed" a woman without consent would be banished and fed to the Freaks. But topside there are gangs, and as Fade warns her, "they'll want to breed you…. That's all they think girls are good for. There are no rules about it up here, either. You have no power" (x). When they encounter such a gang, the leader, Stalker, claims Deuce for himself. They plan to hunt Fade for sport and rites of passage. Tegan, a girl who has been used for the gang's breeding, helps Deuce to escape. Tegan has been abused and has little physical strength and doesn't know how to fight. She has been traumatized "just because she was born a girl" (163). But she ends up being a survivor as well.

In *Ashes*, one of the characters, Lena, who is beginning to transition into one of the Changed, is on birth control and wonders if this contributed to the reasons why her stepfather and religious leader, "Crusher Karl," "dared" to rape her. "No inconvenient little pregnancies to try and explain away" (277). When the "world crashed" she didn't have a way to get any more pills and she wonders if her illness is PMS, "which would be just so her luck"

(277). It's not; it's pregnancy. Not only is Lena's rape revealed, Lena confesses to stabbing Karl to death, arguing, "He visited a lot" (346). The Bishop and ministers decided to cover it up. "Karl was just gone, like he'd never existed. I think they were secretly glad I'd gotten rid of the asshole" (346). Eventually Lena is killed in action after she changes.

These overt acts of violence, and acts of state violence like imprisonment, bombing, and mass shootings, are only the most obvious forms of violence. Coleman notes that "it is important for critics of YA dystopia to be aware of 'slow violence' to better understand how Smith shapes a highly contemporary and sophisticated understanding of setting" (9). Not all violence can be measured in gunfights and blood shed, which are also present in Orleans. The violence that slowly works its victims to the bone is just as effective. Katniss knows this violence; her family, and her community, are starving. For Lena in *Delirium*, Saba in Dustlands, and Bea and Alina in *Breathe*, their marginal social status translates to a marginal existence. For many Girls on Fire this slow violence makes change mandatory to survival if not also an improved quality of life. While violence is inevitable, and while violence works against the bodies, minds, and hearts of so many Girls on Fire, *The Interrogation of Ashala Wolf* makes a deliberate intervention in the use of violence as a means toward social change. As they brainstorm their fight, Ember asks Ashala, "when will you understand? We can't change the world with violence. Only with ideas" (32). Ashala wonders "how ideas are much use against armed enforcers" and jokes that she'll "talk your philosophy" when she's captured. Ember's philosophy may not be useful in Ashala's immediate circumstances as prisoner; however, as the story unfolds, we know there is a bigger plan— a war of ideas. Later, Em reminds her again of the importance of "chang[ing] how people think": "You can't transform a society for the better with violence, Ashala. Only with ideas" (190). In Girls on Fire novels, state violence is prevalent, individual violence is self-defense and survival, and collective violence is rebellion, even revolution—a means toward change.

Social Control/Power

Amidst the often bleak environmental conditions and other material challenges Girls on Fire face, corrupt political structures are often the structural reality that matches the bleak environmental conditions. As a defining element of the larger dystopic tradition, social control shapes the conditions that define the struggles that the Girl on Fire will face and the potential of what comes after struggling, fighting, and surviving. But it is never as simple as the single arrow that President Coin gives Katniss for the execution of the deposed President Snow. The arrow find's Coin's heart instead since she is just another version of the same corrupt leader. But this one murder cannot change a whole system. Moylan notes, dystopia's ability to "reflect upon the causes of social and ecological evil as systemic…. In its purview, no single policy or practice can be isolated as the root of the problem, no single aberration can be privileged as the one to be fixed so that life in the enclosed status quo can easily resume" (*Scraps* xii). With no isolated root, the systemic issues that the Girls on Fire face have no easy answers or clear cut solutions. Things are messy.

Even in these messy times, most books offer a central figure of control, power, and corruption, or pure evil. While not all of the evil or authoritative or abusive characters are men, and not all the women who act as power-hungry villains are patriarchal, overwhelmingly, men play the role of Hegemon. I use this term here as a purposeful connection to the characters in Orson Scott Card's *Ender's Game* and subsequent books in this series, as well as the use of the word by cultural critics and intellectuals like Frantz Fanon. The Hegemon is the face, symbol, and source of power in YA dystopia.

When women are in the role of Hegemon, like Sylum's Matrarch in *Prized* or President Coin in *Mockingjay*, they are acting out the markers of masculine power and control, or they are mentally unstable like Janis in *The Forgetting* and Queen Levana in The Lunar Chronicles. Men—often fathers of the love interest (and sometimes the long-lost father of the Girl on Fire, like in Partials and Eve)—are overwhelmingly cast as the villain and are corrupt, evil, and ruthless. This reflection of reality mirrors the ways in which dystopia shadows our contemporary world in the U.S. (but also other places). Men comprise the vast majority of CEOs of companies, especially in the Fortune 500. They commit the majority of violent crimes. They make up the bulk of police forces, military troops, elected politicians, and just about any other position of power and authority. They make laws that restrict women's bodies and popular culture texts that exploit women' bodies and poison our minds. While these roles and circumstances are slowly changing, in YA dystopia this reality morphs into tyranny through the role of malicious, corrupt, and selfish leaders. Our collective experience of oppression along gender lines is personified in YA dystopia's Hegemon.

Those with power have a variety of means of controlling their populations. Control through resources like food and medicine are powerful tactics and the hallmark of the Hunger Games series. The tessera—the meager supply of grain and oil—that children from ages 12 through 18 can request (and increase their likelihood of their name being drawn in the Reaping) is a direct reflection of the control of the population that complements the brutal spectacle of the Hunger Games. These forms of control can go further, utilizing medical and genetic manipulation like when the Capitol brainwashes Peeta or when the evil queen in the Lunar Chronicles genetically modifies Wolf until he is almost no longer human. Both of these examples show the ways in which the boys, the love interests, are manipulated and abused, at least as much as the Girl on Fire is abused and manipulated. Peeta and Wolf are both able to overcome their brainwashing, in part because of the love of their Girl on Fire. Along with the "divide and conquer" strategy, starvation and physical and mental abuse are "classic" forms of control.

Propaganda and mass brainwashing are also effective; a controlling ideology shapes the limits and expectations. As a number of articles ranging from *The Huffington Post* (Crum) to *Wired* (Geek's Guide to the Universe) to *Bitch Magazine* (Mirk) noted after Trump's acceptance of the Republican nomination for president, Octavia Butler wrote about a future where a candidate uses the slogan "Make America Great Again" to manipulate voters. Trump's policies are not far off and the sudden turn to the idea that "alternate facts" are legitimate is most certainly a move from dystopian politics. But many mentions of Trump's similarity to right wing dystopian dictators fail to note that, in time, Jarett's reign ends and things move toward better, in part, because of the growth of Earthseed. The community ideals, the focus on literacy and education, the shared ownership, and more counter the fascism of Butler's fictional candidate/president. Most YA dystopia books portray the kind of power that has oppressed for generations; many of these examples include dictators. Girls on Fire navigate this power to varying degrees, but they make it clear that such power is not particularly desirable, nor is it inevitable.

Power, in the world of YA dystopia, often targets difference, creates difference (like along economic lines), and fears those it cannot so easily control. In *The Darkest Minds*, the adults fear the children whose abilities cannot be controlled, let alone understood. Their instrumental, tangible power is still controlled by fearful and corrupt adults, even when they succeed. The special abilities do not translate into political power, not even in the end. In *The Summer Prince*, the Aunties use their power and control to keep the wakas in their place. In conversation with her mother, June realizes that politics are all about "advantage and placement and promotion" and wonders: "is anything real?" (193). She expects her mother to "yell back at me about irresponsible wakas and accepting the world the way it is and not the way I want it to be" (193), but her mother is resigned to be "just a housewife" (194) and thinks that it is "a terrible system … but it's the best we have" (194). The grandes are content with the way things are, but June thinks, "that's why she's a grande and and I'm still a waka. Because she can accept that./ I won't" (194). And, as queen, June will have an opportunity to change this system in ways that most other Girls on Fire never will.

Katniss impacts her world, but she lives to see that it doesn't change all that much. She just no longer has a central role. In the second book of the

Birthmarked series (*Prized*), Gaia finds that matriarchy can be just as dangerous as patriarchy. When she seeks a new power structure, she leads a movement that results in her reproductive organs being removed, her body violated and her "woman parts" stolen. In The Selection, America and Maxon will continue to have a central role as they now are in the position to use their power for the good of the people, breaking down the caste system and giving people more choice. Saba's New Eden chooses a council of "nine wise women" (419). She says, "They try to choose me, but I won't be chosen" (419). When power fails, perhaps empowerment keeps the fire burning. The abstract, the metaphorical, the literal meanings of choice, are all explored by Girls on Fire as one means to fight, or at least endure, corrupt power structures.

Choice

We might begin to wonder, in YA dystopia like in reality, whether choice is just a myth. Historian Howard Segal illustrates the "persistent association of utopianism with lack of choice" (123) in his book *Utopia*: "Beyond the obvious question of whether specific utopian schemes could ever be implemented has come the traditional concern over forcing individuals, groups, and societies to adopt values, institutions, and ways of life that many might otherwise reject" (123). One group's utopia is another's dystopia. The grand vision of one constituency seems to inevitably lead to the inevitable oppression of another. As Hunter notes in *Crossed*, "You have to remember that people back then *chose* the Society and its controls as a way to prevent a future Warming event, and as a way to help eliminate illness" (316). But the lack of choice in dystopia not only has the element of a failed utopia, it also has the power to unlock the entire system. Illness cannot be eliminated and "future warming events" are not easily avoided without drastic, collective, planet-wide changes.

Choice is a key element in many of these books, particularly around the lack of choices manufactured by the corrupt power structure. In *Delirium*, Lena's best friend Hana critiques their lack of choices while Lena defends that lack by saying at least they have choices. They are given a list of marriage partners to choose from. Later, in *Requiem*, Hana's not given this choice; she is forced into an abusive relationship with the Mayor. In *Matched*, on the other hand, each person is only provided with one perfect match, which is how all the trouble starts for Cassia in the first place. If only Xander's face had popped up, she might never have questioned anything. Because Ky is an Aberration in an otherwise flawless system, the entire system is suspect. These romantic choices, or lack of them, speak to Seifert's identification of choice as the dominant narrative in the three YA dystopia novels she examines. Choice about who to marry, in these books, corresponds with bigger ideals about choice—the right to live as we choose, to love as we choose, to be who we choose. So many Girls on Fire choose the well-being of others over their own like Tris, in *Allegiant*, who chooses to take her brother's place in a mission sure to lead to death. (In fact, that's why Caleb was chosen for the particular assignment.) And, of course, Katniss chooses to take Prim's place in the Reaping and overcomes her inevitable death sentence twice, even though Prim does not ultimately escape this fate.

Choice also plays a role in Juliet's sense of self at the end of *Shatter Me*: "I'm wondering when I became a motivational speaker. When I made the switch from hating myself to accepting myself. When it became okay for me to choose my own life" (332). And this sense of self is directly connected to her commitment to fight for a better world: "Things are changing, but this time I'm not afraid. This time I know who I am. This time I've made the right choice and I'm fighting for the right team. I feel safe. Confident./ Excited, even./ Because this time?/ I'm ready" (338). Even in a highly controlled world, the choice to fight is still a choice.

The trope of choice is not always limited to the social control and power that shapes these dystopic words, or the way these worlds reflect our own. Choice is a feminist principle toward self-actualization as well as self-determination. Sometimes this principle can inject language that echoes these progressive politics. For instance, at the end of *In the After Light* (the Darkest Minds), Chubs (Charles), the nerd of the group, argues: "'It's what a person chooses to do with their abilities that matters. By locking someone up for making a choice about their body that they have every right to make, what you're essentially saying is that, no, you don't trust us'" (526–7). These words come from a young man, in a different context, but also echo the fundamental feminist right to choose what happens to one's own body. Other books, like the Eve and Birthmarked series, make the feminist principle of choice more overt as Girls on Fire fight for reproductive rights. As a midwife, Gaia provides women with choice even when her own choice is taken in the end.

Marotta also describes choice in the neo-slave narratives of *Tankborn* and *Orleans*. She argues that Fen chooses death. "In her own way, by embracing her ability to choose, even Fen escapes her state of bondage" (68). This is a fair assessment of Fen's little bit of power. She chooses Enola's life over her own. But Marotta stretches this self-sacrifice. She argues, "Her consciously chosen act of self-sacrifice, her life for Baby Girl's, reveals her desire to protect Orleans society and to ensure its survival" (68). Fen isn't protecting society; her death has no connection to, for instance, the guns that are on their way into Orleans. It has some connection to a possibility that Daniel might inform someone in power about the lush resources that *Orleans* holds and those with

Ambiguous, symbolic, and layered, these three covers reveal nothing physical about Gaia, their Girl on Fire. The cover of *Birthmarked* features the ribbon with the code that Gaia breaks to reveal birth records that her mother was keeping. The cover of *Prized* displays the symbol of the Matrarc's power. The more ambiguous cover of *Promised* showcases a ring, which could be the symbol of a promise of marriage, but it might also represent what Gaia loses in the end (Square Fish [Macmillan]. Cover photographs © istockphoto.com and shutterstock.com. Cover design by Faceout studio, Tim Green).

power will somehow improve conditions for the people in Orleans because the Outer States wants its resources. But this is a stretch. Further, Outer States intervention is more likely to lead to decimation of Orleans than rescue. Ultimately, it is Fen's promise to Lydia that Baby Girl will have a better life that causes her to sacrifice her own. This act gets Enola across a wall with Daniel; the rest is up to him. But what is the future for Orleans? For all we know, tribal warfare decimates the area and the Outer States infiltrates the area to extract the riches that exist there. Or, simply, Orleans continues on, surviving as it has for decades.

Kayla's choice in *Tankborn* does not have the same fatal weight to it. As Marotta argues, Kayla "chooses the freedom of another over her own" when she gives the remaining cure to her friend, Mishalla, also assuring that Mishalla can have the life and love she desires. But Kayla is only delaying her own transformation. The cure exists. So, Kayla may demonstrate "that she not only embraces her identity, but also that she is willing to work as an activist, helping to transform her society into one that values equality instead of intolerance and the community over the individual" (69), but the book's conclusion makes it clear that Devak is going to be able to get Kayla the cure. He has resources, and he loves her. How could he not move mountains for her?

Men as Hegemon, Boys as Consciousness

We might think that the message of the Hegemon in these books is an uncritical acceptance of men and masculinity as toxic and irredeemable and power is always corrupt. The role that women play in positions of evil, power-hungry dictators certainly mitigates this accusation. Most often these women, like Dr. Cable in *Specials* (of the Uglies series), is basically playing out a masculine role; other times they are the classic maniacal evil queen like in The Lunar Chronicles. Clearly, the role of the Hegemon is not about men—it is about patriarchy. While in real life justice in the face of rich white males often fails, in YA dystopia most of the time, these figures fall from grace as a direct result of the actions of the Girl on Fire. In fact, even when the future outlook is still cloudy, at the very least, the Hegemon has fallen.

In these books, men are often symbols for the larger wrongs of society and these stories shape a fictional future and reality that reflects a version of our contemporary world. But, there is hope—the extreme masculinity and violence of the Hegemon makes the boy a path to consciousness. The younger generation has better morals and more heart—at least the boys our Girls on Fire love. The young man reveals the hidden truths, the corrupt actions, the hidden stories. He has a respect for women, generally, and recognizes the power and potential of the Girl on Fire specifically. The boy is often the key that unlocks—or at least exposes—the power of the man. He pulls back the curtain that shrouds the Girl on Fire from the truth. He is the romantic ideal and often the political ideal. He is a rebel or a revolutionary.

Girl on Fire and Boy Love Interest
(and Other Characters)

Book/Series	Protagonist	Love Interest and Boy as Consciousness* (There is often more than one love interest though mostly as a means for conflict)	Other Important Characters Include Friends, Siblings, Parents
The Hunger Games	Katniss, the girl who was on fire	Peeta (the boy with the bread and the dandelion) Gale?	Gale (the best friend) Prim (sister) Rue (ally) Haymitch (mentor)
Delirium	Lena (Magdelena)	Alex* Julian (son of leader of *Deliria*-Free America)	Hana (best friend) Grace (younger cousin) Raven (leader)

Book/Series	Protagonist	Love Interest and Boy as Consciousness* (There is often more than one love interest though mostly as a means for conflict)	Other Important Characters Include Friends, Siblings, Parents
Legend	June	Day (Daniel Alton Wing) The Primo Elector's son	Metias (brother, murdered) Thomas (friend turned enemy)
Birthmarked	Gaia	*Leon Will and Peter (brothers in Sylum who are interested in Gaia)	Maya (baby sister) The Libbies (marginalized women of Sylum)
What's Left of Me	Eva/Addie	Devon/Ryan*	Hayley/Lissa Dr. Lyanne (ally) Henri (foreign reporter)
Ashes	Alex	Tom Wolf (Chris)	Ellie (younger girl) Wolf dog
Eve	Eve	Caleb* Charles (father's employee)	Arden (friend from school and then leader of the resistance).
Enclave	Deuce	Fade* Stalker (conflict and misunderstanding)	Momma Oakes (adopted mother) Tegan (rescued)
The Darkest Minds	Ruby	Liam (Lee)*	Charles (Chubs) Zu (younger girl) Vida (frenemy) Cole (Liam's brother)
Dustlands	Saba	Jack (Seth) DeMalo Tommo (estranged son of DeMalo, teen with crush on Saba)	Lugh (brother) Emmi (sister) Auriel (shaman) Maev (leader of the Free Hawks)
Cinder *Scarlett* *Cress* *Winter*	Cinder Scarlett Cress Winter	Prince Kai Wolf (Alpha Kesley) Carswell Thorne (outlaw) Jason (royal guard)	Iko (Cyborg friend)

Book/Series	Protagonist	Love Interest and Boy as Consciousness* (There is often more than one love interest though mostly as a means for conflict)	Other Important Characters Include Friends, Siblings, Parents
Shadows Cast by Stars	Cass	Bran (son of chief)	Paul (brother) Madda (mentor)
Orleans	Fen de la Guerre	None or Lydia (leader of the O Positives; dies giving birth to Baby Girl).	Daniel (tourist and scientist from the Outer States) Baby Girl (Enola)
The Summer Prince	June	Enki* (but it's more complicated)	Gil (best friend) Babel (rival/frenemy)

Boys are often a key that unlocks the body of the Girl on Fire as much as her mind. In The Hybrid Chronicles, Devon/Ryan (and their sister, Hally/Lissa) help Eva gain the ability to use the body she shares with her sister, Addie. More importantly, they give Eva a sense of self and individuality. She has to learn to be responsible and accept her shared existence. So does Addie. They negotiate head space, body control, relationships, choices, and beliefs. In *Shatter Me*, Juliet, who has been locked up after accidentally killing a child she was trying to help, has been isolated and untouched for years. Adam is the first person who has made her feel like something other than a monster. "I try to understand the confidence he has in who he thinks I am and realize his reassurance is the only thing stopping me from diving into a pool of my own insanity. He's always believed in me. Even soundlessly, silently, he fought for me. Always" (177). After Warner tries to test Juliet's skills, Adam tries to convince her that she is not a monster and confesses his love. "He's kissing away the pain, the hurt, the years of self-loathing, the insecurities.... The intensity of our bodies could shatter these glass walls" (175).

In *Eve*, boys are alien. After being segregated from men for over a decade, she notes that men are "strange and unfamiliar creatures ... so much taller and broader than women. Even their gait was different, heavier..." (39). And when she finds herself living among boys who are segregated in similar and different ways, Eve realizes that her education has been skewed: "Sometimes it seems like all the things I need to know, I don't. And all the things I do know are completely wrong" (142). She can see how her life—and even her self—may have been different in different circumstances: "Maybe here, in this dugout, away from Teacher and the lectures, the book would be different. Maybe I'd be different" (143). Her eye opening begins with a rebellious girl in her school, Arden, but her education in the ways of the world and the lies of her upbringing are certainly stoked by Caleb. She recognizes what she learns from Caleb and why this knowledge is so important. "My real education had begun with Caleb. I felt as if I was only getting started; the truth was something I couldn't yet imagine" (246). And Eve is an interesting example because she must kill her father and act as a leader when she thinks that Caleb is dead. Of course, he is not dead. He is her happy ending.

In *Delirium*, Alex is a similar source of information for Lena. Together they plan their escape, but Alex is captured. Later, they are awkwardly reunited. In *Enclave*, Fade plays a similar role. When Deuce gets kicked out of the enclave and is doomed to death, he helps her find the surface and survival. In *Under the Never Sky*, Perry reveals to Aria her heritage and where she fits in among the Savages with special abilities. In *Matched*, Ky shows Cassia his story through writing and art (in a kind of graphic novel) and unravels the world she knows and the future that she has imagined for herself. He teaches her how to write, and further unlocks her critical consciousness. In *The Darkest Minds*, Liam is Ruby's rock and reminds her: "Now isn't the time to change yourself to fit into the world.... You should be changing the world to accept you. To let you exist as you are, without being cut open and damaged" (234). For June, in *Legend*, Day models the impact a prodigy can make, and when he is beaten down by the power structure, June must do the fighting for both of them. All of these relationships are challenged by doubt and insecurity as much as the dystopic conditions they are forced to navigate. But, in the end, their love endures and there is space to explore a new version of their relationship in a new world—except for June in *The Summer Prince*. Her love affair with Enki is not simple (her best friend, Gil, is also in love with Enki and has his own affair); it is not enduring (Enki is sacrificed by the Hegemon). Enki upsets June's privilege and challenges her sensibilities. But, in the end, a part of Enki lives on through the city that June now leads so her relationship continues in a new way.

The powerful role that boys play as consciousness is not to say that the Girl on Fire does not sometimes see the truth for herself without the help of the boy. And, certainly, once she has a different perspective a lot of the pieces make more sense to her and she is able to figure out many things for herself. But, this plot line—as much as it might seem to simply reinforce heteronormative and patriarchal arrangements—captures a real socio-cultural phenomenon. Social scientists—as well as real-life Girls on Fire—have noted the ways in which men or boys have been a catalyst for their own development of oppositional consciousness. These may be interpersonal relationships or inspiration from artists, musicians, philosophes, and fighters. For instance, France Winddance Twine's study of "brown-skinned white girls" reveals that many girls did not identify as black or as something other than white until they went to college and began dating black men. Many of these girls had been isolated in adolescence, being passed over for dates in favor of their white friends. In college, they found people who shared their experience of systematic oppression and they found tools to help them see how their previous experiences had been shaped by racism. In life we get "brown-skinned white girls"—girls of color who are raised, socially and culturally as "white." YA dystopia also shapes Other girls as amalgams of unknown heritage and as defacto white, as well as defacto heterosexual. The boys make an impact. The boy raises consciousness, provides tools, gives unconditional support. The Girl on Fire shapes herself into a conscious being and social actor and she fights and finds her own way.

* * *

Personal experiences with oppression and privilege shape the lives and experiences of girls and shape the ways in which they develop critical and oppositional consciousness. For girls who experience privilege, something or someone is needed to shatter illusions, which can be painful as well as redemptive. The role of boys and men—of masculine challenges—are important to consider in addition to the role of feminist consciousness and female role models, accomplices, allies, and frenemies. The boys in YA dystopia— the boys that complement the Girls on Fire—may just be a new breed of men that challenge old markers and meanings. They are poised to change toxic masculinity, in part because they are often so brutally (and literally) beaten down by the Hegemon on a personal and political level. These stories illustrate that masculinity is flexible and boys, too, are sometimes conscious, sensitive, broken, brave, thoughtful, and complex. The Girl on Fire attracts the broken boy through her brokenness and her strength and ability to cope with, and even overcome this brokenness; she often keeps the boy from falling apart.

Gay makes a compelling argument about broken men (like Sandusky and like professional athletes more generally) and the damage they do to individuals as well as to our culture. She notes a story about a father who beat a man to death when he found this man sexually abusing his daughter. He was not charged. She argues that "broken men are everywhere...." And alongside these broken men are the "women who all too often become broken too. It's a spectacle in every way" (159). While Gay means this quite literally, she taps into a trend that YA dystopia's Girls on Fire challenge, and maybe even shatter. The broken men attempt to break their boys, and they almost do. But, those broken boys don't break the young women who love them. In fact, those Girls on Fire often heal the broken boys. Or, like Peeta and Katniss, they are broken by a bigger system and they console and heal each other. It is actually quite striking to track how frequently the love interest is a character who has been abused by their father (or mother), and how often this abused boy is beaten not only by their father figure, but also by the figure of political dominance—their father is often also the corrupt leader, the Hegemon who is killing citizens ruthlessly. He is not the protected son he might appear to be, like Maxon, the prince and soon-to-be-king, who hides the scars and welts from his father's beatings from everyone including his mother in The Selection series. When he shows America his back, he is revealing a very intimate part of himself. He has been beaten many times before he takes a beating for her rebellious actions. The hidden marks show his strength and humility as much as his powerlessness.

In *The Hunger Games* Peeta is beaten and emotionally abused by his mother; in *Catching Fire* he is abused by the games again, and in *Mockingjay* he is abused and brainwashed by the Capitol. In *Birthmarked*, Leon is abused by his father. Tobias (Four) in the Divergent series, is beaten and emotionally abused by his father, so much so that Marcus is one of his four fears. In Eve, after a childhood of forced labor, Caleb barely survives repeated beatings and may not walk again. In the Darkest Minds, Liam has been abused by his father, but also mentored and supported by his stepfather. In *Shadows Cast by Stars*, Bran is so brutally abused by the men who capture his father and steal his father's spirit that he is a shell of his former self and Cass barely recognizes him. And the list goes on. Is this because a boy who has been physically beaten and emotionally scarred has the capacity to see the hypocrisy of the power structure better from his vantage point? Does it make him more vulnerable? Does it excuse his sometimes rash behavior, his inability to open up to the Girl on Fire who so readily offers her love? Or, his abundance of love in the face of her indifference or indecisiveness? Does he love so loyally because he is made whole by the Girl on Fire?

The dystopic conditions that Girls on Fire survive are often enough to oppress the characters of YA dystopia, but the boys have the added layer of physical and mental and emotional abuse in far more frequency than the Girls on Fire. The Girl on Fire has the power of feminist consciousness-raising behind her; she is strong. The Boy as Consciousness cannot live up to the expectations of patriarchy and violent masculinity that are so often modeled to him. He often refuses to play the game, or finds another game. Are these boys shielding Girls on Fire from this harsh aspect of reality? Sometimes they quite literally do act as shield, as protector or as sacrificial lamb. But, most often, the love interest is solid, unwavering in his love and devotion. Comparing Peeta to Gale (who does not even get a modicum of her attention), Roxane Gay notes, "Peeta, on the other hand, is everything. He frosts things and bakes bread and is unconditional and unwavering in his love, and also he is very, very strong…. Peeta is a place of solace and hope, and he is a good kisser" (138). He is also a symbol of a hopeful future—the dandelion. The Boy as Consciousness is, perhaps, even more powerful when he is sacrificed, which rarely happens. When it does, like Enki in the *Summer Prince*, even killing him cannot contain his power as Boy as Consciousness. He lives on as a part of the City.

Girls on Fire as Girlfriends

At their best, feminists argue for an importance of fostering female friendships, especially in the face of a culture that fosters competition between females that begins in girlhood and continues into womanhood. I originally found Roxane Gay's book, *Bad Feminist*, through "How to Be Friends with Another Woman." This chapter is a list of more than 13 points—sometimes humorous; always insightful. The second item on the list reads "A lot of ink is given over to mythologizing female friendships as curious, fragile relationships that are always intensely fraught. Stop reading writing that encourages this mythology" (47). If only it were so easy.

It is also easy to see the "specific formula" that Ann M. M. Childs identifies: "the female protagonist is pulled into rebellion by a best friend only to abandon her female friend for heterosexual love, succeeding in creating hope while the hopeless consequences befall her friend" (200). Childs argues that this pattern "endorses sexism in terms of the way female characters relate to one another, implicitly accepting rather than challenging society's preconceptions of female friendships as intrinsically shallow" (200). While Childs's argument erases the nuances of the specifics, she is certainly not wrong. I'd like to be able to point to Girls on Fire as triumphant leaders in this realm of female friendship, but these texts—like our real world—are more limited. Even so, an exploration of female friendships reveals deeper aspects of these texts, and the nature of female friendship. We can look, again, to Olamina for perspective. When she is first developing Earthseed, and she dares to speak to her best friend about preparing for survival outside their walled home, her friend betrays her and tells her mother. Lauren's father sternly cautions her against talking about her ideas, but they do negotiate some ways to educate the community without scaring them. Later, Olamina develops friendships with women like Zahra and Allie. She appreciates their council, but she always keeps some distance through her role as the leader of Earthseed.

Some Girls on Fire are girlfriends to male friends who are their best friend—like Katniss and Gale in the Hunger Games and June and Gil in *The Summer Prince* (and Tally and Ruby Iyer)—but most girls don't have very many friends in the first place. Saba and Cass have brothers as close friends; Saba's brother (Lugh) is controlling while Cass's brother (Paul) is haunted by the dead. Many are isolated from other girls by circumstance or choice. For instance, Nadia avoids people generally as a result of her ability to remember what she witnessed when the last Forgetting happened. Gaia is an outcast with a friend who won't be seen with her in public. Katniss spends her spare time in the woods with Gale, but she has a connection with the Mayor's daughter, Madge. When Madge was left out of the films, the possibilities of what Madge's friendship might mean are erased.

Friendships with younger girls are often easy for Girls on Fire, perhaps because they can play the role of protector. Katniss and her love for her sister helps spark friendship with Rue. Ruby develops a friendship with Zu, who chooses not to speak until Vida helps her tell her story. Alex with Ellie. Nadia with her younger sister. Many of these younger girls offer levity in tense situations and an overall love and support; they are protected by their older sisters but they also offer these sisters a source of support. Without these younger girls, Girls on Fire are more independent; these girls make them vulnerable because they can be used as leverage against Girls on Fire.

Some girlfriends are "Girls as Consciousness." In *Eve*, Arden is the impetus for Eve's initial questioning. When a girl on fire has seen behind the curtain, through the fog, she can no longer be the same. Arden, a girl who came to school later than the others, has seen through the veil and she knows what fate the girls wait for. Arden is rebellious and doesn't fit in. She plays pranks that can be mean and cruel at times, and she isolates herself as she talks about the parents that wait for her in the City in the Sand. (Later we find out there are no parents; these were only stories.) When Eve finds Arden preparing to escape the day before graduation, she confronts her and finds out the truth. Women are considered sows. Eve sees this for herself before she escapes and she and Arden find each other outside the school. When Eve compromises their position, Arden distracts the soldiers so that Eve can escape. Eventually, Eve realizes that she has to help to free her friends from their inevitable reproductive slavery. Arden, it turns out in *Rise*, is the rebel leader. She is not just the rebellious girl from school; she is a force in the transformation of society.

Cinder's friendship with Iko's artificial intelligence across different bodies is largely based on Iko's unwavering loyalty. In fact, Iko is Cinder's only friend. Kayla surrenders her cure to Mishalla who has always been steady and loyal. Tris and Christina stand up for one another when targeted by the Dauntless bullies, and later have a falling out when Tris inadvertently kills her friend, and Christina's boyfriend. Eventually, Christina forgives her enough to establish a new friendship. Some Girls on Fire alienate their friends, like Charlie in *The Essence* after she becomes queen. Other girls are separated from their girl friends by circumstance, like Lena and Hana in *Requiem*. At the end of the novel, Lena tears down the wall while Hana wanders aimlessly away from the life that was arranged for her.

The frenemy is also present in some of these books, like Babel in *The Summer Prince*. She is June's competitor for the Queen's award and June can't help but dislike her. However, she and Babel develop an understanding when Babel tells her that competing with June makes her work harder and create art at her best. In The Chemical Garden series, Rhine and her co-wives help each other; they have lost everyone and everything and have little life left to look forward to. In the Darkest Minds series Ruby is forced to work with Vida, and eventually they develop what could be called a friendship, offering unsolicited advice and support as well as an occasional reality check. Later, when Ruby is struggling with who she is and what she has become, Vida assures her that she is different from the other Oranges, that the very evidence is that she is questioning herself and how she goes about using her mind-control abilities. "The key difference," Vida tells her, is that "you are *not alone* ... even if it feels that way sometimes. You have people in your corner, who care about you like crazy. Not because you forced them to feel that way, but because they want to" (*After Light* 373–4). Ruby can trust Vida to tell her the truth and this frenemy is part of a group of friends and Ruby's support system.

What's Left of Me is more complicated by bodies shared by more than one personality. Addie has carried Eva around with her and they have shared many aspects of life; when Eva starts wanting autonomy, the two clash. Even so, they realize their shared dependence and partnership and learn how to navigate by sharing life. In *The Interrogation of Ashala Wolf*, Ember and Ashala work together closely even as they disagree on what approach is best for changing their world. The second and third books in the series focus on Ember and Georgie. They are a trio of friends and comrades and a part of a bigger Tribe.

Many friendships are close, developed over a lifetime. Friendships give girls support, comradery, a sounding board, a companion, but the possibility of female friendships is limited by the structures of a culture that pits women and girls against each other in a variety of ways. *Beauty Queens* offers the shining example—a diverse group of girls forced to live and work together toward survival. The novel itself constructs a story without a lone protagonist. While Alina is a central character connecting other characters, and Taylor is the (self-appointed and later elected) leader, each girl has her own story line. Within the story friendships, alliances, competition, and stereotypes are played with and re-imagined. The girls are all, in a way, searching for themselves and the island provides the perfect backdrop. As explored in chapter four, disaster becomes an opportunity to re-make the world.

Among the diverse girls of *Beauty Queens*, rivalries become friendships like when Shanti and Nicole start out as rivals as the only two girls of color in the pageant survivors and Nicole notices "the only other brown girl was giving her an eyeful of attitude" (14). Shanti's sharp competitiveness bucks up against Nicole's desire to be something other than the sassy black sidekick.

For Shanti, "it was as if she were in constant competition with herself./ But she couldn't control everything" (74). Shanti knows that "the Top Five would never hold both a black and brown contestant. No matter what they claimed, the pageants were not multicultural-friendly" (74). These realities of racism exist in the pageant world, an extension of our manufactured mainstream world of comfortable difference, but the girls make friendships outside of these rules and expectations. When they are both neck deep in mud, staring their impending deaths in the face, they bond and co-self-rescue themselves, forming a new bond.

Even when some of the girls are upset and feel betrayed by Petra's "not technically a girl. Yet" (106) secret, they are more upset about being lied to and breaking rules from the pageant than they are about Petra's penis. In fact, Mary Lou comes to Petra's defense, saying that there is "no specific rule against a transgender contestant" (107) and Adina, Nicole, and Jennifer band together before Taylor settles it with a vote. Democracy in action.

Even when reality TV pirates land on the island and the girls scramble to share the razor and shave their legs, there are no cat fights or desperate attempts to gain the attention of the boys. The relationships that develop are as diverse as the girls themselves. Adina gets tricked by a "casanova" even as she fully and freely engages in sexual intercourse with him. When he tries to apologize later, she is unforgiving. Some of the girls simply make new friends or possible future connections like Nicole and one of the pirates, Ahmed. And the most masculine, most powerful pirate, Captain Bodacious himself is a new breed of man—one who loves Petra's former boy band and loves her for who she is. He is well-read, obnoxious, and open-minded. Petra wanted "her chance to compete like any other girl, to make a statement to the world that there was nothing wrong with her, that she was beautiful through and through" (105). Rather than have to hide who she is and compete for an arbitrary title, Petra is able to make this statement through heterosexual romance—ground zero of female competition.

Beauty Queens on Fire

Beauty Queens demonstrates the ways in which girls can work together and establish friendships even in competitive environments. Most importantly, this book showcases a diverse cast of characters that play with and challenge stereotypes.

Girl on Fire	*Diverse Characteristics*	*Example*
Adina Greenberg, Miss New Hampshire	Jewish, wants to be a journalist. Sarcastic and cynical. Bass player in a punk band. Jaded by her mother's five marriages. Joined the pageant	Adina realizes that with each new husband her mother "was really trying to fill in the sketchy parts of herself and become somebody she

Girl on Fire	Diverse Characteristics	Example
	to take it down from the inside.	could finally love. It was hard to live in the messiness and easier to live in the dream. And in that moment, Adina knew she was not her mother after all. She would make mistakes, but they wouldn't be the same mistakes. Starting now" (375).
Taylor Rene Krystal Hawkins, Miss Texas	Miss Texas, daughter of a military man, abandoned by mother when six years old. Determined to win Miss Teen Dream in her last year. Self-appointed leader and general bad-ass. Proficient with guns, martial arts, and gymnastics.	"I was voted Most Likely to Rule the World in a Scary Way. But I am used to dealing with petty jealousy" (201).
Petra West, Miss Rhode Island	Former Boyz Will B Boyz! band member, J.T. Woodland. Transgender. Mother's cancer and manager's embezzlement left her family broke. Entered the pageant with the support of a transgender rights group (Trans Am) to make a statement and to get money for her surgery.	"I'm not in drag! This is who I am" (100). "She'd wanted her chance to compete like any other girl, to make a statement to the world that there was nothing wrong with her, that she was beautiful, through and through and through" (105–6).
Sosie Simmons, Miss Illinois	Hearing impaired, loves to dance, doesn't define her sexuality, but is attracted to people rather than gender.	"She figured out early that nobody liked an angry disabled person" (136). "When she was dancing, Sosie felt as powerful as a superhero. Her body did what she wanted it to without her having to say a word" (139).
Jennifer Huberman, Miss Michigan	A lower class, lesbian, "at risk" teen. Good with mechanics and electronics. Loves comic books. Joined the pageant when a guidance counselor suggested it. The first and second place girls were unable to continue so Jennifer found herself in the Miss Teen USA pageant.	"She knew what they thought when they saw her: Trash. Wrong side of the tracks. Dyke. Juvenile delinquent. Rehabilitation project…. No one expected anything from girls like Jennifer, except for them to drop out, get pregnant, fuck up" (121).

Girl on Fire	Diverse Characteristics	Example
Nicole Ade, Miss Colorado	The only black girl in the pageant. Wants to be a doctor. Joined the pageant for the scholarship money and to make her mother (a former Lakers Girl) happy. Haunted by the place of the sassy black sidekick stereotype.	"Nicole hated that she could never quite feel like she was just herself, just Nicole, but she was somehow representing an entire race. That's how they saw her, as a 'they' and not a 'she'" (48).
Shanti Singh, Miss California	Indian American. Wants to be a scientist. Entered the pageant because she had won everything else and wanted a challenge. In a search for "likeability" she creates a personality: an "American underdog," a "happy assimilation story" (76).	"I'm not Indian enough for Indians and I'm not American enough for the white people. I'm always somewhere in between and I can't seem to make it to either side. It's like I live in a world of my own. ShantiBetweenLand" (191).
Mary Lou Novak, Miss Nebraska	On the surface, a nice, respectable, mid-western girl. Under the surface, a wild girl, an independent girl (runs in her family). A vegetarian. Contains herself through distraction and her "purity ring." Finds love with a native of the island who accepts her as she is.	"She did not want to follow her mother's advice and sleepwalk through the days. Was it really so terrible to be a wild girl? Could it be any worse than lying about yourself?" (169). "All those things she'd been taught about feeling shame were wrong. It was not a curse to fully inhabit your body. You were only as cursed as you allowed yourself to be" (173).
Tiara Destiny Swan, Miss Mississippi	Participated in her first pageant when she was two weeks old. Insists that her parents are acting in her best interests. Not the sharpest, but struggling to find herself after a lifetime of being controlled and abused on the pageant circuit.	"Don't tell anybody, but sometimes, I just don't want to sparkle" (145). "I've learned that feminism is for everybody and there's nothing wrong with taking up space in the world, even if you have to fight a little bit" (335).

Miss Alabama, Brittani Slocum, is often confused with Tiara, Miss Mississippi; they look alike and make innocent/ignorant remarks often. Miss New Mexico, Miss Ohio, Miss Arkansas, and Miss Montana also play roles, but they have only their pageant titles, not first names or back stories.

Regardless of the competition all around them, the girls establish friendships and working relationships. The story shows that not only can women get along, they can also collaborate, lead and follow, disagree, build things, remain friends after break ups, create a society and more, when given the opportunity. A conversation about what they would really say if they could speak their minds turns to make-overs (which Adina wants to dismiss) which turns into plans for Girl Con, an event with "wicked cool workshops—writing, film, science, music, consciousness-raising" (152). Based on all they accomplished on their island, the girls imagine what they could do in the real world. Nicole says, "'It will be like we proved ourselves, like all those heroes' journey stories about boys, only we're girls" (154). And, in the end, after escaping gun fights, bombs, a ruthless dictator, a power-hungry politician who is a former beauty queen, an inept Corporation agent, and more, the girls get a final curtain call—one of their making, showcasing their talents as well as their accomplishments. The ending is one of solidarity as the girls all rush the stage: "It is a delightful chaos of bodies.... Everyone contributing something ... leaning into one another in affection as much as support, a great chain of girl" (389). As they are captured in a final image, they are leaping as one: "mouths open, arms spread wide, fingers splayed to take in the whole world, bodies flying high in defiance of gravity, as if they will never fall" (390). And they won't because they hold each other up.

Six

Othered Girls Toward Intersectional Futures

Interdisciplinarity assumes a degree of intersectionality, but it does not necessarily assume a critical stance that interrogates race, class, gender, and sexuality or white supremacy, patriarchy, or capitalism. Intersectionality asks us to look beyond identity to consider the ways in which the individual and the structural are connected. Considering the work of Patricia Hill Collins, Dill and Zambrana explain that intersectional analysis "is characterized by the following four theoretical interventions":

> (1) Placing the lived experiences and struggles of people of color and other marginalized groups as a starting point for the development of theory; (2) Exploring the complexities not only of individual identities but also group identity...; (3) Unveiling the ways interconnected domains of power organize and structure inequality and oppression; and (4) Promoting social justice and social change by linking research and practice to create a holistic approach....

While most YA dystopia struggles with the first two theoretical interventions, the third and fourth are hallmarks of YA dystopia. Each book unveils and often dismantles "interconnected domains of power" and promotes social justice and social change. If we can do better to start with stories that illuminate "lived experiences of people of color" and consider how these stories speak to groups, we can better tap into the power and potential of YA dystopia's Girls on Fire.

In "What Scout Wished For? An Intersectional Pedagogy for *To Kill a Mockingbird* and *The Hunger Games*" Heather Hill-Vásquez explains, "recognizing that many elements of identity and experience function together in a given situation, intersectionality explores the ways in which these elements—including, importantly, forms of oppression—interact" (16). Oppression points to the structural as well as the impact on the individual. She continues, "An intersectional approach can thus also reveal how one form of oppression may be connected to another, such that ideas, perceptions, and mindsets about groups and/or individuals my overlap in who is oppressed and how" (16). We must not, however, practice what Roxane Gay (and others) have called the "Oppression Olympics." We are all in the same boat, so to speak. But there is a major problem with this boat. As Ytasha Womak explains in her book about Afrofuturism,

> It's one thing when black people aren't discussed in world history. Fortunately, teams of dedicated historians and culture advocates have chipped away at the propaganda often functioning as history for the world's students to eradicate glaring error. But when, even in the imaginary future ... people can't fathom a person of non–Euro descent a hundred years into the future, a cosmic foot has to be put down [7].

YA dystopia also chips away at the propaganda that functions as the future. This cosmic foot is still trying to find its ground. And it can be complicated.

Donna Haraway's "A Cyborg Manifesto" speaks to what a future might look like if we were formed in a different social reality: "gender, race or class consciousness is an achievement forced on us by the terrible historical experience of the contradictory social realities of patriarchy, colonialism and capitalism" (296). This historical experience is an individual and collective endeavor and is connected from generation to generation. However, patriarchy, colonialism, and capitalism are not natural. They are not the only systems that might exist in the future; and if they do exist, they will likely be different. Maybe gender, race, or class consciousness will no longer be a "forced achievement." Perhaps there will be more freedom or new challenges. Changing the "terrible historical experience" might be possible, at least YA dystopia lets us believe so.

While I have argued that all Girls on Fire are "Othered" in some way, and while I have illustrated many intersectional futures, there are particular aspects of popular books that strongly point toward intersectional futures. More, there are many less-well-known books that take intersectional futures as the starting point for the worlds the author creates. These lines are blurry and they are blurred through competing interpretations by readers and critics; but the ways in which authors, characters, and stories challenge the narrow ideas and ideals of race and sexuality in the future, are worth a closer look. Further, the ways in which Othered Girls on Fire negotiate community and fight from their position of oppression is an important contribution to the genre and to our visions of the future.

Love and Romance as Sex and Sexuality

In an age when sexual attitudes are loosening, gender identities are flowing, and sexual identities are exploding, the tired tropes of virginity that

Seifert critiques might not be the only meaning that we extract from our favorite stories.[1] "Sex-positive literature" is described by Seifert as "YA novels with characters who engage in sex but do not represent fetishized ideas about virginity" (119) and "actively works against" (120) these tropes. Sex-positive literature presents "girls who have multiple physical, emotional, and intellectual qualities that make them attractive and interesting" (120) and features a "range of intimacies" including "first-time" sex that is "not just intercourse" (120). These are also characteristics of many YA dystopian novels; we just have to look deeper into the "popular"—and beyond the popular.

Sex-positive literature is not popular because "complex portrayals are simply less accessible and maybe even less enjoyable than books that follow our accepted sex scripts" (Seifert 139). And, the "fantasy world" that these books help us to inhabit can still be complex. They are not so didactic, perhaps. They leave room for interpretation. But, as Seifert argues, and cites Campbell, critical reading/deep reading is necessary to fully understand these YA novels in their richness (152–3). "Scholars, educators, parents, and readers alike bear the responsibility" of giving their youth the tools to read "against the grain" (154). If we consider how ideas about sex and sexuality that counter mainstream's narrow definitions can change the ways in which we read sex and sexuality in these books, we can begin to show the value of such "against the grain" readings.

In many ways, in these books romance is a stand-in for sex and sexuality. But romance is also a marker of self and identity. In Rachel Hills's journalistic study of sex, and the ways in which Millennials navigate within and around "the Sex Myth," she shows how much sexuality has come to define "the essence of who we are" and how "normality is the barometer" (55). Hills argues that "it's time to forge a new brand of sexual freedom, a freedom that incorporates the right *not* to do as much as the right to do" (214; original emphasis). But Hills's argument should not be misunderstood as a return to outdated morals. Instead, she is arguing for "the ultimate freedom" where sexuality is only one part of "the puzzle of who each of us is, instead of the load that defines us" (214). Many of our female protagonists are able to embrace this kind of multidimensionality, but many are able to embrace this because their sexuality is underdeveloped and adheres tightly to accepted norms. Lust, passion, desire, desperation, are often described in detail and sometimes proceed beyond passionate kissing. And there is almost always passionate kissing.

A kiss (or many kisses) is standard in almost every novel and there is almost always a "hot" scene when that kiss finally happens. Katniss may have performative and confusing kisses, but other girls surrender themselves to the kiss. Lena gives into the feelings despite her fear of disease. Ruby kisses Liam to put herself back together. And some examples are like in *Winter* when Cinder's cyborg brain keeps track of the number of times she and Kai kiss. She eventually disables this function and stops keeping track. The power of the kiss in *After Light* speaks to the power of the Girl on Fire. When Ruby wiped Liam's mind of memories of her and them in *The Darkest Minds*, she could not remove the emotions attached to those memories. He was basically torturing himself trying to remember why he loved her so completely, but he could not remember why. When they are united, he feels like he is going crazy; he is terrified. Ruby has a kind of Prince Charming effect on Liam when her kiss—or their kiss—causes her to almost inadvertently return his memories to him. At first the kiss is "hard" and "there was nothing gentle about it" (384). Ruby explains, "every thought in my head exploded to a pure, pounding white, and I felt the dark curl of desire begin to twist inside me, bending all my rues, snapping that last trembling bit of restraint" (384).

But then the kiss changes: "when I found him again, it was deeper, and softer, and sweeter. It was a kiss I remembered, the kind we used to have when it felt like we had all the time in the world, when the roads stretched out just for us" (384). When she gives into this feeling, she does so not caring if it makes her "weak, selfish, stupid, terrible" (384). As she remembers what it used to be like, she finds herself in Liam's mind, and when she realizes where she is, she realizes it is too late. Essentially, Ruby is in a state of such pleasure that she cannot keep her walls up. She cannot keep her control of the situation. She cannot continue to manipulate Liam into not knowing their past; she cannot keep him from the truth of their present and future, and his choice of where he wants to be.

Gaia, in the Birthmarked trilogy, Ruby in the Darkest Minds series, Cassandra in *Shadows Cast by Stars*, Aria and Perry in *Under the Never Sky*, Deuce and Fade in the Razorlands trilogy, and Saba in the Dustlands trilogy all have consensual sex. Saba is manipulated, but not unwittingly, while Gaia is a willing participant. Liam is patient with Ruby (the boys are always patient when waiting for permission to have intercourse), like Four is with Tris. Tobias and sex appear on Tris's fear scape, but that fear is bigger than a fear of sex. For Deuce, sex is something that she has been cautioned against. In her society, Hunters, Builders, and Breeders are the roles and only Breeders have sex, and only sanctioned sex. People don't really know their "sire" and "dam" and there are no families, only bratmates. She grants Fade "exclusive kissing rights," which is how she describes a romantic relationship.

While Deuce lacks information about "breeding" for a variety of reasons, this future-based ignorance speaks to the ignorance that exists in contemporary contexts, like schools that offer little to no sex education, which is often abstinence-only based. For instance, as Fade is working to overcome his PTSD, in his sleep he snuggles up to Deuce. She notes, "I was surprised by what he must be dreaming. Or maybe there was no mental aspect needed. For all I knew, males might wake up in the morning, ready to breed. I had very little information on such matters" (65). But, she has some sense. When he wakes, he says "Don't move.... I just ... need a minute." As she notes, "I took that to mean he was extremely interested in breeding, a fact I could confirm through our double set of blankets" (66). Before they go to war, they "breed." She says, "I don't want either of us to regret that we never did" (363). She even notes that "it hurt a bit, but I'd had worse" (365). (But before this she says, "I knew if I asked, he would stop," reinforcing the importance of consent.) To further emphasize the message of consent and safe sex, this series even includes discussion of birth control. As Momma Oaks explains, her "monthly" tells her she is not "breeding." Deuce continues, "I made a mental note to ask her how to prevent brats.... I wanted us to be ready when we had our own" (386). Deuce is planning for a future responsibly and Momma Oaks is happy to provide the information: "She startled me by providing the information in detail" (399). This is also information that Gaia provides to her communities in *Birthmarked* and *Prized*. These books challenge the silence around sex and encourage girls to be informed.

In all cases, these books make clear that these girls are *choosing* to have sex. After discovering Charles and Vida have been hooking up, Ruby notes: "If nothing else, this one thing—this one choice—wasn't made under pressure, or fear, or even desperation. It was something I wanted. To be as close to him as I could, with nothing standing between us. I wanted to show him the things my words were too clumsy, too self-conscious, to really convey" (415). The author makes it clear that Ruby's choice is her own and sex is a part of the narrative: "the overwhelming gratitude I felt that fate had given him to me ... left me unable to speak again. So I kissed him and told him that way, over and over again between breaths, as he moved over me, inside of me, until there was nothing in the world beyond us and the promise of forever" (416). End chapter.

In *Shadows Cast by Stars*, Cass lets Bran know that she does not need taking care of and that if he can't deal with that then he can just leave. She tells him she "wants [him] to stay, but only if we're equals" (229). Cass shoulders tremendous responsibility for herself, her family, and her community. She is up against patriarchal leadership structures and ancient powers of indescribable evil. Like so many Girls on Fire, she's an over-thinker. She doesn't let go; she can't. But when she is with Bran and she feels safe and free, when she is "floating naked under the sun, strangely unashamed" she tries to tell herself "*Don't think. Just feel*" (238). She is still caught up in her head: "I don't know this dance. I want to let go, to let myself feel him ... to give myself over, but I can't. Every muscle in my body is tense as I fight—not against Bran, but against myself" (239). When Bran reminds her "we can wait. There's no rush," she knows there is immediacy. She knows "that this is the moment" (239). And when Bran asks her to stop thinking, "just like that, for the first time in my life, I do. I stop thinking, and just feel" (239). This is a significant moment for Cass, perhaps the only moment in her story when she is free from her burdens and responsibilities.

These romanticized sexual encounters are not described in much detail, but it is very clear that they have heterosexual intercourse and that this is sex. In fact, passionate kissing may be more detailed and drawn out than sex. Further, the messages about love, sex, and romance aren't applied to all sex, but to the particular circumstances of the book. Girls can see examples of being treated with respect, of consenting to sex. Being allowed to consent to sex in our rape culture is rarely explored. We might consider that these novels do not reinforce virginity but redefine sex. Sex is no longer simply the heterosexual penetrative act that has defined it. Kissing is sex. Love in the midst of war, famine, or disaster is powerful resistance. Bill Clinton redefined sex. Millennials are redefining sex. Girls on Fire are navigating sex within the confines of strictly controlled and tightly defined realities, and the confines of the YA genre. Some Girls on Fire challenge these confines.

Sex Outside the Boundaries

While some of these Girls on Fire push the boundaries of what is acceptable sexuality, some protagonists—and some interpretations—reveal a more radical sexuality. Chris Donaghue describes this kind of sexuality in his book *Sex Outside the Lines: Authentic Sexuality in a Sexually Dysfunctional Culture*: "When you learn to have sex without limits, you will open yourself up to more options for sexuality and relationships, the ability to challenge current sexual categories, and finally, a liberation of your sexuality from shame. Authentic sexuality means that 'normal' is not the goal" (xii). Gaia feels shame for her scarred face, but not for her (veiled) sexual acts with Leon. Saba refuses to feel shame for her escapades, even when her actions might put everyone's lives in danger. She has sex with DeMalo despite how she feels about Jack: "I lose myself. In the touch of him, the taste of him, the smell of him, till I feel the moment when the edges of me start to blur. I let go. An I melt into the dark, blank heat" (341). She feels differently in the morning, but DeMalo is clingy and desperate, hardly the ruthless Hegemon: "You gave yourself to me, he says. And I gave myself to you. Freely. Not just our bodies, it's more than that. Much more. You felt it too. I know you did. We're going to be so beautiful together, he whispers. So perfectly beautiful. In our perfectly beautiful, perfect new world." Saba is part of his delusions of power; she knows this. When she explains to Jack, he tells her that he is in no position to judge her. She repeats her plan from earlier: "I ain't no soft girl. I don't know no soft words./ Be with me Jack. That's what I'll say. Burn with me.

Shine with me" (165). When she has a chance to say the words, the result is "and he does./He does" (423).

Donaghue further argues that "there is psychological brilliance in those who do not internalize cultural norms and instead create their own paths of growth" (6). One of the cultural norms in YA dystopia is the love triangle. Girls are often "prized" like Gaia in *Prized*, America and the other contestants in *The Selection*, Eve in the Eve series, and Saba in The Dustlands trilogy. But the love triangle is also challenged. In Ashes, Alex has a relationship with two boys. There is little promise of any individual surviving in their harsh world, but the relationship that Alex has with each boy speaks to a different aspect of her personality as well as her stake in the future. She loves Tom, but the monster in her head loves Wolf/Chris and she cannot exist apart from the monster in her head. Nor can the world survive without her monster. She balances these two boys like she balances the two worlds she lives in.

Brilliance is reflected in *The Summer Prince* though we might argue that the characters in this book have internalized cultural norms for their future dystopic society. As NPR reviewer, Petra Mayer, writes, "And how deliciously unusual to read a YA dystopia that's comfortable with ambiguity and nuance. This is a book that doesn't condescend. Gil, June and Enki find themselves having to tread carefully as they work out their own answers to a host of questions about love, art, technology, tradition—even sex." Johnson describes that her original thought was a "bisexual society" but that she would probably describe it now as "pansexual"; regardless, the "default was not straight" because she "wanted it to be more open" (class visit). Only *The Summer Prince* approaches sexuality from a space of liberation of sexuality and a new norm. For the reader—a product of our conflicted, damaging culture—the characters are creating "their own paths of growth" that inspire us. Sex and sexuality are far more open and ambiguous than in our own world. There seems to be no judgment, almost no taboos (though it seems problematic for June that Enki prostitutes himself for mods). During the course of the story she also exhibits independent sexuality when she pleasures herself. When Enki finds her, she is embarrassed not by her act, but by what she was thinking about—Enki. Even though June does eventually have a sexual relationship with Enki, and even though she is in love with him beyond her school girl crushes, June's story does not end with her place at Enki's side. Enki has chosen to die to give her power. Ultimately, she learns that love is much bigger, much wider, than most romance narratives will allow for—it's as big as a city and beyond.

* * *

Othered expressions of sexuality from masturbation to intercourse to same-sex relationships are scarce. Hills urges readers to "dismantle" the Sex Myth, to "cast off the stories and the symbolism, and let yourself be" (214).

This Millennial-friendly philosophy comes with a modicum of privilege and can be seen in the romance elements of YA dystopia as well as the Girls on Fire who "cast off the stories and the symbolism" that are propagated by heterosexual, quasi-monogamous, vanilla sex and sexuality in YA dystopia.

Exploring the sexual possibilities in texts like these are important to not only ferret out unintentional homophobia, but also to reveal the undertones that might be made into overtones through reader's interpretations, fan fiction representations, and future writers' less-closeted writings. Butler incorporates homosexuality into her novels through the suspicions that her brother, Marcus, is gay, and through Allie and Mary's relationship. She even admits that under different circumstances she might have fallen for one of the women she is recruiting to Earthseed. These are not central narratives, but they are important for showing how heterosexuality is not the overwhelming norm. It makes space for the marginalized to move toward or to the center.

Some popular books about Girls on Fire push up just against the edge of heterosexuality (perhaps unintentionally) and some fall short. Some attempts to interrupt heteronormative narratives are overt while others take some creative interpretation. While it may be too much to read sexual possibilities into some of the female friendships of these novels, these markers can actually be quite insightful. We can imagine alternate possibilities for our favorite characters. Henthorne notes, "Numerous writers of fan fiction also seem to find a queer subtext and build upon it…." and while most of this is centered on Peeta and other male characters, some "writers of slash fiction imagine a relationship developing between Johanna Mason and Katniss and some read Madge Undersee as having an unrequited love for Katniss" (54). We might see the undertones of the mockingjay pin that Madge gives to Katniss before she leaves for the games, a kind of pinning of the corsage, as a version of heterosexual prom traditions.[2] Of course, Katniss is going to her death, which she will fight for in the Hunger Games arena. Madge could have been another romantic choice for Katniss; at the very least she interrupts the love triangle.[3] In fact, there are many cues in Hunger Games that point to a sexuality that may not be heterosexual, which speaks to its power as a text. Nakia explains the ways in which Katniss is able to embody her shifting understanding of her own sexuality:

> When I first started questioning my orientation and as I went from struggling to acceptance, the types of books I needed shifted…. Having Katniss Everdeen represent my communities is an important start and while many people might argue that she doesn't count as canon representation because her orientations weren't explicitly defined in the books, she's consistently helped me feel not so abnormal.

Because Katniss and her sexuality (and her race and gender) can be read in multiple and even conflicting ways, there is more room for fictional characters and stories to provide ambiguity and room for exploration. Writing for *MTV*

News, Victoria McNally points out, "since the books first became popular, many members of the asexual and demisexual communities have embraced Katniss as a relatable hero for them to rally behind."

Perhaps most YA, generally, and dystopia specifically, is not ready to break the heterosexual mold and so flashes of Madge or a close female friendship stay undeveloped or under-developed. In *Delirium* and *Pandemonium*, the ways in which Lena's and Hana's friendship is described is in a similar language of love that the book uses to describe the way Lena feels about Alex, her mother, and her cousin, Grace. Further, in *Pandemonium* Lena describes Bram and Hunter: "In Zombieland, we would have called them Unnaturals, but here their relationship seems normal, effortless. Seeing them reminds me of pictures of Hana and me: one dark, one light" (67). While this could simply be a comment on their physical differences, the fact that this comparison comes in relation to Unnaturals underscores this aspect of Lena and Hana's close friendship. In *Requiem*, we get Hana's voice as she shares narration with Lena. Hana describes her friendship with Lena, asking: "Why were Lena and I best friends? What did we talk about? We had nothing in common. We didn't like the same foods or the same music. We didn't even believe in the same things./ And then she left, and it broke my heart so completely I could hardly breathe. If I hadn't been cured, I'm not sure what I would have done" (55–56). But this is post-operation. Hana is quick to explain that "I can admit, now, that I must have loved Lena. Not in an Unnatural way," (56) but as a reader, I don't buy her explanation. It almost feels forced when she describes her feelings about a boy she was getting to know before going forward with her cure, "the drop in my stomach whenever he looked at me" and "a hand on the inside of my bare thigh" (52). The way she describes how she feels about Lena is far more passionate: "my feelings must have been a kind of sickness. How can someone have the power to shatter you to dust—and also to make you feel so whole?" (56). As Hana escapes, after helping Lena escape, she wanders the streets alone; without Lena she is aimless, lost.

The relationship between Tally and Shay in the Uglies series is similar, but it takes on stereotypes that are insidious, if not unconscious, in its portrayal of Shay in relation to Tally. Shay comes across as mentally unstable and the potential relationship is unhealthy and obsessive on Shay's part, even without reading lesbian undertones. The implications, either way we read the relationship, are problematic. Both Tally and Shay are desperately lonely after their friends leave to either have surgery and become pretty, or run away to the Smoke. They become fast friends, literally and figuratively, as Shay teaches Tally how to hoverboard. After Tally has mastered the needed skills, Shay takes her to the Rusty Ruins. This all seems like thrill-seeking, especially when Shay takes Tally on the rollercoaster. But Shay is working hard to convince Tally that she should run away with Shay to the Smoke. Shay wants to go, the reader is told, because Shay is interested in David, but maybe she really wants Tally.

If we consider Shay as a lesbian, the book also takes on some interesting dimensions. First of all, if Shay were a lesbian, we get no clues in any of the books that this would be okay in this future society. Sex and sexuality are virtually invisible except as they manifest in the romantic/rebellious kisses that Tally shares first with David, and then with Zane. There are also hints that "sex" may be going on in the pleasure gardens or in the exploratory fun of new pretties, but these elements are left undeveloped. The YA genre's overall lack of engagement is a good excuse for such lack of development, but these are also missed opportunities.

There are some other markers that make Shay a character with, at least, a questioning sexuality. Shay has all male friends or at least no female friends of consequence until she meets Tally. Shay's bonding with Tally is around the tricks and pranks and adventures that can be found mostly by hoverboarding, but also include bucking the system and questioning what they have been told all of their lives about the world, past and present. When Tally gets to the Smoke she suspects that maybe Shay was interested in getting to the Smoke not only because she wanted a choice in her life, but also because she suspects Shay is romantically interested in David. But David is not a romantic crush, he is a symbol of freedom because he can only be himself. This is what Shay really wants—to be herself. This is an obvious interpretation, even if the book pretends Shay is distraught over being rejected. Shay is distraught, perhaps, because Tally has chosen David over Shay. She has lost a friend and an idealized vision of life away from the Pretty society.

Many aspects of these books expose Shay as a jealous girlfriend. In each of the books Shay and Tally have disagreements and arguments that mostly stem from Shay's obsession with Tally, but also could be explained by "irrational" female behaviors. Shay accuses Tally of stealing her boyfriend and she suspects Tally of being a traitor (which, of course, she mostly is). In the second and third books she accuses Tally of being selfish and having a huge ego. She is upset with Tally when she shares her cure pills with Zane instead of with her, even though Shay turned down the cure herself. Toward the end of the second book, after this betrayal, Shay takes up cutting as a way to cure herself. (The resemblance to contemporary trends of cutting are certainly worth further consideration.) And she uses this trend to start her own clique, and then to leverage more power (and more perception) as an elite branch of Special Circumstances. She then uses this influence to force Tally to become a Cutter and Tally is turned into a Special, mostly against her will. Shay makes Tally in her own image—not in the image of who Tally wants to be.

While Shay eventually finds her niche as a non-special Cutter in *Specials*, for most of the three books she is obsessive, emotionally manipulative, clingy, jealous, petty, and erratic. She fits many stereotypical aspects of repressed lesbian sexuality. However, it is unclear if this is a purposeful aspect of Shay's character and of the book series, or if this is simply a stereotypical representation of an adolescent girl that is based upon the author's knowledge of girls as developed through mainstream popular culture. Is the author (a man) simply depicting what he sees as being the nature of female friendship, or is he aware of the ways in which he has created a foil to the Girl on Fire that depicts repressed sexuality? Either way, Shay is a problematic representation of a female character. This dysfunctional female relationship undercuts the positive female relationships in these books. Further, it fails to imagine a relationship between Tally and Shay that is healthy, sexual or not.

* * *

Libba Bray, Nalo Hopkinson, Alaya Dawn Johnson, and Malinda Lo expand the possibilities of friendship, love, sex, and sexuality. In *The Chaos*, sex is talked about frankly and the protagonist navigates slut-shaming. At the same time, examples of sexuality outside of the confines of heterosexuality are clearly present in the novel. In *The Summer Prince*, polyamory, bisexuality, and openness about sex and sexuality are norms of the culture. In Malinda Lo's work, sex is part of a rather ordinary life made extraordinary by circumstance. In *Adaptation* and *Inheritance*, not only is non-heterosexual romance an element of the story, the negotiation of a three-way polyamorous relationship is part of how the female protagonist resolves her feelings between David and Amber. By the end of the story, David and Amber are dating Reese and the three of them have to figure out how their polyamorous relationship works—it's a new alien world as well.

In *Beauty Queens*, a range of sexual identities and opportunities exist alongside the diversity of the Girls on Fire more generally. Some of the girls engage in sex; some of them do not. For instance, Adina is struggling to make sense of her mother's inability to exist autonomous of her husband and, as a result, is now in her fifth marriage. Adina eventually lets her guard down with Duff, and a lengthy scene develops as she negotiates sex with him and the war of her body and mind (258). She finds herself enjoying the "surrender" (258) and insists on a condom, which Duff eventually locates after Adina shames him about how "uncool" pressuring someone for sex is (259). Adina is a fully present participant and notes "that she could be both completely vulnerable and totally in control was mind-blowing" (261). When she finds out that Duff had videotaped the encounter for his video diary on his reality TV show, Adina is furious—with herself as much as with him.

Sexuality outside of heterosexual norms is also explored through the relationship of Jennifer, an out lesbian, and Sosie, who "had crushes on both girls and guys" that were "person-specific infatuations" (174). When Sosie finds Jennifer's artwork depicting the Flint Avenger and her sidekick, Sosie asks Jennifer if she is gay and when Jennifer asks Sosie the same question, Sosie finds it "odd" that she "had to make some sort of hard and fast decision about such an arbitrary, individual thing as attraction" (174). The friendship that she has developed with Jennifer makes her sure of one thing: "she was, however, a Jenniferian. And so she leaned forward and kissed her" (175). While Jennifer reads this kiss as "a silent communication full of meaning" (175), Sosie's feelings for Jennifer eventually fizzle and she breaks Jennifer's heart. Later they re-establish a friendship that endures beyond the island.

For Mary Lou, sexuality is a secret she keeps and a feeling she tamps down with her "purity ring." While this symbol is seen as another means of controlling girls' sexuality by the cynical feminist in Adina, for Mary Lou, the ring is something that helps her keep control of herself: "she had taken the vows that were supposed to keep her safe from her own impulses and desires" (161) and her feeling that she is "too much for one body to hold" (163). While Mary Lou seems like she might be a self-righteous, middle-America stereotype, she is actually a wild girl, "the curse that had plagued women in her family for generations" (161). The control that Mary Lou's ring symbolizes in culture-at-large plays out righteously in her story line. Her mother's cautions had led Mary Lou "to be afraid of her own body" (161), but she discovers that her body is not something that she has to feel betrayed by. She does not need to be afraid that "the prince would never want a cursed girl like her" (167). When she meets Tane Ngata, ornithologist and eco-warrior (and of the native people who have been forced off the island), she finds a man who can love a wild girl. After he performs oral sex on her, she confirms that "all those things she'd been taught about feeling shame were wrong. It was not a curse to fully inhabit your body. You were only as cursed as you allowed yourself to be" (173). And Mary Lou gets her prince, after she rescues him, and they do live happily ever after—but she also gets to live her dream of being an "adventurer" and a "Pirate Queen" (384) and living "outside the rules" (158). Mary Lou wants to have it all, and since it's her story, she gets what she wants.

* * *

Cynics can write off the ways in which young love can impact political and cultural consciousness-raising, the ways in which boys and men have often been responsible for bringing out the "bad" in a "good girl." More so, boys and men are often the means of transgression from a life of superficial conformity. And more novels might begin to recognize the ways in which girls (and maybe women) can also be that catalyst. More novels might make space for Other versions, ideas, and ideals about love, sex, and sexuality in the future. More novels might make space. Period.

White Supremacy: Unshakable Structure?

The absence of race in dystopia reflects the unrealistic desire to ignore/minimize race in the present and is perpetuated by the largely white population of writers, editors, publishers, and readers in the U.S. Garcia and Haddix question the lack of diversity in literature "given the growing diversity of readers" and ask what this means for dystopian societies or for "societies that are unreal and imagined" (211). What is at stake when even our imaginations are limited by white supremacy?

An easy assumption to make in dystopia is that the people of the future U.S. are racially indistinguishable. Whether from racial mixing or from a changed system of racial hierarchies and categories of identity, we might assume that "race" is unimportant. And maybe race as we know it is unimportant; however, some other system will likely be in practice. Any "American" dystopia that does not account for racial dimensions to future identities, and does not weave this element into the story, is missing an important component. This erasure is a result of a contemporary mainstream culture where race if often assumed to be irrelevant, racism is thought to be over, and too many (mostly white) people think that racism supposedly only continues because people of color keep talking about it. Racism continues because it is embedded in our social, cultural, and political institutions.

The Forgetting creates a future scenario where the meanings of race from the past are most certainly erased. After all, every 12 years people forget who they are and how their world works. They have to re-learn all about themselves and their lives from the books that they keep on their bodies at all times. While not a lot of ink is spilled describing the physical attributes of characters in ways that show the visual diversity, when Nadia and Gray discover the knowledge that has been lost and scroll through the people who were chosen on earth to make the journey, it is clear that the people of Canaan were originally "diverse"; they were selected from all over the world. The result of 75 men and 75 women procreating for several generations (not to mention the confusion that happens during the Forgetting) has created a mix of people who are racially ambiguous in this future. They have no concept of racial difference; this was not an aspect passed down to them from their parents, their society, their culture, or even their home world. They are defined by their occupation or, rather, the occupation of their parents. Those without books, without a history, are The Lost, and they are essentially the slave population of the society. Janis created this class; it was not a part of their original settlement or its utopic vision. The many colors of people mixed together when the ethnic (cultural) ties were broken by Forgetting. But, it is not always so easy to forget.

Lavender argues that "science fiction is actually transmitting assumptions of racism even in stories that are ostensibly envisioning a future where race has become irrelevant" (20).[4] Certainly race can be woven in a heavy-handed way, an incomplete way, a problematic way, etc., but if we do not engage in race as an element of dystopian texts and criticism, then we are perpetuating old systems and structures. As Alaya Dawn Johnson notes, "one of the big problems going on with YA is that the vast majority of the writers are white and so the vast majority of the worlds are getting written from that perspective and they are not trying to get outside of it" (Gay YA). Getting outside of a white perspective requires a change to American culture and institutions. The future is open to a rewriting and reimagining of race. An awareness of what Hampton describes as the "complexities and contradictions embedded in our imaginations and employment of race" (182) is necessary to imagine new possibilities.

Just as "most of the people writing literature in America right now are white," (Gay YA) when scholars and critics consider dystopia, we often frame the lessons of race from the perspective of white America. Moylan explains, "Butler and other sf writers like her use sf to move us outside of our normal comprehension and allow us to see how race operates culturally. This kind of writing takes us beyond the scope of our ordinary experiences and forces us to mediate between what we already know about race and what we can learn about it by reading sf" (Scraps 22). While we can all grow from the opportunity to "move outside our normal comprehension," Moylan assumes that this allows us to see how race operates culturally. But people of color, and more generally people with critical consciousness, see this operation in every text. "Normal comprehension" is greatly limited by a plethora of cultural stereotypes, a lack of attention to race in educational contexts, and historical amnesia. "What we already know" is shaped by our racialized realities, what we are exposed to, and what we have the opportunity (or drive) to learn about. So, what "we" can learn about race and "what we already know" are conditional. If we assume Moylan is writing about what "we" white people can learn, he is arguing that we need science fiction to take us outside of the ordinary experiences of white supremacy, and into texts where race is engaged in a meaningful way rather than ignored, sublimated, whitewashed, or written out of existence. And he is right.

Texts that engage race in a meaningful and thoughtful way model what YA dystopia can be with more critical consciousness and critics that hold texts accountable for a lack of engagement with race in the future. But, of course, considering race and white supremacy is one aspect of a multidimensional, intersectional approach. We cannot ignore or dismiss race, as so many authors and critics are prone to do. Culturally conditioned readers most often assume that the character is white because we have been conditioned by ongoing cultural legacies that the default is white and cover art and promotional materials help paint that picture. We need to interrupt these assumptions and traditions. But we also cannot shrink our lens down to only consider race, at least not if we want a fuller picture of the texts and its multiple shifting and overlapping contexts. We may *assume* a character is white, but we can also *imagine* that she is not white. We can imagine different racial designations, categories, and meanings, as some YA dystopia authors do.

* * *

A variety of controversies surround the casting call for Katniss, the casting of Rue, and fans' interpretations of what their favorite characters should look like, as well as what those visual cues might mean in contemporary and dystopian contexts. It is complicated and difficult terrain. And difference is tolerated and celebrated to a point. Garcia and Haddix argue it is the "polite" and "politically correct" reading to claim that "a character's racial identity does not affect one's reading of a text" and that this kind of reading "maintains the hegemonic culture, where whiteness is the norm" (214). This hegemonic norm is a (problematic) "color blind" claim that could be used to argue for representations of race being defacto white. But as Garcia and Haddix remind us, it is not enough to acknowledge, we must also "attest to, speak up for, and challenge the absence of revolutionary images of youth of color" (216). We need to see the color that is there and think critically about what race means now and what it might mean in the future.

The Hunger Games is a prime example of the complexities of racial representation. Many readers did not read Katniss as white; they point to her olive skin and brown hair, her marked difference from the lighter skin and hair of her mother. Some fans were upset that the blond, fair-skinned Jennifer Lawrence was cast as Katniss, and some fans even have created alternative castings and fan art that depict Katniss as a girl of color. But in "The Revolution Starts with Rue: Online Fandom and the Racial Politics of the Hunger Games," Antero Garcia and Marcelle Haddix argue, "Rue's identity as a nonwhite, powerful woman are ignored by most readers and film goers" (216).[5] In the mainstream, Rue is not seen as the Mockingjay; she is often not seen as more than a version of Katniss's sister, Prim. Readers who refuse to see race might even imagine Rue is not black. Certainly there are many readers not paying attention to race because they have the privilege of imagining a "color-blind" world. Garcia and Haddix argue that the outrage over Rue's casting and rejections of "her skin color as anything but white" is precisely connected to the central role that she plays in the plot (212). They further argue that if Rue was marginalized, a background visual intended to prove there is "diversity" in the text (like many characters of color), then readers would not be so upset about her being black in the text and portrayed by a black girl in the film. As much as we can read race onto characters, in the case of Rue we don't need to. Collins already has. And online fandom has created spaces that read race into spaces where it has been whitewashed.

* * *

The physical books (and official websites) are one of the starting points for whitewashing. Considering the covers/art work of some key books illustrates the problems with representation at the first impression—the cover shapes our expectations. Annie Schutte argues,

> If a YA book features a white, female protagonist (and this accounts for a not insignificant portion of YA released each year), it seems inevitable that the book cover will display an idealized and airbrushed masterpiece of her on the cover. And when a YA book actually does have a protagonist of color, too often one of three things seems to happen: 1. The cover is "whitewashed" and shows a Caucasian model instead of a person of color; 2. The cover depicts someone whose race seems purposefully ambiguous or difficult to discern; or 3. The character is shown in silhouette.

Schutte illustrates these points through several examples with commentary. A survey done by Kate Hart illustrates this trend as well (Huffington Post). Analyzing 624 book covers from books published in 2011 "She found that 90 percent of covers featured a white character, 10 percent featured a character of ambiguous ethnicity, 1.4 percent featured a Latino/Latina character, 1.4 percent an Asian character, and 1.2 percent a black character." While covers are vibrant and colorful, they continue to perpetuate whiteness. Further, many YA books also have different covers for the adult market and the teen market as Garriott notes, "YA texts have become so popular for readers who do not identity as young adults, that popular YA texts are often republished with 'adult' covers ... [that] emphasize the either/or status of the young adult and adult, revealing our culture's reliance on easy categories" (245). Covers targeting adult audiences might be more ambiguous or symbolic, but some of these symbolic covers also perpetuate the ways in which girls and women are portrayed in popular media—in parts instead of as a whole. The cover of Cinder features her lower leg with an x-ray view that reveals her cyborg parts and the Uglies series includes a set of covers with up-close faces as well as a set that features parts—a face covered by a sheet, a leg, an eye. Beauty Queens highlights a sexy mid-section, perhaps the most common piece of girls and women to adorn pop culture images, but also undermines this symbol.

Many include symbols of white, fairy-tale fantasies like The Selection series—each a different, elaborate dress. Even though her class status signals and shapes her otherness in her story, America's signature red hair is the main element of difference projected from these covers where she is draped in luxury. Books where the protagonist is definitively described as being white, like Delirium, reflect a white identity clearly on the cover, often

Each cover of The Selection series features the same model in an elaborate dress. Shadow figures of the other girls who are a part of "The Selection," a competition to become the wife of Prince Maxon, haunt the background. The dress attracts readers and represents the role that luxury plays in this book, but it also masks the political aspects of the book—the commentary on class systems and brutal dictatorships (Harper Teen. Cover art ©2012 by Gustavo Marx/Mergeleft Reps, Inc. Cover design by Sarah Hoy).

through a close-up of a face. Some covers obscure the face and offer it in pieces like The Hybrid Chronicles which offers two faces in one image, an optical illusion used to represent the two souls of Eva and Addie. Other covers are misleading, like *Partials* where the protagonist is definitely not white, but the cover centers a rear-view of a girl with long dark hair and light-ish skin who may or may not be white. Many covers silhouette girls in a way that obscures racial identification like on the cover of *Partials* and to some extent, *Orleans*. Many covers avoid problematic racial representation because they are abstract or symbolic, like the Hunger Games series, the Enclave trilogy, and *Shadows Cast by Stars*.

Even when the image on the cover features a girl of color, assumptions of whiteness can happen. One of my students noted that she thought that the cover image of *Parable of the Sower* was a trick or featured another character. Even though a black woman is on the cover, she still thought the protagonist was white. In fact, many of my students read Olamina as white because they are white and they have been programmed to unconsciously default to white when they read. However, other covers like *Tankborn*, *The Interrogation of Ashala Wolf*, *Orleans*, and *The Summer Prince* celebrate the girl of color with less ambiguous covers. While book covers can be limited by the demands of marketing, there are some ways that fans and critics push back. Fan art, found on a wide variety of social media sites like Pinterest, Instagram, and Tumblr,

These three covers all present a clever optical illusion—a face that is two faces in one, which perfectly represents the Girl on Fire, Eva/Addie. Eva narrates the story and begins to gain equality in her body with her sister, the dominant soul. The covers show a dominant face and another that requires a closer look. Eva's story is the one revealed upon deeper inspection—the triumph of a Girl on Fire who grew from a flame that was supposed to expire (Harper [Harper Collins]. Jacket art © 2012 by Maxime Quoilin. Jacket design by Erin Fitzsimmons).

give fans space for imagination and some even challenge whitewashed racial representations.

Charts, lists, infographics, and search engines also reflect whitewashing. Katniss is only one girl—one female protagonist—in a body of work that allows for a diversity of girls. This diversity of girls is not always recognized in a selection of the most popular and accessible novels. Many infographics and flow charts can be found online to lead readers to dystopian books they'll be interested in. Search engines like Maine Marvel's NoveList Plus and www.literaturemap.com can also be used to find books like the Hunger Games or other popular books. One resource that was created by the YA librarians at the Lawrence (Kansas) Public Library "maps out the entire universe of hit YA fiction," explains Andy Lewis in his *Hollywood Reporter* piece, "If You Liked 'The Hunger Games' Flowchart Maps World of YA Fiction." Lewis explains, "The chart starts by asking to choose between a male or female narrator and then the choices branch off into fantasy, environmental disaster and futuristic before adding other categories like cloning, space and paranormal." The charts are limited and the flow does not fit with the split of male and female choices. The updated charts are better. There is no longer the choice of a male or female protagonist, perhaps because so many of these books are about girls. However, neither the original, nor the updated include any of the Othered Girls on Fire. Pinterest and other social media sites are full of "must read" and "if you like" collections of book suggestions—and after Trump's election lists like "Here Are the Books You Need to Read If You're Going to Resist Donald Trump" (Lee) and "Pop Culture Prepared Me: The Trumpocalypse" (Grossman-Heinze) began to appear—and few include Othered Girl on Fire texts.

Making YA dystopia more accessible to young readers is one of the goals of *What Should I Read Next?: 50 Dystopian Books for Teens,* an e-book by Kim Trujillo (who also writes religious guide books). This resource, provides a particular selection of works according to the author's tastes, which are biased toward stories with male protagonists. She is certainly upfront about this, providing a brief summary, a rating, and references to her favorite books. The author further reinforces the dominance of stories with male protagonists, tending to rate books with male protagonists (and/or more dominant male characters) higher and recommend more of these books as favorites. For instance, Trujillo remarks that Gaia (Birthmarked) seems too young to be a leader and one of the guys should have been the leader. Further, virtually none of her picks include characters of color or writers of color.

* * *

Many texts completely side step the question of race or ethnicity. Some offer small clues or distractions like Cassia Reyes, whose last name could give her Latinx roots, or like Saba whose dark features are compared to her brother Lugh, the golden boy: "If you seen me and Lugh together, you'd never think we was the same blood./ Never think we grew together in the same womb./ He's got gold hair. I got black./ Blue eyes. Brown eyes./ Strong. Scrawny./ Beautiful. Ugly./ He's my light./ I'm his shadow./ Lugh shines like the sun…" (3). This future is far flung and race does not exist in this future world; this physical difference may be only that of dominant and recessive genes. In *The Way We Fall*, however, Kae's physical difference is described but not attributed to racial difference, except in passing. For instance, she is described as "some girl with light brown skin" (221) and notes that this is "the first time [she's] outright wished [she] was the same color as just about everyone else on the island" (221). The full implications of what this means for the character are not explored.

Other books make small nods to differences of skin color, hair texture, or other tangible differences that are associated with race in contemporary America—most often in descriptions of non-central characters. For instance, Vida, in the Darkest Minds Series is described as having supermodel looks. Vida is "honest-to-God lovely, some perfect mix of ethnicities—her skin a glowing brown that reminded me of a warm autumn afternoon, almond-shaped eyes, hair dyed an electric blue" (*Never Fade* 26). Vida has "the kind of face you'd expect to see in a magazine: high, bold cheek bones and full lips that seemed always fixed in a small smirk" (*Never Fade* 26). Like Allison (in The Immortal Rules) who is described as "exotic," Vida's racial and ethnic difference adds to her beauty. And like many stereotypical roles for girls of color, Vida also has attitude.

A few YA dystopia texts overtly tackle the topic of race and its related topics. It should come as no surprise that the majority of these books tend to be less popular than texts that feature white protagonists (which are also texts that don't typically engage race). And many are written by women of color: *Orleans*, *The Summer Prince*, *Shadows Cast by Stars*, The Immortal Rules, Legend, *The Lost Girl*, and *The Interrogation of Ashala Wolf*. Garcia and Haddix "emphasize that public imagination often cannot see racialized life in young adult literature and [illustrate] how this genre can incite critically conscious identity formation for readers" (204). More diverse representations, more reflections of young people of color in meaningful, revolutionary roles is a start. Engaging with what race *looks* like in the future is one strategy.

Most books by white authors largely fail to engage with racial difference, and a few sprinkle in difference as an afterthought; however, minimizing race in the future in not just done by white people. Ignoring or minimizing race can be a strategy of assimilation or passing or a declaration of American identity. As I illustrate in "Othered Girls on Fire," Marie Lu does not embrace an ethnic identity for herself, she stakes an American one. She writes: "Day is an American who happens to look half-Asian. His race has absolutely no effect on his personality, actions, opinions, and preferences. I'm pretty sure I wrote him like this because *I* feel like an American who happens to be Asian." Lu's creation of her male protagonist, Day, speaks to a non-racialized "American" identity that Lu identifies as her own. She sees her physical Asian characteristics in Day and celebrates him as unique—in the way he looks and in the way he fights for freedom and justice. On the surface, this series includes diverse racial characteristics as well as what might be considered more progressive gender and sexuality. Lu writes in her blog,

> [T]here are two things about the Republic that are more utopian than our own society: 1) there is zero gender/sexuality discrimination, and 2) there is zero racial discrimination.... The Republic could care less what race or gender or sexual orientation you are. The Republic only cares what your *class* is. Misogyny, anti-gay bigotry, and racism are replaced here by severe class discrimination.

This is Lu's vision, but these elements are not replaced; they lurk in her text as well. Still, the story she creates pushes gently against the racial politics of our time. But what I read as overt integration of race—and imagine as a political act—is simply an exercise in general diversity. Lu explains,

> I think back on when I first created Day for *Legend*, and I honestly cannot remember thinking much of his race.... In hindsight, I'm a bit embarrassed that I thought so little about it, that at the time I knew almost nothing about YA or the issues of race/lack-of-PoC [People of Color] characters in the book world. It just ... didn't occur to me. I simply wanted a diverse cast with varied races and characteristics, for the same reasons that you might want a cast that don't all have brown hair or all have green eyes.

Lu's ignorance of "YA or the issues of race/lack-of-PoC characters in the book world" is disappointing. As I argue in "Othered Girls," Lu has every right to be an American, and to (re)define what it is to be an American. But what is her responsibility? What responsibility does an author of young adult literature generally, and dystopian literature specifically, have when it comes to representing a vision of the future where the violent realities and structured inequalities—as well as the empowerment, community-building, and consciousness-raising—of race, ethnicity, gender, and sexuality have not simply been swept away and replaced by simple visual diversity and less politically-charged fictional future struggles?

Some authors of color opt for white protagonists, but these texts often incorporate racial and ethnic difference in other important characters and more awareness of not erasing racial difference in the future. For instance, Kristen Simmons focuses her story around a white protagonist. Even with its sub-par plotting and character development and its heavy-handed lessons, it is difficult to fault the author when she writes in her acknowledgments

As demonstrated here, the covers of all three books in the Legend trilogy are austere and military-looking. They do not feature June, the Girl on Fire on the cover, perhaps because she shares the role of main protagonist with a male, Day. To show them together might unduly influence the reader's perception of the story, which includes romance but is not dominated by it. June and Day live in future Los Angeles and this cover speaks to the setting and tone of this militaristic dystopia (Speak [Penguin]. Cover design by Lori Thorn).

section: "And finally, thank you to the people who, in the face of hardship, fight. Who turn surviving into thriving. Because of you I now live stronger and wiser, with the knowledge that hope is working through us all, even in our darkest moments" (364). This optimism, spirit, and comradery is exactly why I love YA dystopia and this Asian American social worker/writer is exactly the kind of person we should hope will continue to write about possibilities of the future.

Like Malinda Lo and Marie Lu, Kat Zhang writes a female protagonist who is a rather ordinary white girl and saves the Others for her supporting cast. In her dystopia, anyone who looks "foreign" is suspect in a country with closed borders and a fear of difference. In other words, anyone who is not visibly white is suspect. Hally/Lissa and Devon/Ryan look foreign and this foreignness is vaguely connected to their father who would tell stories about the origins of the world. But a language other than English is just as suspect. Henri, a reporter from outside the Americas who has dark skin and African origins, also has a French accent. He does not speak unless behind closed doors. With the exception of Henri and the siblings, no other characters are described as looking "foreign" or with any descriptor that distinguishes them as not being white. We are to assume that after the Great Wars, the Americas closed their borders and that somehow all of the diversity that already existed in these spaces somehow disappeared? In short, the development of this scenario is less than fleshed out. As a result, the ways in which otherness is used in this novel is underdeveloped. In some instances it seems the author is making an argument against discrimination and oppression—this is the struggle of the hybrids, after all. But the argument is in the realm of vague arguments for freedom.

Malinda Lo's *Adaptation* also opts for a white female protagonist but offers a rare example of an overt critique of white privilege as her Girl on Fire, Reese (whose name could not be more white), considers race for the first time in her life. After she goes to a party with David, she realizes that she had never really thought about how many of David's friends are Asian just as she had "never thought of herself as white" (150). Reese clarifies, "It wasn't that she thought of herself as NOT white; she simply never thought about it. She realized that was probably the biggest sign of all that she was white" (150). This small example speaks to Reese's development of consciousness and an understanding of the importance of thinking about power and privilege in addition to thinking about race.

There are some exceptions to erasure or superficial hints or inclusion. For instance, two white authors—Karen Sandler and Dan Wells—feature race in their books. In the Tankborn series, Sandler uses the Indian caste system as a model for a future world where cyborgs have taken on some of the same discrimination of the lower castes in the racial hierarchy. Dan Wells creates a somewhat racially ambiguous character, Kira Walker, who later discovers her racial and ethnic heritage at the same time that she discovers her status as a Partial—a cyborg created, rather than born. Sandler's text is obviously a critique of racism, but it is more subtle. Partials, however, uses not only artificial life to comment on race, Wells also overtly identifies and condemns signs of racism that look like our contemporary examples. For instance, the prejudice that humans have against Partials is described as racism since "racism had all but disappeared since the Break, with humans of every shape and color working together freely because there was literally no one else to work with" (274). The shift in circumstances ends one form of racism and creates a new one. The new divide between human and machine leads to "sweeping racist statements" (259–60) and the choosing of sides. However, some Partials are more evolved than humans, as a Partial soldier (Vinci) explains, "I have recently learned to make my allies along ideological, rather than racial lines" (*Fragments* 464).

Through these examples, we can see that racial representation is more a matter of consciousness—of the reader and the author—than the individual's physical characteristics. While the overwhelming whiteness of most authors absolutely reflects the overwhelming whiteness of the genre, assumptions that we might make based on authors' names, appearances, or experiences may not hold true to their text. This is true for some white authors who challenge contemporary racial categories as well as some authors of color who don't. All of these examples speak to diversity—to difference, to representations that reflect the spectrum of American identities and heritages—but they do not necessarily reflect intersectionality. Intersectionality asks us to take the character as a whole, to examine the many aspects of their identity including race, class, gender, sexuality, and ability as well as personality traits, socialization and cultural context. Characters, like people, are multidimensional. The range of Girls on Fire give us a collective diversity that speaks to America's dystopian future—the themes, patterns, prisms, and interruptions that shape the collective landscape for YA dystopia. Girls on Fire illustrate diversity and multidimensionality as well as similar challenges and negotiations.

Race-ing the Future, a New Lens

Past, present, and future, our character—our identity—is a product of our times. For instance, set in the 1960s or 70s, Lauren Olamina might have been torn between Black Power and Feminism. She may have found her niche with black feminists, a group whose ideas implicitly inform Olamina's character, values, and beliefs in *Parables*. But in the science-fictional future, even as race divides people, Olamina does not have to be confined by identity politics, especially in world where there are bigger problems than identity and identification. Economics, poverty, and socio-economic class divisions are some of these problems, and one's identity tends to be defined by vulnerability and perceived wealth or ability. For instance, as children in the 2010s and 2020s of *Sower*, it was the "fashion" to be dirty and to be clean was to stand out in a negative way. Likewise, when traveling north Olamina notes that their packs are too clean and could make them vulnerable to attacks. If you appear to have something worth stealing or if you appear to be unable to defend yourself, you are a target. Even so, racism exists and Olamina must navigate that as well.

In *Parables*, while all colors of people are impacted by the social, economic, and environmental chaos and upheaval of the "Pox" people of color are disproportionately affected. Therefore, despite these markers of class, it is still dangerous to be, for instance, a mixed-race couple. Zahra, one of the survivors of *Sower*, notes that on the streets such couples attract the wrong kind of attention. People are suspicious of difference and are locked into the effects of the "divide and conquer" strategy of the Hegemon. It is also, of course, dangerous to be a woman. This is one reason why Olamina disguises herself as a man when she is traveling. Because of her size and strength it is easy for her to pass as a man; however, her disguise does not fool those close to her, only those who might judge her and assess her/him from a distance. Later, Olamina toggles between male and female as she "seduces" Earthseed followers through a kind of door-to-door campaign. Through this strategy the aspects of Earthseed's ideas about community, education, politics, the environment, and family become opportunities for recruitment. Race becomes less important as *Talents* progresses and Earthseed transforms people and grows communities and impacts social, cultural, and political change. The novel is optimistic even as individual struggles with identity continue.

Girls of Color as Girls on Fire

Book/Protagonist	Elements of Race—Identity, Social, and Cultural/Author Info	Quote That Represents Approach and Understanding of Race
Legend/June	While June is assumed to be white, Day is explicitly of mixed race. Marie Lu: "*I feel like an American who happens to be Asian.*"	June describes Day: "His face is perfectly symmetrical, a mix of Anglo and Asian, beautiful behind the dirt and smudges" (125). Day describes June: "I can't tell what she is, which isn't unusual around here—Native, maybe, or Caucasian. Or

Book/Protagonist	Elements of Race—Identity, Social, and Cultural/Author Info	Quote That Represents Approach and Understanding of Race
		something. She's pretty in a way that distracts me" (112).
Tankborn/Kayla	Inspired by Indian Caste System: Trueborns, demi-status trueborn, and low-status trueborn. Kayla is at the bottom—a GEN (genetically engineered non-human).	Skin color charts, clothing, and bali earrings mark one's status. "Darker color was better, but only to a point ... too-light skin would bump a trueborn into minor status" (25).
Partials/Kira Walker	Race is a visible plot element and protagonist of Indian origins. Cyborgs used to highlight the contemporary racial system in the U.S.	"Racism had all but disappeared since the break" (274).
The Many Lives of Ruby Iyer/Ruby Iyer	Takes place in India. Self-published Amazon bestseller.	"Not that being called *Madrasi* is derogatory. It had just felt uncool in South Bombay.... I had grown up there surrounded by good-looking people, all tall, and fair, bearing genes of their Aryan forefathers from the north of the country. My own family looked very different. We may have been from another planet, the smells and sounds of my home were that alien to them" (9).
Beauty Queens/Multiple characters	Diverse cast of characters including Adina (Jewish), Nicole (black), Shanti (Indian American).	Shanti gave a rueful laugh. "Don't you know the other trope?... The brown people die first" (192) ... "both Shanti and Nicole managed to free their hands for one last, sisters-in-non-white-dominant-culture-solidarity hand clasp...." / "'You can't ... trust ... the man,' Nicole said with her last breath, as she and Shanti sank beneath the quicksand" (193). [Don't worry; they escape on the next page.]

Book/Protagonist	Elements of Race—Identity, Social, and Cultural/Author Info	Quote That Represents Approach and Understanding of Race
The Chaos/Scotch	Afrofuturism.	She is black, but not as dark as her mother, brother, boyfriend, or best friends. After the Chaos passes, she is pleased to be darker (239).
Orleans/Fen de la Guerre	Race as re-imagined along the lines of blood type.	Fen: "Lydia say I pass for a boy, if not for the braids she do for me, all wrapped up in a top knot on my head to keep out of the way" (15).
	Smith's mother was a survivor of Hurricane Katrina.	Daniel: "For the most part, the rules of blood make race irrelevant. Blood types cross all ethnicities" (207).
The Interrogation of Ashala Wolf/ Ashala Wolf	Aboriginal Australian roots.	"*Before* the Reckoning? There weren't any Illegals back then. Although there were different peoples—different races, they were called. Ember had told me about it, once—how things like my skin not being the same color as hers or the way Pen's eyes were almond-shaped used to mean something. After the end of the old world, when there were so few humans left, everyone stopped worrying about things like that" (111–12).
Shadows Cast by Stars/Cassandra	Canadian Indigenous roots.	"Above, through the smoke hole, the moon peers down at us: Cree, Den, Anishinaabe, Métis, White, half-breeds, some with the names of their native tongues, some with names given to them by the white man, some with names that I've never heard before. We're a strange stew, but we all wait together to see what the moon has to say" (185).

Book/Protagonist	Elements of Race—Identity, Social, and Cultural/Author Info	Quote That Represents Approach and Understanding of Race
		"We are now just what the name means: mixed. Half-breeds. Not red enough to be red, and not white enough to be white" (45).
The Summer Prince/June	Afrofuturism. Set in future Brazil. June is as light as a citizen is allowed to be.	June: "Her skin is light, like mine. Usually that means you're poor, but sometimes it just means you have a strange papai" (35).
		"Appearance regulations" exist but Enki's mother arrived too late to use tech to conform to these standards (12).
		Auntie Yaha insists that "we don't wallow in our differences the way flatlanders do" (12).

In "Othered Girls on Fire" I argue that "the Girl on Fire brings critical attention to the limitations and possibilities of mainstream representations. The 'Othered' Girls on Fire complete the picture" (234). But here I want to note the value of the "Other," to make her center. Marotta argues that "SF texts featuring African American female protagonists still appear infrequently" (234). And they do, but several books offer an intersectionality that challenges the racial norms of YA dystopia, particularly *Orleans* and *The Summer Prince*. It is no coincidence that these texts are black—written by conscious black women, about consciously black characters, in racial futures that speak to the complexities of race and possibilities of intersectional identity in our world. They both engage with racial issues of today by imagining what race might look like in the future. Both texts also draw on the tradition of Afrofuturism, described by Ytasha Womack as "an intersection of imagination, technology, the future, and liberation.... Both an artistic aesthetic and a framework for critical theory" (9). Afrofuturism is at work in these texts, but the critical theory aspect impacts the whole tapestry of Girls on Fire. Placing black people and dystopia into this framework reveals the diversity of the genre as well as the future. It is Afrofuturism, as Alaya Dawn Johnson describes: a "method of imagination" (class visit), but it is also American in its cultural roots and part of the American imagination.

Womack also highlights the importance of imagination:

Afrofuturism is a great tool for wielding the imagination for personal change and societal growth. Empowering people to see themselves and their ideas in the future gives rise to innovators and free thinkers, all of whom can pull from the best of the past while navigating the sea of possibilities to create communities, culture, and a new balanced world. The imagination is the key to progress, and it's the imagination that is all too often smothered in the name of conformity and community and standards [191].

Many Girls on Fire feel smothered by standards set by corrupt leaders and power structures that need re-imagining. They become innovators and free thinkers. Readers become innovators and free-thinkers—pulling from the past and imagining a "new balanced world."

Lavender underscores the importance of looking for stories from Othered spaces especially when considering social justice: "If science fiction is about social change, let us talk about how this change comes about from an 'other' space, a black space" (7–8). If we practice the Afro-futuristic "method of imagination" and look to black spaces, many possibilities to interrupt popular (hegemonic) readings exist. One such reading is explored by Antero Garcia and Marcelle Haddix in "The Revolution Starts with Rue: Online Fandom and the Racial Politics of the Hunger Games." The authors make a radical argument that "Katniss is not the revolutionary matriarch we are led to believe across the Hunger Games trilogy. Rue is" (204). This is supported by their online research where a Tumblr post that makes this claim garners "hundreds of thousands of repostings" and a comment: "SOMEBODY FINALLY SAID IT" (208). In a hostile online space where fans express disappointment over Rue being black (Holmes), this reading goes beyond proving the fact that Rue is, in fact, black; Garcia and Haddix create a revolutionary function for Rue's character. Garcia and Haddix argue that "Rue's death sparks change; Katniss is simply there to stand witness as Rue's disciple" (204). We do not hear Rue's voice in the narration, but we hear her song—those few simple notes—that echo throughout the text—and especially through the films.

If Rue is the Mockingjay, this is a bit of a stretch—but it is a necessary stretch. We should consider how different perspectives can help us layer meaning and reveal truths that may not be contained in the text. As Garcia and Haddix argue, "Not seeing and not naming race in novels … also limits readers' comprehension of the text" (214). Basic understandings of race and racism in the American past, present, and future would go a long way to changing the landscape of YA dystopia, and YA more generally, and American culture as a whole. Culture can empty a text or character or plot of meaning, but the readers and the reader-fans can imbue a text with more meaning than the text originally contained. When we consider the Other Girls on Fire, we don't need to stretch so much.

* * *

Both *Orleans* and *The Summer Prince* offer female protagonists who are immediately identifiable as non-white and both are multi-layered, flexible, and adaptable to the circumstances that shape their stories and their worlds. They are black, but what this means is different in their future. For Fen, in *Orleans*, blood type determines tribe and life; for June, her lighter skin signals a European ancestor and "usually means you're poor" (35); she is not poor, but she is "as light-skinned as anyone is allowed to be" (26). The imagination of talented, conscious authors helps us consider race in the present and future. The vision of a different system recognizes the ability for the system to change in the present as well. Race is socially constructed so, at least in theory, it can be consciously reconstructed. It only makes sense that dystopia should perform such an act.

Marotta cites a generic field of scholars who "have criticized science fiction as a genre for the failure to clearly identify the ethnicity of their protagonists" and notes that Smith "partially" extends this trend with her "ambiguity about Fen's race" (63). But Fen's race is not so much "ambiguous" as it mixed and projected into a future where race means something different, even though all the old markers are still there. Marotta juxtaposes this with *Tankborn*, noting that Sandler places race in the foreground as she introduces Kayla and Jal.... "Kayla is black, female, and a GEN" (63). Marotta's reading of how *Orleans* takes on race is based on our contemporary racial structures andd limits the impact of the racial commentary and conversation that this novel provides.

Discussing racial representation, Marotta argues that "the grouping of individuals is reminiscent of segregation but, at first, they look as if they have been selected for self-protection rather than forced by racial discrimination" (57). Organizing for self-protection, however, has historically been done along racial lines; self-protection cannot be so easily divorced from "forced racial discrimination." Marotta also argues, via Leonard, that "race tends not to be highlighted, but instead appears as one of the character's physical attributes" (57).[6] Since race is defined by physical characteristics and imbued with meaning by culture, a character's physical attributes are the most obvious connection to race. As Coleman, who also writes about this novel within the context of African American YA literature, notes, "*Orleans's* divergence from other popular YA dystopias is further apparent through its protagonist's ethnicity" (4). He recognizes that what composes Fen's character is not so much her race (her skin color and hair texture) as it is her language and culture, and the context of her story within a society that is divided along the lines of blood-type. Fen's rich ethnic character also signifies her race; it has ties to the past even as it means something different in the future.

Fen is immediately identified as non-white in terms of her skin color— her "bare brown arm" (13)—and the voice she uses to tell her story: "not everybody willing to die. Somebody want to take my blood, they got to go through the veins in my neck or thigh. They can only bleed me once and I be dead. But that better than being a blood slave" (17). Perhaps the lack of a direct reference to her blackness in this description is "ambiguous." However, the regional cues make Fen not only "African American" but also an amalgamation of the diverse racial and ethnic region that was New Orleans and has become Orleans a couple of decades into the future. Fen is recognized as black/African American by context within the book and within our cultural frames for Katrina. And, because race means something different, *Orleans* embraces Afrofuturism at its roots. While in Tankborn Kayla may be unmistakably black, the caste system and Indian cultural references mean that while Kayla's story is a neo-slave narrative, it is not necessarily an American neo-slave narrative; however, the author's national affiliation means that there are American echoes. The author's American roots merge with her appreciation for, and celebration of, Indian culture amidst her critiques of caste generally and specifically. These are important challenges but YA dystopia can do more. And it does.

Intersectional, International and on Another Level

There is almost nothing about *The Summer Prince* that is anything like other YA dystopia novels. The story takes place in future Brazil. The protagonist is culturally sophisticated and of the upper classes. She is an artist. She is not white, but her class gives her social power and privilege. June lives in a world where race has similar meanings and functions to our world. But she lives in a world where women rule, the males are "beautiful boys" who are allowed to cry and dance, and sex is not a big deal as it is culturally accepted that the "wakas" (the under-30 youth) sleep with whomever they want whenever they want. She also lives in a world where women bear the responsibility for creating a better future, and the young are needed to intervene in this future-making. For all these reasons and more, *The Summer Prince*, adds to the richness and complexity of the genre and provides an important lens for considering YA dystopia.

Wrapped up in this story of politics and power, corruption and transgression, is an interesting construction of gender and sexuality. The women hold power and give the men a modicum of freedom. Men destroyed so much (including themselves) and the women have held power for 400 years. Palmares Três is proud of its equal numbers of men and women, but men continue to be oppressed much in the fashion of women in contemporary American contexts. Boys are beautiful and are allowed to cry and dance and sing. They can become Uncles and can hold positions of political and social importance, but women (Aunties) tend to dominate politics and positions of importance. Because Aunties' lives are long, change happens slowly. Men are placated with the few boys who become kings and they are allowed to perform ritual suicide when they feel they have lived out the narrative of their life.

Even the name of the novel undercuts the power that men have. Enki is the Summer King, and some Aunties try to lessen his power rhetorically—by referring to him as the Summer *Prince*—as if this demotion in title is enough to disempower him. But Enki's power does not come from his title; his title gives him opportunity. He comes from a class that has very few such opportunities while June is economically and socially advantaged. She lives on Tier 8, far above where the lowest class lives: "We call it the catinga, the stink, but they call it the verde. Green" (13). June's entitlement is called out by Enki, by June's school principal, by a girl from Salvador. June knows she should win the Queen's award. She doesn't question why. She drives herself forward, and along the way she realizes that what's at stake is more than an award, and more than her own individual future.

The Summer Prince is a dystopia; however, as the author has noted, it is also a "complicated utopia" (Gay YA; class visit). The survivors—the women who rebuilt—were trying to avoid the mistakes of the world of men. They made other mistakes instead. Palmeres Três's status as a utopia is questioned by a character from the flat, and war-torn, land of Salvador. She scoffs at the price that Enki pays to live in a Paradise. In her head, June questions this idea of a paradise. Certainly the place June knows could not be described as such. And, yet, June's world has far less violence and far more resources. In comparison, it is a utopia. But this is exactly the point about dystopia—we cannot necessarily recognize it as such when we are in the middle of it. Johnson means for this future to be both a utopia and a dystopia—two sides of the same coin. This complex world is not unlike ours in this respect. June, too, is complicated.

June is just like all the other wakas in her adoration of the summer king, but she also sees past the hype. She is a critical thinker: "I don't actually know Enki. I'm not stupid. I'm aware this attachment I feel is the product of emotional investment in the largely stage-managed and manufactured spectacle of the royal election … a thousand wakas are probably crying themselves to sleep tonight, just like me" (33). But she is also an artist: "I live for spectacle, for the construction of emotional states and the evocation of suppressed feelings. I can appreciate what Enki has done with his election—the way he subverted it while simultaneously triumphing within its rules" (33). She cannot help but be swept up in the process, but she wants to be a part of it, not just an observer. At the first event where the three candidates are introduced, June demonstrates her love of Enki and represents all wakas in her love as she and Gil sneak in and display a holo projected above the audience. It gets Enki's attention, but it is not much more than a school girl stunt. Her art becomes more sophisticated; she gets hurt and she expresses this hurt in her graffiti art that features Gil and Enki kissing. She makes these feelings public—but anonymous—in the face of Queen Oreste. Her art grows when she realizes that he is also an artist and partners with him. She explains what kind of artist he is: "You mean that you manipulate, that you express yourself on objects and use them to express you. You mean that when you choose to be the summer king, you choose to use your own body as a canvas that no one can ignore" (68). June wants to use her body as her canvas as well, and she designs a tree on her body by inserting lights under her skin, but her art is easily removed when the state takes control of her body. Enki reminds us: "*a human canvas can't live. It can only flare and make a record of its dying*" (69). Enki is a temporary flare; June must keep the flame burning.

Throughout the novel June struggles between what she wants—the queen's award, the highest honor she can get as a waka within a system tiered by class, and what she thinks is right. She has to figure out what she thinks is right and sometimes she gets in her own way. Enki challenges her to think about her privilege. When their artistic partnership begins, June explains: "This isn't about sex. This isn't a love story. I'm not doing this so a king can choose me and make me special./ I'm doing this so two artists can create work together that they could never imagine alone" (66). Ultimately, love is exactly what June gets with Enki. First as a part of his love for everyone. Again, when he speaks as the city. When she is at her lowest—unable to enjoy the simple pleasures that the other wakas are enjoying—is when Enki gives her love physically. She risks her own life to rescue him and their love affair goes on the road where "our sex is a little death each time he touches me, much longed for" (246). June ultimately gets his love, as his death does exactly what June first admires—he subverts the system while also playing by its rules. Enki makes her queen, which is unheard of in the fictional city of Palmares Três. Ultimately, she doesn't win the queen's award, she wins the queen's position. And there's a lot of hard work ahead of her.

* * *

The Summer Prince is a complex, beautiful work of art, but it lacks the accolades that it deserves. In fact, Johnson notes that it is "very much on the margin" and received "rejections from every publishing house" but that Arthur A. Levine Books "bought it quickly and rallied behind it" (Johnson, class visit). *The Summer Prince* can't be popular; it is too intellectual, too layered, too rich and ripe with history. It takes on issues of race unflinchingly and offers sexuality that challenges mainstream representations. It is also a book about a black girl, by a black author. Marotta argues that "it must be noted that critical examination of YA literature featuring African American characters is lacking" (64). Marotta and Coleman add much to this lack through their examinations of *Orleans* and *Tankborn*, but, unfortunately, while critical examination is lacking, there is some criticism that does not take into account the particular aspects of the genre of YA dystopia. This ignorance sometimes misreads what the author writes and misunderstands why and how the author is writing the text and conceiving of their story. As powerful an example *The Summer Prince* is of an intersectional, revolutionary YA dystopia text, by borrowing from a culture that does not "belong" to her, Johnson has made herself vulnerable to accusations of cultural appropriation. Johnson is a black American, but she is not a Brazilian. She is writing about an Afro-futuristic place that draws from a culture that does not belong to her. She's an outsider looking in. Her position is ripe for criticism. However, cultural appropriation is a complicated dance with shades and negotiations.

In a snarky criticism of *The Summer Prince*, a Brazilian native takes Alaya Dawn Johnson to task for her exploration of a future Brazil that draws upon cultural references that this critic feels are representative of what an outsider would write about. Ana Grilo believes Johnson has "good intentions" and that "she tried to be as respectful as possible," but for Grilo these efforts "go awry." For instance, she argues that "the use of language drove [her] to distraction … we only use those words [mamãe for mother and papai for father] when speaking to children or when speaking to another member of the family." While I can understand the overuse of a term that a reader thinks "made the characters sound like they were either babies—or being ironic and making fun of each other," the idea that these two words could be used so totally differently in a world hundreds of years in the future seems to be lost on this critic. Language evolves. Further, the novel makes a point to show the ways in which the under-30 youth, the wakas, are considered to be too immature to handle the responsibilities of adulthood. If they are using a word that makes them sound juvenile, this makes a lot of sense. But Grilo cannot see beyond her particular cultural context. In fact, she dismisses the fact that the book is set in the future because of the language used (Portuguese); the location is "still in Bahia"; and "the book references Brazilian history and background." She does not understand what Johnson sees as a fundamental aspect of culture: it is a "moving target" (Gay YA).

While Grilo makes a valid point about cultural appropriation, the ways in which she dismisses Johnson and her work are clearly rooted in what she describes are her biases: "I am Brazilian (born and bred), I am White (half-Brazilian, half-Portuguese), I am from Rio da Janeiro, I have a History degree…." While we must remain critically vigilant, vigilance and dismissiveness are not the same. The fact that Grilo does not address any of the aspects of Johnson's novel that highlight the African diaspora speak to her position of privilege. She has much to say about ancient history (her academic specialty) and religion, but nothing to say about racial representation. Further, she criticizes the novel for not recognizing that "Brazil is a place of huge cultural diversity." And yet, she also dismisses the aspects of the novel that illustrate Japanese influence like the use of the term *waka*, which is Japanese slang, and the Japanese architectural approach to the pyramid city (which brings the snark: "Are Brazilians AZTECS now??!"). Ultimately, Grilo holds the authenticity of her cultural roots so close that she cannot imagine the dramatic changes that the future might hold. Early in *The Summer Prince*, June explains that she has "been out in the bay a few times, just to see what we look like from the outside (it's so easy to forget, sometimes that there *is* an outside, and we should never forget)" (12). This wisdom applies beyond the book—when we look from the outside, we see things that the people inside might forget or take for granted.

While it is important to challenge stereotypes and to imagine new worlds, some readers will always lack the imagination needed to see more than "hugely common stereotypes bound together and thrown at my face." Johnson is gracious in the face of such critiques and notes that "it's great that we have spaces where those things [different perspectives] can exist side by side with the book" (Gay YA). In a world where ideas can circulate freely, the Girl on Fire has to defend her right to be different, to be of a future world, to create a new world.

Indigenous Girls on Fire

Dystopia also provides space (about as much space as any other American cultural space!) to consider the future of the first, the original, Americans. What does indigeneity look like in a future built on a past of decimation, appropriation, and celebration? In a couple of novels like *Monsters* (of the Ashes series) Native American (Ojibwe) or indigenous traditions are mentioned, like the use of hallucinogenic mushrooms as medicine, but these are largely divorced from Indigenous peoples. In the Dustlands trilogy, a new age kind of religion echoes Native American symbols like Saba's pet crow, Nero. Mercy gives Saba a heartstone that gets hot when her heart's desire is near. Most obviously is Auriel, a shaman whose grandfather had visited Saba's father and taught him how to read the stars. Auriel guides Saba and reminds her to "stay true to yerself. Who you really are. What you believe. You ain't like nobody else" (338). Saba's sister, Emmi, also discovers her shamanistic abilities that Lugh dismisses as "airy fairy" and Emmi describes as "the earth told me" (159). Such instances only reinforce the contemporary erasure of Native American people as part of the past, not alive and well in the present, and certainly not building the future.

Megan Crewe's dystopian series—which includes the books *The Way We Fall*, *The Lives We Lost*, and *The Worlds We Make*—appears to be about an indigenous girl. In the first book, Kaelyn lives on an island off the coast of Canada. Her mother is referred to as a "darky" (10) and Kaelyn stands out from the other people in the novel. At one point she is identified solely based upon her appearance and difference: "some girl with light brown skin, which narrows the options down to one" (221). At this point she notes: "I've felt uncomfortable and out of place before, but that's the first time I've outright wished I was the same color as just about everyone else on the island" (221). Her described skin color difference is the only clue that Kaelyn might not be white, but even these small descriptions of difference mostly disappear as the subsequent books unfold. Another clue comes in the second book when she recalls a past incident "when that tourist looked at my skin and hair and called me a mutt" (24). This story shares elements similar to *Shadows Cast by Stars*—disease, an isolated island threatened by the government, mixed-race characters. But the Way We Fall series does not make indigenous issues—past or present—an overt part of the narrative so it is unclear what Kaelyn's skin color is supposed to communicate to the reader beyond signifying her difference, and perhaps the unlikelihood that she will become a survivor and a leader. She does survive and she does lead, noting a "nebulous sense of purpose" (239). She protects and delivers the only existing vaccine to the right authority figures. She also figures out that she has the power to make the world that she wants (*The Worlds We Make* 253) and this world is "not just about one person" (*The Worlds We Make* 273).

Shadows Cast by Stars, on the other hand, presents Cass and her brother, Paul, as "half-breeds" and their mixed genes—their very bodies—are the source of the plague vaccine. In the first few pages we learn that Cass and her brother, Paul, are "Others, of aboriginal descent, marked by the precious Plague antibodies in our blood" (1). We also learn that they live the "Old Way" (1), which means they "are the only ones who have stayed, clinging to what little is ours, defiantly living as we always have, without computers and etherstreams and data-nets in our home, without food gels, without central heat" (2). It also means that "the Old Way is a way of work. We have no electricity, no running water, no garbage collection.... It keeps us connected to the earth" (5). Given the traditions of genocide and cultural appropriation, making space for indigenous visions of the future is crucial for American reconciliation.[7] The corrupt power structure stretches back to America's roots and foundations—to decimation, to disease, to war, to broken treaties, and to ongoing cultural appropriation. These are similar challenges in Australia and Kwaymullina explores the possibility of an indigenous future that strongly counters the challenges of the past. An indigenous vision of the future is not easy water to tread.

In *Shadows Cast by Stars*, "Native American" traditions harness the supernatural and the natural power based in nature. Cass can "see the shades" of other people and "when a shade comes to visit, something is about to change" (3). She buries her hands in the earth to stay grounded and in her

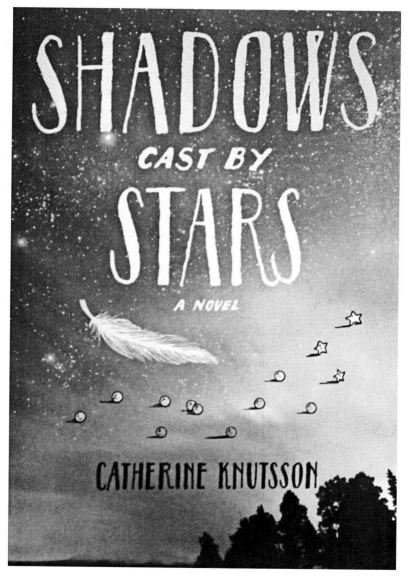

The cover of *Shadows Cast by Stars* has a whimsical, hand-drawn quality that suits the overall tone of the novel. With a starry background as well as hand drawn stars and stones, some of the mystical elements are highlighted. The feather on the cover signals a Native American stereotype and it floats between the title and symbols. The realistic photographic land and trees barely skirt the bottom of the photo (Simon & Schuster. Cover design by Lauren Rille. Cover photography © 2013 by Joe Cantino).

body or to return from the "twilight world of spirit" (3). Nature is a much bigger character in *The Interrogation of Ashala Wolf* where, as Connor notes, "everyone knows it was humanity's abuse of the environment that made the life-sustaining systems of earth collapse" (6). Some of Australia's indigenous traditions are given an entirely new world that, we learn part way through, was created by an original being. As The Serpent tells her, Ashala and her tribe are the last of what we know today as indigenous peoples, and "**might just be the last to carry the bloodline of those I created in the world that was**" (114; original emphasis). The world has become a much different place, evolving and recovering from abuse. The indigenous have survived again. Both of these books are trying to give girls of color a future by digging into the past, recognizing the impacts of genocide and the toll that this long history has taken on indigenous peoples. But because it imagines a future, history stretches.

Shadows Cast by Stars does not shy away from issues like patriarchal abuse of power by tribe elders, abuse of alcohol, and attitudes toward mixed-blood tribe members, but Knutsson also does not make these aspects indictments, just realities that plague (pun intended) oppressed peoples. Knutsson offers a story about the ways in which difference, particularly mixed blood can be both positive and negative. She imagines how magic and myth might look in the future. *Shadows Cast by Stars* is a novel with great intentions and while the plot is a bit messy, and the story doesn't really make total sense, there is a lot of potential here, and I have found that many students enjoy and connect with this novel, perhaps because of that very "native" voice and story it portrays. The novel is full of wisdom, myth, and tradition.

Because of the realities of oppression and violence that Cass continues to face, the native elements cannot be totally romanticized. And even the fated love story is less romanticized. Cass is confronted with the attempted attack (and assumed attempted rape) and stalking of one of the boys. She also develops a relationship with Bran, whose mom is white (and a bit crazy), and whose father is the missing elder and leader. Family is important. She also has a close relationship with her father and her twin brother. Her (white) mother died of the Plague (or, rather, she shot herself rather than suffer to the end). Her father—and family as a whole—is haunted. At times it seems her relationship with her brother, Paul, is a bit too close, like Saba and Lugh in *Dustlands*. Paul is vulnerable, with powers that draw him to the darker side, and Cass feels a responsibility to try to help him. Her father is kind and naïve, and cares greatly for both his children. But Cass's family is shattered like most everything else in her world.

There is also room for Cass to recover something she lost, something that her people—her community—need. She has abilities that are recognized by Madda, and she begins training as a medicine woman. Cass is green in her work as medicine woman, and then she loses the mentor that she thinks she needs. Her skills do not progress much more in the novel, but her struggles do. She relies on what she learned about healing from her mother, a nurse. But it is the spirit world that needs healing, and this is where she has to go to help people, to help herself, and to help humanity. She is forced to face the supernatural world and she navigates "another place, a place of darkness and shadow, with little substance and no rules" (445). In the final battle, she finds her power and knows that "if I want to break the monolith, there is nothing the sea wolf can do to stop me" (448). When she destroys the monolith "its power is now mine, and I will devour it whole and turn it on this creature of nightmares beside me" (449).

The end of the novel (and the author's blog) hint at a sequel, and with the many loose ends, it needs one: "We can't stay here anymore. The boundary has fallen, and this place is no longer safe. The sea wolf knows where we are, and the creature that follows him does too" (455). Cass navigates the battle, but the war is still waging. The novel exudes the pain of genocide and ancestral trauma. Cass gets no breaks; the pain keeps coming. She cannot stop it or control it. But there is some small victory as she and Bran temporarily banish the toxic presence that poisons their people. But Cass wants more: "there is one thing I've learned, it's that we are not bound by the myths created for us. It's time for my own myths.... These are my truths, my myths, my lies. This is my story" (456). Only in fiction can a girl like Cass own her story.

Ashala offers a far future, a much more imaginary place—a much more hopeful dystopic vision. For Ashala, the powers that she possesses are also underdeveloped, but she has a community—her Tribe—and they help each other to better understand their gifts and how they work. Ashala is a leader in ways that Cass is not; she has more resources to work with and better access to the information she needs. But both girls cross into a kind of spirit world and converse with their ancestors, and they have to figure out what to do. They have to hold things together.

While Cass's world carries the wounds of America's past, in Ashala's world the tides have turned. The earth—and its people—have the power to not only resist, but transform. Ashala's world is Australian, but being indigenous it speaks to all First Nations people's as well as to the genocide that happened (and continues) in the Americas.

In her author's note to *The Interrogation of Ashala Wolf,* Kwaymullina considers what the future looks like: "In Ashala's world, where people no longer distinguish among themselves on the basis of race, the word *Aboriginal* has no meaning. But she carries that ancient bloodline and has the same deep connection to the Firstwood that present-day Aboriginal people have to their Counties." In other words, even when a far future erases racial difference, "that ancient bloodline" is, perhaps, the only aspect of "race" that is not socially constructed, that goes deeper than flesh and bone. Even so, in this far future life is valued. "And it is through sustaining caring relationships with other shapes of life," Kwaymullina argues, that "we give substance and meaning to our own existence."

* * *

The two novels in this study that take up indigenous characters, settings, and issues, and the authors' connections to these traditions is stated overtly in their bios. Knutsson is Canadian and "proudly Metis." Kwaymullina is, as her bio notes, "from the Palyku people of the Pilbara region of Western Australia." She also provides an author's note that speaks to her heritage and vision. As a result of her recent discovery of her Metis heritage, Catherine Knutsson's authenticity is called into question by Debbie Reese, "*Learning that she wasn't raised Native and that she's recently been learning about her Metis heritage explains a great deal of what I find troublesome in the novel.*" In a review written for a Native American resource website called American Indians in Children's Literature (AICL), which "provides critical perspectives and analysis of indigenous peoples in children's and young adult books, the school curriculum, popular culture, and society," Reese offers her summary of aspects of the book followed by her "comments" in italics. She attacks stereotypes from this book out of context of the actual book and fails to imagine what a future might look like if the problems of the past and present are manifest in the future. For instance, she rightly questions the inclusion of dreamcatchers as being stereotypical and a "red flag" but takes issue with the men on the Island being "*depicted in derogatory ways. They drink.*" She also takes issue with the lack of compassion shown in the novel to Bran's white mother who is identified as being "a drunk." She considers Cass's special abilities to be "new age" and yet Knutsson's use of the term "apple" ("Red on the outside, white on the inside") as a derogatory word "*signals to me that she's done some research on the tensions within Native communities.*" It does not occur to her that Knutsson might identify with this term herself.

Further, Reese fails to note the reality of indigenous people who are not "full blood." She focuses on the use of the "derogatory term" of "half blood" and "half breed" and misunderstands the use of this term in the text as well as in her own time and context: "*In 200 years, are we to believe there was a change such that the Metis people stopped using Metis and started using half blood or half-breed again?! It doesn't seem likely to me, and, given the family's desire to live in 'the Old Way' it seems that using 'Metis' would be part of that Old Way.*" Later, in a 2016 follow-up note, she speaks of her evolving understanding of this term. She mentions a social media conversation where Daniel Heath Justice (who is "a citizen of the Cherokee Nation and is a professor in First Nations and Indigenous Studies at the University of British Columbia") pointed her toward a source that she looks forward to "spending more time with." Clearly he has more authority on the subject than a writer who "recently learned that she is Metis." This is part of the power of online conversations—to hold critiques accountable.

Because many of Reese's comments are about her confusion, it becomes clear that the lack of development and explanation of a variety of aspects of this novel—related to the Metis and not—are really the problem with this novel. Her "comments" otherwise reveal a narrow vision of who is allowed to write about their identity and cultural heritage. Still she recognizes, in closing, that *"we need Native writers. Ones like Knutsson, who learn of their Native heritage as adults, could give us some much-needed stories, but dressed up in this sort of framework ... it isn't working."* What comprises "this sort of framework" is unclear. The use of stereotypes and new age ideas? Or, the use of mixed-blood Native characters struggling in a world 200 years in the future?

These critiques, like those of Johnson, are fair game, but they are also problematic in a shifting world. We cannot know what the future might look like—what ideas, what animals, what identities, what places might cease to exist or be drastically altered. The safe space of fiction gives us room to negotiate these future possibilities. But if we expect these future visions to adhere to cultural patterns of the present, we are in dangerous territory. As Alaya Dawn Johnson explains, "if you are writing from outside your culture, as I am an American woman writing about Brazil, obviously there are things you are gonna get wrong ... [but] the fact that you are going to get things wrong doesn't negate the value of doing it" (Gay YA). Imagination cannot be bound by the narrow politics of our contemporary world. We *should* expect speculative fiction to give us critical representations that shed light on our present. What we see in that future is not always what we want to see. But Girls on Fire give us prisms, ideas, tools, and comrades. As Ashala says, "I'd thought I was out of options. But I wasn't out of allies" (338).

The Master's Tools

Audre Lorde's foundational essay inquires, "will the master's tools ever dismantle the master's house?" Some Girls on Fire have only the "master's tools" at their disposal. In the case of race, for instance, critics have noted that many narratives are limited by the author's socially constructed notions of race and ethnicity. Even the most conscious writer can only provide the tools allowed by an imagination shaped by a conflicted culture. But YA dystopia gives Girls on Fire room to maneuver outside of the strict confines of cultural rules and expectations. She can begin to access tools that the

Master did not necessarily endorse. In fact, girls themselves are this very weapon and tool. Girls are underestimated, by our culture and by our selves. In YA dystopia girls can explore their full potential.

Some Girls on Fire have powers that the master cannot contain, powers that are developed from any number of sources. The Dark Minds series, Ashes, Shatter Me, Cinder, and The Essence. These special powers are discovered, negotiated, tested, and the Girl on Fire ultimately has to come to terms with her power. Most often this power is an unexpected side effect of some kind of government scheme, a mistake or an oversight. Most often it comes with a price as Cassandra reminds us, "there's always a price to pay in the world of spirit, and a sacrifice to be made" (452). In Under the Never Sky, some people have evolved special abilities—improved sight, smell, and hearing. They are considered Savages by the people of Aria's world, but her father was one and she inherits his abilities. Kayla, in *Tankborn*, has a special strength sket (26)—a genetically-enhanced ability that helps her carry out her assigned job (as a slave). Some of these powers have metaphorical implications like those developed in the Ashes series. An electromagnetic pulse alters the brain chemistry of young people, but not everyone experiences this shift in the same way. Alex develops mental powers that end up being the only thing that can stop the corrupt adults who are using and abusing all of the kids, transformed or not. A similar plot in the Darkest Minds series involves the government poisoning the water supply and causing a kind of birth defect in children who either die or develop special *abilities* as a result of their mothers' consumption of the tainted water. Some kids can harness and control electricity, some are brilliant at electronics and computers, and some can move physical objects with their minds. The dangerous kids can manipulate people's brainwaves (bioelectricity) or produce fire; the former (Oranges) are slaughtered and the latter (Reds) are manipulated and controlled for use by the Hegemon. The protagonist, Ruby, struggles with the implications that her abilities have and the ways in which others (all boys) have used this power for personal control and power. In Shatter Me, Juliet also struggles with her powers but finds a community. Castle tells her: "this is where you belong. Because you need to know that you are not alone" (309). The others have powers as well: Castle has psychokinesis, Kenji can be invisible, Brendan is electric, Winston is highly flexible, and the only other girls are twin healers—one heals the mind and the other heals the body. In the future, man-made mistakes and manipulations lead to powerful tools that can no longer be contained and controlled.

The tools that counter the master are not always tools rooted in reality or accident; here the power of fiction gives girls the ability to fight on a different playing field altogether. Cassandra in Shadows Cast by Stars has abilities to cross over into the spirit world; she can also heal people, however underdeveloped her abilities are. Ashala Wolf has the ability to transform her reality through Sleepwalking and to take other people with her. Other Illegals and members of the Firstwood community have other kinds of abilities; Robyn Sheahan-Bright explains, there are "Firestarters who control fire, Rumblers who can cause quakes, Boomers who make things explode." Some abilities are connected to animals and "animal-speakers often start to resemble the animals they communicate with." Some have more nuanced abilities like Georgie's Foretelling ability and Ember's ability to "take others' memories and share, change or invent new ones" (Sheahan-Bright). But Ashala's abilities go beyond her Sleepwalking. As Ember tells her, "you transform things in a way no one else can" (202). Moreover, she can "make dreams come true" beyond the ways of her ability: "You have changed the world, and you didn't use your ability for any of it. So maybe Sleepwalking is an extension of who you are inside" (207). The abilities of the Illegals supposedly threaten The Balance, but they really only threaten those who control the world—those who make the rules and enforce them with the power they have manufactured.

Ordinary Girls and Special Powers

Lauren Olamina's "specialpower" is a disability not a power.	"It isn't magic or ESP that allows me to share the pain or pleasure of other people. It's delusional" (11). "I get a lot of grief that doesn't belong to me, and isn't real. But it hurts" (12).
Ordinary girls are often emphasized.	**Lena**—*Delirium*. "I'm not ugly, but I'm not pretty, either. Everything is in-between" (15). **Tris**—*Divergent*. "I am not pretty—my eyes are too big and my nose is too long—but I can see that Christina is right. My face is noticeable" (87).
Some girls seem ordinary or claim to be nothing special, but also have a developed and valued skill.	**Katniss**—*The Hunger Games*, bow and arrow. **Gaia**—*Birthmarked*, midwifery. **June**—*Legend*, prodigy (trained soldier). **Cassandra**—*Shadows Cast by Stars*, a medicine woman (and more). **Kayla**—*Tankborn*, a GEN (genetically engineered non-human) with a strength sket.
Some Girls on Fire have special abilities of a supernatural quality.	**Aria**—*Under the Never Sky*. Heightened sense of hearing and other auditory abilities. **Charlie**—*The Essence*. Royal powers that only the women have. **Ruby**—*The Darkest Minds*. Ability to manipulate people into doing what she wants them to do. **Juliet**—"~~My touch is lethal~~. My touch is power." **Cassandra**—*Shadows Cast by Stars*. "Share[s] the

power of the sisiutl, the strongest of the spirit
creatures" (447–8).
Ashala—*The Interrogation of Ashala Wolf.* Sleepwalker: able to go places and do things in a state of
altered consciousness.

Octavia Butler offers another important tool to counter the Master, a
tool that the collective of Girls on Fire helps to foster. As Olamina travels
north in *Sower* she recognizes her "natural allies"—not simply "people of
color" but racially mixed couples and groups. Although most of her allies are
people of color, this is not the defining factor in friendships, comradeships,
or community. Color is, in many ways, a default of the extreme poverty and
social chaos, conditions that affect everyone regardless of color. The dispro-
portionate rates of people of color in poverty in the present have, at this
point, been more evenly distributed though it seems that the rich and privileged in this science-fictional future (like the present) tend to be white. While
color continues to be a problem in a world where people are taught to be
fearful of what is different from themselves, color is not an issue in these
ways for Earthseed's followers. In *Sower* Olamina notes that the kids in her
neighborhood would have started to look mixed and it is just such mixing
that characterizes Acorn. Olamina wonders if the children of Acorn will grow
up to see racial mixing as the norm; however, we cannot know since Acorn
is destroyed by the very forces that have problems with racial mixing. And,
as *Talents* concludes rapidly there is little room for a developed discussion
of identity, race, gender, or sexuality; but perhaps this is because the diversity
of the Earthseed community is assumed to exist as much as it is assumed as
one of Earthseed's strengths.

The idea of natural allies, and the communities these ties can form, are
important ideas for an imagined future—both the fictional ones we imagine
and the real one(s) we make. Quoting Maxine Greene's 2000 collection of
essays, *Releasing the Imagination*, Garcia and Haddix note that "imagination
is what, above all, makes empathy possible" (215).[8] Essentially, this is what
María Lugones suggests when she argues that "travelling to someone's 'world'
is a way of identifying with them because travelling to their 'world' we can
understand *what it is to be them and what it is to be ourselves in their eyes*"
(401, original emphasis). This kind of empathy can be found in many of our
Girls on Fire and, no doubt, in many would-be world-savers. "World-travelling," for Lugones, describes "a particular feature of the outsiders existence:
the acquired flexibility in shifting from the mainstream construction of life
to other constructions of life where she is more or less 'at home'" (390). While
this is a presumed condition for women of color, Lugones notes that "this
flexibility is necessary for the outsider but it can also be willfully exercised

by those who are at ease in the mainstream" (390). Mainstream expectations require flexibility, adaptation, and the ability to be a chameleon.

In and out of the mainstream, empathy produces a counter to the Master's Tools of division and difference. Empathy is exactly what distinguishes Ruby from the other Oranges: "it involves being vulnerable to the other person having access to your memories, some sort of natural empathy on your end" (345). Ruby's powers can wipe a person's memory clean or compel them to do something against their will. Empathy is the only way to keep this power in check. For Ashala, empathy is an integral part of herself. As Georgie explains to her, "you feel things deeply—all the way to your bones" (205). Georgie knows that "caring about people, helping people, that's what brings [Ashala] back to herself" (206). Ultimately empathy is why Girls on Fire persist; they fight for other people before they fight for themselves.

* * *

Love is, perhaps, the most obvious counter to the Master's hate, and the most undercut by romantic representations of love that don't take into account the power of love beyond our narrow definitions. Feminists have explored the importance of love as pedagogy and methodology. Love, bell hooks argues, is "a combination of care, commitment, knowledge, responsibility, respect, and trust. All these factors work interdependently. They are a core foundation of love irrespective of the relational context" (131). The relational contexts for Girls on Fire include boys and men, fathers and mothers, siblings, friends, animals, and even enemies. I explored the relationships of Girls on Fire with their Boys as Consciousness and their female friends (as well as with the Hegemon); however, these relationships—as well as those with mothers and fathers and siblings and adopted families—deserve far more consideration. Love can heal, as it does for Juliet in *Shatter Me*: "Being around so much love has managed to thaw my frozen parts into something human. I feel human. Like maybe I could be a part of this world. Like maybe I don't have to be a monster. Maybe I'm not a monster./ Maybe things can change" (235). And love can lead to a bigger sense of hope and responsibility in addition to survival and acceptance.

In "Foreword: Birth of a Revolution" Sheree Renee Thomas explains, "In its essence, social justice work, which King embodied and Butler expressed so skillfully in her novels and stories, is about love—a love that has the best hopes and wishes for humanity at heart" (1). This is the love that Ashala Wolf embodies as a leader. Ember explains: "People come to the Firstwood all hurt and scared and angry at the world, but the only thing you see is the good in them, the greatest version of themselves that they could be. And somehow, most of them grow and change until they start becoming that person" (138). Ashala brings out the best in people and, Ember notes, "if Ash has to die to protect everyone she cares about, then so be it. You have to let her love. Because it's the only thing more powerful than hate" (203). As powerful as Ashala's love is, her hate is equally powerful and potentially destructive. If "very distressed" she can "go into something called a dissociative state" (205). The problem is, when Ashala uses her power as a Sleepwalker, Ashala "mov[es] through the world in an unconscious state, seeing everything as part of a super-intense dream" (61). When she is unconscious, she is disconnected from her core of love and empathy.

The contexts for love are also the violent realities that Girls on Fire navigate. In writing about "love in violent times" Inga Muscio argues that love "requires imagination, a sense of humor, creativity, resourcefulness, openheartedness, and figuring out how to make the very, very best out of the very, very worst" (261). This description speaks to the qualities of the Girl on Fire— creative, resourceful, openhearted. And Girls on Fire's ability to make the best of what are almost always dire situations—environmental devastation, endless war, devastated communities, limited resources, and tightly controlled social and cultural regulations. Through all of the trials Tris faces in the Divergent series, ultimately she recognizes "I don't belong to Abnegation, or Dauntless, or even the Divergent. I don't belong to the Bureau or the experiment or the fringe. I belong to the people I love, and they belong to me— they, and the love and loyalty I give them, form my identity far more than any word or group ever could" (*Allegiant* 455). Of course, this love is also the source of her untimely demise. Eve comes to a complementary conclusion: "I had believed that love was a liability—something that could be wielded against you. [But] love was death's only adversary, the only thing powerful enough to combat its clawing, desperate grasp" (270). Love is bigger than the stereotypes of romance that shape and define the genre.

Ultimately, our discomfort with the subject of love—as something more complicated and more simple than can be understood with one word—is an extension of, and function of, our larger problems with understanding and defining love in a culture where one word is expected to represent all of the various inflections, dimensions, and shades of "love." In *The Summer Prince*, June forgets that love can be bigger than romantic love. When the city tells June that it loves her because "Enki used the love of you to tie my external sensors to my municipal energy production unit" (185), Enki clarifies: "what she means is that she loves you because I do" (185). June is still skeptical: "what if his love is something more than just his mods? Nothing would make me happier, and nothing would scare me more" (185). Love can be revolutionary, but even when romantic and stereotypically hetero, love can be a tool toward personal, individual transformation.

* * *

In her "Introduction" to *So Long Been Dreaming: Postcolonial Science Fiction & Fantasy,* Nalo Hopkinson describes a conversation she had about Audre Lorde's "Master's Tools." She paraphrases what she's told by a recent PhD student: "'We've been taught all our lives how superior European literature is. In our schools, it's what we're instructed to read, to analyze, to understand, how we're taught to think. They gave us those tools. I think that now, they're our tools, too" (8). This exchange gave her "a lot to think about" (8). She rethought, and rewrote, her story with this in mind. She remarks, "In my hands, massa's tools don't dismantle massa's house—and in fact, I don't want to destroy it so much as I want to undertake massive renovations—then build me a house of my own" (8). Girls on Fire are working to build their own houses as well as communities and worlds where we can all live free, if we don't die trying.

From Survivors to Community Organizers to World-Makers

To be a survivor is to overcome hardships and persevere; the degree of success is dependent upon the conditions that await the survivor. Sometimes she has agency and sometimes she can only continue to survive. Some Girls on Fire are barely holding on, only hoping to survive, and we are often unhappy with their outcomes. As I argue in "Othered Girls on Fire," "Most of YA dystopia's girls are just barely scraping by, scavenging food and supplies, trying to hold themselves together, let alone the people they have taken responsibility for" (238). Some girls survive only to find there are more challenges ahead of them. A couple, like Tris in *Allegiant* and Fen in *Orleans,* don't survive at all. But other girls not only survive; they are poised to take on the world, to be leaders, to shape the future.

In "On Secrets, Lies, and Fiction: Girls Learning the Art of Survival," Kerry Mallan is "interested in how literature for young people depicts survival as a complex activity that negotiates silence, subjugation, and subjectivity" (36). While her focus is not on dystopian novels, YA dystopia includes a range of complex activities that girls engage in and these books are an even more powerful as a complex that "negotiates silence, subjugation, and subjectivity." Girls on Fire bear the responsibility of the problems of their world. As Becky Thompson explains of survivors of trauma, "Absorbing the world's pain is both a quality and a liability (since it places us at the center somehow, responsible for responding to, and fixing all that is wrong)" (63). Or, in Katniss's case, blaming herself for all that has gone wrong, even when she had no control over the trajectory of the rebellion. In fact, many Girls on Fire (like Alex in *Ashes* and Ruby in the *Darkest Minds*) blame themselves for the big problems that are out of their control. In *The Forgetting*, Nadia blames herself for not being able to save Gray. However, toward the end of the book, after Gray's memory has been returned (by Nadia), she says: "'I tried to save you, and I couldn't save you.' *I can never save you*" (385). Gray answers: "This, Dyer's daughter, feels very much like being saved" (385). Nadia is the only person in her world who cannot choose to forget and to not remember. She is the ultimate survivor. Though Nadia was a survivor of trauma when the novel begins, at the end, she speaks to this trauma more powerfully. She notes that "the past is never really gone.... It only lies in wait for you, remembered or forgotten.... It comes to me most often in my nightmares, when I wake up screaming and sweating during resting" (396). She is not the only Girl on Fire to suffer from nightmares, a symptom of PTSD.

Blythe Woolston also considers trauma and PTSD in "Bent, Shattered, and Mended: Wounded Minds in the Hunger Games." She discusses the brain, the way the brain makes sense of the world around us, and what happens to the brain when it experiences and tries to process trauma: "Many disaster survivors experience anxiety, nightmares, and other symptoms of PTSD" (171). We see these symptoms in many different Girls on Fire. But Woolston also illustrates the ways in which stories can help to heal trauma. She argues, "Making narratives is a way to make sense of events, and dreams might just be efforts to tell a story, to put the pieces together" (182). The stories of Girls on Fire complement our own stories and also inspire the capacity to write new stories, to imagine different worlds. She sees some power in the end of the series: "[Katniss is] imagining a future. That takes more courage than being a girl on fire" (178). And yet, imagining a future is exactly what defines a Girl on Fire.

Becky Thompson's insights about survivors of trauma can tell us a lot about the unique qualities of the Girl on Fire survivor. Thompson notes that "one of the unique survivor qualities is being able to sense that the world is on fire—the earth, our people, are in trouble" (63). Thompson must have been writing about YA dystopia's Girls on Fire because this description is so in tune with these female protagonists, their books, and the symbol of fire that is woven throughout so many of these stories. The other qualities she identifies also speak to the power of Girls on Fire: hyper vigilance, "having a heightened sense of awareness, a self-consciousness that creates a kind of insight and sensitivity" [Alex in Ashes]; "often recognize others in distress" [Gaia in Birthmarked]; often gifted healers [Cassandra in *Shadows Cast by Stars*]; "often at the center of building creative communities" [Cassia in Matched]; "see the world more rather than less accurately than the less traumatized" [Ruby in the Darkest Minds]; "have a way of keeping hope alive" [Katniss, and so many other Girls on Fire!] (43–4). Perhaps most notably, "Trauma survivors also understand compassion, not just for themselves but for those who injured them" (41). For instance, Nadia can't help but protect her father from the punishment he would receive for his manipulation of his family's books, but his abandonment hurts her every time she sees him. Eventually she learns his reasons, and they are the same reasons as everyone else: they were manipulated by Janis, the brutal and controlling Hegemon. Girls on Fire, in order to survive, cannot wallow in the past; they have to actively make the future.

As trauma has been put on the national radar, Thompson argues, a kind of doctrine has been created that runs the risk of "putting the emphasis on what is wrong with survivors.... " But, "Survivors are not, as individuals, the problem.... Survivors are the canaries in the coal mine, not the poisonous gas that kills the miners" (41). So, too, are Girls on Fire the canaries in the coal mine; what they survive in fiction tells us what we may have to survive in real life. Like us, Girls on Fire have not created the circumstances of their dystopia, but they have to take responsibility for the mess they have inherited.

* * *

In "Brown Girl in the Ring as Urban Policy," Sharon DeGraw argues that "in her 'everywoman' role, Ti-Jeanne serves as a model for survival. Engage in the community, look to family and faith for support and guidance, do not over-rely on science and technology for 'quick fixes,' and make tough decisions about personal finances and consumerism" (210). These notes on survival apply as much today as they do in this fictional future. But survival and community-building is not easy for Ti-Jeanne. As Thompson notes, "Survivors do much emotional, physical, spiritual, and mental work to stay in the world, to be present. That takes guts" (43). Ti-Jeanne loses her family and inherits a legacy with her community. She could lose herself to madness at times; instead, she relies upon spiritual traditions that have been passed down to her. DeGraw continues, "You may not end up with the traditional American dream, but returning to your 'roots' can be a sustainable alternative" (210). Sometimes, however, there are no roots to return to. Sometimes staying alive is the best a girl can do. And sometimes staying alive means building community.

In *The Forgetting*, everything is at stake. Nadia witnessed the ways in which the community tears itself apart approaching the inevitability of the Forgetting. And, if she does not succeed in getting out the truth and getting people to take shelter, the community will be decimated again, not only because of the Forgetting, but also because Janis has selected her "best" 150 people, has attempted to burn the Lost alive in their housing complex, and to kill the rest of Canaan's people with a poisoned grain supply. Janis is one Hegemon who is a woman, and she wields her power like any other dictator—

brutally, discriminately, and through fear. Nadia describes Janis's actions "to shape the truth as she pleases. To bend us to her will like a piece of melting glass" (238). But Nadia is the foil to her plans: "there's at least one person in Canaan who will no longer be bent. Who can shape the truth for herself" (238). Nadia knows that despite Janis's ability to remember, her remembering has been skewed. Her understanding is described as childish. She has not had access to the truth, so she has evolved her own. But Janis's vision belongs to the old world and Nadia is able to get people to safety, to restore the memories of those who choose to remember. Together the survivors work on building a new society.

* * *

Hardships, starvation, violence, even zombie attacks, these Girls on Fire survive some tough stuff. Some girls have special powers; many are just gifted leaders or have a special talent that helps them succeed. Still others are just "ordinary" girls who rise to the occasion. At the end of *The Worlds We Make*, Leo feels happy and wonders if that feeling is wrong given the state of the world. Kaelyn replies, "I think that's how we stay alive" (280). But before that moment, Kae wonders if this world "where all that mattered was being the strongest, biggest pack" was "a world I wanted to save" (238). Some Girls on Fire never stop to ask this question; survival is like putting one foot in front of the other.

Some girls survive but face the impossibility of their new world. For Miranda in the Last Survivors series, there is little to make a world from. All she can hope for is love and "family," even though the definition of family has expanded. When Gaia leaves Sylum and heads back to Wharfton, she is acting as a survivor; she is looking to build a new community by merging her old world and her new one. In *Shadows Cast by Stars*, Cassandra is a survivor and she will need to be a world-maker. June in the Legend series and June in *The Summer Prince* emerge with real power and influence. In *The Summer Prince* June is the new queen and Enki's blood has literally been spilled to get her there. Through her art, her love, and her realization that the system is not acceptable, June survives differently. She survives being charged with treason. She survives the long journey on foot to Salvador. She survives imprisonment.

So many of these survivors are poised to create new ideas of community. Kaelyn feels a sense of purpose and responsibility. Toward the end of *The Worlds We Make* she says, "the sense of purpose I'd felt before flooded me, twice as strong. For such a long time, the responsibility of carrying the samples had felt like a burden. But it was actually a gift" (253). She is given a great responsibility, but it takes time for her to understand and accept this fact. She continues, "I'd spent all this time intending to just hand it over to people with more authority than me, but I didn't have to.... I didn't have to let them ... decide how the world should be. I could at least try for the world *I* wanted" (253). She develops some sense of agency and the world that she wants is one that also takes into account the needs of other people.

Some girls have the optimism or the opportunity to re-construct a world, most often within the confines of a new or evolving community structure. In response to an interview question about the tendency of YA dystopia to reinforce "an ideology that privileges the individual at the expense of the social collective," Smith affirms that "*Orleans* is more concerned with picking everyone out of the muck, rather than just one shiny soul" (Conners 39). And, yet, we could argue that Enola functions as that one shiny soul. She is not compromised by Delta Fever, so she is shiny in this regard. She is worth Fen's sacrifice. But Enola is also symbolic, a sign of hope where there is little. She represents a community that has been more than disenfranchised. She might be a key to a new world; she might be a link to a forgotten community. She might be nothing but an ordinary girl in the Outer States with no idea where she came from.

The work of community happens beyond the pages of the fictional futures of Girls on Fire, but these texts also inspire those of us who navigate our real world(s). Womak describes the work of Detroit community organizer adrienne maree brown. brown notes, "For me, as an organizer, what gets me through has been immersing myself into these sci-fi worlds'" (178). But she doesn't just use it as a tool for escaping the challenges of her activist work, she also applies ideas from Butler's *Parables* books as a "template for change agency in desperate communities" (179). This text informs "community farming, building relationships with neighbors, and essential survival skills" (180), as well as "door-to-door relationship building that is nonjudgmental" (181).

Womack also notes brown's recognition of a community that is "not rooted in one place, but rooted in a shared ideology" (181). This community organizing, brown notes, is like the Zapatistas. It is a structure that fits a future world, a transcendent community. The shared ideology of Girls on Fire in YA dystopia that I explore here connects with the real-life struggles of women, of feminists, and of marginalized peoples of all kinds. It connects with the millions of women who organized, gathered, and combined their voices across the U.S. and around the world the day after Trump took office. One of the women who dances to Alicia Keyes's "Girls on Fire" song in my fitness classes at the Bangor YMCA told me that she was grateful to have been exposed to this song. She would not have known it otherwise when Keyes broke out into song after her motivational speaking. At this moment— on the mall in Washington, D.C., among thousands of other women—she was able to share this connected knowledge, this shared cultural text and symbol, and she was able to connect back to her home community and to

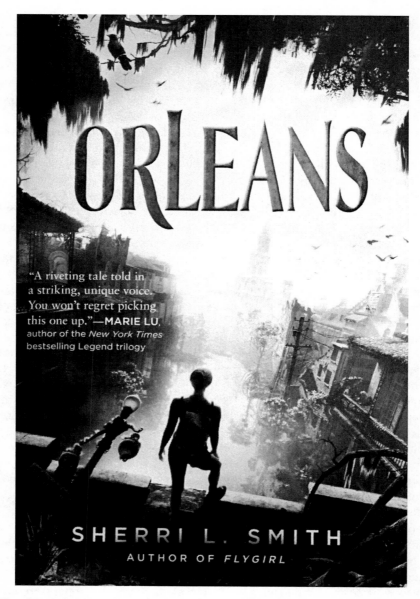

Place looms large on the cover of *Orleans*, the ambiguous Girl on Fire surveying the defining landscape. A streetlamp for Bourbon Street has fallen over and the streets below are flooded. Amidst the devastation, there are signs of life—the dilapidated buildings are flanked by bright green trees. Fen de la Guerre is shown looking away, but she is poised for movement (Penguin. Cover art © Michael Heath. Cover design by Danielle Carlotta).

the way we move our bodies and minds as a part of a community of women dancing. There is power everywhere.

* * *

The community that Olamina creates sets a standard that is difficult to live up to in life and in fiction. For Acorn, and Earthseed as a whole, every member serves the community and is responsible for teaching and rearing the next generation. Everyone works—at a trade they choose and on community projects like building houses. Everyone shares—food, language, art, skills, stories, lives. The system is small-scale but it grows mostly because of the need for such places. Everyone gets a share of the profits. Everyone at Acorn is free to join, or not join, Earthseed. Everyone is valued and community members look out for each other. In the future, Earthseed offers an alternative to violence, corrupt power, and self-interest.

Change is the only constant. And no one understands better than Olamina the "thorny tie[s]" that community creates as she laments her failures as a leader and the necessity of dispersing the community to avoid more violence, repression, and forced slavery. Then again, as Joy James notes, "in the face of isolation, exploitation, and abuse ... prisoners recreate new forms and meanings of 'community'" (30) and many Girls on Fire find themselves imprisoned figuratively, if not also literally, but never permanently.

Katniss is also a symbol that speaks to community. Katniss is "a girl with an uncanny (and often unwitting) ability to create a sense of community wherever she goes" (243), as Bree Despain argues in "Community in the Face of Tyranny: How a Boy with a Loaf of Bread and a Girl with a Bow Toppled an Entire Nation." As Despain notes, the Hunger Games also illustrates how powerful community can be in the larger struggle: "If you destroy the ability, or simply the desire, to give or to share amongst a group of people, you will destroy the heart of the community. And if you destroy the heart of the community and replace it with fear, then you will control the people" (238). Girls on Fire all face tyranny and build community or at least find new communities where they can be active participants. And community is a powerful tool. Despain argues, "The problem with allowing a sense of community to spring up in an otherwise oppressed society is that once it has started to take root, it's almost impossible to stamp out" (245). The communities that sprout at the end of Girls on Fire stories embody this impossibility.

Many of our YA dystopia stories end with ashes to build from or with structures to re-make. The building of new communities is the work for the girls to inspire and will fall to the next generation. The future Girls on Fire make offers a vision, and re-vision of a multi-colored, multilingual community that some critics today imagine as "the oppressed" (Sandoval) or the "new wretched" (Kelley), a community that crosses old lines of identity and culture, time and place.

Community is central to present and future understandings of identity and power. As Audre Lorde's powerful words remind us:

> Without community, there is no liberation, only the most vulnerable and temporary armistice between an individual and her oppression. But community must not mean a shedding of our differences, nor the pathetic pretense that these differences do not exist.... It is learning how to stand alone, unpopular and sometimes reviled, and how to make common cause with those identified as outside the structures, in order to define and seek a world in which we can all flourish. It is learning how to take our differences and make them strengths.

If we consider community as something less tangible, YA dystopia is a scattered yet connected community. Girls who survive become our leaders and have the responsibility to build a future community together, "a world in which we can all flourish."

Girls on Fire begin by standing alone "unpopular" and "reviled"; they are composed of a variety of individuals who are "outside the structures." But YA dystopia's stories "make common cause," because it "take[s] our differences and make[s] them strengths." YA dystopia's Girls on Fire are able to survive, grow, and prosper as a collective. These girls are able to lead the way toward a better future—a fictional future that is every bit as real as the future that so many authors so eloquently create from the scraps of history and the present. But the ideas of YA dystopia's Girls on Fire, as complemented by theories and historical analyses and perspectives, provide a kind of guide to reconstruction. Here, the science-fictional future and the real past inform the kinds of changes that need to happen in the present in order to create the kind of future worth fighting for. Again, *Parable of the Talents* reminds us that all we can do is "live in the world that is and try to shape the world that [we] want. But none of it is really easy" (273). Then again, if we focus on transforming/reconstructing identity, power, and community, maybe such a world is closer than we think.

SEVEN

Off the Page and
Into the World

The influence of (YA) dystopia—as a literary mode and as a cultural phenomenon—is at its peak cultural moment. It is easy to declare this trend "dead," as some critics have proclaimed (Corsetti). We are apt to make such declarations when something extends beyond its allotted sphere of influence in the cultural or popular culture realm and starts to impact, for instance, politics and revolutionary change. But the power of these ideas are not contained by their cultural forms, and the seed has been planted. When we read critical dystopias we are changing ourselves in ways that often make us want to change the world; we might even develop practical ideas about how we can transform the world, and actions toward doing so. As Moylan argues, critical dystopias "teach their readers not only about the world around them but also about the open-ended ways in which texts such as the ones in front of their eyes can both elucidate that world and help to develop the critical capacity of people to know, challenge, and change those aspects of it that deny or inhibit the further emancipation of humanity" (*Scraps* 199). In other words, texts reveal truths and empower transformation.

We might wonder if texts can have so much power and influence, but the mountain of evidence that illustrates the power and influence of texts makes this more a question of how, and to what ends, than it is a question of whether texts can change us or change the world. Moylan notes that "by means of their creative speculation, these hopeful texts help to revive and expand the popular political imagination in the name of progressive transformation," (277). The popular political imagination has been the focus of my arguments. This imagination is malleable and collective, and the voices of the marginalized are often not given credit or attention in the popular political imagination. The voices of Girls on Fire change this popular political imagination and elucidate the kinds of progressive transformation that can be bolstered with attention to these kinds of texts. Moylan continues, "They offer the prophetic challenge to go and do likewise, to become aware and fight back, possibly in a world that is not (yet) as bad as one on their pages" (277). And it might just be this "not (yet) as bad" quality that makes this genre so powerful. Further, this genre lets us imagine that if we act now, we can change this inevitable trajectory.

The role of dystopia toward the practical nature of transformation can be seen in other YA texts like *Green Valentine*. *Green Valentine* is not dystopia, but it is YA. It is largely formulaic like every good YA book tends to be—it follows the formula, but Astrid's story offers something different at the same time. It is cross-cultural and part of the American imagination. *Green Valentine* offers a love story as well as a partnership, a happy ending as well as a growth in consciousness and a realization of community. There's even a few good dystopia plots like the evil Mayor (Boy as Consciousness, Hiro's mother) and her scheme to corporatize Valentine and, on the other hand, the hypocritical anarcho-primitivist "soldiers battling for the earth" (184) who inspire plenty of critiques and conversations regarding violence and working within the system rather than destroying it. While Astrid is optimistic and proactive, Hiro is cynical and detached. The over-achieving, popular, beautiful protagonist Astrid Katy Smythe explains, "Living in Valentine was like living in a bleak dystopian wasteland" (7). Hiro sees Valentine as a dystopia, but he is more in tune with the fascist political and educational systems that are "keeping us docile" (40) and he describes his world "like a cross between *1984* and *The Hunger Games*" (41). The multiple references to dystopia not only underscore the novel's theme of environmentalism, but also give the reader a deeper layer of resonance. The reader of *Green Valentine* is most certainly familiar with *The Hunger Games* and with YA dystopia. The reader can take away real-life tactics of guerrilla gardening and community organizing.

In the end, Astrid—with the help of Hiro and her friends—brings the community together in all of its diversity: "crammed in together like one giant, swirling mass of colour [sic] and weirdness" (271). She tells this crowd: "growing our own vegetables is an *act of resistance*. And it's not a negative resistance like a boycott or a strike. It's *positive*. We're *creating other options*, opening up new pathways to live and be" (274). And Astrid is a leader who inspires her community first through guerrilla gardening and then through political organizing. She grows herself as well (as she also notes) and realizes that she needs new tactics. She notes, "Local government. Grassroots politics. Getting involved with the community. Changing the world from the bottom up. That was something I could get behind. The fight wasn't over, but we'd won this battle, and I was totally up for more" (278). Though Hiro steps to her side to share the feeling of "this whole saving-the-world business," Astrid keeps her voice and centrality. She says, "I was finally making a difference. I took that feeling and held it inside me, so it burned with a bright, joyful flame. I held it gently, letting its warmth spread through me./And I knew I would never, ever let it go" (279). Astrid is clearly a Girl on Fire. They're growing. We're everywhere, and not just in fiction or in the future.

Not Just for the Young

In a blurb on NPR's *All Things Considered*, former librarian, Janet Jones, makes a summer reading suggestion that speaks to the connections adults find to YA dystopia. In a review of *Why Grow Up?: Subversive Thoughts for an Infantile Age* by philosopher Susan Neiman, Jones notes that "one of the things that [Neiman] says is that 'Maturity means finding the courage to live in a world of painful uncertainty without giving in to dogma or despair. A grown up, 'Neiman writes' helps to move the world closer to what it should be while never losing sight of what it is." Jones identifies with this idea because, she notes, "I'm a grown up … but I also keep my childhood-ness with me too." However, this idea of "maturity" demonstrates how adults tend to underestimate young people, and the assumptions we make about adults. "Maturity," which comes with experience more than age, could be synonymous with coming of age. It could also be another way of separating adults from children and adolescents. If someone gives in to "dogma or despair," they are not mature? If someone struggles to keep perspective they are not adults? Young adults can have this maturity and perspective. In fact, young people who face adversity in their lives are forced to grow up more quickly. They have to act like "adults" even if they may not feel like adults. In *The Worlds We Make*, Kae and her friends come across a younger girl. Kae notes that "she looked hungry—not for food, but for information. Reassurance…. These days, at eleven or twelve, maybe you had to *be* one of the adults" (152). Today's world also requires many children to shoulder adult responsibilities, often because the adults are not holding their own.

Quite obviously, YA dystopia is not only enjoyed by young adults or teens, it is also read by women (and men) for any variety of reasons—the engaging characters, the fast-moving plots and quick-turning pages, the romance and the love and the hope. As Sean Connors writes about his edited collection, *The Politics of Panem*, "As this book attests, [Collins's] dystopian narrative about a teenage girl unwittingly caught between competing political ideologies continues to capture my imagination" (2). He's not the only scholar who feels this way. In *Bad Feminist* Roxane Gay describes her obsessive love of the Hunger Games trilogy and her anticipation for the first film:

> I am not the kind of person who becomes so invested in a book or movie or televi-
> sion show that my interest becomes a hobby or intense obsession, one where I start
> to declare allegiances or otherwise demonstrate a serious level of commitment to

something fictional I had no hand in creating. Or I didn't used to be that kind of person [138].

Gay declares herself "Team Peeta," gushes a bit more, and then continues, "After finishing *The Hunger Games*, I quickly read the next two books in the trilogy—my obsession, at this point, was raging and white hot. I was so invested I couldn't stop talking about the books" (139). My obsession is not unlike Gay's; however, I am invested in a whole collection of works and will always be "Team Katniss." We can all find the parts of YA dystopia's Girls on Fire where we are engaged and invested, but we can simultaneously appreciate the whole diverse band.

This trend of middle-age women loving young adult literature disgruntles some like YA author Anthony McGowan whose rant about middle-aged white women at a YA conference sparked an argument that not only occupied much of the conference, but continued online afterward. Sian Cain writes in the Children's and Teenagers Books blog for *The Guardian*,

> [Anthony McGowan] lamented speaking to "monocultural audiences" of white, older women at YA conferences. Some misogynistic, cause-and-effect musing began: most YA bloggers were women, all his editors were women, "so there is a huge amount of energy directing these kinds of texts, texts that may well appeal to women in their 20s and 30s rather than to teenagers. We've got this female-dominated world producing texts that reflect themselves, for other young adult women," McGowan said, perhaps unaware of the significance of making links between gender and perceived quality.

McGowan contests Cain's observations of misogyny in a blog post titled "Why I am a Misogynist." He repeats a similar version of what Cain reported and writes, "It's the kind of slur that's very hard to shift from one's back." Regardless of whether McGowan meant or intended misogyny, it appears. But so does elitism. Cain further quotes McGowan as saying: "I don't think adults should read YA stuff…. I think they should move on and read Tolstoy and Dostoyevsky or Dickens and stop reading Twilight and the Hunger Games…. It is part of being a grown-up, you leave those things behind." These sentiments clearly assert patriarchal power and elitism and are certainly not unique to McGowan.

McGowan's comments are rather mild compared to those made about a week earlier by Joe Nutt in a piece called, "Why young-adult fiction is a dangerous fantasy." Nutt's thoughts on the current state of YA are clearly dismissive and misogynistic:

> Several generations of teenagers, especially boys, have been effectively prevented from ever becoming literate adults by a publishing industry that has decided young adult readers have an insatiable appetite for what amounts to nothing more than gossip fodder, the endless recycling of petty anxieties and celebrity confessions that choke the pages of magazines placed strategically at the supermarket checkout. So

much young adult fiction is little more than a florid expansion of those headlines about the new love in Jennifer Aniston's life, Taylor Swift's dietary obsessions or Kim Kardashian's latest sex tape.

Nutt not only blames women for watering down the pool of literature, but also gives them responsibility for preventing generations of mostly boys from literacy. Not only is his description of YA lit dismissive and not accurate, it is ignorant and dangerous, especially when we consider that the majority of people teaching literacy are women.

Dunn shares an example of connecting with a male student over a shared love of Lois Lowry's *The Giver*. She writes, "Lowry is from a generation different from mine and my student's, but her powerful speculative fiction reached both of us. Lowry creates a space in which the mind can wander through the visual imagery and fantastic worlds she imagines" (15). Books are powerful tools of connection across generations.

The attraction of YA dystopia is, at least in part, an attraction to hope and the possibilities of the future that adults and mainstream culture can often take for granted. Boys and girls and women and men are attracted to these messages. Marotta notes, "As Elphick (2014) observes it is not the adults with their past societal notions that will be successful, but the youth of the present with their new outlook on life" (58). This plays out in *The Summer Prince* as June discovers that her waka perspective is being interrupted by sensibilities not fit for a waka: "this is a grande sound for a grande love and I wonder what it says about me that I can feel it vibrating in my throat" (183). Adults should also be reminded to questions the way things are. If we see the challenges to hegemony as the realm of the youth, if we cling to past societal notions (like sexism), if we dismiss the "dangerous fantasy" of YA, we condemn future generations to living dystopia.

Inspiring the Next Generation of Writers

Many books and websites include interviews with authors and, inevitably, they are asked to give advice to readers who also want to be writers. Again, Octavia Butler leads by example in her essays, "Furor Scribendi" and "Positive Obsession" inspiring writers to dedicate themselves to writing every day while also highlighting the challenges for writers who are poor, female, and/or black. She writes, "I saw positive obsession as a way of aiming yourself, your life, at your chosen target. Decide what you want. Aim high. Go for it" (*Bloodchild* 129). Authors like Kat Zhang, Marie Lu, Veronica Roth, and Alexandra Bracken illustrate that young women can be successful in the genre. Many of these authors are active online with their fans and readers. Some writers are accessible, like Alaya Dawn Johnson, who has done several online interviews and was a guest speaker in my "Race, Class, Gender, and Sexuality in American Culture" class (via video conference). In these contexts, writers inspire us. Johnson inspired me and my students through sharing the practical aspect of her work—her ability to make a (frugal) living as a writer—as well as the tools she has as an artist and storyteller to "make [the] conversation bigger" and "break certain assumptions." These are the kinds of motivation that inspires and motivate Girls on Fire.

The YA dystopia trend has inspired a plethora of material and a slew of self-publishing on Amazon.[1] One of the most successful of these books is *The Many Lives of Ruby Iyer* by Laxmi Hariharan. It has so many hallmarks of the genre: evil mother turned power-hungry megalomaniac, gay best friend, unexpected development of a super-power. While the story lacks depth and substance and the writing is a bit forced, the diversity it infuses into the genre is exciting. And there is plenty of action to entertain the reader. In the Ruby Iyer series, book 0.5, Hariharan describes Ruby Iyer as "just another scared, screwed up teenager growing up in Bombay, till a terrifying encounter propels her from her everyday commute into a battle for her own survival. Hariharan creates a world for herself and her readers, explaining how she composed the Ruby Iyer Diaries: "Ruby wrote almost daily from the age of ten till she left home at sixteen-and-a-half. It is from here I picked scenes from her early life." And Hariharan continues to grow Ruby Iyer's story.

Fan fiction inspired by YA is also a means to foster young writers, and writers more generally. Inspiration is in our favorite characters and readers can grow stories through online forums for aspiring writers. Cromwell notes of *Orleans* that "an uncertain future beyond the novel's end, encourage[es] its young readers to create their own ending, one that might include the ecofeminist ethic that the novel advocates" (29). Extending our favorite stories might also extend transformative ideas. In the extension of stories and in the re-working of them, there is power and potential. One of the assignment options I give for *Orleans* is to write the afterword or the next chapter of Fen's story. This assignment produces some interesting results from Daniel bringing Enola to Fen's sponsors to Daniel deciding to raise Enola himself to Enola returning to Orleans to face her future through her past. Sometimes Fen even survives.

In general, my Girls on Fire class attracts and inspires the students who want to be writers, and many of our students want to be writers (or are already writers, sometimes published). When the math department offered a contest to represent Pi, it was the perfect opportunity to inspire students to cross disciplinary lines and write about YA dystopia themes related to this mathematical concept. One student took me up on the challenge and her short story won the first place prize (a free 3-credit class). She continued to pursue this passion, was accepted to the Stonecoast Writer's summer workshop (and got a grant to attend), and later applied to the MFA program. Other students develop projects that grow beyond the one-semester class. Students sometimes further their projects through independent studies and inspire new directions and representations. Many students explore same-sex relationships or challenge other limitations of the genre. Girls on Fire and YA dystopia keep alive the dreams of many of us (perhaps myself included) who fantasize about *being a writer.* This inspiration can also inspire other realms of being and acting and creating.

Inspiring Pedagogy: The Power of Girls on Fire

While my scraps of fiction will most likely never find their way into the world, Girls on Fire inspires my teaching and research. Beginning with the texts themselves is our most powerful pedagogical tool. Many books include reading guides or discussion questions—in the book or online. More pedagogical tools are needed like the Tribe Education Resource Booklet written by Robyn Sheahan-Bright for Walker Books Classroom and produced with assistance from the Australian Government's Council for the Arts. It also includes context provided by the author through a "cultural and historical background" essay. This booklet includes background on the books, the cultural context, a framing through critical literacy, and ideas for classroom applications like themes, key quotes, discussion questions, and activities. Considering the strict curricular demands of the public school system in the U.S. and the competing demands on students' time, pedagogical tools and links to classic American literature texts help bring the future into the past-focused contemporary classroom like in Heather Hill Vásquez's "What Scout Wished For? An Intersectional Pedagogy for *To Kill a Mockingbird* and *The Hunger Games.*"

In *Zombie Seed and the Butterfly Blues: A Case of Social Justice,* R.P. Clair describes the various kinds of connections that literature has allowed students to make in her classroom. Clair argues that in part this Zombie theme (or "rhetoric") reaches students "because it speaks to the mind-numbing aspects of the traditional educational system" (xviii). A critical eye on one's own education is a solid start to critical consciousness. The subject matter of fiction can inspire students when it reflects the social, cultural, or political issues of our times, like R.P. Clair's Zombie theme. YA dystopia speaks to both an imagined world and the real world in all its complexity. A plethora of academic articles and books speak to the power and influence of YA dystopia and Girls on Fire in our classrooms, even if we use other language or different texts.

* * *

Girls on Fire is also a powerful—and multifaceted—theme. It certainly catches students' attention when they are registering for classes. It is also a kind of symbol that students can hold onto. The idea of the Girl on Fire can be a powerful archetypal image for girls and women in ways that we may not anticipate. In a section of *Minds Made for Stories: How We **Really** Read and Write Informational and Persuasive Texts* entitled, "Becoming Heroes of Our Own Stories," Thomas Newkirk argues that "constructing causal narratives also allows us to imagine ourselves as agents, even heroes, in our own life stories, which can be purposeful and coherent ('things happen for a reason')" (28). He supports this idea through psychology and then through anthropology, arguing that this need might just be "hardwired" into our brains and biology. This powerful element of stories—the ability to, through our imaginations, be the heroes as we read about them, might just transfer into heroic qualities in our lives. "Of course," he argues, "events are not in our complete control, and humans face trauma and tragedy" (29). Trauma and tragedy is an immediate reality in Girls on Fire's stories and my students' lives. Even if we cannot have complete control, having control over our story can be an important component of empowerment on an individual level. Newkirk argues, "Not surprisingly, a 'healthy' explanatory style is associated with increased motivation, persistence, and educational achievement. How we tell our stories matter" (29). But it is also important on a collective, cultural, and structural level. How we tell the stories of girlhood, and the stories of Girls on Fire, matter.

In my Girls on Fire class, my diverse non-traditional students note what this symbol means and what it can mean in their lives as well as in the lives of others and extrapolate what the Girl on Fire can be to young people, how she can inspire and promote social justice. Many students take this inspiration to heart. Confidence in voice, for instance, is inspiration and can be shared and students bring ideas from class to friends, family, and public forums. Students are quick to see the value in the symbol of the Girl on Fire within and beyond the text. As Mariah MacDonald explains,

> These girls we have read about have been able to stand up and go against the powers above them to find change. We are seeing this in today's media as well. People are standing up for what they think is right and that is a great thing to see. We should question things and have open ideas on the rules we are dealt and if we think there is something wrong let's stand up and fight for what's right. We can learn a thing or two from all of these reluctant heroes in our books.

Mariah also makes connections between our world and our need for real-life heroes:

> All of these books show us how we should move forward in society and question things we are not sure is right. Like we have seen time and time again the higher up powers are doing what they think is right and that is not always the case. They are

not living in the same conditions as some of these people so they are making an une-ducated guess for what is right and wrong. Those who are living it should feel okay to think and question the rules. These books can teach us all a lot of standing up and taking a stand when we think something may be wrong or needs change.

The Girl on Fire is the symbol that speaks to the need for change. The Girl on Fire takes on epic proportions, in part, because her strength, power, and influence can be seen across multiple examples. Reading one book or series is inspiring, but the symbol that emerges from across the genre is more powerful.[2]

Students who are familiar with these books might see them in a new light through the Girls on Fire lens. One student who had previously read the Hunger Games describes how she reconsidered the books through the Girls on Fire lens. She saw new value in this book and what her daughter might get out of it. Her first read was of teenage rebellion; her second saw a survivor and a hero. Another student, Michelle Cloutier, a teacher in her own classroom, makes similar connections as she describes how her middle school students understand this symbol and how it also resonated with her personally:

> My students immediately connect with this symbol. I think it is ever so important to expose young women to positive role models and leaders—people who are going to spark change in our world. I am thirty-eight years old and I felt empowered after reading the Hunger Games series. Who wouldn't? Girls on fire can help us face the future through their actions no matter how subtle they are....

Students are able to make personal and structural connections. Students describe the ways in which this course reveals the connections between how we live our lives and the direction the world is heading. Students start to see the ways in which privilege works, even if they don't use the word privilege. They see the denial that helps to support privilege. But most of my students do not live in worlds of privilege.

For some of my students, whose lives are filled with hardships that some-times are not a far cry from dystopic challenges, the Girls on Fire can resonate on a personal level. One student had to take an incomplete with me in two classes when she had a particularly rough semester. This is not unusual where I teach and I am excessively generous with incompletes. But few students fol-low through on the work to actually finish the course. Lacey Stone is one stu-dent who persevered and finished the work for both courses. When I got to her final paper for Girls on Fire, I found that she veered from the prompt. She writes:

> During the fall semester when this class was going on I was struggling. I was strug-gling as a woman to understand my world and my emotions. I have been raising my son basically on my own and struggling with relationships outside of the toxic one

with his father. I read these novels and cried. I found so much of my confused self in the main characters of these books. The maternal protector in Fen de la Guerre in *Orleans* struck me because I am a mother. Trying desperately to survive so someone else can too, Fen takes the role on without question. Katniss and her love for two different men in two different ways, and also fighting for survival in an arena where her every move is watched. At the time I felt as though I was living in a fish bowl and all eyes were on me. Fighting an abusive ex and trying not to lose my mind in the process was much like being in the Hunger Games themselves. Leaving a world behind that I had known for so long and venturing out into the unknown to survive and hopefully thrive like Lauren did in *Parable of the Sower*. I was finding myself while reading these books. I cannot express what kind of comfort they brought me. I'm still surprised at the way I internalized these characters and made such connections with them.

The comfort Lacey describes finding demonstrates the personal connections that we can make with a book at a particular time in our lives. Sometimes these books challenge what students think they know about themselves and about the world and some students are willing to look at themselves critically, to grow and change but also consider the bigger influence in how we can live better as a society. The simple connection of readers and text can provide a life-line.

These texts can also illuminate our experiences, helping us to get perspective on our accomplishments. Another student, Tiffany Schofield, describes the way in which my Girls on Fire class helped her get perspective on her professional experience:

For the last 15 years of working in the publishing world and managing a small publishing imprint, I've seen growth and changes that I had not dreamed possible. I embraced our struggling fiction list and continued to push forward with various marketing and promotional ideas on a shoestring budget because I fully believed in the writers and their fine talent for storytelling. No matter how many times I was told that "things just couldn't change" or that "no one really cares about that imprint" it only fueled my fire to fight harder. The journey of our small publishing imprint has been fraught with challenges the entire way (internally and externally) but I was not willing to give up. Until your enlightening *Girls on Fire* class, I had not considered my own role in our publishing program's "rebellion" to go against the grain and prove itself to the world (reluctant 'hero' syndrome, I suppose … lol). I simply knew I believed in the imprint and its writers and refused to give up. At some point along the way others finally started changing their perception(s) of our emerging publishing program and followed my lead to believe in the imprint and put some real support behind it./ I can proudly say that I've seen success in being a Girl of Fire for our small press. In 2012, one of our mystery authors landed on the finalists list for the MWA Edgar Awards* (this one still thrills me!), in 2013 we received the Lariat Award from Western Writers of America, in 2014 two of the five finalists spots for the Nero Award, and in 2015 we were named "Best Historical Western Publisher" by True West Magazine./ This incredible journey is also what inspired me to return to college to augment to my business degree with a bachelor's degree in English Literature. I feel like I have finally found my true calling in life and want to explore and enjoy every inch of my journey. And it all started with a small idea ... a spark that ignited a blazing revolution for my personal and professional life!

This student was able to put her passion and drive into perspective, to put her support behind something she believed in, and to see herself as a Girl on Fire. Another student, Emily Shull, had a similar reaction: "I have always struggled with rebellion and bucking against the norm. I like to think I have a little bit of girl on fire in me." So many of my students act as Girls on Fire, but they don't necessarily see this in themselves before making these kinds of connections between these books and their lives.

These are the sentiments of many students. Many actually think that Girls on Fire is more than just an academic theme or pop culture catchphrase. The connections between the characters and real girls—like the students themselves!—is a powerful one. One student, Cherise Letorneau notes:

> We all have it in us to be Girls on Fire, we simply have to stand up for what is right and not be afraid of baggage of a word like 'feminist,' which is slowly being reclaimed by a new generation of women or being called a 'nasty woman' as a way to bring us down only for millions of women to wear the badge, or rather—shirts happily.

This student makes connections between what she learned in class and what is going on in the world around her. Girls on Fire was an obvious connection to feminism, to politics, to social change, and to rebellion and hope.

Pedagogy: Action Projects

In all of my classes I include "action" projects, and I have written several articles that describe these civic engagement projects and their impact on students and on education more generally. This staple of my curriculum and pedagogy allows students to put ideas from class into action. In my Girls on Fire class I have used both the open-choice project as well as the proscribed project. Both produce new ways of understanding these texts and new ways of circulating their ideas outside of the classroom. Through their academic work for Girls on Fire, students can be empowered in myriad ways and can make an impact outside the classroom. In my *SIGNAL* article I conclude, "The Girls on Fire theme can inspire students to fight for a better world—and more diverse books—or, at least, discover (and maybe even share) a world of books that are often dismissed or overlooked" (52).

Students take on a variety of projects including designing lesson plans, engaging in social media campaigns, creating library displays, and collecting and sharing resources. Some students host film showings and discussions with friends or with their children and their children's friends. Many students work in libraries and schools and they take Girls on Fire into these spaces, creating displays, pathfinders, bookmarks, and handouts. Some students write stories, giving voice to the Avox of the Hunger Games, for instance. Or they create art projects that bridge the struggles in their world and the perseverance of the Girls on Fire in books. Students also create unique, inspired projects. For instance, one student created fliers with statistics about the capital vs. the districts that illuminated today's world and left them in books at stores and libraries—a kind of covert consciousness-raising. Another student wrote and illustrated a children's book version of Katniss's story for kindergarten-age children. My favorite project was a "guerilla gardening" project. The student assembled a variety of garden-related quotes from the Hunger Games and printed them on stickers. She put these stickers on small envelops full of seeds that included a variety that would grow something in any climate. She spread these seed packets at a Detroit art show and I continue to distribute these seeds to students and to promote our campus community garden project.

Some of these projects make powerful interventions in people's lives. For instance, one student used the action project as a way to connect with other military wives—young women who gave up their life ambitions, at least temporarily, to follow their military spouse to Italy. The student reported that the women were able to discuss the ways they felt about losing their fire and how they worked to stay true to themselves even when they feel isolated and alone and far from home. Some students use the action project to express themselves artistically and therapeutically, processing domestic violence experiences and other trauma.

In addition to turning inward and locally, students can see the power of taking ideas from class into the world—the one requirement of this project. Students recognize the importance of sharing knowledge toward a better world. One student, Michelle Corriveau, also notes that the action project is often the component that is missing in academic classes:

> The action education projects were very unique in themselves. I've taken literature courses my entire life because I love the worlds and characters and complex social issues. This is also why I've taken all psychology and sociology based subjects in college. However, this is the first class where we didn't just sit to talk about it and analyze it. We had to break the fourth wall of our classroom, so to speak, and live it.

The third and final time I taught this topics course I made some changes to the action project aspect of the course. In the first two iterations students chose their projects from a list of general suggestions and shaped these projects to fit with their time and interests. In the third iteration, I created a set of action assignments that connected to the weekly materials, largely derived from the kinds of projects students completed in the first two iterations.

Instead of completing only one project over the course of the semester, students chose any two projects that fit their interests and time.

Girls on Fire Action Projects: Connections and Extensions

Book	Action Project
Parable of the Sower, 1st half	Ask at least three people what YA dystopia is and whether this is a topic that interests them. Find three online sources that describe/explain what YA dystopia is. Write about 300–500 words about what YA dystopia is and why it is a topic that is important to consider in American studies and/or women's and gender studies. Share what you learned with at least three people on social media or IRL.
Parable of the Sower, 2nd half	Do some research about one of the real-life problems that contribute to the conditions of dystopia: climate/environment, economic, war, disease, technology. What is the problem and what are people doing (or not doing) to address the problem? What do you think can be done to address this problem? How does dystopia help us understand the problem, what is at stake, and what can be done?
The Hunger Games *Catching Fire* *Mockingjay*	Host a book discussion group or film viewing and discussion for one of the HG series books at your home or at a campus or center. Invite friends, family, other students, or community members to participate. Briefly describe what you did: how you promoted/invited people, what you planned, what you did, how it went. Reflect upon what you learned through this discussion and how you were able to share ideas from class with the people who attended this event.
"Othered Girls on Fire: Navigating the Terrain of YA Dystopia's Female Protagonist" and the Introduction to *Female Rebellion in Young Adult Dystopian Fiction*	Create a collage of images (cut and paste IRL or compile images and create a digital collage) that represents the "Girl on Fire" or the "Female Protagonist." Include some analysis of your collage and share with at least three other people on social media or IRL.
Prized	Ask 3 to 5 people what the world would look like in the future if women were in charge. Considering these responses in relation to *Prized*, explain how/why the world might be different if women were seen as the primary leaders. What are the problems and promises of matriarchy? How does this vision compare to *Prized*?

Orleans	Write an afterword for this book. What is the next chapter for Fen or for Enola?
Shadows Cast by Stars	Cass learns the lesson of the importance of self-care. Do something for yourself that is a practice of self-care. Briefly describe what you did (went for a walk, took a yoga class, meditated...) and consider Cass's experience with learning about the need for self-care in order to be present for yourself and for others. How can self-care practices help Girls on Fire?
The Summer Prince	Public Art: June is a public artist: "I live for spectacle, for the construction of emotional states and the evocation of suppressed feelings ... and I am done with fairy tales. I want art, pure and clean and uncompromising" (33). Create your own public art project.
End of class reflections	What books are popular and well-known (HG, Divergent) and which are less well known (SP, Orleans, Shadows Cast By Stars)? Why? Share a less well-known YA dystopia book with friends, family, or community. Create a post to distribute via social media or create a library display or make a flier or book insert. Reflect upon why this book is less well-known, how it can be better known, and why it is important to share books like this.

Cherise Letourneau describes her project and how she drew inspiration from *The Summer Prince*. She writes:

> I started an art project myself based on these images. I'd been trying to bring awareness to these causes for awhile online to followers. But thanks to June and her need to paint and create pieces of art as a symbol, I decided to do the same. I paint these famous images, redesign them to convey emotions. Though so far I've kept them to myself, I felt a need to paint such emotional scenes and get the emotions I feel about this country on paper. If I hadn't had this class this semester, I might not have had this sort of coping method since election night to get through such feelings of fear and anger and sadness. June while drawing on pieces of paper in a way of coping with the soon to be loss of Enki and possibly in the person who she had known as Gil becoming a shadow of his old self with grief, she drew them both.

Students are able to see and articulate the connections between action and education and value this aspect of the class. They can make connections between what they read and what they see. Students can see how small acts can make a big difference; they can be part of a bigger struggle. They can feel powerful; they can be Girls on Fire. Alexandra Ireland describes,

> I think that seeing those parallels between real life and fictional individuals created or rather changed part of my world view. I've read a lot of young adult novels, dystopian and otherwise, and at the end, I'm able to close the cover and walk away.

Doing these projects, seeing that some of what's happening in these novels are not some distant part of our future, but rather something that is happening *right now* changed something in me. I read novels now and I relate what's happening to a real life conflict. It not only enhances my reading experience, but it also enhances how I see the world and how I look at world issues. Somehow, I'm better able to relate to world issues through novels. I think we see the news and because it's so bad all the time, naturally, to protect ourselves, we try to gain distance from it. All that really does, in the end, is allow us to deny that certain atrocities are happening around the world, some of them in our own backyard, and half the battle is just being aware of and acknowledging them.

These books aren't abstract. When Cherise Letorneau posted about the Dakota Access Pipeline in relation to the project connected to the 2nd half of *Parable of the* Sower she noted:

I now look at a lot of my reading and look for similar undercurrents on matters such as these. Is there a political message in there? Is it hinting to history repeating itself? I look at these matters and I see them on the news. I watch as our Earth becomes sicker and watch people like those at Standing Rock fighting to try and keep us as a people from becoming sick with it. All of this can be seen as hints to futures that aren't so far away from these books.

Making these specific connections to what's going on in the world, helps to show the relevance of these books and the importance of being an active participant in making the world we live in as well as the world we want our children and future generations to live in. Many students took the advice that Madda provided to Cass and applied it to their own lives. And many others made connections beyond themselves. Courtney Koller explains,

Looking back on the action/education projects I have accomplished, I have discovered that too much of anything results in disorder. The action/education projects have illustrated that balance is the key to survival of society as a whole. The YA dystopian genre acts as a physics crystal ball, the genre is illustrating what our future society can potentially look like if we continue to allow technology to advance at the rate it is going without applying restrictions and limitations.

In the classroom, the power of Girls on Fire and the YA dystopia books also gives students room to consider the possibilities of change, of the power of ideas. As Lara Naisbitt notes,

I really liked doing these assignments because they very much solidified my understanding of dystopian literature, and specifically the Girl on Fire, as political art, as subversive in the sense that they uncover truths of our own world; provide us with the lens to see certain global problems, structures of power, and categories of inequality that exist in our societies. We desperately need more books like these because they make us *think*. And for girls in particular, they make us aware of our own entrapment by the dominant culture and give us alternative perspectives of girlhood.

Lara gets to the heart of what these books are about and why I built a class around them. Students raise their consciousness, building on a solid base or seeing through power for the first time. Alexandra Ireland, a student who came to class with solid critical thinking skills, extends our class discussions and speaks to the need for people to "wake up":

> Theoretically, I understand that in history, revolutions are built on the backs of dead men and women, but ideologically, I like to think that something as extreme as death isn't necessary for change, but in YA dystopia (and in real life, I suppose) it seems to be the only thing extreme enough to wake people up. People want a singular, significant, and sudden event to spark change, and what event is more significant, finite, and impactful than death? Birth, I suppose, but do we need death to begin a (re)birth? Are the two events so intricately connected that we cannot have one without the other?

These big questions become more important every day, but the classroom is often ahead of the world we inhabit, particularly the world represented by mainstream media.

From Print to Screen

For years, Hollywood has produced films that focus on the actions and exploits of men. In *Terminator 2*, Linda Hamilton kicks some serious ass, but she is also "crazy" and shortsighted. In the *Star Trek* and *Star Wars* films and franchises more generally, a woman or two get to have a brave and powerful moment, if she looks good doing it. In many films, women are barely present and/or are motivation for returning home or fighting the good fight (sometimes they also kick ass): *Oblivion* (Tom Cruise), *The Matrix* (Keauna Reeves), *Looper* (Bruce Willis), *Mars* (Matt Damon), *After Earth* (Will Smith), and *Edge of Tomorrow* (Tom Cruise with Emily Blunt kicking ass). Every once in a while a woman will get a central role like Sandra Bullock in *Gravity* or Charlize Theron in *Panthenon* or Sigourney Weaver in the *Aliens* franchise. Sometimes TV versions make more room for women like in *Battlestar Galactica's* 2005 remake where the Starbuck character is female (Katee Sackhoff), or *Star Trek Voyager* with Captain Janeway (Kate Mulgrew). Starbuck is conflicted, reckless. Janeway is poised, accomplished; she's also the least popular Star Trek franchise.

Men carry the action and the starring role in most science fiction films, but it is typical for mainstream dystopian stories to end with a female figure as the hope for the future. Films like *Book of Eli*, *V for Vendetta*, *Children of Men*, *Waterworld*, *Snowpiercer*, *In Time*, *Dredd*, and others give girls a bit of space—some education in the ways of survival in the dangerous world—but they do not give her agency over the film or even over her own story. It is rare to see a dystopian story that centers the girl or woman, where she starts the story and finishes it, or passes it along to the next generation. In *Waterworld*, the young girl does not speak, but the map to solid land is a part of her body. She is hope for the future. In *V for Vendetta*, vigilante V leaves Evey (Natalie Portman) to take up the political resistance he has dedicated his life to. She is a guarantee it will continue. In the film version of *Children of Men* (where the book and film vary greatly)—in a world where no babies have been born for 17 years—the hope for the future lies in the womb of a young, black, immigrant woman. In *The Book of Eli*, Eli (Denzel Washington) saves Solara (Mila Kunis) from being raped and/or sexually enslaved and she takes up his fight. In all of these films, the girl or woman is threatened physically if not also sexually. In *V for Vendetta*, V tortures and imprisons Evey to reveal the truth and secure her loyalty. She can almost forgive him. In most of these films, the man dies to help ensure that the girl carries the torch, but the story often ends before the girl really gets to do anything besides look prepared or hopeful—maybe even locked and loaded, like Solara—for the future.

YA dystopia's Girl on Fire offers a central character—a story that is all hers. She shares it, but there is no doubt about who is the center. In the realm of film, Katniss and Tris are unique. For many Hunger Games and Divergent fans, the story of Katniss and Panem, and Tris and the Dauntless, comes through the films without the context of the fuller story and reading experience. What do these films mean without the depth that the books provide?

Ex Machina (2015), *Lucy* (2014), and *Mad Max: Fury Road* (2015) might offer new feminist hope for (white) females in science fiction films. Or they might repeat many old restrictions for women—beauty (even despite physical "imperfection" or disability), agency post-narrative, a place in a bigger story and plot where men run the show (literally and figuratively). *10 Cloverfield Lane* (2016) is an interesting example of a dystopian (officially fantasy/mystery, or thriller) film that simultaneously offers feminist hope while also being a show run by men. Michelle (Mary Elizabeth Winstead, known for her "scream queen" roles) wakes up chained to a cement wall after a break up with her fiancé and a car accident. The film leaves many elements to imagination and assumption as she tries to figure out what's going on. She fights back against her captor, even when she finds out that the air outside is poisonous. She designs and assembles a contamination suit using her skills as an aspiring fashion designer. When she finally escapes, she discovers that there has been an alien invasion and she has to fight to stay alive. She triumphs over the familiar—a conspiracy theorist/doomsday prepper/navy veteran who may be a pedophile or just a lonely, abusive wanna-be father—and the totally unfamiliar—alien beings. In the end, a Molotov cocktail defeats the alien. And while her abductor led her to believe the world had ended, humanity is surviving and fighting back and winning and rather than flee to the "safe zone," Michelle joins the struggle. Like so many other dystopian films, her story is really only beginning, but she had to defeat The Man and rescue herself. As Tasha Robinson writes in her excellent analysis of the film,

> But ultimately, the ending fits because it's the necessary completion of a meaningful arc. The film is Michelle's story. It starts with her, it sympathizes with her throughout, and it dismisses plot points that aren't related to her story, or important in her character's mind. It doesn't end with Howard because it was never really about him. It's about the long-term effects of abuse, and how one person overcomes them. In the end, the aliens aren't as important as the journey they symbolize, and help complete.

10 Cloverfield Lane is ultimately Michelle's story and Michelle is certainly a Girl on Fire.

* * *

While the Hunger Games was popular before the films, Katniss has certainly become an icon through the films. And because of its success, other Girls on Fire stories have been made into films or purchased with the promise of a film. The popularity of the Hunger Games and YA dystopia in the world of books has helped bolster a number of books that have been made into films or TV shows since 2012: The Hunger Games series (2012, 2013, 2014, 2015), the Divergent series (2014, 2015, 2016, 2017), *Ender's Game* (2013), *The Maze Runner* (2014), *The Giver* (2014), *The 5th Wave* (2016), *The Host* (2013), *Z Is for Zachariah* (horribly skewed, 2015), *The Selection* (2012 TV movie). Several online articles offer lists of the many novels that are in the process of being made into films or television series: *Legend, The Forrest of Hands and Teeth, Cinder, Incarceron, The Darkest Minds, Matched, Partials, Shatter Me, Uglies, Under the Never Sky,* and *Slated.* Many of these optioned books will never make their way to the big screen, and the small screen may be a more likely fate, as the final installment of Divergent hints. These films set the stage for an army of Girls on Fire films but the choices of what books get film offers follows along some of the same lines as the whitewashed trends I examine throughout this book.

Critics note that the final installment of the Hunger Games franchise did not do as well as expected and none of the other films have reached the peak of *Catching Fire.* Critics also note that splitting the final book in the trilogy into two films was most likely the death toll for the Divergent Series. After *Allegiant's* unsatisfactory showing in theaters, the last film was diverted straight to DVD with promises of a TV pilot. Since Tris dies before *Allegiant* ends, she has no place in an ongoing series, unless this element of the plot changes. Can you have a series about a Girl on Fire if she dies before it begins? Perhaps we are not telling the most compelling stories that Girls on Fire have to offer.

Feminist hope in popular culture—in film, in particular—resides in the films of the Girls on Fire not yet made. For instance, Lauren Olamina's story is epic. It could be a trilogy of films. *Orleans* would also translate well to a single film. *Beauty Queens* offers an opportunity for a cast of multi-cultural characters who are both beautiful and compelling as well as diverse. Tankborn started as a film script; it could certainly be re-imagined as one. The Partials' action would entertain viewers at least as well as any film about cyborg war. What all these stories have in common (girls of color) reveals the limitations of popular culture which are stricter than books. And yet, there is some progress, as Lily Herman demonstrates in an article for *Teen Vogue*, "Tomi Adeyemi Talks YA Fiction Publishing Deal for 'Children of Blood and Bone.'" Reporting on her seven-figure book deal (which also includes a film), Herman describes:

> The young adult West African fantasy book follows the story of Zélie, a young girl who's fighting against her oppressive monarchy to bring magic back to her people. If her mission fails, her community could be wiped out.... But aside from a compelling plot and a strong-willed heroine as the protagonist, the book deals with larger themes, like race, police brutality, oppression, and power, that are being discussed in real time.

This book certainly provides a Girl on Fire and dystopian elements as well as a context outside the white western world. And the author provides further fuel. Herman quotes Adeyemi, "For me, this is how I try to help the world. This is how I can protest and how I can say something. Often problems like racism or police brutality feel so much bigger than one person, and we ask how we can deal with these [issues]. If I write this and I can make people understand, then I feel like I'm doing my part to fight this and I feel like I *can* fight this." Further, Adeyemi notes that her inspiration for writing came from seeing the backlash against the casting of Rue and Thresh in the Hunger Games films. Adeyemi continues, "When these prejudices are depicted in an entirely other world, you're able to see things in black and white and then empathize and understand. With a story, that's the closest thing we have to being in someone else's head." As a young woman of color, Adeyemi's contributions to the popular imagination signal a necessary shift toward empathy.

The cultural trends of films and books last longer than the present moment. The films simultaneously spread the fire and squelch it. In films we are able to live the books in new ways. In media more generally, we can continue to experience the books we love, make connections, create tributes, and inspire new ideas. But, these books survive; we come back to them. We relive them and extend them.

The End? (Spoiler Alert)

I hate when a book or series ends. I can't wait to get to the end—to see what happens—but when I get there I lament that I can never go back. And yet, I go back. I re-read books, and not only because I am teaching them. I read them again to enjoy them again; sometimes I enjoy them even more. Many of these books, particularly those that are a part of a series, employ the convention of cliff-hangers. (Some do so better than others.) We can't stop turning the pages. We stalk the library or book store waiting for the next book, the last book, the new book. Or we have all our electronic books at our fingertips. Paper or digital, these books also resonate outside of their textual world, which makes them even more powerful cultural texts.

The resolution to our favorite series may not meet our expectations or desires though many of these books include the requisite happy ending, even as many of these happy endings are open to interpretation. Sometimes happy endings are fitting and necessary like at the end of the Lunar Chronicles. We have been given so many fairy tale elements that we have earned our happily ever after. And we get those very words on the last page even if the happy endings are a bit more complicated and contingent. Cinder and Kai don't end with a marriage proposal. In fact, as Kai kneels, Cinder warns him that he better not ... but he is presenting her with her foot—the proof of their perfect fit and a symbol of the past (and a twist on the glass slipper). Cinder accepts the possibility of someday being an Empress and she drops the foot of 11-year-old Cinder into the lake where the previous evil queen sent her victims.

We often crave happy endings. I am also a "bad feminist," and I am just as guilty. I was beyond annoyed when I picked up *Allegiant*, the third book in the Divergent series, only to find that there was duel narration. I could only conclude that Tris was not going to survive this book. I could hardly finish reading the book after her death. Many readers were disgusted with Veronica Roth. Some readers applauded her bravery and integrity while other readers refused to read the third book, or any of her other books ever again. It can be difficult to let go of the characters we love. Some books allow pretty much everyone to survive and to find a happily ever after. Some books kill off one peripherally key character (like Christina's boyfriend in *Insurgent*), but let the others live mostly happily. But other books, like the Hunger Games' *Mockingjay*, disposes of character after character, including Katniss's beloved sister, Prim—the one she entered the Hunger Games to save in the first place, the one who seems to also want to help people to the detriment of her own safety. And Prim's death is further complicated by the question of whether the bomb that killed her was from the capitol or the rebels. The former is bad enough; the latter is too much to bear. Plenty of characters in the Hunger Games live to build, or at least see, the future, but the ending could hardly be understood as happy. Many books have endings that keep us busy debating, like the Hunger Games. Some people read this ending as romantic and happily ever after while others read it as dismal, a compromise, the slowly burning embers of a fire that has long been extinguished. Bree

Despain argues, "in the end she's so broken it's shocking … although not surprising considering that most dystopian stories end with a dead or destroyed protagonist" (250). The end of the Hunger Games trilogy keeps us thinking—it is a powerful and unsettling ending. It is both shocking and not surprising, but in the worlds of YA dystopia's Girls on Fire this is not the fate of "most" protagonists.

Ambiguous endings that allow for multiple interpretations and offer endings that mirror the complicated circumstances of the story, are the best endings. For instance, in *Requiem* the Delirium series ends with a connection, a clarification of misunderstandings—a declaration of love—and the collective tearing down of the wall that has been built to reinforce the divide between the haves and the have nots. Lena calls for the reader to "Take down the walls…. All of you, wherever you are…. Find it, the hard stuff, the links of metal and chink, the fragments of stone filling your stomach. And pull, and pull, and pull" (391). This call to action is a powerful way to end a book series that has shown us a world that we definitely don't want to live in, but more importantly, also shows us that such worlds can be changed.

Some books offer a vision of freedom in the end. As *The Forgetting* concludes, Nadia works to help reconnect families and to "create a history" (396), but neither she nor Gray can be contained by the walls any longer. They set out to explore the planet and find the remains of the ship that brought the first humans to their new home. They "leave it to lie" and move beyond. Nadia notes, "I never imagined the unknown could be so beautiful. I want to write it down" (403). And just at that moment, Gray says, "Let's run" and Nadia concludes the novel: "And we do" (403). This last image is one of freedom and the impending discovery of the unknown as well as love and partnership and hope.

Some endings are too easy like *Article 5*. If the book had ended at the end of chapter 17, "We were going back to the resistance" (359), it would have set up the sequel while also leaving us with hope as well as a sense that Ember would be facing struggles that she is now better-prepared to face. The whole book was a very drawn-out process of coming of age and coming to consciousness. We know Ember is ready for the next stage. But the final chapter tries too hard to convince us. On the future, "the time to fight was coming, but until then we'd been granted a moment of peace; a deep breath before the plunge" (360–1). Many Girls on Fire have this kind of moment—often a stolen moment when they can just be, and just be with the one(s) they love. Here, the fight and the plunge lack the revolutionary potential of other struggles. But, it's only the first book in the series.

Other endings are more difficult to swallow. Just as very few books kill off the female protagonist, very few kill of the male love interest. In fact, a few temporarily fool us into believing he may be dead. At the end of the first book in the Delirium series, Alex is surely dead as he is mobbed by enforcers and Lena barely escapes with her own life and is then nursed back to health by other Invalids. But, Alex is not dead and his reappearance causes some drama. In *The Interrogation of Ashala Wolf*, Conner is dead and Ashala is devastated. "The entire world shifted, breaking apart and leaving me falling into nothingness" (347). Ashala asks her grandfather for help and is filled with sound; she saves him with a kiss, in the style of Sleeping Beauty: "the song poured into the word and the word poured into the song, and it all poured out of me" (357). And this kiss becomes an epic kiss:

> Electricity sparked between us, and I was burning, but not with rage this time. Everything seemed to vanish, until there was nothing except the feel and the taste of him, and the music pulsing through us both. The boundaries between his self and mine disappeared, and for a glorious moment, I was the angel and he was me, and the two of us together were the whole world [357].

This is not the only book where epic love overcomes death but near-death is a common trope.

In *Once*, the second book of the Eve series, we are led to believe that Caleb is dead. His death is hard to accept, but when Eve does accept it, she is reinvigorated in her quest for justice and the last book turns back to the feminism of the first book. She knows she needs to rescue the girls, kill her father, and aid the rebellion. The resolution of the Eve series shocked me in its overt pandering to the happy ending expectation. Just as the series is coming to a close, there is hope. Eve runs to find the survivors of the Dugout and there he is. His legs don't work, but he's still alive. The doctor was ordered to let him die, but he keeps him secretly alive instead. The book concludes with Eve answering the question about who she is with the answer: "I'm his wife" (310). This unbelievable moment—definitely worthy of throwing the book across the room—is somewhat mitigated by the "new epilogue," which revisits the story five years later.

We can accept death when it makes sense for the plot and other aspects of the book; for instance, Enki's death is slowly dragged out over the course of the novel. It would not make sense for him to live. But I still refuse to believe that Fen is dead at the end of *Orleans*. I ask my students to write the afterword and sometimes I can experience a different ending for Fen. Other critics see her death as perfectly clear and unambiguous. Coleman writes, "Fen is instantly killed from the gunfire" (26). *Orleans'* ending was, for me, open for interpretation. For most of my students and for critics, this open possibility was obviously closed. Coleman notes that "Orleans does not end neatly. In fact, the ending is left ambiguous" (29). But, he is not referring to Fen's death; he is referring to Enola and Daniel's escape. Coleman describes the ending with Enola's fist as having "positive undertones" and Enola's gesture having a "nascent environmental activism" even if the "gesture is ambiguous"

(29). For Marotta, this gesture is not ambiguous: "She leaves her readers with the image of resistance, of Enola "'waving her small fists at the weeping sky,' the resilience of the next generation, and the symbol of the fight to escape oppression still to come" (62). This fighting spirit is hope.

Marotta also finds hope in Fen's death: "Fen chooses her own version of freedom—she elects to die by the hand of the soldiers while saving her community rather than succumb to the plague…. Fen gains control of her commodified body and chooses to surrender her life in exchange for her child's freedom" (62). A kind of freedom is certainly what Fen exercises, but the stretch to saving her community is not supported by the text. As I note earlier, nothing about this exchange impacts the greater community of Orleans. But, this is the power of stories and our many interpretations. The author's perspective can add another layer.

Smith finds it "interesting" that her interviewer, Sean Connors, sees the ending of *Orleans* as "ambiguous" (39–40). (What might she think of my argument that it is "open for interpretation"?) Smith describes the ending in relation to the character's trajectory within this solo novel: "Fen completes her journey from survivor to willing sacrifice. Daniel moves on from trying to save a brother that died long ago to saving a living baby. Enola is … the future. And it's wide open" (40). The future is wide open because the baby, Enola, represents that expansive hope. But, in Fen's former world, violence is encroaching. In Daniel's world, scarcity and extinction are causing conditions to worsen. The wide open, Smith notes, is "hopeful, but at a cost, and with more to do" (40). This is the only realistic kind of hope at the conclusion of YA dystopia. Even the happily-ever-after endings are often contingent.

Some books end pointing toward possibility, and none of them assume that radical change is going to be easy. At the end of *Resist*, Bea notes, "And he's right. We all have a lot to do. A lot to learn. A lot to still be afraid of. But today, I'm glad of the rain on my hand and my own shallow breath./The elements finally belong to us all./And for now, that's good enough" (360). With the freedom to breathe restored, there is hope that society can be rebuilt. *Echoes of Us*, the last book in the Hybrid Chronicles, also ends with conditional hope as Eva notes "the dissolution of the institutionalization system" which is, Hally notes, "a start" (350). Eva continues, "the other things—the tolerance, the fading of the hatred and the fear—would come later. I believed in that" (350). *The Summer Prince* points overtly to hope with Enki's death literally marking June as the next leader. We know that she will be able to implement change and that the future might not be perfect, but it will be better. Enki's sacrifice will interrupt a long tradition of slow change and evolving corruption.

Regardless of the endings of books, they point toward the future, the hope and strength we need to survive and transform ourselves and our worlds.

But not all books, not all endings hold the same weight or inspire the same action. In her comparison of dystopia and volunteerist YA literature, Heather Snell shows how "young people not only cultivate an other-regarding ethic but also transform themselves into 'good' global citizens" (122) but she also finds that these novels fall short of "any real solution" (122). Further, they often reinforce the "magic" of returning home and the conservative values" of the American family. We see this type of ending in the Darkest Minds series. After Charles publicly contests the "communities" that are nothing more than new prison camps, Ruby's friends hurry her off to "forget for a little while. Outrun the hurt" because "everything will be different going forward" (534). Liam shifts into some kind of old-fashioned world where despite their adult endeavors and independence for most of their childhood, if they want to see each other he will have to get "permission to take the car" and she'll have to "run it by [her] parents to get their okay" (534). And so for a few moments they are carefree and together: And the open road rolled out in front of us" (535). There are hints that however the U.S. moves forward, it will have to take into account the toll that trauma will take on the children who have lived through this violent ordeal. But after surviving such a level of violence—after leading the other children and working with the adults— it's difficult to believe they'd be content to go back to being children. Instead, Snell argues, "perhaps what is needed most right now are not books that begin the difficult process of imagining alternatives only to rewind us back to an imagined past, but rather, books that take greater risks by modelling present and future worlds, which, while not perfect, inspire us to take a radically different direction" (123). Some of these inspirations can be found in the realm of the online world.

Beginnings from Endings: Social Media and Activism

Endings seem like logical points of conclusion. But these endings are also potential points for beginnings. As Rebecca Solnit notes in her 2016 foreword to her 2004 book, *Hope in the Dark: Untold Histories, Wild Possibilities*: "Hope calls for action; action is impossible without hope" (4). For some readers, these books open us to the real problems in our world and inspire a desire to make this world a better place. As Solnit notes,

Changing the story isn't enough in itself, but it has often been foundational to real changes. Making an injury visible and public is often the first step in remedying it, and political change often follows culture, as what was long tolerated is seen to be intolerable, or what was overlooked becomes obvious. Which means that every conflict is in part a battle over the story we tell, or who tells and who is heard [xvi].

Girls on Fire are changing the story of what the future looks like and who fights for that future. They make individual and collective injury visible and point the way toward progressive political change. Almost every plot that Girls on Fire navigate includes a shift in perspective so that what was long tolerated or overlooked becomes intolerable and obvious.

There are many ways that these books inspire transformation. My students investigate these throughout class as they find examples online and share them. They also create opportunities to put ideas into action through their projects. Sometimes these projects reach into social media—a realm whose full power remains untapped, but continues to grow through education and organizing. In this space, fans babble, teens express, critics break down, artists innovate on characters' images and personalities, activists build campaigns. As Samantha Dunn explains, "Readers today advocate, celebrate, and interact with books in many ways for many reasons. The ways novels, authors, and readers communicate seems to have changed in the Internet era" (1). She continues, "readers can place their reactions to and interpretations of the text online through multiple outlets. Using blogs, comments, web posts, and tweets, reader-fans articulate their opinions to the global community" (8). In these spaces, YA dystopia shapes interactions and tests ideas.

Fan fiction and art and culture are another way that readers explore the worlds of their favorite books. Dunn notes that "through reading and writing fan fiction, fans become more active in their communities, more open to new ideas and theories regarding interpretation of source material" (5). This shifting interpretation and openness makes YA dystopia more powerful—what we imagine is possibility. Dunn also notes an example of the role fan fiction might play toward exploring sensitive issues and developing identity (6): "A teen who is exploring her sexual identity, for example, may read fan fiction that incorporates new romances into the commercial text to understand her own interaction and reactions better" (5). Whether connecting to favorite characters, connecting to other readers, or connecting with oneself, fan fiction extends YA dystopia into life.

These online spaces may be merely celebratory; they may be hero worship. But fans tend to also be critics and many use social media as an opportunity to challenge or expand as much as celebrate. Many authors thank their fans and readers for helping them write better books. Dunn argues that "new media has also created a space in which authors can reach readers in a more immediate way" (13). Some authors actively engage online and some create works that grow online spaces regardless of author involvement. Henthorne discusses fan communities and the developments to such communities as a result of digitization of texts. He notes that Collins is "very much a twenty-first century writer, a writer who regards readers as creative partners, constructing narratives that can accommodate the narrative desires of others"

(155). Online spaces extend the authors' work. Readers today, Henthorne argues, "increasingly contest the author's authority over a text. Rather than simply try to discern an author's meaning—decoding as it were—or rely upon critics or commentators to decode for them, readers assert meanings themselves, both individually and as part of fan collectives" (139). These spaces become empowering sites of creation and negotiation as well as conversation. The act of making meaning is centered.

Dunn compares the online interactions of three YA authors including Lois Lowry, whose interaction largely comes from classrooms where teachers create "learning communities" (20); J.K. Rowling, who built a "global franchise" (23); and John Green, who is quite active via YouTube videos and "promotes lifelong learning" and "positive, active spaces for adolescents to explore literature and life" (28). The power of authors, especially when connecting to large fan bases, cannot be underestimated. Dunn certainly does not underestimate: "One author, one book, has the power to build a global community" (46). Dunn notes that "both Green and Rowling have fan-made and fan-supported charities to raise money, awareness, and the spirits of individuals in the global community" (42). Authors help to raise awareness and provide outlets for fans to engage with and beyond their texts. But fans do the real work.

Fans also work to keep authors, publishers, and culture-at-large accountable. Antero Garcia and Marcelle Haddix, make an interesting case for the power of online spaces in their chapter "The Revolution Starts with Rue: Online Fandom and the Racial Politics of the Hunger Games." The authors argue that "online fandom communities help challenge hegemonic readings" (205) of texts like the Hunger Games. Their chapter "attempts to problematize hegemonic readings of the Hunger Games" and "emphasize that public imagination often cannot see racialized life in young adult literature and how this genre can incite critically conscious identity formation for readers" (204). The divide between "public imagination" and readers' individual "critical consciousness" is negotiated in social media spaces.

The particular tools and interactions of online communities are important and Garcia and Haddix explain the role that memes play in these spaces: "memes are important cultural literacy performances for youth engagement" (206). They are also "multimodal" and "multi-authored" (209). The authors cite several studies that show memes are "'a new literacy practice' with significance for 'enacting active/activist literacies'" (206). They also analyze several memes and consider the exchanges that happen in these spaces. While they focus their chapter on "incit[ing] critically conscious identity formation for readers," they also illustrate the potential power that online communities can have in interrupting monolithic, hegemonic readings of popular books and films like the Hunger Games. The individual gains in identity formation for young readers of color are utterly important, but the ways in which these conversations move the larger ideologies and power structures—and how they can do so in more powerful ways—are worth further consideration.

As Garcia and Haddix note, online communities help our favorite books to "function as more than a site for consumption"; they can allow "critical voices to share in the meaning making" of a book (210). This kind of collective and contested meaning-making is important in the case Garcia and Haddix discuss—Rue as a young woman of color and Rue as Mockingjay. As I note earlier, challenging hegemonic readings in the classroom and in online communities is key to diversifying our reading material as well as our world. Some of these challenges can even seep over into the space of reality.

* * *

The issues raised in texts can be exploded in media spaces and charitable solutions develop in response. The Hunger Games cast members, Jennifer Lawrence and Josh Hutcherson (Peeta) partnered with the World Food Programme and Feed America for a video public service announcement and a new website. As the WFP website notes,

> "This partnership will help us spread the word that hunger is the world's greatest solvable problem," said Nancy Roman, Director of Communications of WFP, adding that millions of readers identified with the characters in the Hunger Games trilogy.... "We want to tap into that excitement.... If all of us did just one small thing to fight hunger we could end hunger around the world. We are deeply grateful for the support of Suzanne Collins, who writes as though she understands hunger in the world, as well as Lionsgate™ and the Hunger Games cast—who have the power to change lives as they feed people worldwide."

The potential power of celebrity is one resource that non-profits and other community-service organizations can tap into in order to expand their reach and sphere of influence. However, more is needed to expand this influence beyond a website that primarily collects donations.

The Harry Potter Alliance attempts to connect activist campaigns like "The Hunger Games Are Real"; "Odds in Our Favor"; and "We Are the Districts" with fans who would like to work toward progressive change. In fact, the mantra "The Hunger Games Are Real" echoes across the internet (Acronym TV). We can see the parallels with our world and we want to help change them. As its website states, "The Harry Potter Alliance turns fans into heroes. We're changing the world by making activism accessible through the power of story. Since 2005, we've engaged millions of fans through our work for equality, human rights, and literacy." The work that the Harry Potter Alliance does also inspires individuals and organizations. As Van Jones notes, "the imaginary world of Panem does not seem so far away. Is it any wonder that some striking workers at Walmart and McDonald's have adopted the

Hunger Games symbol of resistance, the three-finger salute? Or that people have begun sharing their own stories of economic distress with the #MyHungerGames hashtag on Twitter?" Even established groups like AFL-CIO have tapped into the popularity of the Hunger Games with the "#WeAreTheDistricts" campaign and a call to submit photographs with the three-finger salute—"the symbol of solidarity of the working people." As Van Jones notes, we see "President Richard Trumka toss three-finger salutes, while the Odds in Our Favor campaign combats inequality." As the AFL-CIO website states: "Working families, union members and leaders are joining the online movement to lift up these issues of economic inequality and poverty using the 'Hunger Games' as a jumping off point." Ultimately, Jones argues, "These books are not popular because we want to escape to Katniss Everdeen's world. They are a phenomenon because we suspect her world is our own."

Political symbols and actions outside of the U.S. can also be developed in relation to books and the stories of Girls on Fire. In 2014, a young woman in Thailand was photographed holding up three fingers—the gesture that the people of District 11 use to communicate their support to Katniss and the gesture that symbolizes rebellion and resistance. In a *New York Times* article, Seth Mydans notes that "one of the detained students, Natchacha Kongudom, told reporters, 'The three-finger sign is a sign to show that I am calling for my basic right to live my life.'" The fictional symbol transgresses the boundaries between life and fiction and it was used effectively enough to prompt a reply by the authorities. Mydans explains, "The salute, which in the movies is a daring act of silent rebellion, began to appear here in the weeks after the May 22 coup. The authorities warned that anyone raising it in public could be subject to arrest." A picture and the story of Natchacha Kongudom and her friends (and fellow activists) circulated social media spaces. This was not simply a spontaneous act of protest; Mydans notes that "the students were members of a protest group that said it had bought hundreds of tickets to a showing of the film and planned to hand them out free, according to The Bangkok Post." The film, and its revolutionary message, were being used as a platform to bring awareness to the community and country; the theater company thought so and cancelled the showings. But this was not an isolated event and protestors continued to use the symbol as well as other references to George Orwell's *1984* (Mackey, Mydans). As Mackey's news story illustrates through multiple images, these protests were captured and spread via social media.

* * *

Yvonne Bynoe argues, "Activism … is not merely caring about a situation or being informed about an issue. Nor is it talking about problems ad nauseum, yet never implementing any solutions or alternatives" (100). Sometimes online spaces lend themselves to talking; sometimes online spaces provide opportunities for acting and working toward solutions. Bynoe also notes, "An activist is someone who decides to affirmatively act in order to improve his or her community and by extension the world" (100). How we choose to "affirmatively act" varies according to our talents, passions, and capacity for risk. Solutions, alternatives, and acting affirmatively takes time and energy. Dystopia keeps us focused on the future. As Solnit notes, "It's always too soon to go home. And it's always too soon to calculate effect" (3). In other words, even when we cannot see the end goal that we are working toward, we are still moving forward.

Solnit reminds us that "what we dream of is already present in the world" (xvii). And Girls on Fire continue to develop stories, to inspire us and to remind us. Solnit also reminds us that we should "recognize what a radically transformed world we live in, one that has been transformed not only by such nightmares as global warming and global capital but by dreams of freedom, of justice, and transformed by things we could not have dreamed of" (2). If we lose sight of how much the world has changed, we might also lose sight of how we can work to change it. A long life helps to see the scope and impact of this change; thus, one of the drawbacks of youth is a lack of lived experience in a changing world. When we are young, we live in the transformed world without knowledge of how the world got to be the way it is; we can see that it needs still more change. We can learn the past and we should, but we should also remember that history is "a crab scuttling sideways, a drip of soft water wearing away stone, an earthquake breaking centuries of tension" (Solnit 3). We can't imagine that we know exactly how cause-and-effect turns out. As the dedication to *The Forgetting* reminds us: These books are "For all who remember they can change their world."

From Inspiration to Consciousness

Girls on Fire are inspiring figures; their action are often activism in their worlds and can inspire activism in ours. YA dystopia like the Hunger Games, Rodrigo Joseph Rodríguez argues in "'We End Our Hunger for Justice!' Social Responsibility in the Hunger Games Trilogy," can "work to 'awaken' readers to social problems and instill in them a sense of social consciousness" (158). This social consciousness might inspire a variety of actions. Reading about girls who change their world, or even just change their lives, makes us more willing to fight for our world. When Alina's first line in *Breathe* is "Breathing is a right, not a privilege, so I'm stealing it back" (1), we can't help but align ourselves with her. In our world, we take breathing for granted; we might just be part of the problem. The fact that these are fictional inspirations does not reduce their potential for inspiration. In fact, they might just increase this potential. Some girls model activism; as Marotta argues, "Through their activism, both Fen and Kayla assist in securing freedom for future generations" (68). But more importantly, Girls on Fire books individually and collectively develop a consciousness poised to resist oppression and challenge the status quo.

Rodríguez explains: "Coming into consciousness calls for new ways of seeing and understanding the complexity of the world. It also entails searching for ways to work within and, if necessary, to subvert existing power structures to act for change" (158). Rodríguez argues that the Hunger Games is a book that can raise consciousness in these ways. He argues that in Katniss Everdeen, "Panem finds a hero who is socially conscious and who offers readers a model of resistance" (159). Rodríguez also reveals what he thinks is obvious about this text: "Collins's message is clear: only by becoming socially conscious and working together can people liberate themselves from the chains of oppression" (159). Rodríguez sees the citizens of Panem as the oppressed group; when the districts come together to fight the Capitol, they are working to liberate themselves from their chains. As I have shown throughout this book, freedom from hegemonic control, freedom from slavery, freedom of choice are all important themes. But without consciousness, this freedom will only account in a new version of the same forms of oppression that have existed in the past.

Rodríguez also makes a direct connection between liberation and consciousness: "Collins's message is clear: to maintain order one has to strip people of their social consciousness. To retain the ability to think critically and ask questions is to reserve the power to challenge the status quo and replace it with a new social order" (162). Many dystopian conditions develop because of a lack of social consciousness, often beaten out of people for generations. People fear regimes, starvation, separation of families. Rodríguez continues, "Critical literacy aims to equip people with the tools necessary to name the reality they live and challenge the oppressive conditions they face" (164). So many girls discover the truth that has been hidden from them and from their society. They unlock secrets like in *Incarceron* and *The Forgetting*. Gaia solves codes to reveal truth. Cassia reads into a poem to find truth. Girls on Fire model critical literacy and inspire it as well.

Our Girls on Fire grow consciousness in the realm of their stories; readers grow consciousness through reading, reflecting, discussing, and imagining. Individual development of consciousness builds toward collective understanding and action, but understanding the community of Girls on Fire through more collective ideas of consciousness highlights possibilities beyond the text. As I note earlier and in "Othered Girls on Fire," almost all of our Girls on Fire are "othered" in some way. Recognizing this shared status of oppression—Lauren Olamina's "natural allies"—is not meant to mitigate the oppression that girls of color experience or to conflate their experiences of otheredness, but it does unite girls through their oppression and potential empowerment. And the voices and experiences of Girls on Fire are crucial to the group status and collective consciousness of all Girls on Fire.

* * *

The critical concept of "the oppressed" gives us another way of considering the powerful potential of the concept for Girls on Fire, and the potential of this identity toward social justice. In *Chicana Without Apology* Edén Torres describes "the oppressed" through the following description:

> People who rise to political consciousness out of oppressed groups join a global community of revolutionary thinkers and activists who have been employing what Chéla Sandoval calls 'the methodology of the oppressed' for a very long time—even as they may separate from their home cultures [117].

Torres describes "people who *rise to political consciousness* out of oppressed groups" by thinking about groups, rather than individuals. Girls on Fire rise to political consciousness through struggle against oppression. Together, with the "mothers," they compose a "community of revolutionary thinkers." They separate from their home cultures because they are forced out—through violence, or circumstance, or knowledge, or a refusal to submit or conform. "Revolutionary thinkers and activists" may separate from their "home cultures" for any number of reasons, extending and re-imagining the idea of "community." In fact, the conditions of dystopia themselves cause a separation from home. Homes are changed. Homes are lost. Homes are rebuilt. In YA dystopia, geographic isolation, walls, factions, and tribes falsely or conveniently divide people whose interests are shared. Sometimes, in the face of absolute power, difference becomes less important on common ground. As consciousness develops from this space, it is also transformed. Consciousness, rather than identity or even history, becomes the uniting and transformative factor. The Outcasts, Others, Invalids and Savages work with those who have lived relatively privileged lives. Tribes unite. And consciousness is exactly what YA dystopia's Girls on Fire raise.

The Oppressed and the Hegemon and the Hope

Book(s)	The Oppressed	The Hegemon	The Hope
The Hunger Games	The districts (in hierarchy)	The Capital President Snow (then Coin)	Katniss is the symbol of the Resistance.
Eve	Everyone outside The City of Sand, especially girls	The King	The resistance is successful.

Book(s)	The Oppressed	The Hegemon	The Hope
	who are confined to breeding centers and boys imprisoned in labor camps.		
Delirium	The Invalids	The government Mayor Hargrove	The wall is torn down, literally and figuratively.
Breathe/Resist	The Auxiliaries	The government; The Premiums	The Resistance is successful.
Cinder	The lower classes on Luna and the people of earth	The Evil Queen, Levana	Cinder is the true queen of Luna.
Legend	The poor or slum sectors	The government of the New Republic; the Elector Primo	June is a prodigy.
Matched	The Aberrations and Abominations	The Society	Cultural changes Voting
Orleans	The People of Orleans	The Outer States; La Bête's tribe of ABs	Baby Girl (Enola)
Birthmarked	People in Wharfton (outside the wall)	The Enclave government	Gaia begins to see through the lies.
Prized	The men and Libbies of Sylum	The Matrarch	Democracy
The Summer Prince	The people of the catinga (the wakas?)	The Aunties	June is queen.
Shadows Cast by Stars	The Band, Others	The government; the Seekers; the Corridor.	Cassandra has power in the spirit world.
The Interrogation of Ashala Wolf	The Illegals, The Tribe	The government	Ashala and the Tribe.

In the foreword for *This Bridge We Call Home: Radical Visions for Transformation*, Sandoval shifts the methodology of the oppressed slightly by referring to it as a methodology of emancipation, thus dislocating "the oppressed" as a defining category and focusing instead on the anticipated results of this methodology—freedom. This move obscures the agents' identities and places the importance on the shared goal (a fitting tactic in the right circumstances). This shift is important if we are to move toward a common goal from a diversity of positions and this diversity of positions is, essentially, what YA dystopia's Girls on Fire create. Emancipation ends oppressive regimes. But this shift in language also takes the ownership away from "the oppressed" whose conditions created the need for emancipation, and whose theories and cultural products begin to make such emancipation possible. However, imagining a collective "oppressed" in the first place blurs lines and draws disparate peoples together much like Earthseed does. But in many of these novels protagonists gather allies from across class, and from across the new kinds of social, cultural, economic, and political divides. Emancipation is a shared goal.

Emancipation is ultimately the defining condition of an "oppressed" that is no longer oppressed. For some Girls on Fire emancipation becomes literal, but for Earthseed emancipation is also about fulfilling the destiny—to take root among the stars—and they are able to do this once they escape enslavement and circumvent their oppressors. Eventually, the social, economic, and cultural climate shifts to make room for Earthseed, in part because of their efforts. Some stories, and some realities, offer opportunities not just for individual, but collective emancipation. In Ashes, when Alex destroys the means to control the Changed, a new social order can develop. A balance will have to be struck. In Matched, the Poet, the Pilot, and the Physic bring together methods toward a shared solution and a future with choice. Ashala fights for the Tribe and for the world.

Toward these ends it is helpful to imagine "the oppressed" through complementary conceptualizations, like Robin D.G. Kelley's "new wretched of the earth," which he describes in *Freedom Dreams* as the "very multi-colored working class" who are rebuilding, reinventing, and reconfiguring "in ways that radically challenge the status quo" (12). Kelley's "wretched" are grounded in the revolutionary struggles of the working class throughout the history of the U.S., a history that informs and shapes YA dystopia's futures as well. The Girls on Fire are almost all "wretched." The idea of the "new wretched" is, perhaps, a more empowered or empowering viewpoint of "the oppressed" as it carries with it the radical and revolutionary roots from Frantz Fanon's pivotal and highly influential book *The Wretched of the Earth*. In this work, Fanon brings important dimensions to the idea of "the oppressed."

The conditions of oppression that exist under the "postmodern"—crises surrounding shifting identities, limits on power and resources, polarization of wealth, and state-sanctioned violence—continue to speak to the need for flexible social, cultural, and economic change across American institutions. The problems of the past and present are also those of the future. YA dystopia reflects what needs to change in our world. As Fanon writes, "the need for this change exists in its crude state, impetuous and compelling, in the *consciousness* and in the *lives* of the men and women who are colonized" (35–36; my emphasis). YA dystopia provides a kind of consciousness that undermines colonial systems and ideologies that affect people's lives and consciousness and promotes a radical oppositional (or differential) consciousness.[3] Fanon not only unites "the oppressed," but also recognizes the similar consciousness that defines the lives of "the wretched of the earth." Girls on Fire grow consciousness throughout their stories and struggles. They inspire the growth of our own individual and collective consciousness, a differential consciousness that, Sandoval argues, shifts to meet the circumstances.

Throughout *The Wretched of the Earth* Fanon argues that "European [white] peoples must first decide to wake up and shake themselves, use their brains, and stop playing the stupid game of the Sleeping Beauty" (106); otherwise they will be swept away in the currents of social, cultural and economic movements of "the oppressed." Essentially, this is what happens in many Girls on Fire YA dystopia texts—a quick, violent revolution that allows at least some rebuilding or shifting of the ways in which the game works. The catalyst—the spark—to end the games that Girls on Fire navigate. White people need to "wake up" and shake themselves and YA dystopia contributes to this mission. Few YA dystopia Hegemons would admit this. However, in Butler's *Parables* the oppressed are able to overcome the colonizer's grip by circumventing the established power structure at a point of weakness. The economic conditions and social and political turbulence provide the needed ideological space to develop critical, oppositional consciousness. As fascism's grip loosens, Earthseed's influence grows and its destiny is at least partially realized when Olamina witnesses the first shuttles leave earth for other worlds. For this to happen, racial barriers at the individual level are shattered and the oppressed come together to effectively transform individuals, communities, and structures. Here, power is a result of empowerment and this kind of power ultimately trumps that of fascist violence. Consciousness is ultimately the key in and beyond texts.

Consciousness into Action, In and Beyond Fiction

Throughout this book I have shown the ways in which fiction can relate to our contemporary world and can potentially change the world we live in—

from the themes and contexts of Girls on Fire stories, to the feminist roots laid by first wave feminists like Charlotte Perkins Gilman, to the work of critics and fans. I have also tried to show, as Naomi Klein argues, that "young people have a critical role to play because they'll be dealing with the worst impacts of climate change…. And when young people find their moral voice in this crisis, it's transformative" (Geek's Guide). There are many subjects and topics, problems and challenges that we might take up in the collective struggle toward a better world and a better future.

I have also shown many connections, forward and backward, that authors, critics, fans, and activists have made with Octavia Butler's work. For instance, *Diverse Energies* and Ytasha Womak note a foundation and scholarships named for Octavia Butler that carry on her legacy. One connection to Butler's work is key to an understanding of just how powerful fiction can be. *Octavia's Brood: Science Fiction Stories from Social Justice Movements*, edited by adrienne maree brown and Walidah Imarisha, is a direct connection between fiction and activism, and the book's dedication illustrates just how pivotal Butler's work has been to social justice movements, and to activists and organizers: "To Octavia E. Butler, who serves as a north star for so many of us. She told us what would happen—'all that you touch you change'—and then she touched us, fearlessly, brave enough to change us. We dedicate this collection to her, coming out with our own fierce longing to have our writing change everyone and everything we touch." Butler's work has transformed the world because it has transformed people who work for change. As co-editor, brown notes that the editors and contributors have read Butler's stories as "case studies" (281) for social justice struggles. They are activists who turn to fiction.

In "Foreword: Birth of a Revolution" Sheree Renee Thomas explains, "With incisive imagination and a spirited sense of wonder, the contributors bridge the gap between speculative fiction and social justice, boldly writing new voices and communities into the future" (2). Bridging this gap is a purposeful endeavor. Like many other visionary writers believe, the power of fiction is both real in its influence and unrealized in its potential. Co-editor Walidah Imarisha adds: "We believe this space is vital for any process of decolonization, because the decolonization of the imagination is the most dangerous and subversive form there is…. Once the imagination is unshackled, liberation is limitless" (4). This power of imagination exists in many fictional forms, but dystopia and utopia—removed from the present—extend that imagination into the real world. The real world needs the power of imagination.

Thomas also notes that "in their other lives" the contributors to this collection "work tirelessly as community activists, educators, and organizers" (2). In fact, the editors of the collection approached community organizers and asked them to write their experience and ideas into "visionary fiction," a term they differentiate from science fiction or speculative fiction. In her Introduction, Walidah Imarisha explains, "We want organizers and movement builders to be able to claim the vast space of possibility, to be birthing visionary stories" and "build a future where the fantastic liberates the mundane" (3). Whether we call it dystopian fiction, science fiction, speculative fiction, or visionary fiction, fiction that imagines a better tomorrow makes today survivable.

Like the sentiments of Hopkinson and Mehan in their collection of science fiction and fantasy by postcolonial writers, in her "Outro," adrienne maree brown writes, "We hold so many words inside us. So many futures. It is our radical responsibility to share these worlds, to plant them in the soil of our society as seeds for the type of justice we want and need" (279). This is exactly the philosophy that Butler imagines through Lauren Olamina's philosophy and religion, Earthseed. In addition to planting these seeds through fiction, and connecting fiction to the work of social justice warriors, the editors note the importance of collaborative work in developing tools. In her "Outro," brown describes three tools, the first of which is visionary fiction. The second is "emergent strategy," which is "intentional, interdependent and relational, adaptive, resilient because it is decentralized, [and] fractal" and "uses transformative justice, and creates more possibilities" (280). The editors also hold writing workshops where they practice what brown describes as "collaborative ideation." Participants brainstorm a particular context and parameters; they write their own story about what happens in this co-created world, and then they share their stories and get a diverse perspective on the world they have created. As brown argues, "if we want worlds that work for more of us, we have to have more of us involved in the visioning process" (281). We need more visioning, we need more emergent strategizing, and we also need to take care of ourselves so that we don't burn out when we set ourselves on fire.

Developing Self-Care

There are plenty of examples of triumphant heroines in YA dystopia—they get their boy/man; they make a positive impact on society. Girls are often either super-human or a broken shell. For instance, Tally is a superhero of sorts. At the end of the third novel, she takes on the voice of the protector of all of humankind, becoming a kind of eco-terrorist and legend. Because the last book in the series takes place just three and a half years after the end of the third book, Tally is still a factor, and while she has been an ugly hero, a pretty hero, and a special hero, she takes on an extra special hero status in the last book. She is the only real special left—the only one who can save humanity from themselves. Katniss, on the other hand, has a bittersweet ending as she lives with the psychological impact of her experience well into her future. Girls and young women who sacrifice themselves, often to near death (or sometimes death), are the Girls on Fire of YA dystopia. There are few examples of girls recognizing the need for balance. For example, the closing lines of *Allegiant* belong to Tobias (Four): "Since I was young, I have always known this: Life damages us, every one. We can't escape that damage. But now, I am learning this: We can be mended. We mend each other" (526). Tris cannot be mended.

Most Girls on Fire operate through the burning need that comes with what Octavia calls "positive obsession." She writes about the "unwritten rule" that "you're supposed to know you're as good as anyone…. Act tough and confident and don't talk about your doubts…. Fake everyone out. Even yourself" (*Bloodchild* 132–3). But Girls on Fire can't help but be authentic. Instead, like Butler, we "[do] a lot of thinking—the same things over and over" (133). Butler is not only navigating the self-doubts that come with being a woman in American culture; she is also navigating the doubts that come with being a "Black person, a Black woman" (133). Being a Black woman writing in the world of science fiction where "nearly all professional science-fiction writers were white men" (133), it is no wonder that she is driven by positive obsession: "I couldn't stop. Positive obsession is about not being able to stop just because you're afraid and full of doubts. Positive obsession is dangerous. It's about not being able to stop at all" (133).

Olamina never finds balance and her daughter resents her for it. Many girls are used up by the end of their story. Katniss is powerless to choose even her own destiny. In the Darkest Minds series Ruby recognizes the need to not bleed herself dry, but she struggles to keep herself in check: "I knew what I'd been when I'd found them: a terrified splinter of a girl who had been shattered a long time ago. I had nothing, and no one, and no real place to go. Maybe I was still broken and would always be—but now, at least, I was piecing myself back together, lining up one jagged edge at a time" (297). Ruby comes to find she needs a physical outlet; she needs to continue the training that made her body and mind hard. She spars with Liam's brother, Cole, in order to get out the aggression they both feel at the pent up abilities they cannot (and will not) use freely. Cole tells her, "cut yourself some slack before you literally run yourself into the ground? Take care of yourself so you can help me take care of them, all right?" But like many Girls on Fire she wants to do everything, be everything, save everyone. Similarly, in the Lunar Chronicles Winter suffers physically and mentally because she refuses to use her Lunar gift. She knows what Ruby learns: you might think you are helping someone by manipulating their mind, but those manipulations come with unforeseen side effects and consequences.

Ruby tries to deal with her mind/body conflicts; she remembers her training: "when you're working that hard, you're focusing on every movement your body is making, trying to train each and every muscle to be as sharp as a knife. You get out of your head for a little while" (142). This need to get out of her head is important because her mind is a source of power and influence that she struggles to accept. But she does recognize that "there had been a window of time when it had all come together for me—I'd been strong, mentally and physically" (142). She tries to find that moment by going back to the physical practices like running and sparring. Like Ruby, in the Razorlands series Deuce relies on her training to keep her balanced and remind her who she is. Deuce is not sure of who she is when her skills as Huntress no longer define her identity: "Sometimes I wondered what—and who—I would be without my blades" (*Horde* 193). She has to learn to balance this part of her identity with her lived reality: "I'd chart a new course from here, guided by the gentleness I'd learned from Tegan and Momma Oaks" (*Horde* 342). Gentleness, rather than fighting, is the path she chooses. Ruby, on the other hand, struggles with her mental abilities in the Darkest Minds series. She continually beats herself up. When she tries to explain and apologize to Liam, she recognizes that she "thought I could fix myself with the cure. That's all I've ever wanted, to be done with this. But now, I just want to be kinder to myself" (406). Being kind to ourselves is an important self-care technique.

Many Girls on Fire feel this conflict between who they are and who they are expected to be. In *Fragments* (of the Partials series), Samm reminds Kira that she has to "figure out who you are" not so she can "choose a side," but because she's "tearing [herself] in half" (260). Cinder recognizes the need for her body and mind to work together if she is going to be effective against Queen Levana; the people of Luna—not to mention all of her friends/family—are counting on her. Because she is a mechanic, she has the knowledge and the tools to fix the part of her that breaks. But she also has to function for some time without her cyborg abilities—a part of herself. Cinder's malfunction is entirely physical; her body cannot keep up with her mind and cannot do the things she needs it to do, like keep herself from drowning. But the mental challenges for Girls on Fire are navigated in every book and these books can also extend into the real world of counseling therapy. Our campus counselor, Jen Mascaro, told me about how she was able to use the factions and personality types in Divergent with one of her clients who was a fan of the Divergent books and films and was struggling to understand herself. The applications of Divergent's ideas in psychology and therapy have also been noted in popular media (Boyle) and are also mocked in this realm (Anders).

In many books, the physical is tied to mental health and well-being as part of self-care. Lena finds a coping mechanism in running. She and Hana fly through the streets of Portland, feeling free and happy (which is what

Alex recognizes in Lena that attracts him to her). In *Matched*, Cassia gets to hike, which is totally different from her structured and limited runs on the treadmill, which she engages in as regularly as she is allowed to, which is, of course, strictly limited. The physical is mandated by many totalitarian regimes to maintain the physical fitness of its citizens. Thus, these runs on the treadmill are never enough to satisfy her mind or her body. In *The Forgetting*, residents of Canaan are required to run around the perimeter of the town regularly; missing a run can lead to punishment. But in other books physical training can be oppositional. For instance, cardiovascular exercise is also a part of the training the resistance uses in *Breathe* and *Resist*. Yoga is also used for survival and resistance. The ability to control breath, to use less oxygen, is an important tool in a world where breathable air is controlled by the rich and powerful. This physical training is also used toward a healing of bodies like Bea and Alina who have been conditioned by limited resources. The state contains and controls bodies but Girls on Fire's minds cannot be so easily imprisoned.

* * *

Girls on Fire, and their struggles to survive and grow, can inspire us toward self-care. As Detroit community organizer adrienne maree brown explains and Womack quotes, "Exploring the future through science fiction can be a great support and healing tool" (178). But, as previously noted, she doesn't just use it as a tool for escaping the challenges of her activist work, she also applies ideas from Butler's Parables books as a "template for change agency in desperate communities" (179). Self-care is especially important for survival and healing as much as for transformation.

Self-Care Lessons from *Shadows Cast by Stars*

Madda's Self-Care Advice	Relevance to Girls on Fire
"You have to take care of yourself—tend your own weeds, in a matter of speaking. It's easy to go too deep, to go too far, when you're trying to help a person, and all that does is weaken you.... Strong in the body, strong in the mind" (124–125).	Madda is teaching Cass the importance of boundaries. So many Girls on Fire give too much of themselves. She also makes a connection between mind and body.
"You getting up and leaving is you taking care of yourself, and if you're going to be my apprentice, if you're going to be a healer, you have to learn that taking someone else's crap because you're afraid of hurting their feelings isn't just wrong—it's dangerous" (143).	Girls and women are, essentially, socialized to take people's crap. Girls on Fire are often people-pleasers and don't want to hurt anyone. Instead, they hurt or blame themselves.

Madda's Self-Care Advice	Relevance to Girls on Fire
"We might not have a lot here in this world, but one of the most precious things we do have is the right to choose how we live, and part of that is choosing the paths we walk on" (147).	Taking responsibility for our decisions, for the way we live and think, can be empowering.
"*Don't think*, I say to myself. *Don't think. Just feel*" (238). (Technically this is not Madda's advice, but she would approve.)	Many Girls on Fire are classic over-thinkers. We don't always trust our feelings, our intuition.
There is "duality in everything." Too much water, fire, food, sun, wind, or rain is as bad as too little (318).	Balance is a foundation of self-care.
"Life is about balance, she said, about walking that line between what is right and what is wrong" (318).	Many Girls on Fire struggle with right and wrong, but too few seek balance.
From Madda's posthumous letter: "See past yourself to the things that need doing, and do them when no one else will. Don't choose the easy route. Choose the one that's true" (357).	While this advice might seem counter to self-care since Girls on Fire take on too much responsibility, the important part here is "the one that's true." A Girl on Fire can only live her truth.

Cassandra learns Madda's lesson: "Healing is more than medicine. Madda always said that healing starts with the heart, and though we aren't healed yet, we're on our way" (453).

In *Shadows Cast by Stars*, a novel where the female protagonist is literally on fire at one point, and bitten by a spirit creature at another, we also find Cass trying to learn the concept of self-care. Her mentor, and later adopted mother, tries to teach her the importance of staying grounded, of giving thanks to the earth, and of taking care of herself so that she can be healthy and strong enough to help others. These self-care moments are few and far between in the lives and stories of Girls on Fire, which reflects reality. Recognizing these moments, embracing the inspiration, giving ourselves permission to take some weight off our shoulders, reminding ourselves that we are only human, can be powerful. Tuning into what we need and taking steps to care for our minds and our bodies (and our spirits) is essential. As one of my friends and colleagues told me, you don't have to set yourself on fire to keep others warm. I keep trying to remember this and keep working to build other fires, fanning the fires of girls and women as I wander by, and teaching fire-building skills.

Conclusion: Utopian Visions for Dystopian Realities

In his book, *Utopias*, Howard Segal's "brief history" and his discussion of utopia is infused with dystopian sensibility. Utopia requires a "radical improvement of physical, social, economic, and psychological conditions" (5), and this is the vision that helped found the United States of America. But this is not the United States that we know today, and it is not the United States—or what is left of the U.S.—that we find in YA dystopia. Instead, we find that the grand visions of the past have not given birth to the grand realities imagined. As Rebecca Solnit argues, "Change is rarely straightforward.... Sometimes it is as complex as chaos theory and as slow as evolution. Even things that seem to happen suddenly arise from deep roots in the past or from long-dormant seeds" (xxiv). We can plant those seeds and foster the seeds that have already been planted. We can also see the utopian vision where it might be resuscitated. We can transform it and move it forward.

Segal presents a compelling account of the U.S. as a utopian venture and the differences between possible and probable. America itself is a kind of utopian dream, Segal argues, "America was to be a *probable*, not merely a possible, utopia that would come about primarily by scientific and techno-logical changes. Indeed, scientific and technological progress equaled *progress itself*, not merely the means to progress..." (75). We have continued this legacy of progress and our literature and popular culture imagine the possibilities and pitfalls of science and technology. The progress, however, that Girls on Fire explore is the development of ideas and practices and policies. Progress is on the axes of identity, culture, and consciousness.

A history of America's utopic vision provides the fabric for an under-standing of our contemporary dystopia. Solnit notes the ways we tend toward pessimism when we consider the future from our present: "We transform the future's unknowability into something certain, the fulfillment of all our dread, the place beyond which there is no way forward. But again and again, far stranger things happen than the end of the world" (1). Every Girl on Fire navigates a particular story about the end of the world. And none are really the end.

Segal "distinguish[es] utopian yearnings and expectations from more conventional ones, not least sheer survival in a very different climate in all senses of the term" (74). As we have seen, survival is often the central task of the Girl on Fire. She is not only fighting for her own survival, but also that of friends and family and society. The conventional expectations of a girl and a young adult, are more strictly limited than the expectations for boys and men, like it is for the larger culture. The utopian yearnings of girls and women have had to include gender equality, which also has evolved since Charlotte Perkins Gillman's early utopian novel *Herland* (that's also kind of a dystopia). Gender equality looks different in the past than it does in the present or the future. Gender fluidity is a promise of the future made in the present.

When the means to progress are not critiqued thoroughly and critically, with an intersectional feminist lens; the utopian dream turns to dystopia. But, as Segal reminds us, "As the idea developed of America as *people-made* rather than as *natural*, utopia became a distinct possibility" (78–9; my emphasis). The people who make this distinct possibility continue to be cut from the same cloth as the ideals of the past; Girls on Fire not only challenge the past to live up to the future, they also challenge the future to live up to our collective visions and the unrealized fantasies of the past. America is romantic, idealistic, and conflicted, but our strengths are reflected in these texts that dare to imagine the American dream "deferred" and renewed.[1] We want better; we want justice. That idea, that hope, that ability to remake "institutions, values, norms, and activities," means that there is still hope for us.

* * *

In his speech to his supporters at the Democratic Convention in Philadelphia, on July, 25, 2016, Bernie Sanders passionately declared that "we want nothing less than the transformation of American Society." His message was timely, and especially appealed to young people. While it is clear that Bernie's vision of transformation is progressive—it seeks equality and justice and an end to racism, sexism, homophobia, and all those other liberal policies—exactly what this transformed society looks like, is not clear. Nor is it easy. It will take work—a kind of world-building. This is the work of the future. It requires imagination.

Meanwhile, similar words can evoke a very different vision. Heather Digby Parton writes, "[Steve] Bannon is a radical white nationalist whose main objective, as he has openly admitted, is to blow everything up—essentially to destroy the existing social and political order." In his first public appearance after Trump's election, Bannon reiterates the "unending battle for 'deconstruction of the administrative state'" (Rucker). Bannon's words are more radical, but they do not sound all that different from Bernie Sanders's words. Radicals on the left have also used the language of, for instance, blowing up the establishment. These are words that can inspire the disenfranchised (for instance, black people) as well as those who perceive themselves as being disenfranchised (for instance, white nationalists). Bannon's words alone do not reveal the sinister motives and ideologies behind them that are so different from what Bernie Sanders' words mean. After Bannon blows everything up, Parton continues, "What that leaves us with after the smoke clears is anyone's guess, since he is notably vague on the endgame." Here too, the future is uncertain. The vision of the future, after leaving the "existing social and political order" in ruins is vastly different for Bernie Sanders compared to Steve Bannon, but neither future is spelled out.

We might understand these two futures in the terms of Utopia vs. Dystopia. Bernie's future is a utopia. We have a difficult time finding utopia in the U.S. and in our fiction—one person's utopia is another's dystopia and utopia can quickly turn to dystopia. Using YA dystopia as a lens is far more helpful. For instance, the futures that Girls on Fire navigate are always a result of forces that are already in process—the environment, our global health, political corruption, social chaos. The world that Bannon seeks to create is the world we find in YA dystopia. In fact, Bannon is a perfect model for almost any of the evil Hegemons as well as the corrupt power structures we find in YA dystopia's fictional futures. He has been compared to Darth Vader and Satan and has said in response, that "darkness is good" (Tani). But these comparisons might be giving him too much credit. His attempts to impose chaos might not be effective, and can remind us that, as Dustin McKissen argues, "If what we are looking at is a government with no one at the wheel, then this is an opportunity for each of us to step up and take our places as the real authors of history." And if the person, or people at the wheel are pure evil, as they often are in YA dystopia, we need Girls on Fire even more.

Utopia has its value toward imagining more, but dystopia reminds us of the urgency of the present. Solnit notes that transformations "begin in the imagination, in hope" (4). Dystopia keeps us accountable, reminds us of our collective responsibility. Dystopia even gives us hope, perhaps a more realistic vision of hope than utopia. Solnit describes hope in ways that mesh with dystopian stories: "Hope just means another world might be possible, not promised, not guaranteed" (4). Dystopia does not take for granted the progress of the past because this progress has, at least in part, shaped the dystopic world. Girls on Fire know that if they fail to act nothing will change. Solnit continues, "To hope is to give yourself to the future, and that commitment to the future makes the present inhabitable" (4). Girls on Fire are a source of hope; and we all have a stake in the future. But we also have to live in this world and keep it "inhabitable" for the present as well as the future.

When the lights go out, who will be left to find a new source of light, to discover that human element of fire again?

The Girls on Fire are keeping the fire burning, stoking the fire and keeping watch to ensure that we don't burn out or burn up.

Appendix 1:
Girls on Fire Books

All of the YA dystopia books featuring Girls on Fire that I write about here are included on this list, grouped by series, in alphabetical order, by the first book in the series (which is often also the title of the series). The title of the series, which can be different from individual titles, is included when relevant.

Other important details are also included, like the Girl on Fire (AKA, the female protagonist), the publisher, the year(s) of publication, and other texts related to the series.

This list can be cross-referenced with Appendix 2, the Bibliography by author's last name and with the index.

Titles: *Adaptation* (2012); *Inheritance* (2013)
Girl on Fire: Reese
[Adaptation Series]
Author: Malinda Lo. Publisher: Little, Brown Books for Young Readers
[Ebook companion novella: Natural Selection]

Titles: *The 5th Wave* (2013); *The Infinite Sea* (2014); *Last Star* (2016)
Girl on Fire: Cassie
[5th Wave Trilogy]
Author: Rick Yancey. Publisher: G. P. Putnam's Sons Books for Young Readers
[Film: The 5th Wave (2016)]

Titles: *The Adoration of Jenna Fox* (2008); *The Fox Inheritance* (2011); *Fox Forever* (2013)
Girl on Fire: Jenna Fox
[The Jenna Fox Chronicles]
Author: Mary E. Pearson. Publisher: Henry Holt and Co.

Titles: *Article 5* (2012); *Breaking Point* (2012); *Three* (2013)
Girl on Fire: Ember Miller
[Article 5 Series]
Author: Kristen Simmons. Publisher: Tor Teen
[Extra scenes from Article 5 available on author website]

Title: *Ash* (2009)
Girl on Fire: Ash
Author: Malinda Lo. Publisher: Little, Brown Books for Young Readers

Titles: *Ashes* (2011); *Shadows* (2012); *Monsters* (2013)
Girl on Fire: Alex
[The Ashes Trilogy]
Author: Ilsa J. Bick. Publisher: Egmont USA

Title: *Beauty Queens* (2011)
Girl on Fire: Alina, Petra, Shanti, Nicole, Mary Lou, Taylor
Author: Libba Bray. Publisher: Scholastic Press

Titles: *Birthmarked* (2010); *Prized* (2011); *Promised* (2012)
Girl on Fire: Gaia Stone
[The Birthmarked Trilogy]
Author: Caragh M. O' Brien. Publisher: Roaring Brook Press
[Internet tie-in stories: "Tortured," "Ruled," "The Mirror Girls: Gaia at Seven,"
    "Porch Meeting: Bonnie at Fifteen," "The Potters' Daughter: Emily at Twelve,"
    "Detention: Leon at Twelve," "Advanced Boys with Matches," "Twins of the
    Dead Forest," "Gaia at Eleven"]

Titles: *Blood Red Road* (2011); *Rebel Heart* (2012); *Raging Star* (2014)
Girl on Fire: Saba
[The Dustlands Trilogy]
Author: Moira Young. Publisher: Margaret K. McElderry Books

Titles: *Breathe* (2012); *Resist* (2013)
Girl on Fire: Bea (and Alina)
[Breathe Series]
Author: Sarah Crosson. Publisher: HarperCollins

Title: *The Chaos* (2013)
Girl on Fire: Scotch
Author: Nalo Hopkinson. Publisher: Margaret K. McElderry Books

Titles: *Cinder* (2012); *Scarlet* (2013); *Cress* (2014); *Winter* (2015); *Fairest* (2015)
Girl on Fire: Cinder (and Scarlet, Cress, and Winter)
[The Lunar Chronicles]
Author: Marissa Meyer. Publisher: Feiwel & Friends
[Extra scenes from Cinder available on author blog. Prequels: "The Keeper,"
    "Glitches," "The Queen's Army," "As Sunshine Passes By," "The Princess and

the Guard," "The Mechanic," "Epilogue: Something Old, Someone New," Short Stories "Carswell's Guide to Being Lucky," "The Little Android"]

Titles: *The Darkest Minds* (2012); *Never Fade* (2013); *In the Afterlight* (2014)
Girl on Fire: Ruby
[The Darkest Minds Series]
Author: Alexandra Bracken. Publisher: Disney Press
[Ebooks: *In Time, Sparks Rise, Beyond the Night*. Film: *The Darkest Minds* (pre-production)]

Titles: *Delirium* (2011); *Pandemonium* (2012); *Requiem* (2013)
Girl on Fire: Lena (Magdelena)
[The Delirium Trilogy]
Author: Lauren Oliver. Publisher: HarperCollins
[Delirium short stories: "Hana," "Annabel," and "Raven" (print and ebook), "Alex" (print only)]

Titles: *Divergent* (2011); *Insurgent* (2012); *Allegiant* (2013)
Girl on Fire: Tris (Beatrice)
[The Divergent trilogy]
Author: Veronica Roth. Publisher: HarperCollins
[Short stories in print and online: Four: The Transfer, Four: The Initiate, Four: The Son, Four: The Traitor, Free Four. Films: Divergent (2014), Insurgent (2015), Allegiant (2016)]**

Titles: *Enclave* (2011); *Outpost* (2012); *Horde* (2013); *Vanguard* (2017)
Girl on Fire: Deuce
[The Razorland Trilogy]
Author: Ann Aguirre. Publisher: Feiwel & Friends
[Ebook short stories: "Foundation," "Endurance," "Restoration"]

Titles: *Eve* (2011); *Once* (2012); *Rise* (2013)
Girl on Fire: Eve (and Arden)
[The Eve Trilogy]
Author: Anna Carey. Publisher: HarperCollins

Title: *The Forgetting* (2016)
Girl on Fire: Nadia
Author: Sharon Cameron. Publisher: Scholastic Press

Titles: *The Forest of Hands and Teeth* (2009); *The Dead-Tossed Waves* (2010); *The Dark and Hollow Places* (2011)
Girl on Fire: Mary
[The Forest of Hands and Teeth Series]
Author: Carrie Ryan. Publisher: Delacorte
[Ebook short stories: Scenic Route, Flotsam & Jetsam, A Game of Firsts, Almost Normal, Hare Moon, What Once We Feared, Bougainvillea. Film: Forest of Hands and Teeth (pre-production)]

Titles: **The Host** (2008); **The Seeker** (reported sequel but no publication date)
Girl on Fire: Melanie Stryder
Author: Stephenie Meyer. Publisher: Little, Brown
[Technically not YA but shared characteristics and library cataloging and author's
    fame put it in this category. Film: The Host (2013)]

Titles: **The Hunger Games** (2008); **Catching Fire** (2009); **Mockingjay** (2010)
Girl on Fire: Katniss Everdeen
[The Hunger Games Trilogy]
Author: Suzanne Collins. Publisher: Scholastic Press
[Films: *The Hunger Games* (2012), *Catching Fire* (2013), *Mockingjay* Part 1 (2014)
    and *Mockingjay* Part 2 (2015)]

Titles: **The Immortal Rules** (2013); **The Eternity Cure** (2014); **The Forever Song**
    (2014)
Girl on Fire: Allie (Allison)
[Blood of Eden Series]
Author: Julie Kagawa. Publisher: Harlequin Teen

Titles: **Incarceron** (2007); **Sapphique** (2008)
Girl on Fire: Claudia
[Incarceron Series]
Author: Catherine Fisher. Publisher: Hodder Children's Books

Titles: **The Interrogation of Ashala Wolf** (2012); **The Disappearance of Ember
    Crow** (2013); **The Foretelling of Georgie Spider** (2015)
Girl on Fire: Ashala (Ash)
[The Tribe Series]
Author: Ambelin Kwaymullina. Publisher: Walker Books Australia Pty Ltd.

Titles: **Legend** (2011); **Prodigy** (2013); **Champion** (2013)
Girl on Fire: June
[The Legend Trilogy]
Author: Marie Lu. Publisher: Penguin Young Readers Group
[Ebook: *Life Before Legend: Stories of the Criminal and Prodigy*]

Titles: **Life as We Knew It** (2006); **The Dead and the Gone** (2008); **The World
    We Live In** (2010); **The Shade of the Moon** (2013)
Girl on Fire: Miranda
[The Last Survivors Series]
Author: Susan Beth Pfeffer. Publisher: Harcourt Children's Books

Title: **The Lost Girl** (2012)
Girl on Fire: Eva
Author: Sangu Mandanna. Publisher: HarperCollins Publishers
[Outtakes on author website: *Beginnings, Hotel*]

Title: *The Many Lives of Ruby Iyer* (2014)
Girl on Fire: Ruby
[The Many Lives of Ruby Iyer]
Author: Laxmi Hariharan. Publisher: CreateSpace Independent Publishing Platform
[Multiple ebook companion novels and short stories including: *Feral, Taken, Untamed, Redemption, Awakened, Origin, Chosen, Exhale, Ugly*]

Titles: *Matched* (2010); *Crossed* (2011); *Reached* (2012)
Girl on Fire: Cassia Reyes
[Matched Trilogy]
Author: Ally Condie. Publisher: Dutton Juvenile

Title: *Orleans* (2013)
Girl on Fire: Fen de la Guerre
Author: Sherri L. Smith. Publisher: G.P. Putnam and Sons

Title: *Partials* (2012); *Fragments* (2013); *Ruins* (2014)
Girl on Fire: Kira Walker
[Partials Sequence]
Author: Dan Wells. Publisher: Balzer + Bray
[Ebook: Isolation]

Titles: *The Pledge* (2011); *The Essence* (2013); *The Offering* (2013)
Girl on Fire: Charlie (Charlain)
[The Pledge Trilogy]
Author: Kimberly Derting. Publisher: Margaret K. McElderry Books
http://www.kimberlyderting.com/pledge.php

Titles: *POD* (2009); **MONOLITH** (working title, no publication date)
Girl on Fire: Megs
[The POD Series]
Author: Stephen Wallenfels. Publisher: namelos

Titles: *Reboot* (2013); *Rebel* (2014)
Girl on Fire: Wren
[Reboot Duology]
Author: Amy Tintera. Publisher: HarperCollins

Title: *The Selection* (2012); *The Elite* (2013); *The One* (2014); *The Heir* (2015)
Girl on Fire: America Singer
[The Selection Series]
Author: Kiera Cass. Publisher: Harper Teen
[Ebook and print novellas: *The Prince, The Guard, The Favorite, The Queen*]

Title: *Shadows Cast by Stars* (2012)
Girl on Fire: Cass (Cassandra)
Author: Catherine Knutsson. Publisher: Atheneum/Simon & Schuster

Titles: *Shatter Me* (2011); *Unravel Me* (2013); *Unite Me* (2014); *Ignite Me* (2014)
Girl on Fire: Juliette
[Shatter Me Series]
Author: Tahereh Mafi. Publisher: HarperCollins
[Companion novellas: *Destroy Me, Fracture Me*]

Titles: *Slated* (2013); *Fractured* (2013); *Shattered* (2014)
Girl on Fire: Kyla
[Slated Trilogy]
Author: Teri Terry. Publisher: Nancy Paulsen Books
[Originally published Slated by Orchard Books (UK, AUS, NZ), 2012]

Title: *The Summer Prince* (2013)
Girl on Fire: June
Author: Alaya Dawn Johnson. Publisher: Arthur A. Levine Books

Titles: *Tankborn* (2011); *Awakening* (2013); *Rebellion* (2014)
Girl on Fire: Kayla
[The Tankborn Trilogy]
Author: Karen Sandler. Publisher: Lee & Low Books, Inc
[Deleted Scenes found on author's website: "Joining Scene," "Flood Scene," "Coffee
    House Scene," "Zul's Journal"]

Titles: *Uglies* (2005); *Pretties* (2005); *Specials* (2006); *Extras* (2007)
Girl on Fire: Tally
[The Uglies series]
Author: Scott Westerfeld. Publisher: Simon Pulse

Titles: *Under the Never Sky* (2012); *Through the Ever Night* (2013); *Into the Still
    Blue* (2014)
Girl on Fire: Aria
[Under the Never Sky Trilogy]
Author: Veronica Rossi. Publisher: HarperCollins
[Ebook novellas: Roar and Liv, Brooke]

Titles: *The Way We Fell* (2012); *The Lives We Lost* (2013); *The Worlds We Make* (2014)
Girl on Fire: Kae (Kaelyn)
[The Fallen World Series]
Author: Megan Crewe. Publisher: Disney-Hyperion
[Collection of short stories: *Those Who Lived*]

Titles: *What's Left of Me* (2012); *Once We Were* (2013); *Echoes of Us* (2014)
Girls on Fire: Eva and Addie
[The Hybrid Chronicles]
Author: Kat Zhang. Publisher: HarperCollins Publishers

Titles: *Wither* (2011); *Fever* (2012); *Sever* (2013)
Girl on Fire: Rhine Ellery
[The Chemical Garden Trilogy]
Author: Lauren Destefano. Publisher: Simon & Schuster Books for Young Readers
[Ebook: *Seeds of Wither,* including prequel short story "The First Bride"]

Appendix 2: Something Like a Rating System

Throughout *Girls on Fire* I try to be fair to the books I am writing about. I try to keep my personal readings and feelings at the edge of my analysis. This is nearly impossible, but I try. (And my opinions are certainly *informed.*) Here I offer some brief sketches of my "likes" and "dislikes" of these books as well as some of the main elements. These sketches might also help to understand and keep track of the large number of books I discuss in *Girls on Fire*. The groups of books I discuss also reflect the dystopia trees (on the frontispiece and page 112) which attempt a visual categorization that models flexibility—strong roots and room for growth.

I don't offer ratings for the books because it is really difficult for me to judge and assign numbers when I enjoy all of these books. (I suffer through grading for the same reason.) But even as I enjoy all of these books, there are certainly some that are better books and more worthwhile reads. I highlight these here and expect that many readers may strongly agree or strongly disagree with my preferences. The kind of rating I do here is along the lines of Trujillo's *What Should I Read Next?* I try to be brief, and to give an idea of the work overall, but our likes and ratings could not be more different and I am not trying (or pretending) to be objective here.

I hope readers will find this helpful to get an overall sense of books and groups of similar books. This list can also be used as a reference for research projects or as a way of finding complementary texts, or finding other books that are similar to the books that readers like best. As I note in my reflections on fangirling, I love all of these books. I hope all readers will too.

* * *

The Hunger Games. A couple of chapters into the first book, I ordered the second and third on Amazon so I didn't have to stop reading. While Catching Fire is my favorite book in the series, the three books move the story in compelling ways. I have read this series a few more times and it is just as good every time. There is so much to discuss about these books; this is why they are so enjoyable and teachable. Social control, cultural propaganda, inequality, identity, love, media representation, gender roles, politics, family. Katniss speaks loud and clear, and she is conflicted, controlled, and emerging.

* * *

Some of the first books I read (mostly by word of mouth or Amazon recommendation) Wither, Delirium, Divergent, and Legend have similar elements to Hunger Games and were easy to find.

Divergent. I really enjoyed the first book when I read it, mostly because I loved the idea of being *divergent*. I had to wait for the second book, and I had to really wait for the third book. It was impossible to get from the library and I waited months longer than I wanted to. The moment I started reading and found that the chapters alternated between Tris and Four, I was angry and disappointed. I knew what this shift had to mean. This dual narration works well for other series, and *Allegiant* is highly controversial among readers. Many readers now love or hate Roth because of this ending. Personality, socialization, social control, violence, lots of action.

I love **Legend** for the world it builds and imagines, playing with contemporary U.S. politics and patterns in interesting ways. I love its strong female protagonist and its compelling boy-hero. I am disappointed by Marie Lu's commentary, a missed opportunity. But these books are enjoyable, complex, and thoughtful. And full of action. Corporatization, corruption, military power, social control, and disease.

Wither is the first book in the **Chemical Garden Trilogy** and continues with *Fever* and *Sever*. While I enjoyed reading it, this is not my favorite series. I didn't find the world a believable or compelling world and things start to unfold in forced ways—becoming an exhibit at a creepy Carnival, a plane crash that kills the boy. Disease, social control, decimation, drug addiction, sexual slavery. *Wither* is one of the few books and series that takes on explicitly sexual elements and also concerns reproductive slavery, but the protagonist is largely spared from these realities.

Eve (also fairy tale), also explicitly takes on questions of reproductive slavery, beginning with a direct reference to *The Handmaid's Tale*. It does a lot of interesting things with female texts and icons, speaks to the social construction of gender (of girls and boys), includes an element of the princess story, and shines a new light on struggles for freedom and reproductive justice. I can't help but love this series, even when it is hitting the reader over the head. The feminist overtones are much stronger in the first and third book.

Birthmarked is another series that I read early in my YA Dystopia obsession. It also deals with reproductive issues as well as traditional female roles like the midwife. Gaia is also marked by a scar across her face, which makes her an outcast in the first book. With the second novel, *Prized*, the story shifts to a new setting and offers a matriarchy to compare to so many of the patriarchal societies in YA dystopia (and the real world). In the second book, she is not an outcast because of this scar; physical imperfections are a norm in Sylum. The third book finds Gaia as a leader, and she pays for this role with her reproductive organs. Genetic manipulation, environmental degradation, patriarchal and matriarchal societies and corruption. I enjoyed this trilogy, and have found that my students tend to love or hate this series.

Delirium is one of my favorite series. Of the many one-word book titles, and series that have multiple books with one-word titles, *Delirium*, *Pandemonium*, and *Requiem*, is my favorite trio of titles for a trilogy. These three simple words perfectly match the content of the books and their place in the series as well as the story arc. After reading a lot of other books, I re-read this series to be sure I remembered it accurately and to make sure it was as good as I remembered. I love the idea of a society that evolves into one that has outlawed love, that has come to the conclusion that love is a disease. Oliver unfolds several clever and fairly believable story lines in this world. However, she falls short of a really revolutionary treatment of the topic of love. The books are focused on romantic love, even as love for friends and family are factored in.

The Way We Fall also deals with disease and I enjoyed reading these books even though they become rather narrow.

Article 5 is the only series where I finished the first book and didn't immediately try to find the subsequent books. I actually have not (yet?) read the rest of the series. The first book had interesting elements and compelling world-building, but the plot was otherwise ordinary.

* * *

I put off reading books like *The Selection*, *Matched*, *Uglies*, *Cinder*, *Incarceron*, and *The Essence* because of my lesser interest in fairy tales and "girly" topics that revel in dresses and princes and guarantees of happily ever after. I made assumptions about these books that sometimes hold true. Some lack political engagement; some scratch surfaces. Others have surprising insights. While I generally find these books less appealing than the more political or sociologically-based books, they do offer some interesting concepts and characters. And, of course, I did enjoy reading them.

Cinder feels very "Disney" to me though the characters are fierce and the story-telling is well-paced and full of action. There are four novels, each named for one of the strong female protagonists—*Scarlett*, *Cress*, and *Winter*—

as well as a shorter book that tells the story behind the evil queen, Levana (*Fairest*). I appreciate that the books take a view of what the world—and universe—might look like in this future. The story is a bit overloaded with tropes of the genre, combining cyborgs, androids, space travel, disease, telepathic abilities, genetic engineering and manipulation, lunar colonization. But despite this overload, these books offer different views of "strength" and a standard, formulaic happy ending with the coupling of the main characters.

Uglies also takes more of a world view and has an interesting premise and a lot of action. Overall, I find it to be over-rated and underdeveloped in its characters, as well as weak on representations of gender or race even though the focus on beauty screams out the need for more attention to these elements. But this may have something to do with how I learned about these books. I was teaching "Girls on Fire" in conjunction with a former student who was teaching a similar "Girls on Fire" literature class at another university. We shared two books, *Catching Fire* and *Orleans*. Her students claimed that Tally was a more compelling protagonist and that the Uglies books were better. Their push back against Katniss irritated me. I read the whole series to prove them wrong. Uglies is a fast-paced story and has some interesting insights on genetic manipulation, brainwashing, environmentalism, development of technology, cultural isolation and evolution. The fast-flying hoverboards and relentless special agents are a bit tiring, but the arc of the story across the four books is interesting. Tally, however, is only a superficial representation of the Girl on Fire.

I expected **The Selection** and **Matched** to be similar and to be too romance-based for my liking. Both series surprised me in their engagement with politics of inequality and in their exploration of the world they build. Overall, The Selection drags a bit and doesn't do enough with the political aspects. America (the protagonist) can be kind of dense and whiny, and the plot is rather weak. Matched has so much potential. The ideas that undergird the story, the use of literary texts and the attention to the negative effects of illiteracy, are compelling. There are also some interesting moments that examine the social construction of gender. And despite what could be seen as rather problematic and weak development of the female protagonist, I really enjoyed reading these books and I love the ideas behind the world as well as the ways in which the stories of three characters are told and woven together. The male characters aren't just props for the female protagonist; they struggle with their role in the unfolding revolution and provide a contrast to each other that highlights an understanding of social inequality. Late in the process of writing this book, I read Zhange Ni's "New Defense of Poetry," a brilliant piece that made me think about this series in new ways. Still, Cassia gets a bit lost as the strands of the story come together.

Incarceron is a kind of fairy tale, but it is quite different. It is set in the far future, but people have chosen to live in an ancient time, at least on the surface of things. This book often felt like a puzzle to me and made me think about the end of the film, *Men in Black*, when the universe is so small it is hidden on the cat's collar.

The Essence also has the fairy tale feel but introduces some elements not often found in these books, including different languages that are used by each of the different social classes. Language acts as a barrier to communication and progress. The first book is certainly dystopia despite the magical elements, but the second book isn't a dystopia so much as fantasy.

* * *

Environmental degradation can, of course, leave humankind with all sorts of problems. In **Under the Never Sky** and **Breathe** and **Resist**, people are living in pods with artificial air systems. Class divisions mean that not everyone experiences pod life in the same way and some people are even left to their own defenses. In other books, where environmental degradation is a major factor, a variety of causes are explored. Both these series do dual narration and shared narration well. *Under the Never Sky, Through the Ever Night,* and *Into the Still Blue* have more fantasy elements while *Breathe* and *Resist* are more within the realm of realism; the books might stretch the magical possibilities of yoga, but if people can develop heightened sense via evolution, maybe yoga can develop in epic proportions as well.

Z Is for Zachariah is one of the early works of YA dystopia and an early read for me as well. Nuclear Holocaust has left Ann isolated and, perhaps, entirely alone. When a stranger shows up at her family farm, she is forced to take care of him while also keeping herself safe and alive. The 2015 film completely changes the story and can't really be considered the same. This book has a simplicity and close proximity. Little happens, but the story is compelling.

I avoided **Life as We Knew It**, in part because of its popularity. When I finally read it I found it to pander to what I think of as stereotypes of adolescence—crushes on boys (this one a figure skating champion from her home town) and conflicts with parents (those with her mother escalate under the pressure of survival and forced togetherness as well as the pressures of gender-segregated chores). Perhaps these are not stereotypes and these elements do speak to teen readers. Or, perhaps, the popularity of this book is augmented by recommendations from librarians, teachers, and parents. Teens read it because they are pointed to it, and they enjoy it because it is a compelling story. But it is limited and limiting. The rest of the series also suffers from these problems, offering Alex's story and then bringing Alex and Miranda together in the third book. There is also a fourth book, *The Shade of the Moon*, that I have not (yet) read.

Dustlands (*Blood Red Road, Rebel Heart, Raging Star*) is set in a vast wasteland where life is hard and people are looking for land that can still be used to sustain life. I read this series shortly after I read the Hunger Games and the covers and online information certainly played on the popularity of the Hunger Games (as have many books post–Hunger Games). This series has many interesting elements and explores relationships in ways that most other books do not. Saba has an incestuous kind of relationship with her brother, a love/hate relationship with the main love interest (Jack), and a sexual/romantic affair with the bad guy. Things are complicated.

* * *

Immortal Rules, Enclave, Forest of Hands and Teeth, Ashes. Despite my disinterest in Zombie stories generally, I cannot help but enjoy these books, in part because the Zombie element is at the edge of the story. Zombies are often the force that keeps change from happening. They keep people penned in, constantly in fear.

Inheritance/Adaptation, The Host, and The 5th Wave offer stories of alien invasion that change the way in which humans live their lives and often create a tumultuous present and an uncertain future. I read about *POD* in a local arts newspaper review, and it seems to be rather obscure and not widely read. One of the few books in this study written by a man, the story alternates between the stories of a girl hiding in a parking garage and a boy confined to his house with his father. *The Host* and *The 5th Wave* have both become movies. The Host is one of the most accurate film translations though it still cannot reflect the depth of the book. The 5th Wave makes changes that ramp up the action and reduce the extraneous characters.

* * *

Slated, The Darkest Minds, The Adoration of Jenna Fox, What's Left of Me, Reboot, Shatter Me. A whole bunch of books explore the manipulations of minds through surgical alterations, chemical influences, or other natural or not-so-natural phenomena. I did not intend to consider these kinds of books when I first started this project, but they are an important contribution to the wide category of dystopia. The social programming we see in other books becomes more insidious when the brains, minds, and bodies of teen girls are manipulated. Sometimes special powers develop and sometimes girls are more shattered.

* * *

The Othered Girls on Fire often call for more complex categorization and these books are given more attention than most throughout this book.

When I came across an essay that considered **Beauty Queens** as an example of dystopia, I was skeptical. But, as I expanded my vision for what fits in this wide category, BQs makes a lot of sense as an example of YA dystopia. It also gives us a picture of how "diversity" can be done well. For instance, it is impossible to identify one Girl on Fire. The stories and voices of many girls bring this book alive. Humor is also done well—a technique not found in most dystopian texts.

Legend and *The Immortal Rules* are both written by women of color but they give rather superficial treatment of race; however, they reference racial difference more than most YA dystopia books.

Partials creates a world where humans and cyborgs are at odds, but they need each other to survive. Racism is overtly discussed and is the central struggle of the series.

Tankborn imagines a stratified society where there are those who are naturally born and those who are tankborn. Kayla eventually discovers that she is not, in fact, tankborn. Instead, she has been modified into a GEN and enslaved as a result. The books include critiques of class stratification and slavery.

The Summer Prince considers an international American location with deeper roots. This is my favorite YA dystopia book and one of my all-time favorite books. It is rich and unpredictable, except in the inevitable outcome of the death of the Summer King. Beautiful and radical.

Orleans imagines the American South after a string of Hurricanes and an outbreak of Delta Fever. It is a flawless piece of literature that touches on many elements of YA dystopia and the future of America as The Outer States.

Shadows Cast by Stars is a bit rough around the edges—plot lines that go nowhere (or wait for further development) but also really resonate with my students.

The Interrogation of Ashala Wolf is ambitious and important. These books were not easy to get a hold of. I bought a discontinued library copy online and could only get a hold of the audio book for *The Disappearance of Ember Crow* (which I did not have time to listen to while finishing this project). As I was putting finishing touches on my manuscript, I found that all three books are now available via Amazon (except I had to pre-order the third book). This is good news!

I write extensively about most of these books, in part because they are worth the critical attention. They tell stories that are left out of all spheres of (pop) culture. They tell stories of the most marginalized and invisible girls.

* * *

Multiple times in this study I attempted to cut myself off, to draw the line and close the loop on the body of books I consider for this Girls on Fire project. The last book I read, *The Forgetting*, is one of my favorites. It shares many elements with other Girls on Fire books, as I discuss throughout this book; however, it offers a different story—a failed utopia that was settled on another planet. There are many unique aspects to this story, and Nadia is a Girl on Fire through and through.

And then I read one more book that is not YA despite its 17-year-old protagonist. *Memory of Water* (2014; first published in Finland in 2012), by Emmi Itäranta, is a Scandinavian dystopia that focuses on water and breaks many rules. For instance, there is no sex. There are no boys except at the periphery or acting as authority figures. The unspoken relationship between Noria and her friend, Sanja, is a subtle same-sex romance between the lines. Noria is the tea master's daughter, and despite the fact that this work is traditionally passed on to sons, Noria chooses to follow in her father's footsteps. She is entrusted with the secret location of a spring that falls under the responsibility of the tea master—the "place that didn't exist" (6). After her mother takes a job in a far-away city and her father passes away, Noria becomes the tea master and shares the secret with Sanja, whose family is suffering from a lack of water. But the whole village is suffering and her generosity extends once the secret is out. At the same time, she uncovers valuable knowledge about the past and about a possible source of water and she pieces together the story and the maps. She and Sanja prepare to go looking for water in the Lost Lands of the past era, but there is not a happy ending to this story. There is hope, but Noria is a martyr to the cause because of a misunderstanding. We imagine there is hope in the story that Noria leaves behind.

* * *

And this is ultimately the lesson of the Girls on Fire—as long as the story survives, there is hope.

Chapter Notes

Introduction

1. Throughout this book I use the shorthand of YA dystopia to refer specifically to the body of work that I am considering which is, more accurately, YA dystopia with female protagonists. Not only is this shorthand for the longer, clunkier description, it is also a political move to situate a larger understanding of YA dystopia through the lens of the female protagonist. It goes without saying that the genre of YA dystopia has been understood through works of primarily male protagonists until Hunger Games changed the landscape.

2. *Female Rebellion* is a pivotal work here. While I critique some of the ways in which *Female Rebellion* makes its arguments, the work that this collection does makes my work deeper.

Chapter One

1. This section includes re-worked excerpts from my self-published book, *Universal Interdisciplinarity: A Handbook for Academia and Beyond.*

2. While all of this is powerful theory, the particular practice—the actual novel part of *Zombie Seed and the Butterfly Blues: A Case of Social Justice*—is just not a compelling story. It is poorly written, plotted, and conceived—full of unbelievable and predictable scenes. If these are the stories that are supposed to inspire interdisciplinary connections and grappling with the "sticky stuff" … the practice might be better realized through, for instance, YA dystopia's Girls on Fire.

3. bell hooks uses this term "critically vigilant" in her work.

Chapter Two

1. Marotta notes a similar trend in the slave narrative genre that she compares to *Tankborn* and *Orleans*, "Unfortunately, the majority of slave narratives tend to be focused on the male experience rather than that of the female. The neo-slave narrative is a way for contemporary writers to reinforce the African American female experience" (56). Indeed, it is "a way" to understand the experiences and cultural legacies, a way that gives us narrow, but enlightening, insights.

2. A collaboration between University of Limerick and the Department of Intercultural Studies in Translation, Languages and Culture, University of Bologna at Forlí.

Chapter Three

1. Seifert also notes that *Forever* has also been published as an adult novel because of its sexual content.

2. Bonus points to the reader who teases out the layered allusion here: the 1992 book by Clarissa Pinkola Estés, *Women Who Run with the Wolves: Myths and Stories of the Wild Woman Archetype,* and the 1992 film *Foxfire* (which makes reference to this book

and the archetype Estés explores), and the Ashes trilogy where some of the Changed adopt wolf-like behaviors and characteristics.

Chapter Four

1. Originally published as a guest blog on the Badass Bookie blog.

2. Thanks to Jessa Edney for pointing out these films as examples related to cyborgs and androids.

Chapter Five

1. Seifert offers a counter to her argument about virginity in a chapter about sex-positive literature, noting that "there are books that break the patterns" (17). But the books that she "discusses in detail" (17) in terms of sex positivity do not represent the YA dystopia genre as a complex whole. Or, perhaps the books that do represent the YA dystopia genre in sex positive ways are not "popular" enough to warrant study.

2. Another astute observation by Jessa Edney in her work-in-progress, "Queering Katniss" that was first developed in my Girls on Fire class and later expanded into a YouTube video for students in subsequent classes.

3. Ibid.

4. In his work, Lavender attempts to "better understand the American heritage of race and racism related to black experiences with displacement, dispossession, and alienation filtered through more familiar racist structures such as slavery, Jim Crow, or offensive language" (20).

5. It seems a stretch here to call this 12-year-old girl character a "powerful woman." In many contexts, 12-year-olds take on adult roles, but is any 12-year-old a "woman"?

6. She also notes the "many twenty-first century dystopian texts featuring [white] female protagonists" (57).

7. I use this term reconciliation in direct reference to indigenous actions toward justice, truth, and sovereignty.

8. Garcia and Haddix note that Greene goes on to describe a concept similar to Lugones's world-travelling, to "look in some manner through strangers' eyes and to hear through their ears" (215).

Chapter Seven

1. Dozens of e-books can be found on Amazon, and many are free on Kindle. In one search, I was able to download more than a dozen books and dozens more were available. Many of these books have prolific writers who produce multiple installations of their stories. *Gone*, for instance, includes five e-books; *Talented* has six. Many of these also have very specific world contexts like the world where obesity is policed in *Gone*.

2. Katniss has inspired many more female protagonists and Girls on Fire who can hold their own with Katniss's voice and story. Because it is more than just a story and she is more than just a character, the Girl on Fire is a bigger symbol. The use of this term by young adult author Robin Wasserman for her 2016 "adult" novel, taps into the power of this terms and, yet, her version of the "girl on fire" is disappointing. The meaning of the term that comes to life in the pages and on the screen is hijacked by this novel which is not really about a "girl on fire" at all. It's about two girls and their trials and tribulations after the unexpected death of a close friend. It is set in the past. Since Wasserman is a YA author, and this is her first book for adults, I can't help but feel disappointed that she used this powerful phrase as a title for this particular book.

3. Sandoval writes about differential consciousness as a kind of consciousness that is able to shift according to circumstances. Rather than be locked into strategies, Sandoval emphasizes tactics which are easier to shift.

Conclusions

1. A nod to Langston Hughes's 1951 poem, "Harlem," or "What happens to a dream deferred?"

Bibliography

Abate, Michelle Ann. "'The capitol accent is so affected almost anything sounds funny in it': The Hunger Games Trilogy, Queerness, and Paranoid Reading." *Journal of LGBT Youth* 12:4 (2015): 397–418. Print.

Acronym TV. "The Huger Games Are Real: We Are the Districts." Online video clip. *YouTube*. YouTube, 17 Dec. 2013. Web. 16 Apr. 2017.

Aguirre, Ann. *Enclave*. New York: Feiwel & Friends, 2011. Print.

_____. *Horde*. New York: Feiwel & Friends, 2013. Print.

_____. *Outpost*. New York: Feiwel & Friends, 2012. Print.

Ali, Maz. "Some Exciting Things Could Happen by 2050. Here Are the 5 Creepy Ones." *Upworthy.com*. Cloud Tiger Media, 26 Jan. 2015. Web. 5 Mar. 2015.

Allen, Judith A. *The Feminism of Charlotte Perkins Gilman: Sexualities, Histories, Progressivism*. Chicago: U of Chicago P, 2009. Print.

Anders, Charlie Jane. "*Insurgent* Is Like Two Hours of Someone Else's Terrible Therapy Session." *io9.com*. Gizmodo Media Group, 20 Mar. 2015. Web. 25 Apr. 2015.

Andersen, Julia. "So You Want to Write YA: Social Responsibility and Young Adult Literature." *ESSAI* 12.8 (2015): 1–18. Print.

Anderson, Mark Cronlund, and Irene Maria F. Blayer, eds. *Studies on Themes and Motifs in Literature: Interdisciplinary and Cross-Cultural Narratives in North America*. New York: Peter Lang, 2005. Print.

Anderson, M.T. *Feed*. Somerville: Candlewick, 2002. Print.

Atwood, Margaret. *The Handmaid's Tale*. New York: Anchor Books/Random House (reprint), 1998 (1985). Print.

Badger, Emily. "The Wealthy Are Walling Themselves Off in Cities Increasingly Segregated by Class." *Washington Post*. Washington Post, 23 Feb. 2015. Web. 16 Apr. 2017.

Bailey, Moya. "Vampires and Cyborgs: Transhuman Ability and Ableism in the work of Octavia Butler and Janelle Monáe." *Socialtextjournal.org*. Social Text Collective, 4 Jan. 2012. Web. 16 Apr. 2017.

Barnes, Jennifer Lynn. "Team Katniss." *The Girl Who Was on Fire: Your Favorite Authors on Suzanne Collins' Hunger Games Trilogy*. Ed. Leah Wilson. Movie ed. Dallas: Smart Pop, 2010/2011. Print.

Basu, Balaka, Katherine R. Broad, and Carrie Hintz, eds. "Introduction." *Contemporary Dystopian Fiction for Young Adults: Brave New Teenagers*. New York: Routledge, 2013. Print.

Bee, Samantha, Host. "March 8, 2017." *Full Frontal with Samantha Bee*. TBS. 8 Mar. 2017. Television.

Bessette, Lee Skallerup. "The 1998 Dystopian Novel That Eerily Foresaw 2013 Detroit." theatlanticwww. Atlantic Monthly Group, 13 Aug. 2013. Web. 23 Apr. 2017.

Bick, Ilsa J. *Ashes*. New York: Egmont USA, 2011. Print.
_____. *Monsters*. New York: Egmont USA, 2013. Print.
_____. *Shadows*. New York: Egmont USA, 2012. Print.
Blake, Caitrin. "Why Are YA Dystopian Novels So Popular with Students?" *online.cune.edu*. Concordia University, 2 Sep. 2014. Web. 22 Apr. 2017.
Boyle, Alan. "We're All 'Divergent': Personality Tests Get a Reality Check." *NBC News*. NBC News, 22 Mar. 2013. Web. 25 Apr. 2015.
Bracken, Alexandra. *The Darkest Minds*. New York: Hyperion, 2012. Print.
_____. *In the Afterlight*. New York: Hyperion, 2014. Print.
_____. *Never Fade*. New York: Hyperion, 2013. Print.
Bradford, Clare, and Mavis Reimer, eds. "Introduction: Girls, Texts, Cultures: Cross-Disciplinary Dialogues." *Girls, Texts, and Cultures*. Studies in Childhood and Family in Canada Series. Waterloo: Wilfrid Laurier UP, 2015. Print.
Bray, Libba. *Beauty Queens*. New York: Scholastic, 2011. Print.
Bridgman, Andrew. "5 Signs We Are Already Living in a Terrible Dystopian Future." CollegeHumorwww. CHMEDIA Connected Ventures, 18 Jan. 2017. Web. 22 Apr. 2017.
brown, adrienne maree. "Outro." *Octavia's Brood: Science Fiction Stories from Social Justice Movements*. Eds. adrienne maree brown and Walidah Imarisha. Oakland: AK Press and the Institute for Anarchist Studies, 2015. Print.
Brown, Kate. *Dispatches from Dystopia: Histories of Places Not Yet Forgotten*. Chicago: U of Chicago P, 2015. Print.
Brown, Patrick. "The Dystopian Timeline to the Hunger Games [INFOGRAPHIC]." *Goodreads.com*. Goodreads, 21 Mar. 2102. Web. 4 May 2017.
Bruce, Nicole. "The Most Insane Abandoned Places in the Midwest." Thrillistwww. Group Nine Media, 14 Dec. 2015. Web. 16 Apr. 2017.
Buckell, Tobias S. "Preface." *Diverse Energies*. Eds. Tobias S. Buckell and Joe Monti. New York: Tu Books (Lee and Low Books), 2012. Print.
Butler, Octavia E. *Bloodchild and Other Stories*. New York: Seven Stories, 1996. Print.
_____."Devil Girl from Mars: Why I Write Science Fiction." *MIT Communications Forum*. Massachusetts Institute of Technology, 4 Oct. 1998. Web. 24 Mar. 2015.
_____. *Parable of the Sower*. New York: Time Warner, 1993. Print.
_____. *Parable of the Talents*. New York: Time Warner, 1998. Print.
Bynoe, Yvonne. *Stand & Deliver: Political Activism, Leadership, and Hip Hop Culture*. Brooklyn: Soft Skull, 2004. Print.
Cain, Sian. "'90% of YA is crap': The Debate That Dominated the Edinburgh Book Festival." theguardianwww. Guardian News, 29 Aug. 2016. Web. 22 Apr. 2017.
Calhoun, Craig, and Cora Marrett. "Foreword." *Interdisciplinary Research: Case Studies from Health and Social Science*. Eds. Frank Kessel, Patricia L. Rosenfield, and Norman B. Anderson. New York: Oxford UP, 2008. Print.
Cameron, Sharon. *The Forgetting*. New York: Scholastic, 2016. Print.
Campbell, Joseph. "The Treatment for Stirrings: Dystopian Literature for Adolescents." *Blast, Corrupt, Dismantle, Erase: Contemporary North American Dystopian Literature*. Eds. Brett Josef Grubisic, Giséle M. Baxter and Tara Lee. Waterloo: Wilfrid Laurier UP, 2014. Print.
Carey, Anna. *Eve*. New York: Alloy Entertainment, 2011. Print.
_____. *Once*. New York: Alloy Entertainment, 2012. Print.
_____. *Rise*. New York: Alloy Entertainment, 2013. Print.
Cass, Kiera. *The Elite*. New York: HarperTeen, 2013. Print.
_____. *The One*. New York: HarperTeen, 2014. Print.
_____. *The Selection*. New York: HarperTeen, 2012. Print.

Cavendish, Margaret. *The Description of a New World, Called The Blazing-World.* London: A. Maxwell, 1668. UPenn Digital Library. Web. 22 Apr. 2017.

Childs, Ann M.M. "The Incompatibility of Female Friendships and Rebellion." *Female Rebellion in Young Adult Dystopian Fiction.* Eds. Sara K. Day, Miranda A. Green-Barteet and Amy L. Montz. Burlington: Ashgate, 2014. Print.

Clair, R.P. *Zombie Seed and the Butterfly Blues: A Case of Social Justice.* Rotterdam: Sense Publishers, 2013. Print.

Clark, Emma McMorran. "Hurts So Good: Why We Love YA Dystopias." LitReactorwww. LitReactor, 21 Mar. 2014. Web. 28 Jan. 2015.

Clark, Leisa A. "Preface." *Of Bread, Blood and* The Hunger Games: *Critical Essays on the Suzanne Collins Trilogy.* Eds. Mary F. Pharr and Leisa A. Clark. Critical Explorations in Science Fiction and Fantasy, 35 ed. Jefferson, NC: McFarland, 2012. Print.

clo0701. "The Rising Popularity of Dystopian Literature." The-Artificewww. The Artifice, 20 Apr. 2015. Web. 16 Apr. 2017.

Close, Murray. "'Hunger Games' Inspires Tough-Girl Toys." *CBS News.* CBS Interactive, 21 Nov. 2014. Web. 16 Apr. 2017.

Cloutier, Michelle. "Final Reflection." Girls on Fire: Gender, Culture, and Justice in YA Dystopia. University of Maine at Augusta. Fall 2016.

Colbert, Stephen, host. "July 21, 2014." Interview with Edan Lepucki. *The Colbert Report.* Comedy Central. 21 July 2014. Television.

Coleman, Micah-Jade M. *Decolonizing the YA North: Environmental Injustice in Sherri L. Smith's Orleans.* MA Thesis. University of Southern Mississippi, 2016. Web. 22 Apr. 2017.

Collins, Suzanne. *Catching Fire.* New York: Scholastic, 2009. Print.

_____. *The Hunger Games.* New York: Scholastic, 2008. Print.

_____. *Mockingjay.* New York: Scholastic, 2010. Print.

Condie, Ally. *Crossed.* New York: Dutton, 2011. Print.

_____. *Matched.* New York: Dutton, 2010. Print.

_____. *Reached.* New York: Dutton, 2012. Print.

Connors, Sean P. "Dreaming, Questioning, and Trying to Find Answers: A Conversation with Sherri Smith." *SIGNAL Journal* XXXIX.1 (Fall 2015/Winter 2016): 41–53. Print.

_____. "Fashioning Worlds: A Conversation with Lois Lowry." *SIGNAL Journal* XXXIX.1 (Fall 2015/Winter 2016): 41–53. Print.

_____. "'I Try to Remember Who I Am and Who I Am Not': The Subjugation of Nature and Women in the Hunger Games." *The Politics of Panem: Challenging Genres.* Ed. Sean Connors. Critical Literacy Teaching Series: Challenging Authors and Genre. Rotterdam: Sense Publishers, 2014. Print.

_____. "Introduction: Challenging the Politics of Text Complexity." *The Politics of Panem: Challenging Genres.* Ed. Sean Connors. Critical Literacy Teaching Series: Challenging Authors and Genre. Rotterdam: Sense Publishers, 2014. Print.

Corlew, Laura Kati. *Finally, a Song from Silence (Poetry from When I Was Young).* No Cube, 2016. Print.

Corsetti, Caitlin. "7 of the Worst YA Dystopian Cliches Ever." *Gurl.com.* Defy Media, 16 Jan. 2015. Web. 28 Jan. 2015.

Couzelis, Mary J. "The Future Is Pale: Race in Contemporary Young Adult Dystopian Novels." *Contemporary Dystopian Fiction for Young Adults: Brave New Teenagers.* New York: Routledge, 2013. Print.

Crewe, Megan. *The Lives We Lost.* New York: Hyperion, 2013. Print.

_____. *The Way We Fell.* New York: Hyperion, 2012. Print.

_____. *The Worlds We Make.* New York: Hyperion, 2014. Print.

Crosson, Sarah. *Breathe.* New York: Greenwillow, 2012. Print.

_____. *Resist*. London: Bloomsbury, 2013. Print.

Crum, Maddie. "A Dystopian Novelist Predicted Trump's Campaign Slogan in the '90s." *Huffington Post*. Huffington Post, 1 July 2016. Web. 16 Apr. 2017.

Currie, Dawn H. "From Girlhood, Girls, to Girls' Studies: The Power of the Text." *Girls, Texts, and Cultures*. Eds. Clare Bradford and Mavis Reimer. Studies in Childhood and Family in Canada Series. Waterloo: Wilfrid Laurier UP, 2015. Print.

Darling-Brekhaus, Keith. "What's the Matter with North Dakota? Rise of a Male-Dominated Dystopia." *Examiner*. AXS Network, 29 Mar. 2013. Web. 17 Feb. 2015.

Darren. "80+ Fantastic Young Adult Dystopian Novels." *Bart'sBookshelf.co.uk*. Bart's Bookshelf, 6 Mar. 2015. Web. 25 Apr. 2015.

Day, Sarah K., Miranda A. Green-Barteet, and Amy L. Montz. "Introduction: From 'New Woman' to 'Future Girl': The Roots and the Rise of the Female Protagonist in Contemporary Young Adult Dystopias." *Female Rebellion in Young Adult Dystopian Fiction*. Eds. Sarah K. Day, Miranda A. Green-Barteet and Amy L. Montz. Ashgate Studies in Childhood, 1700 to the Present. Farnham: Ashgate, 2014. Print.

Dean, Michelle. "Our Young-Adult Dystopia." *NYTimes.com*. New York Times, 31 Jan. 2014. Web. 25 Apr. 2015.

Deegan, Mary Jo. "Introduction: Gilman's Sociological Journey from *Herland* to *Ourland*." With Her in Ourland: Sequel to Herland. Charlotte Perkins Gilman. Eds. Mary Jo Deegan and Michael R. Hill. Westport, CT: Praeger, 1997. Print.

DeGraw, Sharon. "Brown Girl in the Ring as Urban Policy." *Blast, Corrupt, Dismantle, Erase: Contemporary North American Dystopian Literature*. Eds. Brett Josef Grubisic, Giséle M. Baxter and Tara Lee. Waterloo: Wilfrid Laurier UP, 2014. Print.

Derting, Kimberly. *The Essence*. New York: McElderry, 2013. Print.

_____. *The Pledge*. New York: McElderry, 2011. Print.

Despain, Bree. "Community in the Face of Tyranny: How a Boy with a Loaf of Bread and a Girl with a Bow Toppled an Entire Nation." *The Girl Who Was on Fire: Your Favorite Authors on Suzanne Collins' Hunger Games Trilogy*. Ed. Leah Wilson. Movie ed. Dallas: Smart Pop, 2010/2011. Print.

Destefano, Lauren. *Fever*. New York: Simon & Schuster, 2012. Print.

_____. *Sever*. New York: Simon & Schuster, 2013. Print.

_____. *Wither*. New York: Simon & Schuster, 2011. Print.

Dill, Bonnie Thornton, and Ruth Enid Zambrana, eds. *Emerging Intersections: Race, Class, and Gender in Theory, Policy, and Practice*. New Brunswick: Rutgers UP, 2009. Print.

Donaghue, Chris. *Sex Outside the Lines: Authentic Sexuality in a Sexually Dysfunctional Culture*. Dallas: BenBella, 2015. Print.

DuBois, W.E.B. "Of Our Spiritual Strivings." *The Souls of Black Folk*. 1903. New York: Dover Publications, 1994.

Dunn, Samantha. *Fandom and Fiction: Adolescent Literature and Online Communities*. MA Theses. Iowa State University, 2016. Print.

Dvorsky, George. "Why Modern Society Would Appear Completely Dystopian to a Visitor from the Past." *i09www*. Gizmodo Media Group, 26 Oct. 2012. Web. 17 Feb. 2015.

Echterling, Clare. "How to Save the World and Other Lessons from Children's Environmental Literature." *Children's Literature in Education* 47.4 (December 2016): 283–299. Print.

Fanon, Frantz. *The Wretched of the Earth*. Trans. Constance Farrington. New York: Grove, 1963. Print.

"Fasting and Furious." *Odd Mom Out*. Bravo. 27 June 2016. Television.

Fisher, Catherine. *Incarceron*. New York: Firebird, 2007. Print.

Forman, Gayle. "Teens Crave Young Adult Books on Really Dark Topics (and That's OK)." *Time*. Time, 6 Feb. 2015. Web. 27 Feb. 2015.

Garcia, Antero, and Marcelle Haddix, "12. The Revolution Starts with Rue: Online Fandom and the Racial Politics of the Hunger Games." *The Politics of Panem: Challenging Genres.* Ed. Sean Connors. Critical Literacy Teaching Series: Challenging Authors and Genre. Rotterdam: Sense Publishers, 2014. Print.

Garriott, Deidre Anne Evans, Whitney Elizabeth Jones, and Julie Elizabeth Tyler. "Conclusion: Where Can We Go and What Can We Disrupt from Here?" *Space and Place* in The Hunger Games: *New Readings of the Novels.* Eds. Deidre Anne Evans Garriott, Whitney Elizabeth Jones and Julie Elizabeth Tyler. Jefferson, NC: McFarland, 2014. Print.

_____. "Introduction: Taking Up and Entering Critical Space." *Space and Place in* The Hunger Games: *New Readings of the Novels.* Eds. Deidre Anne Evans Garriott, Whitney Elizabeth Jones and Julie Elizabeth Tyler. Jefferson, NC: McFarland, 2014. Print.

Gay, Roxane. *Bad Feminist.* New York: Harper Perennial, 2014. Print.

Geek's Guide to the Galaxy. "Dystopian Fiction's Popularity Is a Warning Sign for the Future." Wiredwww. Condé Nast, 20 Dec. 2014. 1 Feb. 2015.

_____. "Sci-Fi Tried to Warn Us About Leaders Who Want to 'Make America Great Again.'" Wiredwww. Condé Nast, 16 Dec. 2016. Web. 16 Apr. 2017.

Gibson, C. Robert. "The Hunger Games Are Real: We Are the Districts." *Huffington Post.* Huffington Post, 25 Nov. 2013. Web. 16 Apr. 2017.

Gilliland, Elizabeth, "She Was Asking for It: Discussions About Slut-Shaming Fostered by Gothic YAL." *SIGNAL Journal* XXXIX.1 (Fall 2015/Winter 2016): 41–53. Print.

Gilman, Charlotte Perkins. *Herland.* New York: Pantheon Books, 1979. Print.

Gooding, Richard. "Our Posthuman Adolescence." *Blast, Corrupt, Dismantle, Erase: Contemporary North American Dystopian Literature.* Eds. Brett Josef Grubisic, Giséle M. Baxter and Tara Lee. Waterloo: Wilfrid Laurier UP, 2014. Print.

Green, Joshua. "This Man Is the Most Dangerous Political Operative in America." Bloombergwww. Bloomberg, 8 Oct. 2015. Web. 15 Apr. 2017.

Grilo, Ana. "Smuggler's Ponderings: Thoughts on *The Summer Prince* By Alaya Dawn Johnson." Thebooksmugglerswww. The Books Smugglers, 3 Oct. 2013. Web. 23 Apr. 2017.

Grossman-Heinze, Dahlia. "Pop Culture Prepared Me: The Trumpocalypse." *BitchMedia.org.* Bitch Media, 2 Feb. 2017. Web. 16 Feb. 2017.

Grubisic, Brett Josef, Giséle M. Baxter, and Tara Lee, eds. "Introduction." *Blast, Corrupt, Dismantle, Erase: Contemporary North American Dystopian Literature.* Waterloo: Wilfrid Laurier UP, 2014. Print.

Gundell, Sara. "11 Dystopian YA Books to Cure Your Post-'Allegiant' Hangover." *Examiner. AXS Network*, 10 Nov. 2013. Web. 25 Apr. 2015.

Hampton, Gregory. "Imagining Black Bodies in the Future." *Blast, Corrupt, Dismantle, Erase: Contemporary North American Dystopian Literature.* Eds. Brett Josef Grubisic, Giséle M. Baxter and Tara Lee. Waterloo: Wilfrid Laurier UP, 2014. Print.

Haraway, Donna. "A Cyborg Manifesto: Science, Technology and Socialist Feminism in the Late Twentieth Century." *The Cybercultures Reader.* London: Routledge, 2000. Print.

Hariharan, Laxmi. *The Many Lives of Ruby Iyer.* Middletown, DE: CreateSpace, 2014. Print. 29 Sept. 2015.

The Harry Potter Alliance. "We Are the Districts: Our Mission Statement." *Tumblr.* Tumblr, 13 Nov. 2013. Web. 16 Apr. 2017.

Hartland, Dan. "Brown Girl in the Ring by Nalo Hopkinson." strangehorizonswww. Strange Horizons, 30 May 2016. Web. 23 Apr. 2017.

Heit, Jamey. *The Politics of* The Hunger Games. Jefferson, NC: McFarland, 2015. Print.

Hentges, Sarah. "Girls on Fire: Political Power in Young Adult Dystopia." Theconversationwww. The Conversation US, 20 Mar. 2015. Web. 23 Apr. 2017.

_____. "Othered Girls on Fire: Navigating the Complex Terrain of YA Dystopia's Female Protagonist." *Children's and Young Adult Literature and Culture: A Mosaic of Criticism.* Ed. Amie Doughty. Cambridge: Cambridge Scholars, 2016. Print.

_____. *Pictures of Girlhood: Modern Female Adolescence on Film.* Jefferson, NC: McFarland, 2006. Print.

_____. "This Class Is on Fire! (and Online): Teaching YA Dystopia and the Girl on Fire Through Themes, Contexts, and Action." *SIGNAL Journal* XXXIX.1 (Fall 2015/Winter 2016): 41–53. Print.

Henthorne, Tom. *Approaching the* Hunger Games *Trilogy: A Literary and Cultural Analysis.* Jefferson, NC: McFarland, 2012. Print.

Herman, Lily. "Tomi Adeyemi Talks YA Fiction Publishing Deal for 'Children of Blood and Bone.'" *Teen Vogue.* Condé Nast, 12 Apr. 2017. Web. 16 Apr. 2017.

Hills, Rachel. *The Sex Myth: The Gap Between Our Fantasies and Reality.* New York: Simon & Schuster, 2015. Print.

Hill-Vásquez, Heather. "What Scout Wished For? An Intersectional Pedagogy for *To Kill a Mockingbird* and *The Hunger Games.*" *SIGNAL Journal* XXXIX.1 (Fall 2015/Winter 2016): 41–53. Print.

Holmes, Anna. "White Until Proven Black: Imagining Race in the Hunger Games." *New Yorker.* Condé Nast, 30 Mar. 2012. Web. 24 Mar. 2015.

hooks, bell. *bell hooks: Cultural Criticism and Transformation.* Dir. Sut Jhally. Media Education Foundation, 1997. Video.

_____. *Teaching Community: A Pedagogy of Hope.* New York: Routledge, 2003. Print.

Hopkinson, Nalo. *Brown Girl in the Ring.* New York: Grand Central, 1998. Print.

_____. *Chaos.* New York: McElderry, 2012. Print.

_____. "Introduction." *So Long Been Dreaming: Postcolonial Science Fiction & Fantasy.* Eds. Nalo Hopkinson and Uppinder Mehan. Vancouver: Arsenal Press, 2004. Print.

Huston, Aletha C. "A Path to Interdisciplinary Scholarship." *Interdisciplinary Research on Close Relationships: The Case for Integration.* Eds. Lorne Campbell and Timothy J. Loving. Washington: American Psychological Association, 2012. Print.

Imarisha, Walidah. "Introduction." *Octavia's Brood: Science Fiction Stories from Social Justice Movements.* Eds. adrienne maree brown and Walidah Imarisha. Oakland: AK Press and the Institute for Anarchist Studies, 2015. Print.

Ireland, Alexandra. "Final Reflection." Girls on Fire: Gender, Culture, and Justice in YA Dystopia. University of Maine at Augusta. Fall 2016.

Itäranta, Emmi. *Memory of Water.* New York: HarperCollins, 2014. Print.

James, Joy. *Shadowboxing: Representations of Black Feminist Politics.* New York: Palgrave (St. Martin's), 1999. Print.

Johnson, Alaya Dawn. "Guest Speaker at University of Maine at Augusta." Race, Class, Gender, and Sexuality in American Culture. Bangor, ME. April 2016.

_____. "Interview with Alaya Dawn Johnson: Transcript." Interview by Victoria and Kathleen. GayYa.org. Avada, 23 Oct. 2014. Web. 18 Apr. 2016.

_____. *The Summer Prince.* New York: Levine-Scholastic, 2013. Print.

Jones, Janet Webster. "Detroit Bookseller Picks 3 Nonfiction Books for Your Summer." Interview by Kelly McEvers. *All Things Considered.* NPR.org, 2 Aug. 2016. Transcript. 23 Apr. 2017.

Jones, Van. "'Hunger Games,' a Mirror of America's Inequality." *CNN.* Cable News Network, 21 Nov. 2014. Web. 16 Apr 2017.

Kadohata, Cynthia. *In the Heart of the Valley of Love.* Berkley: U of California P, 1992. Print.

Kagawa, Julie. *The Eternity Cure.* Ontario: Harlequin Teen, 2013. Print.

_____. *The Forever Song.* Ontario: Harlequin Teen, 2014. Print.

_____. *The Immortal Rules.* Ontario: Harlequin Teen, 2012. Print.

Kelley, Robin D.G. *Freedom Dreams: The Black Radical Imagination.* Boston: Beacon, 2002. Print.

Kertzer, Adrienne. "Cinderella's Stepsisters, Traumatic Memory, and Young People's Writing." *The Lion and the Unicorn* 40.1 (2016): 1–21. Print.

Kidd, James. "'I don't want smut on the page': Divergent Author Veronica Roth on Sex and Teen Fiction." *Independent.co.uk.* Independent Digital News, 5 Jan. 2014. Web. 7. Mar. 2015.

Klein, Julie Thompson. *Humanities, Culture, and Interdisciplinarity: The Changing American Academy.* Albany: State University of New York Press, 2005. Print.

Knutsson, Catherine. *Shadows Cast by Stars.* New York: Atheneum, 2012. Print.

Koller, Courtney. "Final Reflection." Girls on Fire: Gender, Culture, and Justice in YA Dystopia. University of Maine at Augusta. Fall 2016.

Kowalczyk, Piotr. "Young Adult Books—7 Most Interesting Graphics and Charts." *ebookfriendly.com.* Ebook Friendly, 27 Jan. 2015. Web. 25 Apr. 2015.

Kwaymullina, Ambelin. *The Interrogation of Ashala Wolf.* Somerville: Candlewick, 2012. Print.

Lane, Ann J. "Introduction." *Herland.* By Charlotte Perkins Gilman. New York: Pantheon Books, 1979. v–xxiv. Print.

Lanfreschi, Anna, and Brittany Lloyd-Jones. "'Divergent' & 'Legend' Authors Play 'Yes, no, meh.'" Online video. HLNtvwww. Cable News Network, 5 Aug. 2014. Web. 16 Apr. 2017.

Lavender, Isiah III. *Race in American Science Fiction.* Bloomington: Indiana UP, 2011. Print.

Law, Victoria. "Do Girls of Color Survive Dystopia?" *Bitchmedia.org.* Bitch Media, 22 Mar. 2013. Web. 23 Apr. 2017.

Lee, Marie Myung-Ok. "Here Are the Books You Need to Read If You're Going to Resist Donald Trump." QZwww. Quartz Media, 1 Feb. 2017. Web. 16 Apr. 2017.

Lee, Tanith. *Biting the Sun.* New York: Bantam, 1999. Print.

Lepucki, Edan. *California.* New York. Back Bay Books/Little, Brown and Company (reprint), 2015. Print.

Letorneau, Cherise. "Final Reflection." Girls on Fire: Gender, Culture, and Justice in YA Dystopia. University of Maine at Augusta. Fall 2016.

Lewis, Andy. "If You Liked 'The Hunger Games' Flowchart Maps World of YA Fiction." *HollywoodReporter.com.* Hollywood Reporter, 24 July 2012. Web. 26 Jan. 2015.

Lo, Malinda. *Adaption.* New York: Little, Brown, 2012. Print.

_____. *Ash.* New York: Little, Brown, 2009. Print.

_____. *Inheritance.* New York: Little, Brown, 2013. Print.

Lo, Malinda, and Cindy Pon. *Diversity in YA.* 23 Mar. 2015. Web. 23 Mar. 2015.

Lorde, Audre. "The Master's Tools Will Never Dismantle the Master's House." *This Bridge Called My Back.* Eds. Cherrie Moraga and Gloria Anzaldua. New York: Kitchen Table, 1984. Print.

_____. *Sister Outsider.* New York: Crossing, 2007. Print.

Lu, Marie. *Champion: A Legend Novel.* New York: Penguin, 2013. Print.

_____. "Frequently Asked Questions." 2010. Web. 24. Mar. 2015.

_____. *Legend.* New York: Penguin, 2011. Print.

_____. *Prodigy: A Legend Novel.* New York: Penguin, 2013. Print.

Lugones, María. "Playfulness, 'World'-Travelling, and Loving Perception." *Making Face, Making Soul/Haciendo Caras: Creative and Critical Perspectives by Women of Color.* Ed. Gloria Anzaldua. San Francisco: Aunt Lute Books, 1987. Print.

MacDonald, Mariah. "Final Reflection." Girls on Fire: Gender, Culture, and Justice in YA Dystopia. University of Maine at Augusta. Fall 2016.

Mackey, Robert. "Thai Protestors Flash 'Hunger Games' Salute to Register Quiet Dissent." *NYTimes.com*. New York Times, 2 June 2014. Web. 23 Apr. 2017.

Mafi, Tahereh. *Ignite Me*. New York: HarperCollins, 2014. Print.

_____. *Shatter Me*. New York: HarperCollins, 2011. Print.

_____. *Unite Me*. New York: HarperCollins, 2014. Print.

_____. *Unravel Me*. New York: HarperCollins, 2013. Print.

Mallan, Kerry. "On Secrets, Lies, and Fiction: Girls Learning the Art of Survival." *Girls, Texts, and Cultures*. Eds. Clare Bradford and Mavis Reimer. Studies in Childhood and Family in Canada Series. Waterloo: Wilfrid Laurier UP, 2015. Print.

Marotta, Melanie. "Sherri L. Smith's *Orleans* and Karen Sandler's *Tankborn*: The Female Leader, the Neo-Slave Narrative, and Twenty-First Century Young Adult Afrofuturism." *Journal of Science Fiction* 1.2 (2016): 56–70. Print.

Martinson, Jane. "Gritty in Pink: Hunger Games Inspired Bow and Arrow Toy for Girls." *theguardian.com*. Guardian News, 20 Jan. 2015. Web. 3 Mar. 2015.

Mayer, Petra. "Samba, Spiderbots and 'Summer' Love in Far-Future Brazil." *NPR.org*. NPR, 7 Mar. 2013. Web. 26 Mar. 2015.

McCrayer, Jenika. "What You Need to Know About How Dystopian Fiction Matches Reality." everydayfeminismwww. Everyday Feminism, 1 Feb. 2015. Web. 2 Feb. 2015.

McKissen, Dustin. "Trump Is Behaving Like a 'Maniac' Alright, but It's Not Because He Has Some Master Plan." cnbcwww. CNBC, 3 Feb. 2017. Web. 23 Apr. 2017.

McNally, Victoria. "'The Hunger Games': Katniss Everdeen Is Uninterested in Sex and That's 100% Okay: There's Plenty of Good Reasons Actually." MTVwww. Viacom International, 12 Nov. 2015. Web. 16 Apr. 2017.

Mehan, Uppinder. "Final Thoughts." *So Long Been Dreaming: Postcolonial Science Fiction & Fantasy*. Eds. Nalo Hopkinson and Uppinder Mehan. Vancouver: Arsenal Press, 2004. Print.

Meyer, Marissa. *Cinder*. New York: Feiwel & Friends, 2012. Print.

_____. *Cress*. New York: Feiwel & Friends, 2014. Print.

_____. *Fairest*. New York: Feiwel & Friends, 2015. Print.

_____. *Scarlet*. New York: Feiwel & Friends, 2013. Print.

_____. *Winter*. New York: Feiwel & Friends, 2015. Print.

Meyer, Stephanie. *The Host*. New York: Little, Brown, 2008. Print.

Miller, Toby. *Blow Up the Humanities*. Philadelphia: Temple UP, 2012. Print.

Milner, Andrew, ed. *Tenses of Imagination: Raymond Williams on Science Fiction, Utopia, and Science Fiction*. Ralahine Utopian Studies, Vol. 7. Eds. Raffaella Baccolini, Joachim Fischer, Tom Moylan. Bern, Switzerland: Peter Lang AG, International Academic Publishers, 2010. Print.

Mirk, Sarah. "Dystopian Sci-Fi Author Octavia Butler Predicted Donald Trump's Campaign Slogan." *Bitchmedia.org*. Bitch Media, 1 July 2016. Web. 16 Apr. 2017.

Monti, Joe. "Afterword." *Diverse Energies*. Eds. Buckell, Tobias S. and Joe Monti. New York: Tu Books (Lee and Low Books), 2012. Print.

Morrison, Ewan. "YA Dystopias Teach Children to Submit to the Free Market, Not Fight Authority." *theguardian.com*. Guardian News, 1 Sep. 2014. Web. 28 Jan. 2015.

Moylan, Tom. *Scraps of the Untainted Sky: Science Fiction, Utopia, Dystopia*. Cultural Studies Series. Boulder: Westview, 2000. Print.

Moylan, Tom, and Raffaella Baccolini. "Introduction: Utopia as Method." *Utopia Method Vision: The Use Value of Social Dreaming*. Ralahine Utopian Studies, Vol 1. Germany: Peter Lang AG, 2007. Print.

Muscio, Inga. *Rose: Love in Violent Times*. New York: Seven Stories, 2010. Print.

Mydans, Seth. "Thai Protesters Are Detained After Using 'Hunger Games' Salute." *NYTimes.com*. New York Times, 20 Nov. 2014. Web. 28 Apr. 2015.

Naisbitt, Lara. "Final Reflection." Girls on Fire: Gender, Culture, and Justice in YA Dystopia. University of Maine at Augusta. Fall 2016.

Nakia. "Straight Is Not My Default: Understanding Katniss Everdeen as an Ace Aro." *GayYA.org*. Avada, 29 Oct. 2014. Web. 16 Apr. 2017.

Newkirk, Thomas. *Minds Made for Stories: How We Really Read and Write Informational and Persuasive Texts*. Portsmouth: Heinemann, 2014. Print.

Noah, Trevor, host. "October 31, 2016." *The Daily Show with Trevor Noah*. Comedy Central. 31. Oct. 2016. Television.

Nutt, Joe. "Why Young-Adult Fiction Is a Dangerous Fantasy." teswww TES Global, 19 Aug. 2016. Web. 23 Apr. 2017.

O'Brien, Caragh M. *Birthmarked*. New York: Roaring Brook, 2010. Print.

_____. *Prized*. New York: Roaring Brook, 2011. Print.

_____. *Promised*. New York: Roaring Brook, 2012. Print.

Oliver, Lauren. *Delirium*. New York: HarperCollins, 2011. Print.

_____. *Pandemonium*. New York: HarperCollins, 2012. Print.

_____. *Requiem*. New York: HarperCollins, 2013. Print.

Parton, Heather Digby. "Why Trump's Week of Chaos May Suit Steve Bannon's Bigger Plans." alternet.org. Independent Media Institute, 30 Jan. 2017. Web. 23. Apr. 2017.

Pearson, Mary E. *The Adoration of Jenna Fox*. New York: Henry Holt, 2008. Print.

Percy, Owen. "The Romance of The Blazing World: Looking Back from CanLit to SF." *Blast, Corrupt, Dismantle, Erase: Contemporary North American Dystopian Literature*. Eds. Brett Josef Grubisic, Giséle M. Baxter and Tara Lee. Waterloo: Wilfrid Laurier UP, 2014. Print.

Pfeffer, Susan Beth. *The Dead and the Gone*. Orlando: Harcourt, 2008. Print.

_____. *Life as We Knew It*. Orlando: Harcourt, 2006. Print.

_____. *The World We Live In*. New York: Harcourt, 2010. Print.

Pharr, Mary F., and Leisa A. Clark, eds. "Introduction." *Of Bread, Blood and* The Hunger Games: *Critical Essays on the Suzanne Collins Trilogy*. Critical Explorations in Science Fiction and Fantasy, 35. Jefferson, NC: McFarland, 2012. Print.

Polatis, Kandra. "Living in Uncertainty: Teens' Questioning of Their Future Drives Stories Popularity." *Washington Times* 2014: 6. *Academic Search Complete*. Web. 5 May 2015.

Pollitt, Katha. "Hers: The Smurfette Principle." NYTimeswww. New York Times, 7 Apr. 1991. Web. 23 Apr. 2017.

Pomerantz, Shauna, and Rebecca Raby. "Reading Smart Girls: Post-Nerds in Post-Feminist Popular Culture." *Girls, Texts, and Cultures*. Eds. Clare Bradford and Mavis Reimer. Studies in Childhood and Family in Canada Series. Waterloo: Wilfrid Laurier UP, 2015. Print.

Queper, Jay (@QueperJay). "I'm guessing dystopian tales will be very popular. We need a field guide for the 'New America.'" 19 Feb. 2017, 1:54PM. Tweet.

"Race on YA Covers: Survey Reports a Continued Lack of Diversity." *Huffington Post*. Huffington Post, 21 May 2012. Web. 4 May 2017.

Reese, Debbie. "Catherine Knutsson's SHADOWS CAST BY STARS." *American Indians in Children's Literature (AICL)*. Blogspot, 11 Jan. 2013. Web. 23 Apr. 2017.

Reid, Joy, Host. "Handmaid's Tale Now Amazon Bestseller." *AM Joy*. MSNBC. 19 Feb. 2017. Television.

Robinson, Tasha. "The 10 Cloverfield Lane Backlash Is Missing the Point: The Wacky Ending Is Perfect for the Specific Story It Is Telling." thevergewww. Vox Media, 17 Mar. 2016. Web. 23 Apr. 2017.

Rodríguez, Rodrigo Joseph. "'We End Our Hunger for Justice!' Social Responsibility in the Hunger Games Trilogy." *The Politics of Panem: Challenging Genres*. Ed. Sean Connors. Critical Literacy Teaching Series: Challenging Authors and Genre. Rotterdam: Sense Publishers, 2014. Print.

Rojas Weiss, Sabrina. "Paper Towns Author John Green Weighs in on the YA Gender Controversy." Refinery29www. Refinery29, 20 Mar. 2015. Web. 15 Apr. 2017.

_____. "Women Represented in Movies Are Worse Than You Think." Refinery29www. Refinery29, 22 Mar. 2015. Web. 25 Apr. 2015.

Rossi, Veronica. *Into the Still Blue.* New York: HarperCollins, 2014. Print.

_____. *Through the Ever Night.* New York: HarperCollins, 2013. Print.

_____. *Under the Never Sky.* New York: HarperCollins, 2012. Print.

Roth, Veronica. *Allegiant.* New York: Katherine Tegen, 2013. Print.

_____. *Divergent.* New York: Katherine Tegen, 2011. Print.

_____. *Insurgent.* New York: Katherine Tegen, 2012. Print.

Rowe, John W. "Introduction: Approaching Interdisciplinary Research." *Interdisciplinary Research: Case Studies from Health and Social Science.* Eds. Frank Kessel, Patricia L. Rosenfield and Norman B. Anderson. Oxford: Oxford UP, 2008. Print.

Ryan, Carrie. *The Dark and the Hollow Places.* New York: Delacorte, 2011. Print.

_____. *The Dead-Tossed Waves.* New York: Delacorte, 2010. Print.

_____. *The Forest of Hands and Teeth.* New York: Delacorte, 2009. Print.

Sanders, Bernie. Democratic National Convention. Philadelphia. 25 Jul. 2016. Transcript. washingtonpostwww. Web. 23 Apr. 2017.

Sandler, Karen. *Awakening: A Tankborn Novel.* New York: Lee & Low, 2013. Print.

_____. *Rebellion: A Tankborn Novel.* New York: Lee & Low, 2014. Print.

_____. *Tankborn.* New York: Lee & Low, 2011. Print.

Sandoval, Chela. *The Methodology of the Oppressed.* Theory Out of Bounds. Minneapolis: U of Minnesota P, 2000. Print.

Sarte, Jean-Paul. "Preface." *The Wretched of the Earth.* By Frantz Fanon. New York: Grove, 1963. Print.

Schofield, Tiffany. "Final Reflection." Girls on Fire: Gender, Culture, and Justice in YA Dystopia. University of Maine at Augusta. Fall 2016.

Scholes, Justin, and Jon Ostenson. "Understanding the Appeal of Dystopian Young Adult Fiction." *The Alan Review* 40.2 (Winter 2013). Web. 16 Apr. 2017.

Schutte, Annie. "It Matters If You're Black or White: The Racism of YA Book Covers." *yalsa.ala.org.* YALSA, 10 Dec. 2012. Web. 4 May 2017.

Segal, Howard P. *Utopias: A Brief History from Ancient Writings to Virtual Communities.* West Sussex: Wiley-Blackwell, 2012. Print.

Seifert, Christine. *Virginity in Young Adult Literature After* Twilight. Studies in Young Adult Literature. Ed. Patty Campbell. Lanham: Rowman & Littlefield, 2015.

Sheahan-Bright, Robyn. "Tribe Education Resource Booklet." *classroom.walkerbooks.com. au* Walker Books, n.d. Web. 4 May 2017.

Siesser, Colleen. "Ain't No Party Like a Divergent Party! (Or … How to Throw a Party to Celebrate the Divergent Movie Release)" *Yalsa.ala.org.* American Library Association, 17 Mar. 2014. Web. 4 Mar. 2015.

Simmons, Amber M. "Class on Fire: Using the Hunger Games Trilogy to Encourage Social Action." *Journal of Adolescent & Adult Literacy* 56.1 (2012): 22–34. Print.

_____. "In Your Dreams: Validating the Teaching of Fantasy Novels in the Adolescent Classroom." *SIGNAL Journal* XXXIX.1 (Fall 2015/Winter 2016): 41–53. Print.

Simmons, Kristen. *Article 5.* New York: Tor Teen, 2012. Print.

Simon, Rachel. "How Is 'Z for Zachariah' Different Than the Book? The New Movie Makes 13 Huge Changes from Its Sci-Fi Inspiration." bustlewww. BDG Media, 28 Aug. 2015. Web. 23 Apr. 2017.

Smith, Sherri L. *Orleans.* New York: Penguin, 2013. Print.

Solnit, Rebecca. *Hope in the Dark: Untold Histories, Wild Possibilities.* Chicago: Haymarket, 2016. Print.

Stollarz, Patrik. "Climate Changes Brings World Closer to 'Doomsday,' Says Scientists." *MSN.* Microsoft, 22 Jan. 2015. Web. 3 Mar. 2015.

Stone, Lacey. "Final Reflection." Girls on Fire: Gender, Culture, and Justice in YA Dystopia. University of Maine at Augusta. Fall 2016.

Tani, Maxwell. "'Darkness is good': Inflammatory Trump Adviser Steven Bannon Argues He, Darth Vader, and Satan Are Misunderstood." BusinessInsiderwww. Business Insider, 18 Nov. 2016. Web. 23 Apr. 2017.

Terry, Teri. *Fractured.* New York: Nancy Paulson, 2013. Print.

_____. *Shattered.* New York: Nancy Paulson, 2014. Print.

_____. *Slated.* New York: Nancy Paulson, 2012. Print.

Thomas, P.L. "Afterword: Why Are Strong Female Characters Not Enough? Katniss Everdeen and Lisbeth Salander, from Novel to Film." *The Politics of Panem: Challenging Genres.* Ed. Sean Connors. Critical Literacy Teaching Series: Challenging Authors and Genre. Rotterdam: Sense Publishers, 2014. Print.

Thomas, Sheree Renee. "Foreword: Birth of a Revolution." *Octavia's Brood: Science Fiction Stories from Social Justice Movements.* Eds. adrienne maree brown and Walidah Imarisha. Oakland: AK Press and the Institute for Anarchist Studies, 2015. Print.

Thompson, Becky. *Survivors on the Yoga Mat: Stories for Those Healing from Trauma.* Berkley: North Atlantic, 2014. Print.

Tintera, Amy. *Reboot.* New York: HarperTeen, 2013. Print.

Torres, Edén E. *Chicana Without Apology: The New Chicana Cultural Studies.* New York: Routledge, 2003. Print.

Trujillo, Kim. *What Should I Read Next? 50 Dystopian Books for Teens.* Kim Trujillo, 2013. E-book.

Twine, France Winddance. "Brown-Skinned White Girls: Class, Culture, and the Construction of White Identity in Suburban Communities." Ed. Frankenberg, Ruth. *Displacing Whiteness: Essays in Social and Cultural Criticism.* Durham: Duke UP, 1997. Print.

Wallenfels, Stephen. *POD.* New York: Ace Books (The Berkeley Publishing Group/Penguin), 2009. Print.

Wasserman, Robin. *Girls on Fire.* New York: HarperCollins, 2016. Print.

Weik von Mossner, Alexa. "The End of Life as We Knew It: Material Nature and the American Family in Susan Beth Pfeffer's Last Survivor Series." *Blast, Corrupt, Dismantle, Erase: Contemporary North American Dystopian Literature.* Eds. Brett Josef Grubisic, Giséle M. Baxter, Tara Lee. Waterloo: Wilfrid Laurier UP, 2014. Print.

Wells, Dan. *Fragments.* New York: Balzer + Bray, 2013. Print.

_____. *Partials.* New York: Balzer + Bray, 2012. Print.

_____. *Ruins.* New York: Balzer + Bray, 2014. Print.

Westerfeld, Scott. *Extras.* New York: Simon Pulse, 2007. Print.

_____. *Pretties.* New York: Simon Pulse, 2005. Print.

_____. *Specials.* New York: Simon Pulse, 2006. Print.

_____. *Uglies.* New York: Simon Pulse, 2005. Print.

Wilson, Leah, ed. *The Girl Who Was on Fire: Your Favorite Authors on Suzanne Collins' Hunger Games Trilogy.* Movie ed. Dallas: Smart Pop, 2011. Print.

Wilson, Sharon R., ed. *Women's Utopian and Dystopian Fiction.* UK: Cambridge Scholars, 2013. Print.

Womack, Ytasha L. *Afrofuturism: The World of Black Sci-Fi and Fantasy Culture.* Chicago: Lawrence Hill (Chicago Review), 2013. Print.

Woolston, Blythe. "Bent, Shattered, and Mended: Wounded Minds in the Hunger Games." *The Girl Who Was on Fire: Your Favorite Authors on Suzanne Collins' Hunger Games Trilogy.* Ed. Leah Wilson. Movie ed. Dallas: Smart Pop, 2010/2011. Print.

"The World Food Programme and Feeding America Partner with the Hunger Games." *wfp.org*. World Food Programme, 23 Feb. 2012. Web. 23 Apr. 2017.

Yancey, Rick. *The 5th Wave*. New York: G. P. Putnam's Sons, 2013. Print.

_____. *The Infinite Sea*. New York: G. P. Putnam's Sons, 2014. Print.

Young, Moira. *Blood Red Road*. New York: McElderry, 2011. Print.

_____. *Raging Star*. New York: McElderry, 2014. Print.

_____. *Rebel Heart*. New York: McElderry, 2012. Print.

Zemier, Emily. "Why Do We Love Dystopian Stories So Much?" *Time*. Time, 21 Mar. 2014. Web. 5 May 2015.

Zhang, Kat. *Echoes of Us*. New York: HarperCollins, 2014. Print.

_____. *Once We Were*. New York: HarperCollins, 2013. Print.

_____. *What's Left of Me*. New York: HarperCollins, 2012. Print.

Index

Numbers in *bold italics* indicate pages with illustrations

271